(continued from front flap)

Philip L. White is professor of history at the University of Texas at Austin. Among his publications are *A History of the American People* and *The Beekmans of New York in Politics and Commerce, 1647–1877*.

Beekmantown,
New York

Beekmantown, New York

Forest Frontier to Farm Community

By Philip L. White

University of Texas Press, Austin and London

Library of Congress Cataloging in Publication Data
White, Philip L
Beekmantown, N.Y.
Bibliography: p.
Includes index.
1. Beekmantown, N.Y.—History. I. Title.
F129.B375W47   974.7′54   78-26558
ISBN 0-292-72428-4

Design by Nancy Whittington

The engravings in this book have been reproduced
from *The Pictorial Field-Book of the War of 1812*,
by Benson J. Lossing (New York: Harper &
Brothers, 1896).

*Plattsburgh Baptist Church, as sketched in 1852 by Elizabeth
Mallory. Many families living in the western part of Beekmantown, especially along the Military Turnpike, attended
this church.*

Contents

Preface and
Acknowledgments

Three basic objectives have guided me in completing this study. The most fundamental aim is to report in detail how a particular portion of the American wilderness became a fully settled farming community. I have attempted to tell this story without preconceptions and, unlike Merle Curti, whose study of Trempeleau County, Wisconsin, provided my original inspiration, I have not sought to "test" any of the several hypotheses concerning frontier influences set forth by Frederick Jackson Turner.

The second objective is to describe as fully as I could the various aspects of community life during the period of development. I have done this with the conviction that historians need to know more about the pattern of life in rural communities during the early national period. As late as 1850, 85 percent of the American people still lived in rural communities of less than 2,500 population. We know a great deal about various specialized aspects of life in this period, including farm life, land tenure, political activity, and others, but we have little understanding of interrelationships among such specialized aspects of life and even less of the pattern of life as a whole in rural communities. Surely, it seems to me, this is a useful undertaking in relation to the effort to write history from the bottom up, rather than with largely exclusive attention to various elite groups—political, economic, intellectual, and others—perceived in a national or international context.

The third objective is to identify interpretive hypotheses of broader applicability suggested by detailed study of the history of this one community. These hypotheses, more fully stated in the conclusion, are (1) the economic advantages of the northern forest frontier in the early national period brought a first generation of settlers relatively high in socioeconomic status and that termination of frontier advantages brought a significant lowering of socioeconomic status in the second generation; (2) changes in various aspects of life between the Federalist and Jacksonian eras do indeed warrant characterizing the latter period as the era of the "common man" despite recent revisionist arguments to the contrary; and (3) contrary to Frederick Jackson Turner's assumption that the frontier fostered equality, the influence of the forest frontier in the North during the early national period was to foster economic inequality—especially in relation to land ownership—and that the influence most favorable to equality was the elimination of the economic opportunities afforded by frontier conditions.

What I have not attempted may also deserve a word or two of explanation. Unlike a number of recent studies of small communities, mostly of an earlier time and a different region, mine makes very little effort to measure social mobility, to determine changes in the pattern of family life, marriage, longevity, or other aspects of what is generally called historical demography. The major reason for that omission is that I found none or very few of the kinds of evidence required for such inquiries. Census data were available in quantity only from 1850, the very end of my period. I found only one tax assessment (1798), no significant data on births, deaths, or marriages, no probate records. Candor compels me to add that I did most of my research before the vogue for historical demography was well underway in this country and, consequently, may not have searched as diligently for such materials as scholars would do now.

Two caveats need to be set forth to the reader. The first concerns the relationship between Beekmantown and Plattsburgh. Both the granting of the land and the first settlement of Beekmantown preceded those in Plattsburgh. However, Plattsburgh's location at the mill sites on the Saranac River, plus the dynamic leadership provided by its proprietors made it the metropolitan center for the region. Accordingly, when governmental organization took place in the 1780s, the town of Plattsburgh incorporated the adjacent area then known as Beekman Patent. Beekmantown secured its own town government only in 1820. Even after that time, however, Plattsburgh continued to exert strong and varied influences upon its smaller neighbor. For all these reasons Plattsburgh receives considerable attention in the pages which follow.

The second caveat concerns source citations. In attempting to minimize the number of notes, I have often incorporated into the text the information required to locate material from several sources upon which I have relied heavily. One is the Beekman Family Papers at the New-York Historical Society. When the context makes clear that the source is the Beekman Family Papers, I have included in parentheses in the text the date of the manuscript. No other information is required to locate the source. A second major source for which I have followed the same procedure is the Plattsburgh *Republican*. When the context makes clear that the *Republican* is the source, I have included the date in parentheses in the text rather than refer the reader to a note. I should add also that from the 1870s onward into the twentieth century the *Republican* often published historical documents or reminiscences. Thus, the date cited for an issue of the *Republican* will sometimes be in that period rather than in the period being considered in the text.

Finally, I need to acknowledge a personal interest in my subject of which I became aware rather gradually over the years. Simply stated, the point is that my own "roots" lie in a community with striking similarities to Beekmantown. My paternal grandfather operated a farm near Lander in northwestern Pennsylvania, which was viable only while lumbering operations took place in the vicinity. I do not know that he actually worked part time for lumbermen or that he sold products of his farm to them, although I suspect he did both. I do know that my father in his youth worked both in a sawmill, where he lost a finger and earned a nickname, and as a teamster driving lumber wagons into town. Since my grandfather's death and the roughly coincidental exhaustion of the local supply of timber, no one has ever made a living on the farm which supported him, his wife, and a family of six children. I have more than the usual devotion in mind then in dedicating this effort to the memory of my father, Lloyd Putnam White, and my mother, Della Depew White, both of whom manifested throughout their lives the values of the rural American communities of the nineteenth century in which they were reared.

Since beginning work on this study in 1960, I have accumulated indebtedness to an enormous number of individuals, as well as to a number of libraries and three institutions. The institutions are the

University of Chicago, the University of Texas at Austin, and Harvard University. Chicago provided the funds which launched me on the study. The University of Texas and Harvard University jointly sponsored the year of leave from teaching duties at Texas during which, as a fellow of Harvard's Charles Warren Center, I completed a first draft. The University of Texas has also provided money for typing several drafts.

In collecting information I drew on a large number of libraries— particularly, the New York State Library at Albany, the Feinberg Library at the State University College in Plattsburgh, the New-York Historical Society, the New York Public Library, the Library of Congress, the Public Archives of Canada, the Newberry Library, the University of Vermont Library, the Plattsburgh Public Library, and the library of the New York State Historical Association at Cooperstown, plus those of the three universities. Among reference librarians, G. Glyndon Cole, Alan C. Miller, and Bruce Stark at the Feinberg Library, and Kathleen Blow, JoAnne Hawkins, and Dick Holland of the University of Texas have been particularly helpful. Officials at the Clinton County Court House were also very helpful in making county records available to me.

To a far greater extent than would be the case in a more conventional historical study, I secured extremely important information from individuals living in the area. Preeminent among them were Mrs. Addie Lawrence Shields of Beekmantown, Charles W. McLellan of Champlain, Mrs. Marjorie Lansing Porter of Elizabethtown, Mrs. Jane Lape of Ticonderoga, Mrs. Benjamin F. Sullivan and David Martin of Chazy, and H. Fuller Allen and Mr. and Mrs. Frank Cooper of Plattsburgh. I had assistance of great value from two graduate students, Avery Colt at the University of Chicago and Carole Wynn at the University of Texas. Professor Allan S. Everest of the State University College at Plattsburgh, who has written extensively on the history of the Plattsburgh area, shared his knowledge with me, guided me to many sources I might otherwise have missed, and criticized my manuscript. I drew appreciably also on *North Country Notes*, the periodical publication of the Clinton County Historical Association.

Several other professional historians deserve a special word of appreciation. Oscar Handlin provided encouragement, as well as indispensable financial aid. Edward Pessen, as is his wont, provided blunt but telling criticisms of the manuscript as a whole. Others who provided thoughtful suggestions include Gilbert C. Fite,

David Van Tassel, Karl Kaestle, Joel Silbey, Robert C. Cotner, Howard Miller, Richard Ryerson, Paul Finkleman, and especially Craig Hanyon, whose biography of De Witt Clinton I await impatiently.

Colleen Kain called my attention to numerous faults while typing early versions. My wife, Meda, exercised keen judgment in suggesting numerous revisions. Her father, Orr Lee Miller, spotted significant mistakes which all the rest had overlooked. Laura Bodour and Ona Kay Stephenson typed the final version in a highly professional manner. I owe a special debt also to Sam and Jean Katz.

Prologue:
No Man's Land

Characterizing the area south of the St. Lawrence, Indian friends of Samuel de Champlain described to him in 1608 "a large lake filled with beautiful islands and [bordered by] a great deal of beautiful country."[1] When he himself traversed the area, Champlain made similar observations. Two and one-half centuries later, Francis Parkman would speculate that Champlain had seen, as Parkman had from the same shores, "the glow of the vanished sun behind the western mountains, darkly piled in mist and shadow along the sky; near at hand, the dead pine, mighty in decay, stretching its ragged arms athwart the burning heaven, the crow perched on its top like an image carved in jet; and aloft, the nighthawk, circling in his flight."[2]

The missing element was people. Champlain did see some indications that Indians had been there—but only parties bent on war or hunting. "These places," he wrote, "are not inhabited by any savages. . . . They withdraw as far as possible . . . into the interior, in order not to be suddenly surprised" by enemies.[3] The Champlain valley, in other words, was literally "no man's land." Situated between the tribes of the St. Lawrence valley and their implacable Iroquois enemies living in the Mohawk valley of central New York, the Champlain area afforded permanent homes to neither.

In the great struggle between France and Britain for American territory, permanent possession of the Champlain region seemed likely to go to France. It was part of the St. Lawrence watershed. Access to it was easy for the French in the days when travel followed watercourses. There were rapids in the Richelieu River between the St. Lawrence and Lake Champlain, but the terrain. in general was quite flat. The British faced a short but difficult portage from the Hudson watershed to that of Lake Champlain. Furthermore, the upper (southerly) portion of the lake was hemmed in tightly, especially on the New York side, by rugged mountain country which afforded "scant . . . foothold for farming folk."[4] Only in the north was the valley wide enough to encourage farmers.

For such reasons the Champlain valley was much less attractive to British settlers than the Mohawk valley running west from Albany. The Mohawk valley afforded more good farmland, easier transportation to the port of New York, and less exposure to French attack. British settlement accordingly turned west at Albany. It did not for some time venture northward into the Champlain valley.

From 1689 to 1759, while France and Britain struggled for dominance in North America, the Champlain valley was in fact a principal theater of inconclusive warfare. Such settlement as did take place was largely incidental to the building of rival forts: French Crown Point (1731) and Ticonderoga (1755) and British Fort William Henry on Lake George (1755). Only after the British conquest of Quebec in 1759 did the valley become safe for civilian settlers.

The British settlers of the 1760s were a varied lot. Major Philip Skene, a Scotsman who had served in the British campaigns in the area, got a large grant and began the town of Skenesborough, now Whitehall, at the southern tip of the lake. William Gilliland, an Irish veteran of the British army, bought up thousands of acres of veterans' bonus lands granted by the British government and established a settlement on the Bouquet River about halfway down the lake. Charles Fredenburgh, a German who had been a British army captain, secured thirty thousand acres in the Plattsburgh area and built both a house and a sawmill there. A few New Englanders came through the Green Mountains to settle the Vermont shore. A few French Canadians settled at the extreme northern end of the lake.

The American Revolution revived the military functions of the valley and ruined all proprietors. Surrender of the area to the United States finished Skene, who had been a Tory. His lands were confiscated. Fredenburgh, also a Tory, disappeared after the war. He may have been murdered. His buildings were burned; his land was reclaimed. Gilliland, suspected and victimized by military forces on both sides, became insolvent and languished several years in jail for debt.[5]

In 1784, 175 years after Champlain had first visited the lake, another Frenchman, Peter Sailly, traversed it in search of a place to settle. "I have never in my life seen anything which approaches in beauty the borders of Lake Champlain," he wrote. He noted also that they were "uninhabited." If the area were to be inhabited, he thought, "it will be the finest in the world." Despite premonitions that the area would be devastated in the "first" war with Britain, he decided to stay.[6] Many others were reaching the same conclusion about the same time. The transformation of another portion of the American wilderness into a civilized community was underway.

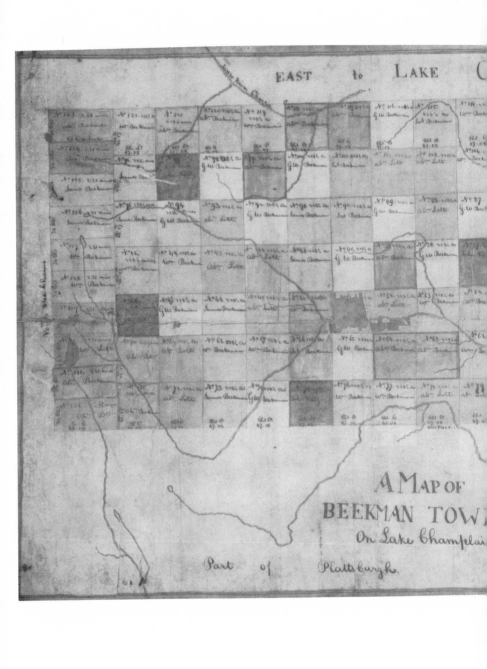

A MAP OF
BEEKMAN TOWN
On Lake Champlain

Part of Plattsburgh.

Allocation of lands among the proprietors (courtesy of the New-York Historical Society)

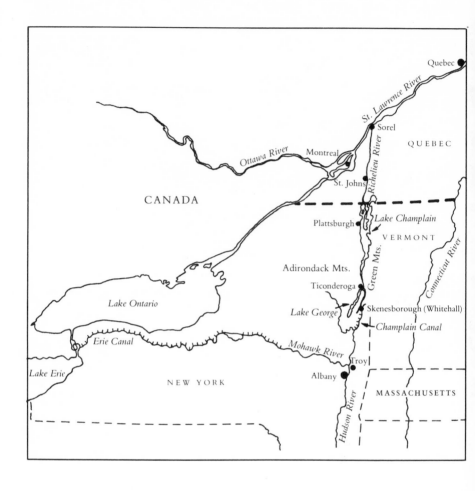

The commercial region of Plattsburgh and Beekmantown

Beekmantown's neighbors

PART 1
Economic Development

Old stone mill, Plattsburgh, one of many mills near the mouth of the Saranac

1

The Proprietors
and the Land

Dr. William Beekman and a number of associates petitioned New York's colonial governor on May 9, 1768, for thirty thousand acres of land on Lake Champlain. "At considerable Expence," the petitioners claimed, they had "discovered a certain Tract of Land situate on the West Side of Lake Champlain . . . also an Island in the said Lake commonly called Long Island [now North Hero], Which . . . are vacant . . . and wholly uncultivated." The petitioners "did humbly pray our said Captain General and Governor in Chief" to grant them as much of the mainland area back from the shore "as will with the said Long Island include the Quantity of one Thousand Acres for each of the [thirty] Petitioners."[1]

Who were the petitioners? Most were relatives, friends, or dependents of Dr. William Beekman, an aged, nonpracticing physician who made his living importing dry goods from England. Three of the signers, William, Jr., Abraham, and James, were sons of Dr. Beekman. All the rest were dummies. Among them were Abraham De la Noy, tavern keeper; his son of the same name; a painter; two clerks; a shopkeeper; and a wig maker.

Notably absent from the list were the names of another son, Gerard W. Beekman, and of Abraham Lott. Together with the other three Beekman brothers, Gerard and Lott were the real investors. Gerard's name was absent because he had petitioned earlier for one thousand acres elsewhere and thus could not openly seek more land because of the limit of one thousand acres on grants to individuals.[2] Lott, a merchant and speculator, also held office as treasurer of the province. He may have had a number of reasons for staying in the background.

Why did the New York City Beekmans, who for many years had invested almost exclusively in commerce and urban properties, turn suddenly to speculation in frontier land? Depressed conditions in commerce may provide part of the answer. Throughout 1767 James Beekman, a merchant like his father and his brother, Gerard W., complained to his British "correspondents" (suppliers) of the "Scarcety of Cash," numerous bankruptcies, and general depression. In 1768 he lamented that goods of all kinds were "a meer Drug [on the market] with us, and are sold out of stores at very little advance, but at the dayly Vandues [auctions] may be bought for less than prime cost."[3] A nonimportation agreement in protest against the Townshend Duties of 1767 did not improve prospects for import merchants.

Political considerations also figured in the timing of the Beekmans' patent. From 1761, when Governor Robert Monckton returned to England, until 1765, when a new governor arrived, New York's administration was in the hands of Lieutenant Governor Cadwallader Colden. Colden made land grants lavishly in that period in order to build up his income from the handsome fees which the land grant recipients paid him but, as one insider noted, the grants which "Old Grey Head" made were "confined to his H[onou]r and his friends."[4] Those friends did not include the Beekmans. Colden was a zealous upholder of British authority. During the Stamp Act riots of 1765, radicals burned his luxurious coach with his effigy on top. A few years later, the younger William Beekman would lend money to the Sons of Liberty, who were chiefly responsible for those riots. His brother, James Beekman, expressed radical sentiments in his letters to British correspondents and would later serve in the provincial congress, New York's revolutionary government.[5]

Sir Henry Moore, who arrived to take over the governorship in 1765, was committed to uphold the British position, but he made every effort to appease the populace which Colden had helped to antagonize. As Colden noted with disgust, Governor Moore "openly caressed the Demagogues—Put on a Homespun Coat, the Badge of Faction and Suffered the Mob to insult officers of Government without interposing."[6] While it is not clear that Governor Moore acceded to the petition of the Beekmans as part of an appeasement program, it is distinctly possible. He had been in

New York for some two years when he approved the petition. Colden, despite his appetite for patent fees, would probably not have approved a grant for such radicals.

Securing valid title to lands on the shore of Lake Champlain required some intrigue on the part of Beekman agents and an incredible amount of luck. In the first place, the French had granted patents which virtually ringed the lake. In a number of places, including the site which would become Beekmantown, they had granted the same land several times. However, no settlement had occurred in the area which the Beekmans sought under any of the numerous patents.[7]

When the area came under British control in 1763, Lieutenant Governor Colden assumed that the French grants were void and began allocating portions of the lake shore to "reduced officers" in accordance with His Majesty's veterans' land program. A cloud appeared over these grants when on July 13, 1764, the Lords of Trade instructed Colden to make no grants in areas claimed by Michel Chartier de Lotbinière under grant from France.[8] Lotbinière's claims encompassed much of the southern portion of the lake region where settlement appeared imminent; consequently, speculative interest was high. Probably the prospect that French grants might be validated operated to discourage patenting of lands claimed by the French farther north. Whether for this reason or because of a prevalent impression that Colden lacked power to make grants of lake shore land, the northern region remained largely free of New York patents. When Governor Moore made an admittedly incomplete map of the overlapping claims in 1767, it showed no New York grants as far north as Beekmantown, although there were some reaching to Valcour Island, not far to the south.[9]

What to do about the French claims posed a problem over which British officials vacillated for several years. Moore declined to confirm a number of French grants, offering his superiors in London a variety of reasons. The enormous size of some of the French grants conflicted with his instruction to grant no more than one thousand acres to any one person. The grants made no provision for quit rents which his instructions required him to include in every patent. Furthermore, they overlapped not only the grants which Colden had made but also—a more telling point—some which the king had made, such as the Fredenburgh grant (see Prologue) to the site of Plattsburgh.[10] Moore begged for a quick decision concerning the validity of Colden's grants "as the Persons interested in them are now under the greatest apprehension of being totally ruined." A decision in their favor, he added, "would give new Vigour to the Cultivation of that part of the Country which has been entirely neglected of late, and will continue to be so, until these claims are ascertained."[11]

Nearly a year later, Moore got his way. The Earl of Hillsborough, secretary of state, wrote him (February 25, 1768): "It is his Majesty's Resolution . . . not to allow any claims made upon the ground of ancient grants from the Government of Canada to Lands which were never acknowledged to belong of right to the Crown of France."[12] An official Order in Council confirming this policy appeared on August 12, 1768.[13] Meanwhile, Governor Moore considered that all the French grants were void and that he could regrant the entire area up to the Canadian border. There was, after all, no part of that area which England had not claimed. Even the saving clause that the French "should not be disturbed in peaceable possession of any Tracts . . . actually settled and improved" constituted no barrier for, as Moore would later observe, "they have no settlements to claim under."[14]

Somehow the Beekmans heard of this new policy decision long before the issuance of the Order in Council which confirmed it. The source of their information was an impecunious Irish lawyer named John Kelly. Kelly was also a small-time land speculator, who bought up veterans' land claims whenever he could. He made it a practice also to acquire marketable information concerning attractive sites for land speculation. This information he conveyed to wealthy individuals whom he then assisted in securing a patent. His compensation was normally the payment of patent fees and conveyance of title to a small portion of the grant which his principals secured. Before the Revolution, Kelly had acquired land in at least twelve New York grants.[15]

Kelly's information concerning the area which would become Beekmantown came from a source which he did not choose to identify. The rich and fertile lands which his informant had located, Kelly asserted, would have been patented long before had it not been generally believed that the old French grants were valid. The informant also told Kelly, perhaps with some exaggeration, that although Colden had been forbidden to grant lands to which the French had issued patents, Governor Moore was not so bound. This information, conveyed in the spring of 1768, was based apparently on knowledge of Hillsborough's letter to Moore dated February 25. The Order in Council confirming the letter was not issued in London until August. In return for this information, Kelly reported, his informant would expect "one name in the petition," that is, conveyance to him of one thousand acres of the land secured plus payment of the patent fees.[16]

In mid-June, a month after getting their petition before the governor and council, the Beekmans received a letter (June 15, 1768) from Kelly's informant. Thomas Nuttman, otherwise unidentified, professed that it was he who had given Kelly what he called "a Location for a tract of Land." His arrangement with Kelly, he wrote, was that he would receive fifty pounds or payment of patent fees on *two* thousand acres to be conveyed to him. However, he expected to share this payment with Kelly. Nuttman wanted William Beekman to confirm the arrangement and to let him know whether or not the grants had been secured.

The Beekmans' petition was working its way through the provincial bureaucracy. Dated May 9, the petition was read in the governor's council and referred to a committee on May 18. On July 13 the council heard a favorable report from its committee and issued the required warrant directing the surveyor general, Alexander Colden, to survey the plot.[17]

Surveying the plot was a crucial step. Kelly had assured Lott that the plot would be "well located" because he intended to supervise the survey himself. Accordingly, the petitioners gave him careful written instructions (July 21). He was to get the actual surveying work done by the "most reasonable of Mr. Colden's deputies you can find" but to avoid the expense of the survey if the lands proved not worth patenting. They wanted him to report in detail on the size and kinds of trees; the quality of the soil; the nature of the terrain; the presence of swamps, springs, creeks, and mineral resources; the depth of the water around the island; and its distance from shore, as well as from Ticonderoga and Montreal. They agreed to pay his expenses and to see that Kelly and his informant received one thousand acres each.

Kelly set out in August accompanied by a surveyor from Colden's office, a chainbearer, a "marker" to assist the surveyor, and several "packmen." On November 19 he reported from the site that the lands on both the island and the mainland were without hills and possessed a deep and very rich soil. By December the survey was complete. Kelly then went to Vermont to look after some of his affairs and, he said, to do favors for both Surveyor General Colden and the provincial secretary, Goldsborough Banyar. Instead of sending the report to Colden as the surveyor general had instructed him to do, Kelly sent it first—unsealed—to Beekman so that he might copy it. Then Beekman was to seal the report so that Kelly's messenger could deliver it to Colden as if it had not been seen by anyone else.

Kelly's advice to Beekman was to get a patent at once. "Delaying," he added, "frequently proves fatal." As for the quality of the land, he thought that there was none better in the province. Furthermore, he was sure that "you can cut as much timber in one season as will pay the patent fees." In a somewhat conspiratorial manner, Kelly added the warning that they should "let no man in either the Surveyor Generals office or the Secretarys office know anything about the quality of the land."[18]

On March 27 the governor and council issued the patent which William Beekman had formally requested on March 1. As usual the king reserved "all Mines of Gold and Silver, and also all white or other Sorts of Pine Trees fit for Masts" for the Royal Navy. Violation of the pine reservation would justify forfeiture of the patent. Failure to settle one family per one thousand acres and to clear three acres in every fifty within three years would also warrant voiding the grant. This provision was virtually impossible to fulfill and was never enforced. The patent also designated the area the township of "Beekman" and endowed it with the usual rights of town government. There was also provision for the payment of quit rents at the rate of two shillings and six pence per one hundred acres.

William Beekman calculated carefully the total cost of securing the patent. The major items were the fees of various government officers:

Governor Sir Henry Moore at £12.10 per 1,000 acres	£375.00
Attorney General John Tabor Kempe at £3 per 1,000 acres	90.00
Surveyor General Alexander Colden at £5 per 1,000 acres	150.00
Secretary Goldsborough Banyar at £4 per 1,000 acres	120.00
Receiver General A. Elliott	5.16
Surveyor General's fees for 18 days at 5 shillings per day	4.10
Total	£745.06

Kelly's expenses of £110 and some outlays for clerical work in government offices brought the total initial investment to £860. Of this total, Lott, Gerard W. Beekman, and James Beekman each paid £159.14.01¾ for six thousand acres each. William and Abraham Beekman jointly paid £266.03.06¾ for ten thousand acres. Kelly, of course, received two thousand acres without any payment but had to pass half of that, or a money equivalent, to Nuttman.

Next, the proprietors had to take care of the dummies. Deeds on file at the office of the secretary of state affirm that Kelly paid £100 each to James Cobham, shopkeeper, and to John Vredenburgh, peruke maker, for his two thousand acres and that William and Abraham Beekman paid eight other dummies at the same rate (£100 per one thousand acres) to secure eight thousand acres, in addition to the thousand which each had patented in his own name.[19] William Beekman's cost figures included no such payments. Those to the dummies were fictitious.

The good fortune of the Beekmans in securing their patent early in 1769 became clear in the light of developments in the second half of the year. In July Hillsborough prepared an instruction to Governor Moore that he was to make no grants "of those Lands on Lake Champlain which are claimed under Title derived from the Crown of France, until the petitions and proposals for such Grants shall have been transmitted hither, and His Majesty's pleasure signified thereupon." The instruction was not actually sent until December, and then it was addressed to Lieutenant Governor Colden. Governor Moore had died on September 11.[20] Had Moore died a few months earlier, arch-Tory Colden would almost certainly have blocked the issuance of the Beekman patent. Had the government changed its policy a few months earlier, the grant would also have been precluded.

As the patentees prepared to seek a profitable disposition of their luckily acquired property, there was a portent of future problems. Upon completing the survey in 1768, John Kelly found it expedient to retain a caretaker, an illiterate named Peter Turner, to prevent the theft of timber from Long Island. In October 1769, some seven months after the issuance of the patent, Kelly took it with him to the spot to "shew our Title to the people of Vermont who have settled on our Island."[21]

How to realize a profit on their investment of £860 was a

problem which perplexed the grantees from the beginning. Should they sell the entire property at once for a relatively small profit? Should they keep title and attempt to settle the grant with tenants imported from abroad? Or should they apportion the land among themselves and allow each to dispose of his portion as he wished, whether by sale or lease? In fact, they attempted each of these courses.

Soon after securing the patent, William Beekman devised a plan (undated) "to settle 124 families together in one town." Under Beekman's plan each family would have a town lot 50 yards by 382 yards. This would include enough land for house, barn, stable, "a Yard for Poultry, a Garden of one Acre and an Orchard or field of near two acres and a half for keeping one milk cow." Six acres of pastureland would be allocated to each family for its cattle and horses; 13½ acres for cropland; 16 for sheep pasture; and 4 acres of woodland "for firing and timber." All of these allocations, however, except for the town lot were of common land or open fields. Beekman provided additional land for a church and church yard, a "Public Hall or Stadhouse," a "publick Granary for wheat to prevent any famine," and a market place. "The Whole," Beekman concluded complacently, "contains a portion of Land three miles square with the town in the middle. And whenever it is fully peopled, another such square may be added to it on any side and so on till the whole country is fully inhabited: and if a small quit rent be paid by every house it will in time rise to a large annual sum." [22]

Small as they now seem, Beekman's allocations were sufficient for the needs and indeed the capacities of most farm families, but there were numerous important factors which he had failed to consider. Most frontier settlers, even in the face of Indian danger, would have no part of communal holdings. Nor was Beekmantown's terrain easily divisible into categories such as Beekman had devised. There were swamps, rock outcroppings, and above all there were trees. According to one reasonable estimate, a man could clear from five to fifteen acres per year, depending on how much other work he had to do. [23] Thus, before the hypothetical tenant of the planned village could utilize fully his "near forty acres" of land in addition to his home site, he would have to spend several years clearing timber. That many settlers would undertake such labor for so long a time with only the prospect of permanent tenancy as a reward became more unlikely every year. Opportunities for "squatting" on absentee-owned frontier land or for purchasing from a myriad of competing sellers were too great to make it necessary.

Impractical as it was, Beekman's plan, nevertheless, reveals much about his values. His plan included no provision for a store, a gristmill, a sawmill, or indeed for any artisan of any kind—only a market place in which, presumably, traveling merchants would offer to exchange their goods for agricultural commodities. The church met the obvious needs of religion—assuming uniformity of belief—as did the "Stadhouse" for government. But, where one might have expected a school, Beekman envisioned a granary—to prevent famine. This suggests an aristocratic disdain for popular education, and it reinforces the impression of extremely naive dedication to creating a subsistence-oriented community of tenant farmers with only minimal participation in world commerce. The sure subsistence would presumably serve the people's basic needs and keep them relatively content, while tenancy would afford both income, authority, and prestige to the absentee owners. Clearly, Beekman's conception of the good society was very much out of date.

About equally out of date, however, were the values prevalent in the Scottish Highlands.[24] Accordingly, a Scotsman named Daniel Macleod made an arrangement with William Beekman (November 1, 1773) to settle Beekmantown with Highland Scot immigrants on terms not too different from those which Beekman had envisaged. For five years Macleod was to pay only the quit rent of two shillings and six pence per one hundred acres. For the next seven years, he was to pay six pence per acre and ever after that, one shilling per acre plus the quit rent. To help him secure settlers from Scotland, the proprietors agreed to lend him £600 for seven years at 7 percent interest. The agreement required Macleod to reserve one hundred acres for a minister, fifty for a "Schoolmaster," another fifty for a doctor, and still another fifty for public buildings. Macleod obligated himself to bring the settlers from Scotland to New York by September 1774 and to keep an agent in New York City to "receive and transport . . . such Settlers . . . as are now in America or shall be brought by him from Scotland" to Beekmantown. Like the "tacksmen" or large lessees in the Highlands of Scotland, Macleod would then be free to impose whatever terms he could upon those who would work the soil.

Emigration from the Highlands to America was flowing torrentially at that time. One reason was that lessors were increasing rents. The increases seem to have stemmed essentially from the conversion of a quasi-feudal economy, which emphasized subsistence farming and service obligations into a more modern, money-centered economy emphasizing cash returns. To some extent the lessors were consciously trying to eliminate the tacksmen as unnecessary middlemen. On the other hand, the tacksmen, it was widely alleged, "by spiriting the lower class of people to emigrate" were seeking to "carry a clan to America." [25]

The willingness of the common people to emigrate was due chiefly to extreme poverty which was, of course, aggravated by the increase in rents. On the island of Lewis, an observer noted many years later that several thousand people still "knew nothing of a chimney, gable, glass windows, house flooring or even hearth stone." In the Hebrides Islands, many thousands lived "in hovels which would disgrace any Indian tribe." [26] Soil and climate were unfavorable. Furthermore, farming techniques were medieval; yet, the population was growing rapidly. An especially severe winter in 1772, plus extremely favorable reports from earlier immigrants, helped to swell the stream of emigration. Biographer James Boswell, touring Skye in 1773, remarked that the local populace did a dance which they called "America." "It goes on," he wrote, "till all are set a-going." The previous year, when an emigrant ship sailed for America, "the people on shore were almost distracted when they saw their relations go off; they lay down on the ground and tumbled, and tore the grass with their teeth. This year there was not a tear shed. The people on shore seemed to think that they should soon follow." [27]

Emigration fever in the Highlands seemed to assure a good supply of tenants for Beekmantown, but William Beekman made it a point to supply Macleod with a letter (December 24, 1773) describing in glowing terms the opportunities which the township afforded. First in his list of advantages was "easy communication by water to a Markett at Montreal, Quebec, or New York." Enthusiasm for attracting settlers apparently induced Beekman in this instance to anticipate by half a century the completion of a canal between Lake Champlain and the Hudson River and to overlook the rapids of the Richelieu River between Lake Champlain and the St. Lawrence. A second advantage was timber—"finest and largest white Oak Timber Trees, for Staves or Ship building also Maple, Beech, Birch, Basswood and other sorts of Trees."

A third advantage of the area was its wildlife. There were "fishes of different kinds, Viz. Salmon, pike, trout, perch and many other Sorts in great plenty in their Season. Likewise Deer, Elks, Buffaloes, Bears, Wild Catts, wild fowls and beavers and many other Annimals." The advantage to accrue to the settlers from bears and wildcats is not self-evident, although each of the others in the list did have its use.

In conclusion, the owners promised Macleod that the "greatest care will be taken of any People you'll send or order to our care here, to settle on these Lands, and the Sooner the better." They wished Macleod "a prosperous voyage home and a speedy return."

Macleod set sail on a ship carrying flaxseed for Northern Ireland in the middle of the winter of 1773–1774. Until the following summer, the owners heard nothing of his fortunes. Then at the end of July, they received a letter which he had written on April 5. It was dated at Raasay Island, off the eastern coast of the Isle of Skye. "I got so far as this," he wrote, "on my way to the Lewise ["The Lews" was local usage for the island of Lewis, largest and most northerly of the Outer Hebrides] after a most Storming winters Voyage, after three weeks and five days to Newry in Ireland. I come by land from Newry to Belfast and Chartered a Ship at Belfast for the High Lands, the Charming Sally of Philadelphia, Captain William Hodge commander. She is really a fine ship of about 400 Tons Burthen, and I expect will carry 400 full passengers easily. I left her at Belfast getting in Provisions, and Beds, etc. and it is to be at Stornoweighers in the Lewise [Stornoway is the principal port of Lewis] about the 20th of this month. We are to take the People at Stornoway and Lock Broom [a coastal town in northwestern Scotland] and about the 15th of May next, I Expect to sett off for your Country."

Macleod was disappointed. He returned to New York without any settlers for Beekmantown. On November 1, 1774, he borrowed £8.16 from Beekman. On the back of the note which he gave is the laconic endorsement: "NB. he was in the Alms House the 7th November." Thus ended the scheme to settle Beekmantown with Scottish tenants.

His own shortcomings or misplaced trust may have contributed to Macleod's failure, but more general factors helped. Powerful landowners had become alarmed at the pace of emigration and were making every effort to slow it. Emigrants arriving at Philadelphia from Lewis in June 1774 "declared that all possible methods were being used to prevent further emigration, including the lowering of rents."[28] The next year the British government prohibited emigration entirely. Perhaps Beekman and Macleod were just a little too late.

Two efforts to sell the patent as a whole aborted before the Revolution, but a third began at its conclusion. One prospective purchaser was Samuel Stevens of Charlestown, New Hampshire. Acting for a group of associates, Stevens pledged on December 15, 1783, to buy the entire thirty thousand acres of Beekmantown at two dollars per acre (Massachusetts money). He was to make four annual payments of $15,000 each with interest at 7 percent.

Almost immediately, however, Stevens began to back out. On January 22 he wrote to Kelly that he had not seen all the people who "engaged me to Purchase BeekmanTown" and, consequently, could not tell what they would do. Those he had seen, he reported, found fault with "the great Price, and the high Interist for the Money and the short Payments. They Suppose that it will be impossible for them to raise so large a sum in so short a time. They are willing to give Twelve Shillings ($1.50) an acre, but want a longer Pay Day, at Six per cent Interist and that not to take place in less than one Year from May next which is as soon as they can Possably make the first Payment, as that depends on their selling their Farms."

Still another objection stemmed from the confusion concerning the status of Vermont. His associates, Stevens reported, "well know that the Government of Vermont have granted Long Island [part of the Beekmantown grant], that a number of Persons are actually upon the Spot, and are making large Improvements, and General Hazen hath taken possession of the Land upon the Main-[land]. . . . I am informed that some time last week the two contending Parties in the Southern Part of the County of Cumberland exchanged a few shots." The next month Stevens retreated even farther. Thereafter, the proprietors abandoned hope for sale through him.

Soon after the collapse of the negotiations with Stevens, the owners received a proposal from John Addoms. Addoms, a surveyor, was one of the proprietors of Plattsburgh. Addoms proposed (October 19, 1784) that the township be surveyed into lots of two hundred acres each and that three roads be run from the lake to the rear of the tract. Precisely what Addoms had in mind is not clear, but it appears that he wanted the owners to award every third lot to him. If this were done, he would put up security to settle within three years one family on each of the lots awarded to him. Exceptions were to be made for lots which were "marshy or not feazable" and "in case of war breaking out against us or interruption by the Savages." In case of Indian attack or war, he wanted equal time after the interruption to effect the settlement. Apparently, Addoms considered that the owners would be amply compensated for the lots he wanted by his own services in making the necessary survey, cutting the roads, and by the increase in the value of the remaining lots which would result from the settlement of those awarded to him. The owners were not yet ready for such concessions, however. William Beekman's note on the back of Addoms' letter states simply: "Putt him off."

That the proprietors did not reject the Addoms proposal outright suggests that they were already considering a policy which they began in fact to implement the following spring. In June surveyor William Cockburn departed from New York City with detailed instructions (June 15, 1785) to lay out lots in Beekmantown. The owners had decided to prepare for the sale of their land in farm-size lots to individual settlers.

The employment of Cockburn, however, did not reflect a decision to abandon all efforts to sell the township as a whole. In 1786, despite the misgivings of Abraham Beekman, the proprietors, for a time, considered selling the entire township to three impecunious men from "Newark Mountains." In 1793 another prospective purchaser appeared, one Peter Dubree, "late of Normandy, France." The terms which Dubree agreed to on March 27, 1793, were quite simple. He was to buy the township for three silver dollars per acre. One-third was to be paid on March 1, 1794, and the remaining thirds on that date in 1795 and 1796. Title was to pass after the first payment, but mortgages on the land were to be given to secure the last two payments.

Despite their many previous disappointments, the proprietors regarded Dubree's undertaking with the utmost seriousness. The Beekmans instructed their local agent to dispossess recent purchasers whose tracts had not been specifically excluded from the Dubree contract. Neither Dubree nor the Beekmans, however, had taken into consideration the international complications resulting from the French Revolution: France was to be at war for most of the next twenty-two years. Dubree wrote (September 1, 1794) to express regret that war had prevented him both from making payment and from leaving France. The letter did not reach Beekman until May 7, 1795. Still optimistic, Beekman then tried to dissuade the trustees of the bankrupt John Kelly from selling his Beekmantown property to apply against his debts. Dubree was planning to return to the United States "as soon as possible," Beekman explained, to complete the purchase of the entire tract. He himself, he added, had recently refused to sell two lots to Judge Thomas Tredwell so that the property could be preserved intact for Dubree.[29] By November 1, 1796, the proprietors had abandoned hope for Dubree's return. On that date James Beekman fixed prices at which he would sell his lots in Beekmantown. There were to be no more efforts to sell the township intact.

The proprietors, it should be noted, lost 7,525 acres of their original grant in 1791. The New York–Vermont boundary settlement approved by Congress in that year awarded Long Island (now North Hero) to Vermont with only a nominal compensation to the New York patentees. The loss was not too difficult to bear at that time, however, for Vermonters apparently had enjoyed de facto possession of the island from the beginning. Furthermore, a transfer agreed to with Zephaniah Platt had added 6,172 acres to the Beekmantown patent; so the net loss in acres was only 1,353. Instead of 30,000 acres, the patentees held 28,647.[30]

Clearly, however, the proprietors' plans for quick profit from their grant had not materialized. There is no evidence that any income resulted from the grant prior to the beginning of sales to actual settlers in 1787. Meanwhile, at the end of 1786, the state had billed the proprietors for nearly £640 in quit rents for the years 1769 to 1787 (excluding the war years). The expenses of Cockburn's survey had amounted to £173.[31] Added to the original investment of £860, these expenses put the proprietors out of pocket some £1,673 for a property which had yet to produce any income after seventeen years. Thus, instead of a speculative venture, the Beekmantown grant had begun to assume the aspects of an investment trust for the heirs of the proprietors.

William Cockburn's departure from New York City in June 1785 to divide the Beekmantown patent into lots symbolized the reluctant decision of the proprietors to prepare for the disposition of their property in small segments to individual settlers. Clearly, the proprietors were unhappy over the decision. Such a policy would entail additional expenses, the employment of a local agent, a long wait for piddling payments from impecunious purchasers or tenants, and interminable correspondence. How much simpler it would have been to sell the entire township, pocket a tidy profit, and invest next time in some less troublesome enterprise. But, having failed in all efforts to arrange such a sale, the proprietors had no alternative. Had they been able to foresee that two generations later the disposition of the property to individual settlers would still be incomplete, they would have been still more unhappy.

Initially, however, prospects were not so grim. Cockburn reported (November 12) that the tract "in general turns out to be a very good one—no mountains of any consequence, and very little waste land Unless about 1500 acres of Drowned Lands [swamps] may be called so."

Cockburn reported one human error which would hinder settlement. Judge Platt, the chief proprietor of neighboring Plattsburgh, "thro' a mistake has run in about one third part of Beekman Town" and "has laid part of it into Lotts and I believe made contracts with several for some of them." However, Platt was willing to compensate the Beekmantown proprietors with lands which he owned on the northern edge of their patent. Accordingly, Platt became the owner of lands in the southern portion of Beekmantown, while the Beekmantown proprietors acquired title to lands across the township's northern border. The net gain to the Beekmantown grantees, as noted, was 6,172 acres.[32] In appraising the agreement later (December 4, 1787), Platt left no doubt as to his feelings. "Your families Estate is £1000 the better in Addition of lands and the settlements I have made adjoining and Building Mills, etc. I only request that you would do something towards settling your land."

In fact, the Beekmans had begun to prepare for settling their lands even before Platt's blunt request. On September 5, 1787, three months before Platt's letter, they had retained Colonel Josiah Throop as local agent. Throop had lobbied for land grants from New York State for Canadian refugees who were fellow revolutionary veterans. With the passage of the desired legislation in 1784, he had become a land agent, surveyor, and attorney for refugees.[33]

The original instructions to Throop (September 5, 1787) were relatively simple. For leases the Beekmans demanded seven pounds yearly per one hundred acres. At Throop's urging, William Beekman grudgingly agreed to allow two years free of rent, instead of one as he had planned. Leases were to run for twenty-one years with provision against cutting valuable timber unnecessarily or otherwise injuring the land. Concerning sales, Beekman had heard that lots "fetch in Cash from 14/ [shillings] to 20/ per acre and that those bordering on the Lake have been estimated at a Guinea per acre; nay that Judge Platt demands 40/ per acre for the Water Lots." In any case he preferred lease to sale "unless some generous Offer be made," such as one-fourth down and the balance in three annual payments, plus interest and a mortgage for security.

Throop's reply (November 20, 1787) was discouraging. While he did report the good news that the first lessee planned to sow an acre or two of wheat that fall, he also observed that Judge Platt had offered somewhat better terms. According to Throop, Platt permitted people "to go on his land 5 years and gett what they can (no rent) and then if they Quitt, he will give them 20/ per acre for what they have cleared and fenced." Furthermore, Platt gave away a number of fifty-acre lots to the first settlers "and afterwards sold other lands to advantage." With reference to the sixteen or twenty who had applied "to go on our Land, esteeming it the best on the Lake," he recommended that the proprietors sell cheaply eight or ten lots two or three miles back from the shore.

Early the following spring (March 20, 1788), the Beekmans altered Throop's instructions somewhat. They approved of the leases he had made according to instruction and urged him to secure more. Now, however, they wanted to bind the lessee to build a frame house, clear a reasonable number of acres, plant an orchard, and cut no timber on land not leased. Furthermore, their preference was now—briefly—for sale rather than lease, if sales could be made at $2.50 per acre, one-fourth down, second in two years, third in four years, and fourth in six years with interest at 7 percent until paid. In 1789, however, a new agent replaced Throop, who had apparently moved west.

To replace Throop the proprietors retained Melanchton L. Woolsey. A native of Queens County, Woolsey had settled in Poughkeepsie (Dutchess County) and married into a lesser branch of the Livingston family. During the Revolution, he was an aide to General George Clinton. Having somehow disposed of a considerable inheritance, Woolsey became bankrupt and migrated to Plattsburgh in 1785 to start over again. He was then only twenty-seven years old. Perhaps because of his "in" with Clinton, who was governor until 1795, Woolsey became clerk of Clinton County and commanding officer of its militia forces. President George

Washington also appointed him collector of customs for the Champlain district.[34]

Woolsey gave every promise of being an unusually satisfactory agent. His first letter to the Beekmans (February 20, 1789) reported that he knew of more than twenty people who were "willing to move on in the spring" if the Beekmans would sell rather than lease. Shortly afterward (March 7, 1789), he affirmed his willingness to serve as agent without compensation or for whatever they chose to pay. In fact, the Beekmans chose to pay him 7½ percent of the money collected for land sold and 10 percent on rents collected.[35]

Eager as he was to please, Woolsey, nevertheless, showed no hesitation in informing the Beekmans when he considered the terms offered unacceptable by local standards. The lease terms which they offered, he wrote (March 7, 1789), were ridiculed by all who heard them and, if insisted upon instead of sales, would prevent settlement. The Beekmans insisted, however, that they could settle the town by offering leases because they committed themselves to sell at a reasonable price at any time prior to the expiration of the lease. But the lessor's labors and even those of his neighbors would in the meantime have increased the value of the property greatly. Not many prospective purchasers were willing to place themselves on such a treadmill, working to increase the "reasonable price" of the property which they hoped to buy, even though they were entitled by custom to compensation for improvements they had made. It was, of course, also true that if a reasonable price could not be agreed upon, the property with its increased value reverted to the owner at the expiration of the lease. Failure to agree on a purchase price under such circumstances would leave the tenant with only whatever compensation he could secure for his improvements, while endowing the landlord with a great appreciation in the value of his land. Few of the New England migrants who were a large portion of Beekmantown's prospective settlers were either so desperate or so unsophisticated as to be willing to accept such an agreement, if they really aspired to buy.[36]

The Beekmans capitulated. Only two days after they had reaffirmed their dedication to their leasing policy, they wrote Woolsey (March 25) that they had decided to accept his advice to sell lands in fee simple. They would give a deed of conveyance at once but "take Bonds and Mortgages from each Purchaser as a Security." The price would be three Spanish milled dollars per acre for the water lots, two and one-half for the next four tiers inland, and two for the remainder. They expected the purchaser to pay the cost of the deed and to pay the mortgage with interest in three years. The next fall (October 15), they became even more reasonable. They changed the sales terms to nothing down, payment of one year's interest at the end of the second year, then the interest and one-third of the principal at the end of the third, fourth, and fifth years.

The lease terms they also changed in response to Woolsey's suggestions. The provision of two years free from rent, which Woolsey had stigmatized as "ungenerous," they extended to three. William Beekman also instructed Woolsey (March 23) to change the requirement that tenants build a frame house. "If you Judge that the restricting them to the Building framed Houses will be a ban to Settlement," he wrote, "let them make good Block Houses to be covered with Ceader or pine Shingles." In an area in which log houses of unsquared timbers would predominate for many years and even blockhouses (squared timbers) were not usually covered with shingles, this was little more than a step in the right direction.

The Beekmans (William and James) continued to insist that no two adjoining lots be leased. They hoped to sell one "to advantage" after a lessee had developed the one adjacent to it. While such a policy was much resented in other places at other times,[37] it apparently occasioned little ill feeling in Beekmantown, perhaps because many of those early settlers who leased lots had no intention of remaining for the twenty-one-year term. Instead, as the following chapter will illustrate, they planned to make what they could from the timber resources—not necessarily of only the leased lot—and to sell their "betterments" (house and clearing) before moving on in a few years. To such settlers the important clause in the lease was that granting them three years free of rent.

Woolsey continued to educate the proprietors in the frontier land business. In the summer of 1789 (July 22), he suggested that they make "some trifling present to Mrs. Ward," wife of the man who, as Woolsey wrote, "has made the first opening in the Woods of Beekman." Such a practice, he added, has been "customary in other places." Whether or not the Beekmans complied is unknown.

In 1791 (February 6), when sales were "very dull," Woolsey reported that many came to view the lands but went away discouraged by the high price. In 1792 (December 23) he strongly urged reduction in the price on behalf of some "very respectable people from Vermont." They wished to purchase, he reported, but objected to the old terms. He thought concessions should be made since "people of such caliber" would help the township, and settlement of the shore would increase the value of the back lots.

In the latter instance, Woolsey's timing was bad. At that time the Beekmans were fervently seeking to sell the entire township to Peter Dubree, as previously reported. Their fervor seems more understandable when one notes that Dubree was to pay $3.00 per acre for the entire plot, whereas Woolsey's most recent instructions fixed that price only for the lots along the lake shore. For the back lots, they had been asking only $2.50 and $2.00, depending on the distance from the lake.

John Kelly argued strongly for the Dubree sale (February 2, 1793) on the ground that the legislature seemed likely to pass a law to "enforce the Settlement of all lands within the state, conformably to the terms of grants or patents under which they are held." Should "New England men" move in as squatters under such a law, he thought it would be almost impossible to dispossess them. Presumably, this meant that a legal action to dispossess a squatter could be met by claims that the proprietors' title was void because of their failure to meet the specifications in their original patent concerning rapid settlement. Kelly's reference to New Englanders in this context seems to suggest that removal of New Yorkers would not be so difficult. In any event such considerations make it rather more understandable that the proprietors were reluctant to abandon hope for the Dubree deal and even required Woolsey to dispossess settlers to whom he had made sales after the dates of the Dubree agreement.

Meanwhile, proprietary rights in the Beekmantown patent were becoming widely diffused. Gerard W. Beekman (died 1781) left his property to five daughters. Bachelors Abraham (died 1786) and William (died 1795) divided their portions among numerous nephews and nieces. John Kelly's bankruptcy put his share at the disposal of a legion of creditors several years before his death in 1799. Of the six original proprietary shares, only those of James Beekman and perhaps of Abraham Lott remained under the management of one person after 1795. Thus, the number of Beekman-town's absentee owners had increased greatly; the difficulty of securing unanimity on policies grew correspondingly.

Defaulting purchasers apparently did not experience speedy fore-closure of their mortgages. Nine mortgages to secure purchases were recorded by members of the Beekman family between 1790 and 1793. Six of these were satisfied. While the sales contracts called for full payment at the end of the fifth year, only one was satisfied in as little as six years. One was indulged for forty-three years, another for thirty-nine, two for twenty-one, and another for twenty years. Of the three which were never satisfied and were foreclosed, one had been outstanding for forty-five years, while the other two apparently represented cases of early abandonment. One was foreclosed within one year and the other, after only two years.[38] Clearly, the Beekmans in those years at least were no great gainers by foreclosures.

The income which the proprietors derived from their property in the period of first settlement is impossible to determine. The diffusion of ownership and the paucity of records for even those with the largest shares make even estimates unreliable. Had they been able to sell all of their land at the reasonable price of fifteen shillings per acre in 1790, they would indeed have gained a tidy profit. Their return would have been £22,500 on an investment of about £1,700. Compound interest on that investment at 7 percent for twenty-one years would have brought it to only £7,039. However, they made sales very slowly and received payment, as the figures on the mortgages indicate, even more slowly. It seems doubtful that they were able to lease much of the property. Consequently, one must conclude that from the standpoint of the original proprietors, the investment meant a considerable capital loss. To the heirs of the first generation, the plots which they received represented appreciating capital assets which could only be liquidated very slowly.

By 1827 Gerard Beekman, one of William's many nephews, was setting terms which were considerably different from those of the 1790s. Instead of payment on sales in three years, he granted seven. Interest was to begin at once, and the purchaser bound himself to a number of leaselike specifications as in the earlier agreements. He was to cut no trees except to clear land for cultivation or for fuel, fences, or buildings. At least twelve acres of the fifty-acre plot were to be kept in woodland until payment was completed.

Good rail or stone fences were to be built around the property; fallow lands were to be seeded with grass; fifty apple trees were to be planted; and the property was not to be transferred to a third party without consent.[39]

Records kept by James W. Beekman from 1837 to 1849 reveal the policies prevailing at the end of Beekmantown's period of development. James W. Beekman was a grandson of the merchant, James Beekman, who was an original proprietor. His holdings in the town were surprisingly large. Sales, after all, had been more or less continuous since 1789, and the property had been divided and redivided among many heirs. As an original proprietor, his grandfather had held only thirty lots. Yet, after almost half a century of sales and subdivision among heirs (James Beekman had nine children), in 1837 James W. Beekman still had an interest in some seventeen lots. Most of these had been sold but not yet fully paid for. Others were leased. Some were still unsettled.[40]

The agent who represented James W. Beekman locally was a highly respected lawyer, William Swetland. Born in Connecticut, Swetland had graduated from Middlebury College in Vermont and then moved to New York. He had practiced in Plattsburgh since 1811 and was highly regarded both for professional skill and for integrity.[41]

Like the original proprietors, James W. Beekman vacillated a good deal over whether to sell or to retain his holdings. Ultimately, he decided to keep farms for each of his two boys but to sell the rest. In the meantime his decisions on whether to sell or to retain particular properties were influenced by several considerations. In the depression year of 1840, he was not eager to sell because he anticipated an increase in value when "money matters" improved. Specifically, he chose (February 10) to retain a farm in badly run-down condition because its location seemed to promise that it could ultimately be sold for twenty dollars per acre, as had an adjacent farm, instead of eight dollars per acre, which was its current value. Swetland had suggested (February 1) that another farm of little current worth might increase in value because it held a large stand of timber and "wood is becoming somewhat scarce." In several instances, improvements were undertaken in order to enhance the value: a well was dug on a farm which had none; a barn was repaired (in the winter while labor was cheap and logs could be skidded on the snow); an "untenantable" log house was replaced by a new building. Much of the labor for the new house, including completion of the cellar, was apparently done by tenants of other properties in return for a rent reduction. A tenant who complained about the log house in which he was living ("a specimen of the antique," Swetland called it) was authorized to build a new one and take the costs out of his rent.[42]

Swetland's valedictory letter (April 5, 1849) reviewed his record at a time when the patent was "almost wholly disposed of." From the beginning of his agency in 1837, he wrote, he had endeavored "not to sell without a degree of confidence in the honesty, industry and economy of the applicant" but then to "give indulgence when required provided that it did not seem likely to result in eventual loss." Rather than resort to legal action in case of default, it was his policy to "judge from the ability of the tenant, of his character for industry and economy whether he would be able to pay in the end with indulgence. [I]f so, to give him time, and encourage him if he seemed to be losing resolution or to seem to despond: and if we thought he could not buy, to endeavor in a friendly manner, to convince him of that fact, and that it was for his interest to give up the contract, and thus take back the land without controversy—and in such cases the land is all that can be obtained. . . . We presume that more than 100 suits might have been brought (and deemed reasonably so) if the course usually pursued had been adopted. . . . But in all the accounts for this office, with all the members of the [Beekman] family, not a single bill of costs can be found charged, nor any tenant turned out of possession by legal process, altho we believe that not one contract has been fulfilled according to its terms." He thought furthermore that all existing contracts would eventually be paid "except perhaps on No. 128 where Squirrels could scarcely get a living."

To illustrate the validity of his policy, Swetland proudly cited the case of Thomas Ryan. "This contract," he wrote, "was made . . . in June, 1835, to run 5 years, annual payments. You probably recollect him as a very small man, who looks as if he would have difficulty in getting a living in any manner. He began without any means whatever. But we found him to be persevering and industrious. He kept gaining by slow degrees: made improvements on his land—saved everything; has continued to live in the same old log house, unfit for any habitation. If we had pressed him at any time within the first ten or 12 years he must have lost his farm. But he was encouraged to persevere, and he has at length paid for his farm, and has paid you $646.83 of *interest* money, and his $1000 of principal, and has quite a good stock on hand, and some means to build with, and is out of debt. It would really delight you to see him. He is as happy as a Prince, to know that his farm is paid for, and full of gratitude for the indulgence he has received. He would do anything, within possibility, to serve you or any of the family. There are many like cases on the Patent."

Swetland took some trouble to justify this lenient policy in relation to the interests of the proprietors. For one thing, it made possible a much higher price. Purchasers often commented, he observed, that "I can have such a piece of land at such a price (considerably less than we ask) and equally good, but if I happen to be unfortunate by a bad crop, or sickness, or loss of stock, I shall be pressed at once, and probably lose my land and what I have paid besides." He argued further that he knew of no case in which a harsher course would have prevented any loss. There had been remarkably few contracts abandoned or forfeited and in only two or three such cases was the property subsequently resold at a loss— "that is, at a less price than the first contract and interest." In those cases he was convinced that the original price had been "beyond a reasonable valuation." On the whole he thought abandoned contracts had resulted in a net gain.

With the antirent riots of the Hudson valley and their record of violence and bloodshed in mind, Swetland affirmed that "one more gratifying result [of his policy] has been that a satisfied, contented and kind feeling prevails throughout the whole tenancy. No one complains of harshness, oppression, or injustice. They regard your family as benevolent friends, and if any of you will come up and pass through the Patent you will find a different state of feeling from what prevails in many places. We venture the assertion that you will not hear one complaint. You will find thriving and grateful tenants who will meet you with sincere and warm gratitude instead of with complaints and reproaches. You will hear blessings instead of curses." [43]

Swetland reported also that he had collected and remitted some $50,000 and that "many thousands more remain in contract," but there is no way of knowing how many owners shared the proceeds. The amounts which Swetland remitted to James W. Beekman varied considerably but averaged only a few hundred dollars yearly.

How, finally, should one assess the role of the proprietors in the development of Beekmantown?[44] From the standpoint of the state, the role of the Beekmantown proprietors was probably quite useful. By making the grant in 1769, the government liquidated an asset which would otherwise have remained frozen for some time. The fees charged for the issuance of the patent helped provide compensation for a number of highly important government officers. The state also secured the services of the proprietors and their agents in surveying the land, advertising its availability, and collecting from those who chose to rent or purchase portions of the grant. In this last respect, the government had clearly saved its officers a lot of headaches. Probably, the government in 1769 had hoped also to buy the loyalty of the Beekmans by bestowing the patent upon them. In that respect the grant clearly failed.

To the proprietors themselves, the Beekmantown venture was essentially an unfortunate aberration from their usual roles as import-export merchants and investors in New York City real estate. They tried vainly to import tenants from Scotland and to unload their property on other investors. After these failures, the proprietors tried to get what income they could from sales and rentals while waiting for the influx of settlers to increase the value of the unsold portions of the grant. Competition from other sellers never permitted them to impose terms which would have brought them high reward. The same factor explains in large measure why it took eighty years to complete the disposition of the land and why during that time there was so little inclination to foreclose quickly on those who were delinquent in their payments—as most usually were.

The role of Beekmantown's proprietors contrasts sharply with that of the men who developed nearby Plattsburgh. Plattsburgh's proprietors (as will become clearer in chapters 2 and 4) were not New York City merchants but men with experience in rural or small town enterprise. They did not secure their land from the agent of a British king. Instead, they bought land bounties paid to revolutionary soldiers by the state of New York, in whose government many of the Plattsburgh proprietors took active parts. Their land was not suitable only for timber enterprises or farming, but it had numerous mill sites which encouraged industrial development. They did not rely on hired managers to act for them but gave personal, on-the-spot supervision to their business. Above all, they did not wait passively for purchasers or tenants to materialize but invested heavily in businesses calculated to help attract settlers. But for the rapid development which Plattsburgh's proprietors fostered, the Beekmantown investors would have fared still worse than they did.

To the settlers, the role of the proprietors of Beekmantown was not very significant. Apart from surveying the lot lines, the proprietors did virtually nothing to help improve the property. Competition from legions of other sellers required the Beekmans to be reasonable, both as to the terms of purchases or leases and to long delays in payment. Furthermore, as the next chapter will illustrate, less than zealous performance by local agents of the proprietors permitted settlers to violate the terms of their agreements and indeed to appropriate highly valuable timber resources which in law belonged to the owners of the patent.

2

Forest Products

Exploitation of forest resources was fundamental to the developing economy of Beekmantown and the surrounding area. When speculators and settlers first began to show interest in the Champlain valley, white oak and white pine timber were the principal objects of their attention. Indeed, utilization of these resources began before any permanent settlement took place. When settlement did begin, potash, an industrial product made from hardwood ashes, became another major export product of the valley.

Together with the capital gain from increasing land values as wilderness became farmland, the marketing of timber products sustained an expansive, prosperous economy through the first generation of settlement, especially during the period of turmoil in Europe associated with the wars of Napoleon. From the mid-1820s onward, however, approaching exhaustion of marketable timber resources and concomitantly of wilderness areas which could be converted into desirable farmland sharply diminished prosperity. For these reasons it is appropriate in attempting to explain how people made a living in Beekmantown to look closely at the forest industries.

White oak grew abundantly in the virgin forests of the Champlain valley, chiefly in areas of good soil. Its wood had two major commercial uses. One was for staves. Nearly everything which moved in commerce at that time traveled in barrellike wooden containers. White oak staves were strongly preferred for such containers because they were hard, tough, durable, and less likely than others to split, shrink, warp, or impart an unpleasant taste to food products. Because of these qualities, white oak staves usually commanded an appreciably higher price than those of other woods. White oak's second major use was in ship construction. Some of the same qualities which made white oak serve so well for staves made it preferable also for ship timbers, particularly for the basic frame of sailing ships. Unlike staves, which could be made from scraps and could be produced and marketed with almost no capital, timbers had to be of considerable size and were so heavy they were difficult for a poor man to transport to market. Consequently, production of timbers was an operation of larger scale and usually of more profit than the making of staves.

White pine was not abundant in Beekmantown itself but grew generally in the sandy soils and the more rugged country to the west and south. Like white oak, white pine had two basic commercial uses. One was for masts. Some white pines grew as high as 250 feet; they were also very straight.[1] These qualities put American white pine in great demand to provide masts for ships of the British navy and for commercial vessels. Because the wood is soft, easily worked, yet strong, white pine was also in great demand as general purpose lumber. In fact, white pine afforded the bulk of the lumber exported from North America.

Some utilization of the valley's timber occurred under the French regime. An expedition searching for timber suitable for ship construction explored the lake shores in 1734. By 1760 the French were using both pine and oak secured from the southernmost portions of the valley. All these operations of the French, however, were on a very small scale; they barely began the exploitation of the valley's enormous supply of timber.[2]

"Soon after the conquest of Canada," wrote geographer Thomas Gordon in 1836, speculators flocked to the shores of Lake Champlain "in quest of pine and oak timber."[3] The ill-fated Charles Fredenburgh (see Prologue) had a sawmill on the Saranac River just south of Beekmantown in the 1760s. Farther to the south, William Gilliland occupied himself in a similar way. Moses Hazen, a transplanted New Englander, operated sawmills and an "ashery" for making potash at St. Johns on the falls of the Richelieu River between Lake Champlain and the St. Lawrence. On the east shore of the lake, Vermonters, including the redoubtable Allen brothers, were also beginning to dispatch rafts of timber to Quebec. In London price quotations for "Quebec yellow pine"—really white pine and much of it from Vermont and New York—began to appear regularly in the 1760s.[4]

In the parlance of the times, the timber business was quite distinct from the lumber business and initially more important. Timber, meaning squared timbers of either oak or pine, was produced for sale in Britain, where it enjoyed a relatively low duty in comparison with sawn lumber. Conforming to mercantilist traditions, the British preferred to reserve to themselves the value added to the product by putting it into finished form.[5]

To produce timber in the form which the British preferred was a relatively simple process.[6] An independent operator might have contracted with a Quebec merchant to supply a fixed quantity of timber or, more often, he might intend simply to sell his product speculatively for whatever it would bring on the Quebec market. At the onset of winter, he would dispatch a crew of ten or twelve men into a promising wooded region, often without bothering to ascertain who owned the property. After the crew had selected and felled the most desirable trees, a "liner" indicated where the cutting was to be done to square the timber; a "scorer" cut notches into the indicated lines at intervals of about thirty inches; a "hewer" armed with a broadax then split off the wood between the notches, leaving the timber squared on two sides. The crew then turned the log to repeat the process on the remaining two sides, ending with a remarkably smooth, square timber and an enormous waste, especially from near the butt of the log. In the case of oak timber, the waste could be transformed into staves.

Getting the timber from the forest to the lake was the job of teamsters, generally local farmers working with their own oxen. Because the timbers were so heavy, this work could be done only when the ground was covered with snow, which served to reduce the friction. The work required great skill, and those who did it commanded premium wages. They preferred oxen to horses for the work because oxen were cheaper, hardier, and moved more deliberately than horses.

Rafting required still another set of skills and posed additional difficulties. Oak timber was often so heavy that it would not float. Consequently, all timber rafts had to include at least some pine. In some instances rafts were built upon the ice. In any case they had to be ready to go at the time of greatest water flow in the spring; later they might well ground at the Richelieu rapids. To construct a raft, about twenty timbers were bound together in several "courses," or layers, to form a "crib." A large number of cribs were then joined together to form a raft some 120 feet wide and often as long as 1,200 to 1,500 feet. Loaded with other export products of the valley—staves, potash, boards, planks, and a variety of agricultural commodities—the rafts departed usually in May. They were propelled both by a number of sails and by the labor of oarsmen. At the rapids of the Richelieu, the raft's cargo had to be landed and portaged for some distance. The raft itself was broken down into smaller segments—each of which then shot the rapids in turn, while the anxious crew hoped it would hold together. If it did not, the oak might well sink and the pine timbers scatter so widely as to make recovery too difficult to be practicable. Below the rapids the cribs were reassembled, and the cargo was reloaded for the remainder of the trip to Quebec. The larger rafts sometimes carried 100 to 150 men.[7]

Upon arriving at the port city, usually in late June, a speculator who had not contracted in advance for the disposal of his product usually let it "hang" anchored in midstream while he arranged to sell it. A number of factors tended to foster a disposition to sell cheaply. In the first place, British buyers tended to prefer timber from the Baltic area. Second, rafts brought their owners significant supplemental income by serving as a form of commercial transportation—the only one economically practical for bulky export products. Furthermore, virtually limitless supplies of the raw material were readily available—free even from the cost of acquiring the landowner's permission, close to the natural avenues of transportation, and capable of being transformed into a marketable product with a minimum investment, as well as good chances for incidental benefits from both the "improvement" of land and from freight charges. Thus, until the market situation in Britain altered with the Napoleonic wars, the Champlain valley timber speculator was usually willing to sell his product at a very low price.

Some of the problems of a contractor who agreed to deliver a specified quantity of timber for a fixed price appear in the correspondence of Pliny Moore, the pioneer developer of the town of Champlain, a few miles north of Beekmantown. Moore and his associate, Royal Corbin, had contracted to deliver a specific quantity of timber and boards in 1793. On May 3 Corbin wrote Moore to urge him to hurry in getting his timber to the rendezvous point near Point au Fer. One reason for haste was that the lake was falling fast; delay would increase the difficulty of traversing the rapids. Equally important was the imminence of the agreed delivery date, apparently May 15. Corbin thought that the merchant with whom they had contracted was not particularly eager to have them meet their contract. The outbreak of war between Britain and France had apparently led the merchants to expect no timber ships that year and, indeed, no more until convoys could be arranged. Thus, the merchant would welcome an excuse not to keep the contract as the timber, if delivered, would almost certainly have to be stored at Quebec for a year. Corbin still hoped to meet the deadline. "We dont Stick working Sundays," he noted, but one of his subcontractors had failed to deliver a promised two thousand feet of oak and adverse winds held him up. On May 21 he wrote that he had returned from St. Johns with his men "in order to forward on the Timber from Chazy and boards that we may come up to our Contract as close as possible." His letter of June 2 indicated that a settlement had been negotiated. But, the bookkeeping was still incomplete, and those who had provided him timber to sell were still clamoring to know how they had fared.[8]

Still more detail on the conduct of the timber exporting business appears in the journal of a young Vermonter who took a raft from St. Johns to Quebec in 1805. Guy Catlin, aged twenty-three, was acting on behalf of a Burlington merchant. At St. Johns he took on a pilot to help get over the rapids. One part of the raft grounded on an island, and damage to one crib had to be repaired. When an anchor cable gave way on a Sunday, his raft drifted downstream with only seven men aboard until it ran into two other anchored rafts which blocked the channel. One of the hands administered a "glazing" to the public official who had harassed the men for violating the Sabbath. With another pilot and fixed sails, the raft completed the journey to Quebec. There, however, Catlin overshot the port and grounded twelve miles downstream. Fortunately, very high tides made it possible to get the raft back to Quebec. There Catlin spent days aboard his raft waiting, as were others on their rafts, for bidders to make their appearance. He finally completed the sale of the timber and of the other products aboard and returned to Burlington in September.[9]

Beekmantown's virgin forest had begun to fall before the Beekmans secured their patent, and it continued to do so in the period before settlement. The chief duty of the caretaker whom the Beekmans hired in 1768, the year before the issuance of the patent, was to prevent the theft of timber from Long Island. In 1772 a traveling British official expressed concern over operations which Hazen, Fredenburgh, and McKay had conducted at the mouth of the Saranac, the future site of Plattsburgh, just a few miles south of Beekmantown. Although the sawmill no longer operated, they had wastefully exploited much of the nearby pine best suited for masts and the most valuable white oak as well.[10] In 1785, when the proprietors instructed William Cockburn on laying out the lot lines (June 15), they asked him to determine, not whether, but how much timber had been cut before the Revolution by Hazen and Gilliland. Finally, Thomas Tredwell, one of Beekmantown's earliest settlers, while acting as agent for the proprietors, blamed the limited value of the remaining timber (April 13, 1803) on the fact that most of the "strait-rifted" white oak, the most valuable timber resource, had been removed before settlement.

The Beekmans themselves, while never interested in investing in timber ventures, gave ample evidence that they knew the value of their forest resources. In instructing Kelly (July 21, 1768) on how to lay out the borders of their tract so as to include as much as possible of the most valuable land, the proprietors listed as the first criterion for appraising its value the size and kind of trees. The suitability of the land for farming came next. When they described their property to prospective settlers (December 24, 1773), the proprietors made no mention of the soil but cited as leading advantages, first, water communication with Quebec and, then, "finest and largest white oak Timber."

Precisely what role these forest resources played in bringing Hazen to arrange the first settlement of Beekmantown is unclear. Surely no man in the region had a significantly better understanding of the prospects for profit from the Champlain valley's vast woodland than he did. But, in arranging the first permanent settlement in Beekmantown, he seems to have had many considerations in view. To appreciate the complexity of Hazen's interests and motivation, a brief account of his career is essential.

Like several other men associated with the early history of Beekmantown and Clinton County, Hazen began life in modest circumstances, rose to considerable wealth and prominence, and then experienced tragic misfortunes late in life. A native of Haverhill, Massachusetts, Hazen had abandoned the role of apprentice tanner to serve in the Seven Years' War. After distinguished service with Rogers' Rangers, he purchased a commission in the British army for £800 sterling. How he acquired that sum of money is not clear.

In any case he soon retired on half pay and engaged in a variety of business ventures in Quebec, mostly in association with Gabriel Christie, a British officer of high status who ultimately returned to Britain. Land speculation in the St. Johns area was clearly one of Hazen's major activities, but he also contracted to supply the British navy with masts and timber, some of which he secured from the shores of Lake Champlain. At St. Johns, Hazen held a number of local offices, built a twenty-room "manor house," operated two sawmills, a forge, and an "ashery" for making potash. After splitting with Christie in 1770, Hazen began to experience acute financial problems. On the eve of the Revolution, British General Sir Guy Carleton characterized him as "greatly distressed in his circumstances." [11]

When the Revolution broke out, Hazen found himself suspected by both sides. Both the British and the Americans, when they could get their hands on him, placed him in custody. He joined the American forces only after they rescued him from imprisonment by the British. Congress then placed him in command of a regiment composed in part of other Canadians—some English in descent, others French—which he led throughout the war.

At the conclusion of the war, Hazen dispatched twelve men from his disbanded regiment to begin the development of what would become Clinton County. Led by Hazen's nephew and former adjutant, Benjamin Mooers, Hazen's settlement party left Washington's camp at Newburgh in the summer of 1783 and arrived at Point au Roche in Beekman Patent on August 19. Mooers and his men, all French Canadians except for Mooers and another Hazen nephew, Lieutenant Zaccheus Peaslee, had cleared some land and built a log house by the time Hazen arrived in October. Except perhaps for a few of the French Canadians, some of whom had abandoned farms in the area at the outset of the Revolution, no one remained during the winter. Mooers and Peaslee returned to Massachusetts. Hazen had problems with the government which required his attention.

Barred by the British from returning to St. Johns, Hazen apparently hoped to make Point au Roche the new center for economic and cultural development of the northern Champlain valley. Point au Roche, he believed, was the "most proper place upon the Lake for a Town." He hoped also to make it the site of a "Coledge and Convent" as well as the seat of county government. [12]

In retrospect it is easier to see why Point au Roche did not become the metropolis which Hazen expected than to understand why he thought it would. The most serious deficiency of Hazen's prospective metropolis was the absence of mill sites. A stream does enter the lake at Point au Roche but, for some distance back from the shore, the terrain is so flat as to provide no opportunity to establish mills powered by the fall of water. By contrast the mouth of the Saranac, where the Platts chose to found Plattsburgh, afforded excellent locations for a number of mills.

Another anomaly in Hazen's selection of Point au Roche was that the land there belonged to the Beekmans and that he seems to have made no effort for several years to come to any understanding with them.

One of many interests which Hazen pursued centered upon land grants to Canadian and Nova Scotian war veterans. By dint of prolonged lobbying—reinforced by desire to keep the refugees off local welfare rolls elsewhere in the state—Hazen and others persuaded the government of New York State to set aside 131,500 acres for those who had left Canada or Nova Scotia to fight for American independence. Some 250 veterans qualified for grants of five hundred acres for enlisted men, one thousand for officers, in a tract which ran southward from the Canadian border, occasionally along the lake shore but more often in the less desirable back country.

Many refugees quickly sold all or parts of their grants to speculators such as Hazen's agent, Mooers, who was in a fortunate position for such efforts. As Hazen's adjutant, he had, of course, known most of those who received grants. Unsophisticated, unfamiliar with English, in some instances illiterate—many of the veterans had in fact chosen Mooers to represent them in collecting back pay, rations, and other emoluments due from the federal government. Now many trusted him to act for them with reference to their land grants. In fact, Mooers sent agents into Canada soliciting authorization to represent others and journeyed there himself in 1792. Despite what would appear an obvious conflict of interest (from which indeed there did arise allegations of fraud), Mooers by 1790 had acquired 20,126 acres at an average cost of seven cents per acre. By 1808 he owned some 30,000 acres, nearly one-fourth of the entire refugee tract.[13]

Fully as ambiguous as the relationship between Mooers and the refugees was that between Mooers and Hazen. Hazen had definitely employed Mooers to begin the settlement at Point au Roche in

1783. The careful exploration of the refugee tract which Mooers made in 1785 was apparently also at Hazen's behest. When Hazen experienced a disabling stroke in 1786, Mooers received his power of attorney and continued to act for him while Hazen lived in New York City and later in Troy until his death in 1803. The extensive correspondence between the two, including statements of account, obfuscates as much as it elucidates concerning their financial relationship. In fact, Hazen's affairs were in near total confusion in his last years, during which he was repeatedly jailed for debt.

Conspicuously absent from the surviving Hazen-Mooers correspondence is evidence of extensive activities relating to the exploitation of forest resources. Nevertheless, it seems likely that such activities did go on at Point au Roche during the time (1786–1794) when Mooers lived there year round as Hazen's agent. In 1787 Mooers cut a "winter road" westward through the Beekman's patent with the approval of the proprietors. The usual purpose of such roads was to get logs or timber from the interior to the lake shore; the configuration of the refugee tract makes it unlikely that the road related to that project. Hazen also claimed to have made improvements worth $3,000 in the Beekman grant and received title to 457 acres (worth at least £457) at Point au Roche in satisfaction of that claim.[14] Such extensive improvement necessarily entailed clearing the timber from many acres. In the same year in which Mooers was cutting the winter road, one Samuel Mix, then "ingaged in getting some Lumber over the Rappits" at St. Johns, gave as one of two addresses at which he could be reached "Mr. More point Derush" (that is, care of Benjamin Mooers, Point au Roche).[15] In 1792 Mooers shipped three barrels of potash and thirteen barrels of the more highly refined pearlash to London, quoted Quebec prices on squared timber, and identified an individual who would take timber to Quebec and hold it until prices rose.[16]

Several considerations may help explain why Hazen and Mooers appear to have done relatively little in the forest industries during the first years of settlement. One is, of course, the preoccupation with land speculation which was indeed highly rewarding for Mooers. Another is that for the years 1786–1788 the legal status of the trade was much in doubt because of a British Order in Council barring "importation of all goods and commodities of the growth and manufacture of the United States into any of the ports of the

Province of Quebec."[17] Only in 1788 did the British explicitly endorse importation of timber and agricultural products into Quebec via Lake Champlain. Still more fundamental in discouraging ventures with forest products in the mid-1780s was the depressed condition of commerce generally. Prices were simply too low to encourage investment in forest industries.

Lumber, as opposed to squared timbers, did somewhat better in the depressed years after the Revolution. In 1785, before any settlement had occurred at Plattsburgh under its new proprietors, Zephaniah Platt and his fellow investors pledged twenty pounds each to finance construction of a gristmill, sawmill, forge, a small boat ("petteauger"), and a fishing seine. By late 1786 they had a sawmill in operation on the Saranac. By 1787—despite troubles with ice jams, desperate shortages of food and clothing, and inexperience—their mill had turned out fourteen thousand feet of boards.[18]

To the north of Beekmantown, Pliny Moore put another sawmill into operation at Champlain in 1788. Alarmed by reports that trespassers were "cutting timber on our land" and convinced that "there will doubtless be repeated incroachments of that kind" until he took up residence himself, Moore moved to the site in the spring of 1788. He had his mill in working order by August despite problems with inexperienced workers and the shortage of food and clothing, such as had plagued the Saranac enterprise the year before. Some of the lumber produced by these early mills found an export market at Quebec, but much, it appears, went into local construction.[19]

The generation of European warfare which followed the success of the French Revolution changed economic conditions in the Champlain valley dramatically. French domination extended farther and farther into the Baltic region, from which Britain had long secured its ship timbers and other forest products. Therefore, the British became deeply concerned to assure the nation an adequate supply of timber, especially for naval construction. In 1795 the government imposed a duty of ten shillings on Baltic timber, about one-third to one-half the advantage which Baltic producers enjoyed in freight charges. In 1804 the duty became thirty shillings. Between 1806 and 1809, Napoleon's Continental System cut off more and more of Britain's Baltic supply. Worried officials raised the preferential duty to £2.14.8, but by then demand had forced prices up to a level which made the duty largely irrelevant. Britain

TABLE I.

Imports into Great Britain from Quebec

Year	Oak	Pine	Masts
1802	387	365	195
1803	1,998	1,350	165
1804	1,954	2,282	1,314
1805	2,466	1,263	535
1806	3,688	1,754	1,152
1807	5,734	2,700	2,753
1808	8,832	9,861	13,333
1809	5,853	17,353	8,333
1810	17,234	38,869	16,680
1811	24,451	52,888	19,025
1812	18,231	32,716	14,019

NOTE: Figures (except for masts) represent loads equal to 50 cubic feet or 600 U.S. board feet or about 2,500 pounds. Robert G. Albion, *Forests and Sea Power* (Cambridge: Harvard University Press, 1926), appendix D. Arthur R. M. Lower concluded that over half the oak timber exported from Quebec between 1807 and 1811 came from Lake Champlain ("Lumbering in Eastern Canada," I, 173 ff.). Fernand Ouellet asserted that for the years 1808 to 1812 only about one-fourth of the oak, pine, and potash exported from Quebec were from the United States; he included the upper St. Lawrence valley as well as Lake Champlain. Ouellet, *Histoire Economique et Sociale du Québec, 1760–1850* (Montreal and Paris: Fides, 1966), 191.

desperately needed timber, and the port of Quebec became a major supplier of its need.[20]

How Beekmantown settlers responded to these bonanza conditions the letters to the proprietors from their local agents make very clear. A foreshadowing of what was to come appeared in the spring of 1803. The proprietors' agent, Thomas Tredwell, wrote then (April 13) to inform them: "Mr. Allen Hackett, who has followed for some time the business of getting square timber for the Quebec Market, wishes to get a raft next winter about the Bay St. Armand [now Treadwell Bay]." He offered twelve dollars per thousand feet for timbers removed from lakefront lots and ten

TABLE 2.

Rafts and Contents Imported at St. Johns

Year	Rafts	Pine Timber	Oak Timber	Pine Planks	Pine Boards
1802	21	95,000	123,522	299,900	327,900
1803	26	163,000	160,720	1,349,500	603,408
1804	44	391,100	202,000	1,703,700	609,411
1805	30	178,000	124,700	1,419,000	1,024,000
1806	28	1,800	282,150	443,700	491,000
1807	37	132,780	453,000	671,700	186,216
1808	25	520,500	98,550	823,200	2,000
1809	23	294,200	35,000	609,000	62,494
1810	102	1,975,800	1,132,000	3,032,800	1,020,200
1811	96	1,559,300	509,050	3,904,200	42,000
1812	72	1,168,140	208,510	2,465,000	20,000

NOTE: All figures except rafts in board feet. Public Archives of Canada, Imperial Blue Books Relating to Canada, 1820–1821, no. 66, p. 6.

dollars for timbers from lots in the interior. Tredwell recommended acceptance and offered both to check the amount taken from each lot and to forward the payment, but William Beekman (June 9) refused. Removal of the timbers would make it harder to sell lots, he believed—despite Tredwell's argument to the contrary—and in a manner unspecified would encourage others to cut without offering to pay.

That others would need no such encouragement, as a contract with Hackett might have afforded, became evident in 1806. John Wilson of Plattsburgh wrote the proprietors: "I have been to examine your Lands and find numerous trespassers cutting and destroying your timber particularly the White Oak which is in great demand at Quebec." He suggested that a compromise be worked out with the trespassers because what they had cut would be ruined "unless used this year." William Beekman authorized Wilson (February 10) to determine the value of the timber cut and to secure compensation. In order to make compensation possible, Wilson apparently had to allow the trespassers to transport the timber to Quebec

TABLE 3.
Value of Timber Products Imported at St. Johns, 1807

Oak timber, 453,000 feet at 1/6 per foot	£33,975
Potash, 3,969 bbls. at £6.15.0	26,790
Staves and heading, 120,000 at £28 per 1,000	3,360
Pine butts, 4,545 at 12-1/2	2,841
Pine boards and planks, 857,915 feet at £2.10.0 per 1,000	2,145
Pine spars, 778 at £2.10 each	1,945
*Oak boards, 7,000 at 1/3 per foot	437
Pine timber, 132,780 feet at £3 per 1,000	398
Pine masts, 20 at £15 each	300
Birch plank, 60,000 feet at £2.12.0 per 1,000	156
*Cherry boards, 1,506 at 1/per foot	75
Shingles, 10,000 at 12/per 1,000	6

*Calculation assumes quantity figures represent board feet; if they really represent boards, the value figures given would have to be multiplied by the length of the boards, but their length is unknown. Some prices were given as ranges: staves and heading, £20 to £35; pine butts, 10/ (shillings) to 15/; pine spars, £2 to £3; pine masts, £10 to £20. Total value of timber exports as here calculated was £72,428. At 8/ to $1.00, this would amount to $181,070. Value figures are calculations based on prices and quantities cited by the contemporary traveler, John Lambert, *Travels through Canada and the United States . . . 1806, 1807, and 1808* (2 vols., 2d ed., London, 1813), I, 260.

for sale (February 8). But, having made the sale in Quebec, they chose not to return to New York's jurisdiction with its proceeds.

In another instance Wilson found a large number of logs which had been cut but was unable to ascertain who was responsible. When he sought authorization (December 5, 1806) to cut more to fill out a raft to get the material to Quebec for sale before it was ruined, William Beekman refused (December 22).

Wilson's next frustration came at the hands of an enterprising individual whom he identified only as Mr. Shefflen. In Wilson's words (January 14, 1807): "Mr. Shefflen has sent into this country an agent of the name of McCoy who by Virtue of a pretended claim of Mr. Shefflen to your land together with other large tracts in this country, has given license to several persons to enter on your lands and the lands of others and to cut and take away any quantity of Timber for Canadas Market. The persons who have contracted with said McCoy have and still are introducing large numbers of Canadians who are spreading havoc amongst the timber in every direction. Yesterday ten of them encamped upon Lot 140 and have marked 180 trees for destruction. Likewise on Lot 143. I went immediately and forbid them. They replied that they should persist and that McCoy had assured them that Mr. Shefflen would make them harmless. The resoluteness of those fellows embarrass[és] me very much; it would occasion a multiplicity of law suits to prosecute them and it seems as if nothing short of that would deter them."

"Mr. Shefflen" was Thomas Schiefflin, a Montreal merchant who had moved to New York City in 1805 and had become a druggist. He claimed title derived from the French Gauchetierre grant to lands overlapping Beekman Patent. The agent, John Mackay (rather than McCoy), was a Canadian who left his employer about the time that the trespasses were taking place. Mackay then wrote Pliny Moore, his prospective successor, that Schiefflin was not to be trusted very far. Moore, who had had business correspondence with Schiefflin since 1801, chose not to involve himself in this affair. Two years later, in *Jackson ex dem. Winthrop v. Ingraham*, the court dismissed Schiefflin's land claim on the basis that no old French grants were valid unless repatented under New York law.[21]

The end of Wilson's agency came soon after his report of these trespasses. On January 14 he requested both an option to buy lot 58 on which he had made improvement "with intent to purchase" and authorization to remove timber from it to fill out a raft. Wilson had previously written (February 8, 1806) that "ill-minded persons among us . . . will inform . . . you that I am getting all the timber I can off your Land." Now, William Beekman apparently became convinced that his agent was not only incompetent but a timber thief as well. He put his reliance again on Thomas Tredwell (June 1, 1807).

Had Wilson salvaged anything for the proprietors from the timber cut by trespassers? Somehow, Wilson had put together a raft composed in part of timber abandoned by trespassers on Beekman lands and got it to Quebec in the spring of 1807, but it brought no income to the proprietors. He had entrusted the income to his partner, explained Wilson (October 19, 1807). But, the partner left Quebec first and squandered all the money on the way home. He then moved to Vermont, where collection would be difficult.

The termination of records early in 1808 makes it impossible to determine whether or not Tredwell was more successful than Wilson in combating timber theft. The few letters from Tredwell before that time were not very encouraging. On October 26, 1807, he wrote that Samuel Tobine, who had signed a lease after being threatened with ejectment in 1804 because of his trespasses, had removed much timber from his leased lot—in contravention of the lease terms. Tredwell hoped to get a little money from Tobine occasionally because he was making potash, but suing him for possession of the product would be fruitless "for he sells it as fast as he makes it." Tredwell also identified James Farnsworth, who was traveling to New York to buy lot 82, as one of the "greatest Trespassers upon the Patent" (November 16). He had stripped not only lot 82 but several adjoining lots of all white oak. Precisely how many trees Farnsworth had cut, Tredwell said, he could not determine (December 2) "till I have an opportunity to get the stumps counted." Tredwell reported problems with other trespassers as well. He could not stop trespassing which had begun on some lots to the north because lot lines had not been run, and it was impossible to determine against which one of the many proprietors the trespass was committed. In his last surviving letter (December 2), Tredwell merely noted that John Wait and Sylvester Phelps had five or six men cutting timber on lot 108.

Timber theft conducted on such a scale and in so flagrant a manner clearly had considerable support in public opinion. The extent to which such support existed in Beekmantown is suggested by the last surviving letters which the proprietors received in this period. They are character references for trespasser James Farnsworth. His honesty and good character, as well as his unquestioned industry, received unstinting praise from James Tobias, a former agent of the proprietors, and from Jonathan Griffin and Peter Sailly. Griffin had recently been Plattsburgh supervisor and was then (1808) a state assemblyman; Sailly had been a member of Congress and was soon to be appointed by President Thomas Jefferson as regional collector of customs.

The embargo and other federal restrictions on commerce between 1807 and 1812 affected Beekmantown's timber business adversely—but rather less than ruinously. The embargo, barring all exports from the end of 1807 until its repeal in the spring of 1809, did reduce the number of rafts passing St. Johns (see table 2) from 37 in 1807 to 25 in 1808, but there had been only 21 rafts in each of the years from 1800 through 1802. Only 23 rafts cleared St. Johns in 1809. During the next three years (1810–1812), the numbers were 102, 96, and 72. Not until 1819, when 113 rafts entered, was even the lowest of these three figures ever exceeded.

Because rafts represented a very large capital investment, often employing over one hundred men and carrying a variety of valley export products, owners were usually men of some standing in the community. Among those who dispatched rafts in 1811 were Levi Platt, something of an economic colossus in the county until his bankruptcy in 1827; Pliny Moore, the principal proprietor of Champlain; and attorney John Nichols. Another was Charles Marsh, future supervisor for both Plattsburgh (1819) and Beekmantown (1823). In addition to Marsh, several other raftsmen of 1811 were probably residents of Beekman Patent. Among them were Nathaniel Chittenden, David Parsons, and in partnership with another man, the trespassing James Farnsworth.[22]

After the war the business of exporting timber and lumber via St. Johns revived strongly. Britain's wartime duties remained in effect, affording Canadian and Lake Champlain producers an extraordinary cushion of protection. In 1820, according to Arthur R. M. Lower, Baltic timber paid a duty which was 130 percent of the price of timber delivered in Britain.[23]

Pine rather than oak was the focal point of the Champlain valley's postwar business. Between 1815 and 1820, oak timber exports were about half what they had been between 1800 and 1805. Even in the peak year, 1819, oak timber exports were less than one-fifth what they had been in 1810. Pine exports, on the other hand, were at their all-time high, both for timber (over two million board feet) and for boards and planks (nearly six million board feet).[24]

Clinton County then, according to the not very reliable United States Census of 1820, was producing more lumber in value terms ($62,190) than any other county in the country. It also had the greatest capital investment in sawmills ($61,150) and paid the highest amount in wages ($9,480), although it employed fewer laborers in sawmills (seventy-six) than did two other counties (each seventy-seven). According to the census, all this was pine.[25]

In 1822 two coincidental developments abruptly diverted Cham-

plain valley trade from Quebec to New York City. After extensive investigation and deliberation, the British Parliament profoundly altered the regulations affecting Canadian trade. Instead of
permitting many products of the United States to enter Canada
free of duty and to be exported as if Canadian, Parliament now
required in the Canada Trade Act of 1822 that heavy duties be
imposed, particularly on timber products, in order to favor Canadian over American producers in the British market.[26]

The second, and more important development of 1822, was the
opening of the Champlain Canal linking Whitehall at the southern
end of the lake with the Hudson River and the port of New York.
Now valley residents could market their products both in their
own country and in their own state. No tariffs, no customs regulations, no Richelieu rapids, no more problem and expense in transferring income from Canada to the preferred purchasing market at
New York. As a busier port than Quebec, New York would
generally afford more competitive purchasing and more expedi-
tious movement of cargo. In 1822, even before it was officially
open, the Champlain Canal carried nearly three times as much
lumber (fifteen million board feet) as had exited via St. Johns in
1819, the busiest of all years on the Richelieu.[27]

An incidental effect of the canal was to put an end to rafting.
Rafts were no longer necessary—as they had been—to navigate
the rapids of the Richelieu, and on the canal they were subject
to a discriminatory toll (double that for the same material in a
boat) because of damage which they inflicted on the banks.[28] Within a short time, the traffic in timber products was almost exclusively by boat.

In a more fundamental sense, rafting was no longer necessary.
It had arisen as a means of traversing the Richelieu and because
of the preference in Britain for squared timber rather than finished
lumber. Thus, Champlain valley producers could now market
more of their product as lumber and plank and less as squared
timber. As early as 1822, the Champlain Canal carried far more
lumber than had the Richelieu, but it appears never to have transported as much squared timber as did the Richelieu in its busiest
years. To the valley this meant more income because of the value
added by transforming logs into lumber or plank. The waste required in hewing pine timbers for the British market also ceased.

Precisely what the opening of the Champlain Canal meant to
the residents of Beekmantown is impossible to determine. It is

clear, however, that timber resources continued to be important for many years. To cite one illustration, the enumeration of sawmills by state and federal censuses shows that the number of sawmills reached a peak about 1840. Specifically, Beekmantown had no sawmills in 1821, one in 1825, five in 1835, ten in 1840, three in 1850, and two in 1855.

Other towns in the county had more mills—larger ones—and had them earlier. Undoubtedly, much Beekmantown timber found its way to them. The probable explanation of the difference is that Beekmantown's streams were inadequate. Few and small, they afforded poor locations for water-powered sawmills. When mills did come to Beekmantown, they probably did so because the available timber adjacent to more favorable mill sites had been exhausted. At least one of the three mills in Beekmantown in 1850 derived its power from a steam engine rather than from water power.[29]

To understand fully the significance of the valley's timber trade, it is necessary to conceive it in a broader perspective. Nationally, lumber exports in the period 1824–1826 were consistently about the same value (roughly $2 million annually) as exports of pork, rice, and all sea products. The only exports consistently of much greater value than lumber were cotton, tobacco, wheat and flour, and "all manufactures."[30] From 1820 at the latest through 1850, New York State led all others by a vast margin in the value of lumber products. In 1840 New York lumber was worth more than twice as much as that of Maine, the second-ranking state. In 1850 second-place Pennsylvania ($7,729,058) produced slightly more than half as much income from lumber as New York ($13,126,759). Within New York State, the Champlain Canal transported about three-fourths of the lumber which came to tidewater. Of this, slightly more than 10 percent came from Canada or from Vermont. Thus, in the period when New York led the U.S. and lumber exports were of considerable importance to the nation, the lion's share of New York's lumber exports came from the New York side of the Champlain valley. In 1835 the ninety-eight million board feet of lumber entering the canal at Whitehall were worth $1,768,184. The next most valuable export of the valley, wool, brought only $215,840. The volume of timber products passing through the canal diminished after 1836, but their value continued to run two or more times that of the second-ranking export of the valley even in the late 1840s.[31]

To Beekmantown settlers and to the nation as a whole before

1830, production of potash and pearlash was roughly equal in importance to production of various forms of lumber. In fact, the European market for potash provided Champlain valley settlers with one of their major sources of cash income.

Potash, a chemical substance which can be derived from hardwood ashes, is the basic ingredient of lye. In the period of Beekmantown's development, its principal use was as a "scouring" or cleansing agent to remove the "yolk," or "gummy secretions," which form a large part of the weight of wool as it comes from the sheep. It was also widely used in bleaching, dyeing, and the manufacture of glass and soap. Demand was greatest in Britain, but potash was imported also by other areas of western Europe, including the Netherlands, France, and Italy. The major sources of supply were the United States, Canada, and the timbered regions of the Baltic, especially Russia.[32]

Production of potash had begun in the American colonies at an early date, but Baltic suppliers dominated the European market. Hoping to secure supplies of this important commodity from within the empire, British mercantilists in 1761 organized a society to foster colonial production by offering premiums for the largest importation from the colonies and by distributing literature describing how to produce it.[33] By 1770 colonial exports of potash and pearlash were comparable in value—as the British customs offices calculated values—to the exports of meat, iron, and barrel staves and considerably greater than the value of exports of naval stores.[34] In Quebec, where production began only in 1767, exports had reached only fifty tons by 1770.[35]

After the Revolution, American mercantilist thinkers concerned themselves with the product. In preparing his famous report on manufactures, Alexander Hamilton elicited much information relating to the production and sale of potash. One of his correspondents informed him that in 1788 New York had exported 13,500 barrels of potash worth "at a very low estimate" $200,000. In his report Hamilton excluded potash from consideration as being "immediately connected with husbandry rather than manufacturing," but he did, incidentally, commend the establishment of inspection systems to protect the reputation of the American product in foreign markets.[36]

New York had set up such an inspection system as early as 1784. The law imposed a fine of ten pounds for resisting the inspector and provided for confiscation of any potash loaded for export without inspection. It was the duty of the inspector to open all containers, grade the contents as first, second, or third "sort," repack the contents securely, and brand the container with his initials and the name of the port. Frequently modified, the law requiring inspection of potash prior to exportation remained in effect until finally repealed in 1843. It never applied to exports from the Champlain valley to Canada, but Lower Canada enacted a similar inspection law in 1795. Thus, after 1795 all Champlain valley exports of potash, whether via St. Johns and Quebec or via Whitehall and New York, were subject to government inspection.[37]

The opportunity which the potash market afforded to the pioneer settler must have seemed almost too good to be true. At the simplest level, the frontiersman could merely burn a stack of hardwood—elm, ash, hickory, or any of several other hardwoods which blanketed the land—and sell the ashes at an "ashery," which would transform them into potash. The price paid for ashes was a few cents per bushel—more for household or fireplace ashes and less for "field" ashes, which were likely to contain more dirt and other impurities. In nearby Franklin County at one time, household ashes brought twelve cents per bushel, while field ashes were worth from five to eight cents.[38] To the settler just "pitching" on a new site, this pittance had remarkable significance. First, it was often paid in cash; virtually all other commodities which he could conceivably produce were merely taken in trade. Second, this cash income enabled the settler to concentrate on clearing land instead of dissipating his time and energy to produce other items with which to trade for necessary supplies.

Enabling the settler to keep at work clearing land was crucial, for clearing increased the value several times. If he owned the land, a settler could then make a great capital gain by selling the land or a portion of it. If he had merely "squatted" on land belonging to the state or to an absentee owner, by local custom he could sell his "improvements," including particularly the cleared land, at a price which was at times comparable to that which the owner could secure by conveying title. For example, one of the earliest settlers of Beekmantown, John Ward, received three dollars per acre from a speculator for improvements on land to which a later settler sought to buy title from the owner at four dollars per acre. In Vermont a settler reported paying $150 to a squatter for improvements on a plot of land while paying only $50 to the owner for the title.[39] Thus, selling ashes brought a quick cash income, which otherwise would probably have been unattainable, and enabled the settler to keep at work on what was often his main enterprise, farm building.

If there were no ashery to which his ashes might be sold within economically feasible range, the settler could, as many did, set up an adequate establishment by himself for the manufacture of potash. There are about as many different descriptions of how to make potash as there are writers on the subject. But, that of 1806 by John Lambert based on observations at Champlain, just a few miles north of Beekmantown, probably best represents the methods in vogue in that area:

> The trees are cut and burnt; after which the ashes are mixed with lime, and put into several large vats, which stand in rows upon a platform; water is then pumped into them, and after filtering through the lime and ashes, it dribbles out of a spicket into a long trough that is placed in front of the vats for that purpose. The water thus drained becomes a strong lye of a dark brown colour, though it gives the buckets which are continually dipped into it a *yellow* tinge. The lye is then put into large iron boilers, or, as they are more generally called, *potash kettles*. Large fires are made underneath, and the lye is kept boiling for many hours, till it approaches a fine claret colour; after which it is taken out, left to cool, and become a solid body, like gray stone, and is called *potash*.[40]

Could the settler secure the necessary vats, the lime, and the iron kettles? Presumably, it was not too difficult to secure a few old hogsheads or barrels—or to fashion some—for use as vats. Limestone was abundant along the lake shore; even in 1850 Beekmantown had two small lime and cement works. To buy a kettle required a considerable outlay but, on the other hand, the investment was likely to liquidate itself rather quickly. In the Genesee country, James Wadsworth provided the settlers of Ogden with two kettles and was highly gratified at what a "spring" they gave to the clearing of land and how appreciative the settlers were.[41] The Beekmantown proprietors never understood their own interest well enough to make such a gesture, but local asheries may have rented kettles as was done in adjacent Franklin County for only one dollar per month.[42]

In marketing his product, the producer of potash in Beekmantown had several options: (1) he could sell it to a local storekeeper; (2) he might arrange to transport it to Quebec on a raft and sell it there; (3) he might commission the rafter to sell it for him; (4) he might sell the product outright to the rafter; or (5) he might sell it to an ashery, which would make it into still more valuable pearlash. This was done merely by baking it at extremely high temperature in a large oven, or kiln.

Storekeepers quite often operated asheries on the side. Peter Sailly ran an ashery as well as a store in Plattsburgh. As late as 1850, Benjamin Simonds, long-time storekeeper in Beekmantown, ran an ashery in addition to his mercantile establishment.[43]

Another marketing outlet for potash and pearlash arose from the fact that merchants preferred to buy their expensive imported items in New York or Boston rather than in Quebec or Montreal. For most rural products, overland transportation for any great distance was prohibitively expensive, but potash and pearlash were highly valuable in relation to their bulk. This, plus the desire of the local merchants to secure credit in New York or Boston, and the need for return cargo on wagons carrying imported goods to the shores of Lake Champlain—all help explain why some potash and pearlash produced in the valley were exported from Boston or New York. After the completion of the Champlain Canal, virtually all Champlain valley exports of potash and pearlash followed that route.

The bonanza period of potash production, as with the timber trade, came with the Napoleonic wars. From 1807, when Napoleon attempted to cut off British trade with the Baltic, until 1812, when the United States declared war on Britain, the demand for potash was apparently insatiable. Prices, normally ranging from about $60 to $100 per ton, rose as high as $300.[44] Spurred by this price incentive and by the relative ease with which potash could be smuggled when necessary, valley producers outdid themselves. In 1808 the number of barrels entering St. Johns was more than twice that of 1807. In 1809 potash imports at St. Johns fell slightly, but the difference was more than made up by an increase in the imports of the more valuable pearlash. Except for the war years, for which figures are not available, imports remained above the 1807 level until 1822, when the Champlain Canal began to divert shipment in the other direction.[45]

In Beekmantown the exigencies brought on Britain by Napoleon's Continental System evoked flagrant conversion of the proprietors' timber into potash, as it also led to flagrant theft of timber. In 1807 lessee Samuel Tobine, as noted earlier, was making potash in violation of the terms of his lease and selling it as fast as he could make it. James Farnsworth, in addition to stripping the valuable white oak from several lots, cut some thirty to forty acres on lot 82 for potash. A low estimate of the damages on lot 82 alone, Thomas Tredwell reported (November 16, 1807), would be $300 to $400. Had Tredwell's letters for 1808 and the immediately following years survived, they would no doubt have registered more complaints of a similar nature.

After the War of 1812, potash remained highly important in the economic development of Beekmantown and the county. A Plattsburgh cooper's advertisement in 1816 seems to suggest the order of importance in his sales; he listed in order: potash and pork barrels, firkins and tubs (for butter). Benjamin Mooers and others seeking legislative action to incorporate a bank at Plattsburgh in 1817 affirmed that the area (several counties) was "productive of large quantities of lumber and potashes, articles which are transported almost entirely to Canada for a market, and paid for in specie. From this source, and from the connexion and intercourse between the merchants of these counties and Montreal [where, it was earlier affirmed, the farmers exchanged their produce for goods] specie may be furnished to supply the calls of a bank at Plattsburgh." A merchant hard pressed for money in the aftermath of the 1819 depression beseeched his debtors to pay him and expressed willingness to accept potash, wheat, and oats in payment on accounts or in exchange for goods. He also sought "House and Field ashes."[46] The state census of 1821 found twenty-two asheries in Beekmantown as opposed to one gristmill, one fullingmill, and no sawmills. There were still twenty-one asheries in 1825 but, in the census of 1835, the number had dropped to one. In 1845 the number had risen to three, had fallen to one again in 1850, and was still that in 1855.

Clearly, until 1825 at the earliest, potash remained a major foundation of Beekmantown's economy. It is interesting to inquire what importance it had in regional, state, and national perspective. Just before and just after the War of 1812, clearances at St. Johns give ample testimony to the importance of potash in the Champlain valley economy. For the 1820s, when traffic began to flow through the Champlain Canal to New York, there are unfortunately no comparable statistics. However, the legislature in these years gave considerable attention to the subject. Members also referred to potash as a "staple of this state," but the export market was "greatly hazarded" by lapses in the state inspection system.[47] Peculiarly enough, even in 1848 only lumber, iron, and cheese entering the canal at Whitehall exceeded the value of potash shipments.[48]

For the nation the statistical situation is somewhat better. Excluding the war years, potash and pearlash exports of the U.S. from 1803 through 1825 averaged well over $1,000,000 yearly in value. The peak was 1825, when exports totaled $1,994,381. In that year potash exports were exceeded in value only by cotton, tobacco, wheat and flour, and the total of all manufactured goods. Important products which were occasionally of lesser value in U.S. exports of the middle 1820s included lumber, pork, rice, and fish.[49] Thus, potash, like timber, was important in the state and national economies as well as in Beekmantown and the Champlain valley.

The foregoing observations suggest, of course, that exploitation of forest resources was fundamental to the economic development of Beekmantown and the Lake Champlain region, but they suggest as well two other points. The first is that exploitation of timber resources was a more important factor in early American economic development than has been generally recognized.[50] The second is that because by its very nature the exploitation of timber resources was a business peculiarly associated with the frontier, it almost necessarily follows that opportunities afforded by timber resources were among the major attractions luring people to new and undeveloped forest regions.[51]

3

Farming

Most of the people in Beekmantown and in Clinton County thought of themselves as farmers. Ninety-two percent of Beekmantown's working residents classified themselves as farmers in the federal census of 1820 and again in that of 1840. Manufacturing enterprises in Plattsburgh and Peru reduced the predominance of farmers in the county as a whole; so in 1820, for example, only 78 percent of the working people of Clinton County called themselves farmers.[1]

Self-sufficiency was clearly the approved goal of farm enterprise in the early years of Beekmantown's development. The conventional wisdom stated firmly that one's farm "should produce every thing necessary to sustain life." To purchase from another what one could produce himself appeared "to be not only bad economy but also doubtful morality."[2] Like mercantilist nations, farm families and their rural communities were enjoined to buy as little as possible from outsiders and to sell to them as much as they possibly could.

Despite the preponderance of farmers and the frequent lip service to mercantilist principles, Clinton County was always a net importer of agricultural products. "Ours is an *importing* rather than an *exporting* county, so far as relates to products of the farm," the president of the county agricultural society observed in 1851.[3] His remark would have been equally applicable at any earlier period in the county's history. Peter Sailly Palmer noted with reference to the local economy of the 1790s that the county imported both meat and grains from Vermont, while it exported potash, pearlash, furs, and timber to Quebec.[4] In 1817 a local tax assessor lamented that we [in this instance residents of Plattsburgh, which still encompassed Beekman Patent] "have not half the number of cows necessary to furnish the butter and cheese actually consumed." In 1843 a speaker at the county fair cried shame upon the county that was "a beggar at her neighbor's door for a large amount of her meat and breadstuffs."[5] Thus, from the earliest times, farmers in the Beekmantown area produced for their own consumption and for sale on the local market in competition with outsiders.

Difficulties in clearing land for farming made self-sufficiency quite hard to achieve in the first decade of settlement. The incentive to clear land was great both to provide subsistence and because of the increase which clearing brought to the value of land. The work of clearing, however, was slow, arduous, and expensive. Normally, a farm family would clear from five to fifteen acres yearly, depending on how many members of the family could swing an ax and what means could be found to sustain the family while the clearing work went on. As late as 1798, Robert Platt of Plattsburgh complained: "I Cant find anybody to Chop by the Job for less than five Dollars per acre and I have not agreed with any yet."[6] Such circumstances explain why Moses Hazen's operations at Point au Roche had not disturbed the Beekmans greatly and why one of Champlain's proprietors in 1787 considered himself lucky to have drawn in a lottery among the town's proprietors a lot upon which a French squatter had made "improvements."[7]

Those settlers not fortunate enough to have had their land cleared for them by squatters of one kind or another had either to buy most of their provisions for the first few years or to leave their families elsewhere until the head of the household had cleared enough land to sustain his family. An early settler of Champlain had "cut over" twenty acres and built a house before he brought his family.[8] In pioneering the settlement of Plattsburgh in 1785, Charles Platt brought provisions with him from Dutchess County but then bought supplemental rations—hay, oats, peas, and flour—for his livestock and himself.[9] He made his purchases at St. Johns but could have secured the same items in Vermont.

Supplies available in those places, however, were not always adequate. In 1789 near famine conditions prevailed. Arriving settlers had bought nearly all the food, fodder, and clothing in the area. "Provisions were Amazing scarce in these Parts," wrote a

Champlain settler at the beginning of the year, "and am pretty Certain that it will be in a Manner a famine." He suggested to Pliny Moore, wintering at Kinderhook on the Hudson, that "if you would Procure a quantity of Indian Corn and Wheat it Would Answer Very well [i.e., sell very profitably] here next Spring."[10] Later in the month, Moore was informed that the French-Canadian who was operating his sawmill "had no provisions and Scarcely any Clothes."[11] Clothing seems to have been chronically scarce. In 1786 Zephaniah Platt had received word from his mill sites on the Saranac that "our french Men is all Naked almost."[12] In the summer of 1789, the Beekmans received word from their agent that the scarcity of provisions had deterred a number of settlers who had planned to move to the area.[13]

Shortages recurred in later years. In 1792, for example, Moore's partner, sent to seize a man's cow for debt, reported that the man had had no bread for four days, had no meat, and that in fact milk was his only sustenance. The partner declined to take the cow.[14] That October Moore's physician reported, "I am entirely barefoot myself and my whole Family" of eight. He thought his six boys could be shod with "Canadian [wooden?] shoes for the present till we get our Timber hewed and ready to draw." In 1803 Moore declined to send to Albany in payment of a debt any of the seven hundred bushels of wheat he then held because wheat was very scarce locally, and "people must suffer" if he did so.[15]

During the 1790s, however, a number of productive farms had come into existence and had begun to alleviate the chronic scarcities. Jurist James Kent, passing through Plattsburgh en route to Montreal in 1795, noted that "the farms all about are excellent." He cited in particular those of his brother-in-law William Pitt Platt, three others belonging to Platt family members, plus those of Melanchton L. Woolsey and John Addoms. He made no comment on the quality of Thomas Tredwell's farm in Beekman Patent, where he dined on his return.[16] In 1797 Charles Platt reported harvests so good in Plattsburgh that the barns could not hold all the sheaves of grain.[17] In 1801 Pliny Moore was negotiating in a dull market at Montreal to sell four hundred bushels of surplus wheat.[18]

Beekmantown's farmers, as they cleared the land and brought it into agricultural production, had three basic sources of income— only one of which was properly agricultural. The first was the timber industries described in the previous chapter. Farmers or their sons could work as laborers in the winter for those who produced forest products for export. Some farmers were able to become wintertime entrepreneurs in one aspect or another of the timber business. The second source of income was farm making or, essentially, real estate development and speculation. According to one estimate, clearing land increased its value from eight to ten times.[19] Most Beekmantown farmers (as will be explained more fully in chapter 5) bought far more land than they could work themselves. They made money by selling part or all of the land they had cleared. If they had merely "squatted" on land without the owner's permission, they could get compensation for their "improvements," as had Hazen at Point au Roche.

Even uncleared land increased in value as settlement approached. Such land in Beekmantown, selling for about two dollars an acre in the 1790s as settlement began, had risen to seven dollars per acre by 1807.[20] An investment of $400 in Beekmantown land in the 1790s might have increased in value to $1,400 by 1807, whereas compound interest of 7 percent on the same sum would have amounted to only $900. Any kind of clearing—even indiscriminate timber theft or cutting to make potash—would have increased the value of the property still more. Thus, most Beekmantown farmers, especially those who moved on after a brief period, were really real estate developers or speculators as well as farmers.

In their more narrowly agricultural roles, Beekmantown farmers produced for their own consumption and also for local sale. Their principal market was the forest enterprises and after about 1810 the iron industries centered at Peru as well. Distant farmers—first, Vermonters; later, those from the Genesee country; and still later, Ohioans—would compete with the local folk in selling human foods to those employed in these industries. They sold especially those foods which were relatively light and expensive—such as butter, meat, and flour—and could bear the costs of transportation. In supplying fodder for the oxen and horses used in industry, however, the local farmers had little competition. Hay and oats in particular were simply too cheap in relation to their transportation costs to permit distant farmers to command any of the market. Consequently, Beekmantown farmers and those elsewhere in the county produced large quantities of hay and oats for sale in their sheltered local market.[21]

Natural conditions for farming in Beekmantown are neither terribly forbidding nor especially favorable. The growing season averages around 150 days, shorter than in some portions of the state but long enough for all of the major grain crops of the temperate zone. The temperature range is from a summer high in the nineties to a winter low in the minus thirties—often too cold for winter wheat. Rainfall averages a moderate thirty inches yearly and is usually well distributed. The terrain is relatively even in the eastern and central portions of the town, rising gently from the lake level of about ninety-five feet above sea level. In the west, however, the ascent becomes much steeper as the elevation rises to sixteen hundred feet. Near the lake the soil is limestone-based and very deep. It has a little too much clay and a little too much water to serve extremely well for grains, but it makes excellent grassland. As one moves inland from the lake, the soil thins until at the western edge of town it has virtually disappeared. There the underlying and outcropping rock is granite, gneiss, and other igneous material. The Cornell University soil classification ranked 29 percent of the land as, in effect, superior, 46 percent adequate, and 25 percent inadequate.[22]

The first significant change in the pattern of agriculture in Beekmantown began about 1809. The immediate cause was the interruption of British-American trade begun by Jefferson's embargo late in 1807. Commercial demand for wool increased greatly as Americans began to produce the expensive woolens previously imported from Britain. The emphasis on quality led to an enormous vogue for Spanish Merino sheep, renowned for the fineness of their wool. Merino wool increased in price from 75¢ a pound to $2 or more by 1814, while "common" wool continued to sell widely for about the old level of 37½¢. Merino rams which had sold for $100 began to bring $1,000 or even $1,500. New York State provided a prize of eighty dollars yearly for the best woolen cloth of household manufacture in each county and a reward of fifty dollars for introducing the first Merino in each county.[23]

Before the Merino vogue was well started, the Plattsburgh town meeting voted on March 28, 1809, "that a Sufficient Sum of money to buy a full Blooded Ram of the Merino Breed and the Expenses of Fetching the said Ram to this Town Shall be Taken out of the Poor Chest and that the Poor Masters shall have the Charge of the said Ram." Presumably, the poor chest was to be reimbursed from the proceeds of a charge collected by the poor masters for the ram's services.

Apparently, this experiment in socialistic agriculture came to nothing, but it is remarkable that the voters approved it at so early a date. It is true that David Humphreys had had a flock of Merinos in Connecticut since 1802 and that Robert R. Livingston had brought some to his Hudson River estate when he returned from his tour as U.S. minister to France. But, neither had had appreciable success in popularizing the breed until after the imposition of the embargo at the end of 1807. Livingston's propagandistic *Essay on Sheep*, which touched off large scale importation, did not appear until 1809.[24]

Although communal endeavor failed to get Merinos to Clinton County, private enterprise succeeded. In the fall of 1811, William Bailey, a prominent figure in the county, advertised in the Plattsburgh *Republican* (November 1): "FULL BLOODED MERINOS," imported the previous fall from Spain and just arrived from New York. By way of testimonial, he observed that Judge Pliny Moore of Champlain and Customs Collector Peter Sailly each had one. "The farmers who are desirous of improving their breed of sheep," the notice continued, "may send their ewes, they paying on the first of May next three dollars for each ewe having a lamb. No charge for the pasture of ewes whether they have lambs or not."

Resumption of trade with Britain at the end of the war soon disenchanted even the most ardent Merino advocates, but production of wool and woolen textiles continued.[25]

Meanwhile, another innovation was capturing the minds of New Yorkers in the years 1819 to 1822. Inspired by Elkanah Watson's record of exciting interest in agricultural improvement through county cattle shows and fairs, New York in 1819 provided a state subsidy for the creation of county agricultural societies. The societies were to award cash "premiums" for what was adjudged at annual county fairs to be superior performance in one or another of the various forms of agricultural endeavor. The state required that to be eligible for the premium contestants must submit a written statement indicating how the results were achieved. Such statements, it was expected, would lead to diffusion of superior techniques, especially as the state planned to select some statements for publication.[26]

Initially, Plattsburgh was quite cool to this agricultural improvement program. Its sponsors at the state level were chiefly Federalists and Clintonian Republicans, while Plattsburgh's leaders were more orthodox Republicans. Only the Federalist towns in the north (Champlain, Chazy, and Mooers) participated in the Clinton County Agricultural Society as it was first organized in 1819. Plattsburgh joined neither in the organization of the society nor in its first Cattle Show and Fair at Champlain on October 14, 1819.[27] During the ensuing winter, however, leaders of the Plattsburgh community began to think more seriously both about the future of agriculture and the role of a county agricultural society in relation to it. The brief depression touched off by the Panic of 1819 probably affected their attitudes. Political considerations (to be considered in chapter 13) also figured in the change. For whatever reason, a "considerable number of Farmers and other respectable citizens of the county" published notice in the *Republican* of a meeting to organize an agricultural society. The meeting convened on December 16, 1819, at Joseph I. Green's tavern in Plattsburgh with Thomas Tredwell of Beekmantown presiding. Those present resolved to seek a reordering of the Clinton County Agricultural Society to include representatives of each town and appointed a three-man committee to negotiate with the existing society.[28]

The three committee members, John Palmer, Anson Sperry, and Robert Platt, prepared a remarkable address in justification of the effort. Beginning with a reminder of the high place of agriculture in the scheme of a "bountiful Providence," the address exalted the cause of improving agricultural production. Its authors affirmed as well that the agricultural societies organized elsewhere in the state had been "eminently successful" in that endeavor. Then with reference to the depression, the authors noted: "It is impossible for your committee to shut their eyes to the present condition of our county, which renders it . . . peculiarly necessary that the attention of our inhabitants should be promptly called to a prosecution of our Agricultural interests, under all the improvements of which they are susceptible. It cannot have escaped observation that the market, both for lumber and potashes, from which this county has heretofore received considerable remittances from abroad, and which has helped to keep us out of debt, for necessaries imported, has of late been extremely precarious, and may reasonably be expected to be more so."

The gist of the argument advanced by the committee was that a county agricultural society would aid the necessary and desirable transfer of the county's economic base from lumber and potash to farming. Attacking continued reliance on lumber and potash, the authors asserted that the market was already precarious and likely to be more so and that the "best Timber" had already disappeared. Further pursuit of lumber and potash threatened "serious and lasting injury from the destruction of our forests." What the committee apparently feared was that destruction of the forests would be carried so far that farms would no longer possess the woodland necessary for their supply of fuel and building material. By abandoning lumber and potash, the argument continued, farmers would be relieved "from the exhorbitant wages of labourers, the depreciation of our stock, and the worn-out and bad condition of our working oxen, which are principally the consequences of lumbering, and which have been felt by them [farmers] as serious obstacles to the profitable management of their affairs."

In defense of farming, the committee argued that it rated higher in the favor of God and man and that it could be pursued indefinitely into the future, while lumbering and potash production would soon be terminated by the elimination of the resources on which they depended. The Champlain Canal, "just opened," the committee rightly believed, would increase the value of exported products for the farmer by reducing the costs of transportation to the seaboard. Appealing to egalitarian sentiments, the committee also contended that, in implied contrast to lumbering, which was conducted on an employer-employee basis, farming opened "a fair field of competition to all." As a final argument in favor of organizing an agricultural society, the authors of the address observed that to do so would entitle "us as a county to the donations which the liberality of our State Legislature intended for our benefit."[29]

Despite these serious arguments, when a mass meeting for the organization of an agricultural society finally took place (February 12, 1820), it was quite apparent that its promoters were far more interested in politics than in farming. A full-page report of the meeting in the politically oriented *Republican* (February 26) begins with the observation that it was held to organize an agricultural society and to "transact other business." The rest of the story reports a successful political rally to support the reelection of Governor De Witt Clinton.

Perhaps because of its utility for political purposes, the Clinton County Agricultural Society did finally become organized on a countywide basis. Its second Cattle Show and Fair took place at Plattsburgh on October 10 and Chazy on October 11. Among the winners of premiums were the following Beekmantown farmers: John How (best milch cow), Samuel Chittenden (best acre of

*Ira Howe's house, Beekmantown, residence of an early settler,
scene of the first fighting in the British attack on Plattsburgh
in 1814*

corn—122 bushels), and Amos Barber (second-best acre of winter
wheat—32 bushels). The award for best farm in Beekmantown
went to James Crook.[30]

In 1821 the third annual Cattle Show and Fair was held at Champlain and Peru, on the northern and southern extremities of the
county respectively. This apparently discouraged potential participants from centrally located Beekmantown. The only Beekmantown winners in the strictly agricultural categories were John How
for second-best cow, Levi Marshall for best acre of broom corn,
and James Crook for second-best bull and again for best farm in
the town.[31]

The last fair of the moribund Clinton County Agricultural Society took place in Beekmantown on October 10 and 11, 1822.
That year John How was esteemed to have the best farm in Beekmantown and to have raised the best plot of broom corn. Samuel
Chittenden won recognition for a superior crop of flax. These
and a second-place award for yearling steers were all the local
residents could garner.[32]

The demise of the society became official in 1823. No fair was held. A half-hearted appeal to the county supervisors for aid from public funds apparently evoked none. A final meeting early in 1824 was to dispose of the small balance in the treasurer's hands.[33] The reasons for the brief life span of the society were several. The state terminated its subsidy. Lumber and potash production were not so badly off as the society founders had believed but continued, at least in the case of lumber, to support the local economy for many years, although apparently at a declining level of prosperity. The rules of the society were discouraging. To be eligible for a cash premium, one had to join the society and also to submit a written statement describing how the approved result had been achieved. Farmers of "parsimonious dispositions and narrow views" looked askance at both requirements. Finally, there is some indication of resentment on the part of "dirt farmers," especially Republican dirt farmers, toward the "gentlemen," usually of Federalist background and with only peripheral interests in farming, who dominated the society.[34]

The social distance between the gentlemen who controlled the society and the farmers whose methods it sought to improve was indeed considerable. In 1821 the published report of the secretary frankly stated that the "experience of three years forces upon us the conviction that it [the society] will not find sufficient support in the great body of farmers, they generally come forward with reluctance, and it requires unreasonable exertion on the part of the secretaries of the society to reorganize it annually, and to obtain a sum sufficient to cover the [matching] state bounty. Indeed but for the liberality of a few individuals (and those were not farmers by profession) in making advances it would not have been effected this year." He referred openly to "enemies" of the society in a context which suggests that he had in mind the poor and skeptical farmers who were disinclined to welcome "improvements" suggested by amateurs, however wealthy and learned. Such farmers probably sensed the irony when at the fair of 1822 Plattsburgh lawyer William Swetland assured them that theirs was the "noblest of all occupations whatever."[35]

Indentifying Beekmantown residents who participated in the agricultural society illustrates that the town contributed to county leadership in this matter and that the movement tapped largely the established leaders. Ex-Congressman Thomas Tredwell presided at the first meeting of the series which organized the society as a county-wide group. James Crook, supervisor of Beekmantown in

TABLE 4.

Improved Land in Beekmantown, 1821–1855

Year	Total Acres	Total Acres Per Capita	% of Potential Arable Land
1821	6,266	4.7	22
1825	8,061	7.0	29
1835	13,937	6.1	50
1845	15,805	5.1	56
1855	24,103	8.5	86

SOURCE: New York State censuses for the years indicated.

1822 and ex officio member of the Clinton County Board of Supervisors, was among the recognized leaders at the outset. Charles Marsh, another participant, was supervisor of Plattsburgh in 1819 and of Beekmantown in 1823. John How, who won many premiums, was a frequent holder of other offices in town government. Only three Beekmantown residents associated with the society as premium winners or otherwise were not political leaders.

The concern for improving agriculture, while not successful in establishing mass membership agricultural societies in the 1820s, did result, nevertheless, in the accumulation and preservation of statistical information on an increasing number of topics related to farming. This statistical reservoir makes possible some generalizations concerning the practice of farming in Beekmantown from 1820 to 1850.

Successive state censuses reveal the rate of progress in converting the wilderness into improved land (see table 4). Somewhat surprisingly, the acreage cleared between 1845 and 1855 was greater than the total for the first forty years of settlement, 1785 to 1825. This rush of land clearing was due largely to relatively high prices for lumber.[36]

By 1850 variation in the size of farms was considerable, but relatively few farms were either very small or very large. The twenty poorest farmers held from 6 to 50 acres. The eighteen wealthiest farmers held from 90 to 250. Only four had over 177 improved acres.[37]

Before 1850 livestock production was apparently never a major

TABLE 5.

Census of Livestock in Beekmantown, 1821–1855

Year	Sheep	Cattle	Swine	Horses
1821	2,466 (1.8)	1,287 (0.95)	—	206 (0.2)
1825	4,278 (3.7)	2,171 (1.9)	1,565 (1.4)	302 (0.3)
1835	4,689 (2.1)	2,788 (1.2)	1,705 (0.8)	811 (0.4)
1845	10,393 (3.4)	3,719 (1.2)	2,084 (0.7)	816 (0.3)
1855	6,491 (2.2)	2,165 (0.8)	1,117 (0.4)	1,085 (0.4)

SOURCE: New York State Census for each of the years specified.
NOTE: Figures in parentheses are per person.

interest of Beekmantown farmers. Sheep were always (for the years in which data are available) the most numerous domesticated animals in the town. But, even in 1825, when the number of sheep per capita was highest, there would still have been only about twenty sheep per family, about the average for a farm in the region.[38] (See table 5.)

Demand for meat rather than wool may have accounted for much of the interest in sheep. A report of 1851 affirmed that "there are [in Clinton County] a few flocks of full blood Merinos, which would not in any respect suffer by comparison with the best flocks in Vermont; but the description of the sheep most raised, is a cross between the Merino and the common or native sheep. For the purpose of mutton, *here the leading object* [italics added], this cross answers a very good purpose."[39] The same report insisted that sheep received much less attention than cattle and horses. Among the twenty poorest farmers in town, the number of sheep owned in 1850 ranged from zero to twenty-two, while among the eighteen richest farmers the range was from zero to two hundred. Only three farms, however, had more than seventy sheep.[40]

The number of swine per capita fell steadily from a high of 1.4 in 1825 (the first census to include swine) to a low of .4 in 1855. The Clinton County Agricultural Society report of 1850 asserted that because of the "high prices which have usually been paid in this county, for all kinds of course grain, our farmers have found it unprofitable to keep more hogs than are required to consume the slops from the kitchen and dairy. The amount of pork made in the county has, therefore, always fallen greatly short of supplying the demand for home consumption."[41] Perhaps the explanation for the decline lies in the improvements in transportation between 1825 and 1855. In the early period, Beekmantown farmers provided pork for their own families if not also for local producers of lumber and potash. Later some Beekmantown farmers found it feasible to purchase, even for their own needs, pork produced in other regions and transported cheaply via the Erie and Champlain canals or by railroad. The number of hogs owned by the poorest farmers in 1850 ranged from zero to seven, while among the richest the range was from three to twenty-three.[42]

Dairying, later to be the foundation of the Beekmantown economy, was not conspicuous at any time prior to 1855. A writer in the *Republican* (February 11, 1837) urged local farmers to stop wearing themselves out with the drudgery of cultivating crops and instead to emulate the farmers of Vermont by raising livestock. By producing wool, beef, pork, butter, and cheese, the writer argued, local farmers could greatly enhance the value of rocky, upland soil. Statistics indicate, however, that farmers largely ignored this advice. They went on producing hay and oats, which they could sell largely without outside competition in the local market. They recognized, as did the president of the county agricultural society in 1851, that "the dairymen of Vermont can supply the demand here for butter and cheese at prices which render it impolitic for our farmers to compete with them."[43] As with swine the number of cattle per capita was highest in 1825 and declined thereafter. In 1855 the ratio was less than half what it had been in 1825. Transportation improvements which exposed the local producers to outside competition may again afford a partial explanation. Another factor in the decline, however, was the switch from oxen to horses as the preferred beasts of burden. Beekmantown's poorest farmers in 1850 owned from zero to seven cattle, while the richest owned from ten to fifty-three.[44]

Horses were always relatively scarce in Beekmantown. But, they tended to increase slightly, while the numbers of other forms of livestock per family all diminished. In 1825 the average family had one horse. By 1855 it had two. Beekmantown's poor farmers owned from zero to three horses in 1850, while the rich owned from three to ten.[45]

Clinton County's most valuable agricultural product in the 1840s was hay. Jonathan Battey, president of the county agricultural society, reported quite flatly in 1851 that for the county as a whole, "the crop yielding the greatest annual income is hay." He estimated that the county produced 75,000 tons, 1 ½ tons per acre on 50,000 acres. Of that amount farmers sold 30,000 tons at prices ranging from $7.00 to $10.00 per ton at their own farms or slightly higher "at the village." Income from that source for the previous year, he calculated to be about $210,000, assuming the relatively low price of $7.00 per ton. Hay consumed on the farm he estimated to have been worth about $200,000 or $4.44 per ton, presumably because it was inferior in quality to that sold. Because hay sold to producers of lumber and iron in the county's "manufacturing villages" yielded no manure for fertilizing farmers' fields, Battey regretted that "the comparatively high price usually paid" had long induced farmers to sell "the greater part of their hay."[46]

In Beekmantown itself, hay production in 1850 ranged from under 10 tons per farm among the poorest farmers to from 25 to 85 tons on the richest farms. One farmer who was not among the richest as judged by land values raised 120 tons.[47] How much of their product these farmers actually sold is not evident. Had they sold about half at $7 per ton, the resulting income would have ranged from under $35 yearly for the poorest farmers to almost $300 for those producing 85 tons.

The most valuable grain crop in Clinton County was oats. "Of all the grain crops," wrote Battey in 1851, "oats may be regarded as the staple product of the county. For many years, it has been rather the main dependence of our farmers for raising money." The market was of course those same "manufacturing villages" because oats provided a major form of sustenance for their draft animals. The bumper crop of 640,000 bushels that year would have brought $204,800 to county farmers if it had all been sold at the somewhat depressed price of thirty-two cents per bushel.[48]

Beekmantown farmers who grew oats in 1850 showed enormous variation in their volume of production. Among the poorest farmers, oat production ranged from none at all to 200 bushels. Among the richest farmers, the range was from 80 to 2,400 bushels. Income from that source, had the richest farmers sold all of their product at thirty-two cents per bushel, would have ranged from $25.60 to $768.00.[49]

Other grains grown in Clinton County were "chiefly for home consumption," according to Battey, but potatoes had recently become a cash crop. Marketed in New York City and other seaboard areas for about thirty-three cents per bushel, Clinton County's potato crop of 900,000 bushels had a value of nearly $300,000 in the previous year.[50]

Potato production in Beekmantown varied as widely as did that of oats. Among the poorest farmers, production ranged from none at all to 300 bushels. Among the richest the range was from 25 to 600.[51] Income from this source among the richest farmers, assuming they sold all their product, would have ranged from $8.25 to $198.00.

Agricultural improvement was a keen interest to the few Beekmantown farmers who participated in the revived Clinton County Agricultural Society in the 1840s. They won many premiums at the annual Cattle Show and Fair and, in accordance with the rules, submitted extremely detailed statements as to how their results were achieved. These statements included minute calculations of their costs so that a reliable profit figure could be shown. Particularly outstanding was S. H. Knappen, who in 1846 won three first prizes (28 bushels of rye per acre; 30 bushels of beans; 32 bushels of barley) and four seconds (83 bushels of corn; 24 bushels of winter wheat; 24 bushels of peas; 191 bushels of potatoes).[52]

The most advanced methods employed locally in dairying were set forth in 1845 by two Beekmantown residents, Thomas Crook and R. O. Barber, who took first and second places respectively in the competition for best butter. Crook's nine cows were a cross of Ayrshire, Devonshire, and Durham with the "best selected common breed." In the winter he fed them as much of the "best hay" as they would eat. For six weeks in the spring, he fed them turnips and potatoes, while in the summer they enjoyed "first rate" pasture well supplied with water. He got 85 pounds and 11 ounces of butter and 33 pounds of cheese per cow between May 1 and September 1. This was better than usual but far below the record of outstanding cows, some of which produced over 200 pounds of butter in a similar period. Barber had eight "common breed" cows which he fed cornstalks, straw, and "roots."[53]

The general enthusiasm for manure was also evident in Clinton County. Jonathan Battey, the society president, lamented the sale of hay and corn because the farmer's manure supply was thus diminished, but he gloried in 1852 that the compost heap had recently won acceptance so that "weeds and all forms of vegetable rubbish, as well as the suds and slops from the kitchen [were perceived to be] worth adding to the manure heap."[54]

Yield per acre in Beekmantown was generally a little higher than the state average. It is probably no coincidence that the crops in which yield per acre was significantly higher in Beekmantown were potatoes and oats, two of the three cash crops of the town. None of these crops, however, was sufficiently profitable to make the area really prosperous. Beekmantown farmland in 1855 was worth $21 per acre. That was above the level in Vermont ($15) but well below the average of $29 in New York State as a whole. Enterprising farmers from Beekmantown, as from Vermont, had long since begun moving in search of better opportunities—to the West or to the cities.[55]

The record of the Clinton County Agricultural Society in the 1840s paralleled closely that of its predecessor in the early 1820s. It began with the stimulus of state subsidy. It attracted few members, most of them representative of the political leadership in the various towns. Ordinary farmers still looked upon it with suspicion. "The array of prejudice and opposition it had to encounter, was really so formidable," wrote one president, "that it did well to survive" its first seven years. It experienced a brief boom at the end of the decade occasioned apparently in part by opening competition to nonmembers (an entry fee was required, however) and by holding the fair jointly with Essex County. A more important cause for the increased interest may have been the establishment of a race track adjacent to the fair grounds. Officers of the society complained that they were "in more than one instance . . . compelled to suspend operations [at the fair] until the return from the 'races.'"[56]

Community leaders continued hopefully in the later years to foresee a shift from timber-based enterprises to farming as the foundation of the local economy. Echoing the agricultural society founders of 1819, the *Republican* editor observed (January 25, 1834) that "as a more speedy means of obtaining the necessaries of life, a large number of our workingmen engaged themselves in marketing the lumber of the country; in which business they have been engaged for a number of years. The material, however, is becoming scarce and they are gradually turning their attention to agriculture. The result is an evident improvement in their pecuniary circumstances and a flattering increase of business in the village." Twelve years later, however, the editor found (March 28, 1846) that "agriculture has not yet received that general attention its importance demands." He thought that in the previous few years

TABLE 6.

Yield per Acre of Selected Crops in Beekmantown (1850) and
New York State As a Whole (1845)

Crop	Beekmantown	State Average	County Average
Wheat	15	14	17-1/2
Oats	30	26	27
Corn	25	25	26-1/2
Potatoes	150	90	137

SOURCE: Figures for Beekmantown are from 1850 U.S. census; those for
county and state are from S. S. Randall's estimates in New York State
Agricultural Society, *Transactions*, 1845, V, 380 ff.
NOTE: Figures are in bushels per acre.

farming had received "a fresh impetus" which had made clear "that
the industrious agriculturalist can *live* and *thrive* in this county."
But, he clearly implied, most farmers pursued other activities as
well. He also noted that Plattsburgh would export over a million
pieces of lumber that year and that most of it would be drawn fifteen to twenty-five miles and some from forty to fifty miles. He
noted further that "much teaming" was also required in other enterprises or, in other words, that the long anticipated switch to farming as the county's basic economic activity was still incomplete.

Nevertheless, the immigrant population of Beekmantown in the
1840s probably approached subsistence farming more nearly than
had the largely native residents at any earlier time. The new arrivals
lacked several of the money-making opportunities available to
those who preceded them. There was virtually no market for
squared timbers and little demand for potash. Even had they been
able to make marketable products from the timber resources as
they cleared the soil for farming, they were for the most part too
far back from the lake to be able to get their products there at a
reasonable cost. If any valuable timber still remained, they could,
of course, sell logging rights to a lumberman; lumbering jobs still
existed in great numbers. Clearing could still make land more valuable, but the quality in the interior was so low as to limit greatly
its value for farming purposes.

Improved transportation, particularly canals but also railroads,
exposed the farmer to more competition in selling his produce

locally and by facilitating migration to western regions, where land was both cheaper and more fertile, tended to keep local land prices from rising very high. Lumbering jobs and selling hay and oats for the lumbermen's draft animals were the chief hopes for cash income for the new arrivals who were clearing the remaining forests of Beekmantown so rapidly between 1845 and 1855. The former Irish tenant farmers among them probably appreciated the fact that 88 percent of the families (425 of 482) were owners of the land they worked.[57]

The history of farming in Beekmantown suggests that two points concerning frontier farming in the early national period receive insufficient emphasis in the works of agricultural historians. The first is that in many areas the earliest settlers were businessmen or laborers, or both, as well as farmers.[58] As in the Beekmantown area, many must have worked as laborers or as entrepreneurs in timber-based industries of one kind or another. Even more were probably in some measure real estate developers, transforming woodland—whether or not they held title to it—into farm homesteads to be sold at a profit. Only after the forest had fallen did the residents become more nearly full-time farmers.

The second point is that farmers on what have been called commercial frontiers probably produced chiefly for sale within their own region rather than for sale to cities or for export, despite the preoccupation of historians with the latter aspects of farm production. Any region lucky enough to have significant lumbering or other industries requiring the use of large numbers of draft animals depended inevitably upon nearby farmers for fodder as well as for some of the cheaper human foods which would not bear the cost of transportation for any appreciable distance.[59]

4

General Economic Development

To complete the story of Beekmantown's economic development, some observations on transportation, commerce, manufacturing, and labor are in order. What they show primarily is the tremendous importance of influences outside the community upon the course of its economic growth.

Transportation problems hindered the development of the Champlain valley quite severely in the early days. Preceding chapters have explained the difficulties in getting commodities to and from Quebec. Those affecting transport to and from Albany or New York before 1822 were still more severe. This was due chiefly to the need to use expensive land transportation between the Hudson and the Lake Champlain watersheds. William Gilliland noted just after the Revolution that it cost eleven pounds to move a ton of freight from New York City to Canada. Of that sum one pound would pay the freight from one end of Lake Champlain to the other, a distance of over one hundred miles, but the charges for carrying cargo from Albany to Lake George, a distance of sixty-five miles, amounted to over eight pounds because of the necessity of portaging between the two watersheds.[1]

Because land transportation by sleigh was cheaper than that by wagon, much commercial traffic between the Hudson River and Lake Champlain in the precanal era occurred in the winter. For example, when Charles Platt left Dutchess County in 1785 to begin work on the mills at Plattsburgh, he traveled in early March with two sleds and two laborers. He reached Skenesborough (the old name for Whitehall) after four days. Deep snow then impeded his progress over the ice on the lake, but he arrived safely at Plattsburgh after four more days.[2] During the winter of 1804–1805, Pliny Moore of Champlain received a request from a creditor in Albany that he send his shipment of potash via Whitehall "during the present Sleighing. The Transportation now," his creditor noted, "is much more reasonable than what it will be with Waggoning."[3]

Poor grazing conditions, however, were a severe handicap to travel in the winter. Soon after his arrival at Plattsburgh in 1785, Charles Platt had to go to St. Johns to buy hay. In 1817 Customs Collector Peter Sailly noted that transportation to Albany in the month of February was very expensive due to the "dearth of forage."[4]

Transportation to and from Albany by no means ceased during the warmer months. Indeed, in 1800 thirty ships were reported to be carrying cargo on the lake despite the high cost of "waggoning" between the two watersheds.[5]

During the spring thaw which normally occurred in April, transportation became still more difficult. Even local traffic largely stopped. In March 1804 Pliny Moore explained to a Montreal merchant that he intended "flouring" soon his large stock of wheat presumably taken in payment for milling services. But, he would be unable to do so until "the throng of Custom [farmers seeking to have their wheat ground for the own purposes] abates by the failure of the Ice." Sailly reported in 1809 that during the embargo of the previous year his predecessor had kept six men stationed at a bridge on a road in the Beekmantown area "much frequented by smugglers in the Winter." But, the guard was abandoned early in April, when "the Roads became impracticable." In 1822 Beekmantown residents petitioned the legislature for permission to change the date of their town meeting from the first Tuesday in April to the first Tuesday in March "owing to the uniform badness of the roads" in April. Assemblyman Benjamin Mooers, looking forward to the end of a dull legislative session in Albany during the spring of 1822, expressed the hope that "the Steamboat may be running by the middle of this month [April] for I expect the roads are getting very bad."[6]

The nature of the transportation difficulties between Plattsburgh and Albany restricted severely the range of commodities which could be exchanged economically. Lumber, for example, did not move southward in quantity before the completion of the Champlain Canal in 1822. In fact, it was impractical even to drive livestock southward to market in the early days.[7] Precisely when the roads became adequate to this form of transportation is not clear. But, as late as 1834, valley residents were vainly imploring the legislature to do something to improve the quality of the Albany-Montreal road through the rugged and sparsely populated region near Lake George. In 1795 James Kent had described that area as "the wildest imaginable and totally unsusceptable of Improvement."[8] It is probably significant that the only commodity prices of which Pliny Moore's Albany correspondent informed him with some regularity were those of wheat, flour, potash, and pearlash—all relatively light and valuable. They served chiefly as the means of making payment for the variety of more valuable commodities which moved the other way—imported luxury items, dyes, and badly wanted articles which the valley did not produce.

Cargoes moving along Lake Champlain, it should be noted, were not necessarily either products of the valley or items intended for sale there. From colonial times onward, there had been some interchange of goods between Albany and Canada. Principally, this trade saw furs moving southward and textiles, hardware, and other items for the Indian trade moving northward. Quantities of tea, tobacco, and other forms of merchandise light enough and costly enough to absorb the high cost of transportation also figured to some extent in the trade between Albany and Canada. Apart from affording some income to teamsters, lake carriers, and their suppliers along the way, this trade was of little importance to the growth of the valley economy.

Getting freight to and from the prospective metropolis of Montreal also posed problems—even for residents at the north end of Lake Champlain, which is only about forty miles from Montreal. The terrain is very flat and affords no difficulties, but the roads were generally abominable. An English traveler who had the misfortune to journey northward on a freight wagon in 1807 reported that the road was "tolerable good" for a few miles beyond the border, but after that "we had to plough through one of the most intolerable roads I ever met with." Among its hazards he listed ruts, rocks, stumps, and fallen logs. "For upwards of ten miles did the poor horses toil and tug through this infamous road, jolting, tossing and tumbling the waggoner and myself in every direction; it was with difficulty we could keep our seats; and the planks at the bottom of the waggon were every moment starting out of their places."[9]

Fortunately, there were easier ways to ship to Montreal. One was to ship only in the dead of winter. Then, as in commerce to the southward, sleighs or sleds glided relatively smoothly over snow-covered and frozen ground, while the ice formed a bridge across the St. Lawrence for roughly three months. Cargoes of flour, butter, cheese, and meat, as well as potash and lumber, reached Montreal from the Champlain valley in this manner. In return Montreal provided much the same variety of commodities which valley residents secured from Albany and New York: dry goods, dyes, spices, and other imported items.[10]

In warmer weather traffic between Montreal and the northern regions of the lake shore moved largely by water. Rafts or lake boats carried cargo to St. Johns. From there some of it moved by wagon—after 1835 by railroad—to La Prairie on the St. Lawrence opposite Montreal, a distance of only sixteen miles. There, of course, cargoes faced the problem of traversing that majestic stream. Alternatively, some cargoes after portaging the Richelieu rapids continued to Montreal by river boat, a distance of about one hundred miles (sixty down the Richelieu and forty up the St. Lawrence). Heavy and inexpensive commodities were of course most likely to take this route. For example, in 1803 Peter Sailly paid fifteen dollars to "Jeremi the boatman at LaPrairie" to bring one hundred bushels of salt from Montreal to St. Johns. Presumably, after carrying the cargo around the rapids, Sailly loaded it onto his own boat for the rest of the journey to Plattsburgh.[11]

Transportation factors help explain why Champlain valley residents preferred to buy at Montreal rather than at Quebec, where they sold their export staples. For river traffic, Montreal was only about ninety miles closer to Lake Champlain than was Quebec. But, for sleighs the distance from Montreal to Plattsburgh was only some sixty miles, while from Quebec to Plattsburgh was well over two hundred miles. As the head of navigation on the St. Lawrence, Montreal in time attracted more ocean-going vessels than did Quebec. Consequently, Montreal became the metropolis to which farmers and merchants from the Plattsburgh area took sleigh-loads of farm produce and potash in the winter and from which they returned with merchandise imported from Europe. Those who sold timber rafts and their miscellaneous cargoes at Quebec, on the other hand, quite often returned with cash or transferred their credits to Montreal or to New York, Albany, or Boston, where conditions for purchasing imported merchandise were better.[12] Transportation to and from Boston or other New England ports was extremely expensive because there was less opportunity for the use of waterways and more reliance upon costly land transportation. In 1786 Moses Hazen employed a long succession of short-haul teamsters to move cargo from Hartford to Skenesborough and then "batteau men" to move it from there to Point au Roche.[13] Much traffic to New England bypassed Skenesborough, leaving the lake at Chimney Point to move some eighty miles through the Green Mountains to the Connecticut River along Lord Jeffrey Amherst's military road of 1759.[14] Even from eastern Vermont, shipping to or from Boston in the 1820s took three to four weeks with four-horse teams and cost from ten to thirty-two dollars per ton. As in the case of trade to Albany, the cost was higher in the summer "with waggoning" than in the winter with sleighs.[15]

Despite these obstacles, some trade between Boston and Plattsburgh took place. For example, an advertisement in the *Republican* (May 7, 1814) offered for sale rum, wines, tea, sugar, spices, and almonds "just received" from Boston. Credits from sales at Quebec may have been transferred to help pay for such imports from Boston, but some potash presumably made the trip by land. The watershed town of Peacham, Vermont, was sending potash overland to Boston as late as the 1830s. Drovers may have taken cattle or hogs from the Plattsburgh area to Boston; a ferry at Port Kent did take such stock across the lake in the 1820s at the rate of twenty-five cents each for cattle and six cents for hogs.[16] In view of Clinton County's usual importation of meat, however, it seems unlikely that payment for imports from Boston often took that form.

Canals began to influence nearly all aspects of valley economy during the 1820s. In 1822, when the Champlain Canal afforded all-water transportation to Troy, Albany, and New York City, the most important result was to provide a substitute market for the valley's timber products just as new British regulations (see chapter 2) were effectively excluding them from their original market in Britain. The new market, however, had several advantages over the old. Reloading from lake boat to canal boat to river boat, expensive as it was, nevertheless, was not so costly as the combined costs of portaging cargo at the Richelieu rapids and suffering damage to cribs of timber as they shot the rapids. By the 1840s, "long boats,"

essentially barges towed by steamboats, carried cargo from Plattsburgh all the way to Albany or New York City without the expense
of transshipment at Whitehall and again at the Hudson.[17] Merchants
found it convenient, as well as more economical, to be able to sell
in the same market in which they bought, rather than to have to
transfer funds from Quebec to New York in order to secure the
advantages of purchasing where the variety of goods was greater
and the prices lower. The new route also eliminated the bother and
expense of customs duties and inspections. Finally (as mentioned in
chapter 2), the new route encouraged the Champlain valley to convert its logs into lumber rather than squared timbers, thus adding
to the value of the product.

In absolute terms the Champlain Canal reduced by as much as
two-thirds both the time and the cost of shipment to New York.
A trip which before had taken twenty-five to thirty days and cost
twenty-five to thirty dollars per ton could be made after 1822 in
ten to fourteen days for about ten dollars per ton.[18] By 1834 freight
from Plattsburgh to New York City was only six dollars per
ton as compared to nearly eleven pounds ($27.50) just after the
Revolution.[19]

The effect of the New York canals on imports was less conspicuous but also highly significant. By lowering the cost of transportation, the Champlain Canal sharply reduced the cost of goods imported from New York City and, by a similar margin, it augmented
the effective purchasing power of the valley. In conjunction with
the Erie Canal, which opened in 1825, the Champlain Canal made
it possible for the valley to secure wheat or flour from the West—
first from the Genesee area and after about 1839 from Ohio—at
prices which induced some to stop growing wheat for sale and others
even to stop producing it for family consumption. By 1849 Ohio
wheat was coming to Lake Champlain via the St. Lawrence and the
Richelieu rivers, using canals around Niagara Falls and the rapids
of both rivers. Freight charges between Toledo and Burlington for
wheat shipped in that manner were 15½¢ per bushel as opposed
to 26¢ by the Erie and Champlain canals.[20]

Passenger service between New York City and Canada via Lake
Champlain was available at an early date. James Kent utilized stagecoach service from Poughkeepsie to Whitehall when he journeyed
to Canada in 1795. Stagecoaches connected St. Johns to Montreal
in the same period. In each case the scheduling of the stagecoach
service was linked—not too reliably—to that of the sailing ships

which plied between the two ends of the lake. Merchants apparently provided much of the business. By 1816 the Red Bird Stage Line afforded a wintertime link between Montreal and New York via Plattsburgh.[21] Such service, operating for some distance on the ice, was feasible only about three months each year, beginning in January. In 1794 William Pitt Platt wrote on April 7 that the man who brought him a letter from Poughkeepsie had come over the ice; he also stated that it was very dangerous and that "the Horses stepped threw repeatedly but arrived safe."[22]

Passenger service was often extremely uncomfortable, to say the least. The experiences of John Lambert, an Englishman who traveled in the United States and Canada between 1806 and 1808, illustrate some of the difficulties which even a wealthy tourist or businessman might encounter. At St. Johns, Lambert missed the sailing of the regular ship for Whitehall. Rather than "remain three days longer in imprisonment at this miserable village," he embarked on a small sloop. Its two-man crew were nautical novices; neither had even been to Whitehall. While they hoped to make a little money by carrying cheese and a few passengers to that distant point, they also seemed to rely on the expectation that their ship would be condemned by the customs officers at Whitehall as unseaworthy. In that event its purchase price would be refunded to them. Their expectation was not without foundation. Lambert noted that the sails were in rags; there was no lifeboat or pumps—only a tin kettle to cope with the bailing problem posed by the numerous leaks. When about midnight they reached the United States Customs House at Cumberland Head (between Plattsburgh village and Beekmantown), they ran the anchorless sloop aground in order to stop.

The necessity of stopping proved unfortunate. It took an hour of hailing to rouse John Nichols, the tavern keeper. When awakened he came out to the leaky sloop in a still more porous canoe, which promptly capsized when the sloop's owner and one of his passengers attempted to board it. Ducked into the water in subfreezing temperatures (it was late November), the three waded ashore, whereupon Nichols raced back to the tavern and "inhumanely ordered away" his prospective guests, who had taken time to rescue his canoe. When the owner of the sloop came back from the customhouse with his clothes "*a solid mass of ice*," it took him two hours to get his ship off the rocks. Meanwhile, the tin kettle was lost and bailing had to be done with a tea kettle.

The rest of the journey was less trying. After a most uncomfortable night aboard, they managed to get ashore at a farmhouse. There for a modest seven pence each they enjoyed "a substantial American breakfast, consisting of eggs, fried pork, beef-steaks, apple-tarts, pickles, cheese, cyder, tea, and toast dipped in melted butter and milk." Although they later had difficulty in finding the proper channel to get them to Whitehall, they did ultimately make port in safety.[23] The regular ship presumably made the journey with fewer hazards.

By 1809 the steamboat *Vermont*, built at Burlington the previous year, plied more or less regularly between Whitehall and St. Johns, affording somewhat better service to travelers. The boat did not stop at Plattsburgh, but anyone who hailed it could board anywhere along the way, presuming he could find someone to row him out to the channel. By 1829 some thirty thousand passengers yearly were traversing the lake on steamboats, but sailing ships still carried most of the freight. Only in the 1840s did steamboats begin to command a major share of the lake's export trade. Until 1849 the Champlain Transportation Company enjoyed a monopoly of steamboat service, first by law and then by buying out or ruining all competitors.[24]

As late as 1846, travel between New York City and Plattsburgh was still somewhat adventurous. A woman who made the trip as a child in that year later recalled: "We left New York City Monday evening by the Hudson River steamboat and arrived at Troy the next morning, stopping at the Troy House . . . for breakfast. The packet boats on the Champlain Canal, left in the morning, but by taking the railroad cars and meeting the boat at Mechanicsville . . . we were able to remain at Troy until noon. There was no railroad depot, but the cars started directly in front of the Troy House, and were drawn through River Street to the outskirts of the city by horses. Tuesday afternoon and night were passed on the packet-boat. . . . My mother . . . sat up almost all night in the stifling air of the cabin, and kept the vermin off from her children. . . . We arrived at Whitehall on Wednesday morning, took breakfast at the hotel and at 10 o'clock, went on board the steamboat at Whitehall." The paddle-wheel steamer, often audible before it could be seen, pulled into Plattsburgh about 7:00 P.M., completing for many of its passengers a forty-eight-hour trip from New York City. It then went on to St. Johns and returned about twenty-four hours later. With two boats in service, there were daily departures from Plattsburgh for either Whitehall or St. Johns.[25]

Railroads, while extremely important in other sections of the country, had had little effect on Beekmantown before 1850. Business leaders in Plattsburgh tried to induce the Boston capitalists who planned a link-up with Ogdensburgh to make the line run through Plattsburgh. However, the financiers understandably chose a direct route through Rouses Point at the northern end of the lake, rather than the circuitous one required to include Plattsburgh. William Swetland, agent for the Beekman family, solicited the aid of James W. Beekman, then a state senator, to secure legislation to bar the construction of the railroad through Rouses Point, unless a branch line were constructed to Plattsburgh. Even before the solicitation, Beekman had made a lengthy speech on the subject—without reference to his own interest in the matter—but to no avail. The road began service ultimately in 1850. A railroad between Plattsburgh and Montreal began operation in 1851. Rail service to Boston from Burlington, the lake's major urban center, had begun in 1849.[26]

When the first store opened at Plattsburgh is not evident, but a remarkable number of prominent early settlers became merchants within a few years. Among them were Charles Platt, who had built the first mills there in 1785, and Benjamin Mooers. Some of these early stores, in particular Peter Sailly's and that of a man named Fontfreyde, were at Cumberland Head rather than at the mill sites on the Saranac. Cumberland Head was closer to the route of through traffic on the lake and, until after the War of 1812, it remained the official port of entry for ships from Canada. By 1811 Plattsburgh was a well-established commercial center. Although it then had only seventy-eight houses, there were thirteen stores, four hotels, and eleven shops and offices.[27]

When the first store opened in Beekmantown is still less certain than is the case with Plattsburgh. Before moving to Cumberland Head, Mooers apparently operated something resembling a store as well as a tavern in conjunction with his operations at Point au Roche. Probably, there was a store in Beekmantown proper by the time it seceded from Plattsburgh. There were numerous other enterprises in the town at that period—including a gristmill, a fullingmill, two taverns, and twenty-two asheries. In 1840 there were two merchants and in 1845 three operated in Beekmantown.[28]

In the 1840s cash payment or "ready pay" began to replace what the *Republican* referred to as "the old and miserable *crediting* business." The development had come gradually. For many years merchants had occasionally advertised certain items for cash sale only. However, in May 1848 W. K. Dana claimed to have begun the first store in Plattsburgh based exclusively upon the "ready pay" principle. His prices on some items, he proclaimed, were 40 percent cheaper than elsewhere in northern New York. Thus, local residents who had cash could purchase at much lower rates. But, for those who could not, there were still many stores which accepted "all kinds of country produce" of specified kinds—"green" hides at the shoemakers, for example, in payment.[29] While Beekmantown merchants never advertised, it seems likely that even in 1850 they were still a long way from adoption of the cash system on an exclusive basis.

That the "ready pay" practice had made so much progress can be attributed not only to improved transportation and the extension of specialized production and exchange but also to an improvement in the supply of money due chiefly to the proliferation of banks. The community leaders who sought in 1817 to secure a legislative charter for the Bank of Plattsburgh presented a strong case. There was no existing bank within 150 miles, and none in the entire state of Vermont. Plattsburgh was the commercial center for Clinton, Essex, and Franklin counties and for Grand Isle, Vermont, as well. Adequate specie for a bank flowed into town from Canada in payment for exports which merchants made of lumber, potash, and other articles. The legislature agreed that a bank at Plattsburgh would "promote the agricultural, commercial, and manufacturing interests" of the three New York counties and accordingly granted the charter. It enjoined the bank, however, to do business only in Plattsburgh and to eschew mercantile involvements and land speculation.[30]

For a number of years, the bank seemed to flourish. Although its stockholders apparently never produced more than $60,000 of the $300,000 which they had subscribed, the bank survived the depression following 1819, when rumors circulated at Albany that it had failed. In the early 1820s, it often paid 4 percent dividends semiannually. But, in 1825 it began to experience difficulty, and by 1828 it was defunct.[31]

The chief cause of the bank's failure was Levi Platt, its major stockholder. In 1822 Platt held nearly six thousand shares of the bank's stock, roughly ten times as many as anyone else. Before the Panic of 1819, Platt evidently had improperly lent a large portion of the bank's money to someone, apparently not a local resident, who proved unable to repay. For years after the panic, bank officers sought vainly to collect the debt, roughly $77,000, from Platt. As late as 1824, the bank had notes circulating in the amount of $188,643, while it had $18,076 in specie in its vaults. By 1826, however, its notes had dropped to $33,694, and its specie amounted to only $248.[32]

To save the bank, its officers instituted litigation against Platt, attempting to foreclose on the mortgage which he had given to secure the debt. Platt took evasive actions which delayed the sale of his properties for about a year, but ultimately the bank secured and sold twenty-one plots of land containing 4,400 acres, forty-nine lots of unspecified size, a gristmill, a plastermill, an oilmill (for making linseed oil from flax seed), a carding and clothing works, and a wharf. The proceeds from selling these properties left nearly $36,000 still due the bank. Meanwhile, Benjamin Mooers, the bank president, fumed privately at the "abominable frauds" committed and at the delay necessitated by the chancery court action in laying before the public "the unjust and unprincipled doings of Levi Platt."[33]

The failure of the Bank of Plattsburgh was doubly unfortunate in that it proved so difficult to gain legislative authorization for a new one. The Panic of 1819, soon after the chartering of the bank, had led to widespread revulsion against new charters, especially for institutions in "country towns and villages." Such banks, legislators believed, were chiefly responsible for the fact that while paper currency was supposedly limited to no more than three times a bank's specie reserve, currency then in circulation had a face value some *six* times greater than the estimated total of specie in the state. About the time the Bank of Plattsburgh failed, the question was to be complicated further by the beginning of Andrew Jackson's famous "bank war," which engendered more antibank sentiment among his supporters. Consequently, while those seeking to institute a new bank in Plattsburgh included representatives of the dominant party, they failed in 1830, 1831, 1833, and 1834 to get the two-thirds vote in each legislative chamber which was then required for a new bank charter. They succeeded in 1836, on the eve of another depression which was characterized by widespread bank failures.[34]

The course of the new institution, the Clinton County Bank, was remarkably similar to that of its predecessor. It survived the onset of the depression which struck soon after its inception, but then it lent excessively to its own officers to finance various speculative ventures. Great loss ensued when the speculations failed and the security given for the lost loans "turned out to be almost entirely worthless." This was the major reason why the bank had to suspend payment from its account in Albany in December 1841. The state commissioners permitted it to reopen shortly with a new cashier and half of its original capital of $200,000. "But after a short time," the state commissioners reported, "it became apparent that its credit had been so far injuriously affected . . . as to force back upon it for immediate payment, its whole outstanding circulation. This it was not prepared to meet."[35] On April 2, 1842, the *Republican* announced that the bank had stopped paying its obligations in Albany and was "paying some 25 per cent to bill-holders at their counter [in Plattsburgh] yesterday." Fearing lest some of its readers might not realize the urgency of taking their currency to the bank for redemption before its resources were exhausted, the editor added the injunction: "Now is your time!"

The failure to establish an enduring bank at Plattsburgh impeded commercial transactions with distant cities. The problem is illustrated by the difficulties which William Swetland experienced in making remittance to James W. Beekman in New York on funds collected from Beekmantown tenants and purchasers of land. Throughout the depression years, 1838 to 1842, Swetland puzzled repeatedly over how best to transfer money from Plattsburgh to New York. The simplest way was for him to write a check to Beekman on the Clinton County Bank. At first, however, Swetland chose other methods because this was both troublesome and expensive, apparently due to the well-warranted reluctance of New York City banks to accept checks on small country banks except at a considerable discount. By 1840 he had come to prefer that method in the belief that banks were then "so situated" as to make such transactions possible without much loss. The demise of the Clinton County Bank within less than two years belied his optimism and made that means of remittance no longer possible.[36]

An alternative method which Swetland had at first favored was to purchase a draft on New York City. That meant to buy an order from someone in Clinton County who had a credit in New York requiring that his credit be transferred to pay Beekman. The bank charged 1 or 2 percent for such drafts. When it closed, Swetland had to scout around himself to find someone who had a credit in New York which he was willing to transfer to Beekman in exchange for equivalent payment from Swetland. In the winter it was virtually impossible to arrange payments in this manner as the flow of commodities to New York upon which they depended was always interrupted by ice. Even when drafts could be secured in winter, it was difficult to get them to New York. Swetland preferred not to send drafts by mail, and reliable travelers were few. One upon whom Swetland had intended to rely was found to be planning to be married en route; Swetland concluded that it would not be "entirely prudent to rely upon the care and attention of a young man so situated." Shortly before the bank failed, Swetland's son-in-law became established as a merchant in New York. The commodities from Clinton County which he sold in New York afforded credits upon which Swetland could safely and conveniently rely in transferring funds to Beekman. Swetland's correspondence makes no more reference to a remittance problem, but the means by which he made the payments was by no means up to date.[37]

Beekmantown residents had always had available to them Asian textiles and spices, Latin American cocoa, West Indian dyes, and a large variety of European products. But, it is evident that by the 1840s the reduction in the costs of transportation had greatly extended the list of exotic commodities available. A prosperous Beekmantown farmer who chose to defy the temperance movement of the 1840s, for example, could choose at will among champagne, cognac, sazerac, a long list of wines and cordials, plus brandies by Leger Freres, Hennessy, and several others.[38] The frontier community of the 1780s was becoming cosmopolitan indeed.

To record the history of manufacturing as it relates to the development of Beekmantown requires some distinction among the three different types which existed. Most conspicuous was manufacturing for export from the region. Here the important items were timber products, including potash (see chapter 2). Next were the articles produced by local artisans for local sale rather than for export from the region. These included boots and shoes, brick, lime, and a large variety of other items which required too much capital or too much skill to be satisfactorily produced by the individual farmer but could not absorb the cost of transportation from other areas. Finally, there was the considerable group of items produced by each family primarily for its own consumption but also for sale when conditions of supply and demand warranted. Among these were butter, cheese, preserved meats, soap, candles, and some items of apparel or home furnishing. Plattsburgh had an industrial focus from the beginning. Financed by the investment of about a dozen proprietors, Charles Platt began constructing a gristmill, a sawmill, and a forge in 1785. He soon had them in operation, but it was difficult to keep them going. He wrote to his brother Zephaniah on January 29, 1787, that the sawmill had not turned since he had left and that the gristmill had also halted. The trouble was apparently an ice jam following a heavy thaw, but obviously both mills had been working, probably since sometime in 1786. In the fall of 1787, Melanchton Woolsey reported to Zephaniah that the gristmill had ground "near 3000 bushels since you . . . left us but we find it exceedingly difficult to man the saw mill" as one man was always busy with the gristmill and the other "very lame."[39]

Manufacturing enterprises such as these seem to have flourished at Plattsburgh and to have attracted others as well. In 1792 an English traveler observed that the residents of Plattsburgh "have artisans of almost every kind among them and furnish among themselves all the materials for building, glass excepted." James Kent in 1795 found two sawmills, two gristmills, and a forge at the mouth of the Saranac. The investment of the mill proprietors had grown by 1797 to about seven thousand dollars, and more mills were constructed within the next three or four years.[40] By 1825 the town was approaching four thousand in population. The state census noted three gristmills, twenty-six sawmills, one oilmill, two fullingmills, two carding machines, three iron works, three distilleries, and fourteen asheries. Unrecorded by the census were several tanneries, boot and shoemakers, blacksmith shops, saddle and harness makers, wheelwrights, tailors, and other artisan establishments which engaged in manufacturing.[41]

Beekmantown, while suffering in comparison to Plattsburgh, nevertheless had a significant amount of manufacturing. Much of it, of course, was the work of artisans to be considered more fully below. But, census reports for 1825 showed that while Plattsburgh had twenty-six sawmills to Beekmantown's one, three iron works to Beekmantown's none, and two fullingmills to Beekmantown's one, the metropolis had only fourteen asheries to Beekmantown's twenty-one. Furthermore, in household production of textiles, as is evident in table 7, Beekmantown was far ahead.

TABLE 7.

Household Production of Textiles

	Population	Fulled Cloth	Flannel and Other Unfulled Woolens	Linen, Cotton, and Others
Beekmantown	1,511	3,207 (2.1)	4,008 (2.7)	4,709 (3.1)
Plattsburgh	3,853	5,148 (1.3)	7,679 (2.0)	6,691 (1.7)

SOURCE: New York State Census, 1825.
NOTE: Figures in parentheses are per capita. Figures for cloth are in yards.

Even household production of cloth normally left certain stages of production to entrepreneurs who hired and supervised workers. That such an enterprise existed in Beekmantown is evident from the advertisement which appeared in the *Republican* on September 1, 1815: "CLOTH DRESSING. The subscribers have commenced DRESSING CLOTH at Beekmantown, where their old customers, and the publick can be accommodated, as they have furnished themselves with a good stock of Dye Stuffs and workmen sufficient to dress cloth with neatness and dispatch. People living on Grand Isle in Lake Champlain can be accommodated by leaving their cloth, with directions how to have it dressed, at D. Flint's Store, on the wharf, Plattsburgh, and have it safely returned there when dressed." The reference to "old customers" suggests that the advertisers had been in the same business before the war.

Encouragement for household manufacturing was a major aim of the Clinton County Agricultural Society throughout the brief period of its existence from 1819 to 1823. Premiums comparable to those for livestock were offered in 1820 for linen, linen diaper, woolen blanket, cotton and woolen blanket, coverlet, woolen cloth, bombazette, straw bonnet, fur hat, fine boots, shoes, and for farm implements such as hoe, ax, plow, and ox yoke. In 1822 the list included, in addition to most of those above, flannel, flannel rose blankets, carpeting, linen check, castor hat, felt hat, straw hat, silk grass bonnet, iron, scythe, cabinetwork, two-horse lumber wagon, machine for pulling stumps, and two-horse harness. Beekmantown residents won prizes in several categories.[42]

What the community leaders wanted was both to foster the self-sufficiency of each home and to reduce the hated dependence on Britain. In the old spirit of mercantilism, they deplored the loss of wealth from the community through payment to outsiders for such relatively expensive commodities. In 1821 an official of the society proclaimed that if the county would progress for twenty years as it had in the last three, it "would be independent of Europe for everything which relates to dress" except cravats.[43] In fact, the county did progress appreciably in the production of cloth for the next four years at least (see table 8), but after 1825 the decennial state censuses show a steady decline in per capita production of textiles.

Equally significant is that although per capita production of textiles in Beekmantown reached its all-time peak around 1825, that peak was not very high. Per capita production of textiles in other towns around the state in 1825 was very often much higher than the relatively modest figures for Beekmantown.

Several other characteristics of household textile production in Beekmantown stand out in table 8. First, cotton and linen were considerably less popular products than woolens. Linen production was especially difficult when compared to the making of woolens and declined as income rose. This occurred even though its raw material, flax, was still grown occasionally in the county in order to sell the seed for the manufacture of linseed oil. Production of cotton cloth was always low, apparently because the cost of the raw material imported from the South was relatively high in relation to the cost of the finished product secured from other sources. The declining price of finished cottons, which came with the rise of the factory system, still further increased the incentive to buy the finished product rather than the raw material. This accounts for the virtual elimination of household production of cotton by 1855.

When the Clinton County Agricultural Society revived in the 1840s, it again offered premiums for a wide range of textile products of home manufacture. But, there no longer seemed any real or even pretended expectation that the premiums would stimulate commercial production. In 1844 a special display of "articles of domestic manufacture" was arranged in conjunction with the annual Cattle Show and Fair. A large "car"—some twenty-five to thirty feet in length—"carpeted and dressed out in fabrics of household and shop manufactures" was drawn through the streets of Plattsburgh by ten yoke of oxen. Governor William Bouck was

TABLE 8.

Household Production of Textiles in Beekmantown, 1821–1855

	1821	1825	1835	1845	1855
Population	1,343	1,511	2,263	3,078	2,933
Fulled woolens	2,433	3,207	3,802	2,869	665
Per capita	1.8	2.1	1.7	0.9	0.2
Unfulled woolens	2,312	4,008	2,362	3,942	2,218
Per capita	1.7	2.7	1.0	1.3	0.8
Cotton, linen, etc.	3,512	4,709	3,002	822	68
Per capita	2.6	3.1	1.3	0.3	—

SOURCE: New York State Census for the years indicated.
NOTE: Figures for cloth are in yards.

aboard. As the somewhat jaundiced editor of the *Republican* observed (October 5), ladies were present in abundance, but fabrics of their production were relatively few. While the Democratic editor stopped short of suggesting it, he left the impression that the object was to promote Whig votes rather than household manufacturing.

In the 1840s local leaders no longer suggested, as they had in the 1820s, that the work of farm families in their own homes was about to achieve self-sufficiency for the county in the production of textiles. In fact, textiles were conspicuously absent from the list of commodities whose importation into the county was so offensive to the speaker at the county fair in 1843.[44] Although the society still offered premiums for much the same range of household textile manufactures at the end of the decade and beyond, the address of 1849 contained overt recognition that the commercial production of textiles in farm households was a thing of the past. "We occasionally hear from the mouths of some old grumblers," said Thomas B. Watson, "sad lamentations over what they are pleased to call the decay of industry among women, and loud complaints that the loom and spinning wheel are now suffered to slumber amid the dust of the garret—just as though our fair country women had not enough of household duties to occupy their time, without slaving themselves in labors that were better left to the looms of Lowell, or the manufactures of Manchester. . . . You do not deserve to have wives, if you wish them to enter into competition with the Steam Engine and the Power Loom in producing cloths, when by exchanging a few of your own productions, you can obtain these with less trouble and at less expense. . . . Therefore should we rejoice that the day of alleviation has in part come, and that the music of the loom and the wheel has in many instances given place to that of the Melodeon and the Piano."[45] Thus did the society at last repudiate the backward idea of family and community self-sufficiency and embrace the principle of division of labor or specialization and exchange as advocated by Adam Smith in 1776.

The federal census of 1850 makes clear that by that time both rich and poor residents of Beekmantown were beginning to heed Watson's advice. Among the twenty richest farmers, four produced no textiles at all. The range of values among those who did produce textiles was from five to seventy-seven dollars. Among the twenty poorest farmers, most showed no household production of textiles at all. The range of values for household production of textiles among the very poor was from one to sixteen dollars.[46]

Few artisans made their living in Beekmantown at any time. Presumably, their numbers grew as population increased, but the proximity of Plattsburgh made it difficult for them to flourish. In 1850 Beekmantown had twenty-one self-employed artisans and sixteen workers employed by them. There were three blacksmiths, shoemakers, and sawmill operators; two persons made lime. Without local competition were a miller, a weaver, a wheelwright, and persons making hoops, iron, wagons, potash, bricks, cabinets, and charcoal. Of the hired workers, six worked in sawmills, four each in the lime and brick works, and one each for a shoemaker and a blacksmith.[47]

An example of what was happening to artisans of another kind is afforded by the advertisements of a Plattsburgh tailor, John White. Alarmed and hurt by the increasing sale of "ready-made" clothing in the later 1840s, White took space in the *Republican* (September 30, 1848) to announce that he too stocked ready-made clothes "manufactured by myself . . . far superior to the refuse clothing sent here from *Troy slop-shops*, and puffed up at other shops as good and cheap articles while in fact they are worthless rags." He made it clear that, as in the past, he would also make clothing to order, cut cloth to fit for "tailoresses" to make, and "no dodging in case of misfits." Other advertisements showed, however, that he was fighting a losing battle.

Food processing in the home held up better for some products than for others. The state censuses of 1845 and 1855 show butter production increasing from 111,892 pounds to 172,695 or from 36 pounds per capita to 59, while cheese production fell from 21,845 pounds to 17,823 or from 7 pounds per capita to 6. The federal census of 1850—perhaps a better guide, in that production figures for each farm are available—indicates that each of the wealthy farms with but one exception produced several hundred pounds of butter and none of the poorer farms failed to produce at least some. Quite a few of the wealthy farms produced no cheese whatever, and none of the poorest farms produced any. Home production of meat averaged around one hundred dollars in value on the richest farms, as opposed to some twenty dollars on the poorest. There were very few farms which produced no meat.

The labor force of bound and hired workers (to be distinguished from self-employed farmers and artisans who also did manual labor) was always quite varied in composition but also very low in "visibility" to the historian. Laborers, of course, shared the hardships common to all the earliest settlers but seemingly suffered more acutely. Those who suffered most from the lack of clothing in the early years, as noted in the previous chapter, were French Canadian mill workers. When an unprecedentedly cold summer in 1816 produced great shortages of grain in 1817, the customs collector, Peter Sailly, noted that "a large proportion of the inhabitants are much distressed for the want of bread whilst the poorer and labouring class are absolutely destitute of the means of obtaining it at the high price it sells for." He took it upon himself to alleviate the shortage in some measure by permitting people to bring in wheat from Canada for themselves and their neighbors without paying duty.[48]

Scarcity of labor gravely concerned the community leaders in the early years of settlement. Laborers who migrated often preferred to shift for themselves as squatters or tenants. Relatively high wages—resulting from the eagerness of those investing in timber enterprises, milling, and land speculation, as well as from the scarcity of workers—enabled many who came as laborers to promote themselves soon to the status of squatters or even land owners. In 1790 Jeremiah Platt wrote back to Poughkeepsie seeking a miller to whom he promised to pay one hundred pounds yearly and two "common laborers that are Sivil and industrious."[49] Robert Platt complained to his father, Zephaniah, in 1798, "I find laborers are not to be had neither for love nor money."[50] At Ogdensburgh in 1809, the proprietor's agent imported laborers from Montreal to work for $13.50 per month but lost them to lumbermen paying $18.00.[51]

In such circumstances, it was natural that the settlers should choose to rely in some measure on various forms of bound labor. The census of 1790, which found eighty-six families in Platts-burgh indicated that there were thirteen slaves. Eight belonged to Nathaniel Platt, four to Melanchton Woolsey, and one to Theo-dorus Platt. Thomas Tredwell, who was about to move to Beek-mantown in 1790, was listed in the same census as the owner of twelve slaves. How many he brought to Beekmantown is uncertain, but he did bring some. Precisely what tasks these slaves performed is not evident, but it is reasonable to assume that they were varied.[52]

The slave population of Plattsburgh did rise for a time, but a state law of 1799 which required gradual abolition of slavery had reversed the trend sometime before the War of 1812. A Plattsburgh tax list of 1798 shows thirty-five slaves belonging to nine different members of the local establishment—mostly Platts but including Thomas Tredwell of Beekman Patent and Benjamin Mooers.[53] From then into the early 1800s, the minutes of the town meetings note several manumissions. In 1814 the state census found fifty-eight free Negroes in Plattsburgh but no slaves. There were in fact only two slaves in the entire county.

Beekmantown seems to have become the seat of a considerable colony of these free Negroes. How they sustained themselves is not at all clear. The fact that many were assessed highway labor along with other residents suggests that they operated small farms. But, if so, it is also likely that they supplemented their farm income by working occasionally for wages as well. The colony numbered twenty-four Negroes in 1825 (about a quarter of the county total) but declined thereafter to a low of ten in 1845. In 1850, however, Beekmantown again had a Negro community of twenty-four, the largest in the county. By 1855 it had increased to forty, but there was still no indication of how these Negroes made a living.[54]

Apprenticeship was a more common form of bound labor. Advertisements for apprentices to be bound to master craftsmen appeared quite regularly in the *Republican*. So did notices identifying runaway apprentices and disclaiming responsibility for them.

"Binding out" as laborers those who had become public charges seems to have occurred quite often in neighboring Chazy but not in Beekmantown. The records of Beekmantown's overseers of the poor for the years 1820 to 1835 make no mention of binding out the poor as laborers. At Chazy, on the other hand, from 1820 through 1824 "all the poor of the town" had been "sold at public sale" during the annual town meetings.[55]

The history of free labor in the Plattsburgh-Beekmantown area can be illustrated by the stories of three migrants who came to the area at different periods. In the earliest years of settlement, Melanchton L. Woolsey, sometime agent for the Beekmantown proprietors, sawed boards, drew logs, tended the gristmill "by night and by day," practiced "both Physick and surgery," and drew deeds. To pay for nails for his house, he also performed other labor of an unspecified nature. He acquired considerable wealth but became a bankrupt after the War of 1812.[56]

John B. Bertrand, except for the extent of his later success, was probably typical of many French Canadian immigrants who worked as farm laborers at a later period. Born in Quebec in 1813, Bertrand came to the United States with his family in 1829 at the age of sixteen. They crossed the border with seven dollars. Bertrand worked as a farm laborer in Clinton County and in Vermont, saved his money, and bought a farm. Dissatisfied with it, he sold it and bought another in Beekmantown. By 1850 he had become one of the wealthiest farmers there.[57]

Michael Shields was more or less representative of the Irish immigrants. In 1846 along with several other Irishmen, Shields received $5.50 for labor at seventy-five cents a day in conjunction with William Swetland's efforts to determine whether or not the iron ore to be found in Beekmantown was of commercial quality. (It was not.) What other labor Shields performed—with or without his horses and oxen—is not evident, but probably his employments were only a little less varied than Woolsey's. Like most rural laborers, he was also a farmer. In 1850 his fifty-acre farm valued at $800 contained two horses, two cows, two oxen, seven sheep, and two hogs worth in all about $200. He produced six bushels of wheat, twenty-five of rye, two of corn, twenty of oats, twelve of buckwheat, plus fourteen pounds of wool, four hundred bushels of potatoes, one hundred pounds of butter, nine tons of hay, thirty dollars worth of meat, and thirteen dollars worth of home manufactures.[58] Thus, he was by no means entirely dependent on his wages for a living.

In each of the four economic topics considered in this chapter, developments outside of Beekmantown and Clinton County exerted the most profound influence upon the pattern of economic change. Completion of New York's trunk canals reoriented Champlain valley trade from Canada to New York City and lowered transportation costs dramatically. The decline in production of timber and potash, quasi-manufacturing enterprises, came about largely because of the exhaustion of resources. However, household production of textiles for sale, as well as for home use, declined due to the rise of the factory system of production elsewhere—aided by both the improvements in transportation and the increase in the supply of money.

Changes in the character of the laboring population also owed much to external developments. In the early period of scarce labor, French Canadians, Negro slaves, and young men from New England or elsewhere in New York provided most of the labor force. By the end of the period, French Canadians were still an important source of labor, but the state had abolished slavery, enabling the few Negroes to become free farmers and probably only occasional laborers. Large-scale immigration from Ireland had provided a new reservoir of poor farmers who were also sometimes laborers. Young men native to New England and New York State were no longer so available. As the next chapter will show more fully, they were moving to the West or to the cities.

PART 2
Social and Intellectual History

Judge Pliny Moore's house, Champlain, residence of the principal developer of the town, also a miller, lumberman, and Federalist political leader

5

People

Contrary to a still widespread impression as to the sequence of arrivals in frontier communities,[1] the first generation of settlers in the Beekmantown-Plattsburgh area was considerably higher in socioeconomic status than the second. Previous chapters have laid a foundation for explaining why this was so. But, both the demonstration that it was so and the explanation as to why it was so need to be made explicit. It is worthwhile to explore as well where the settlers of each generation came from, how they got along with each other, and why so many of the immigrants chose to move on to other areas. Intergroup relations, housing, health, and crime also deserve some attention.

At least seven of the first eighty-six heads of families to settle in the Plattsburgh-Beekmantown community were individuals who had enjoyed higher than average status. Three of the seven were Platts (Charles, Theodorus, and Nathaniel), close relatives of the proprietor, Zephaniah. Reinforced by the arrival of George and William Pitt Platt, the clan would have property holdings in Plattsburgh assessed at about $70,000 in 1798.[2]

Melanchton L. Woolsey, although he did the roughest kind of labor in his early years at Plattsburgh, was also a man of some status. Son of a Long Islander killed in the Seven Years' War, Woolsey had inherited £2,500 but had lost it all during the Revolution. After marrying into one of the lesser branches of the Livingston family of Dutchess County, he came to the Saranac in 1785 with only $4. By 1798 he owned 246 acres, a store, corn crib, smokehouse, and "1 little house" assessed in all at just under $3,000.[3]

Peter Sailly was a "French gentleman" who left France after an unfortunate business experience. He arrived at the future site of Plattsburgh about the same time as Woolsey and Charles Platt. By 1798 he owned 200 acres on the lake shore, a store, a barn, an ashery ("ashhouse"), and three "potash shelters" with a total assessed value of $2,450.[4]

Two of the seven settlers of some status listed in the 1790 census lived originally in Beekman Patent. One was, of course, General Moses Hazen's agent, nephew, and former adjutant, Benjamin Mooers. Mooers lived at Point au Roche year round from about 1786 to 1794; during that time he began the impressive land acquisitions mentioned in chapter 2. The other high-status settler in Beekman Patent was Nathaniel Tredwell. Nathaniel was the son of Thomas Tredwell, who also moved to Beekmantown in 1794. A Princeton graduate who had served with Zephaniah Platt in the state convention which ratified the United States Constitution, Thomas Tredwell was also one of the proprietors of Plattsburgh. In 1790 he was about to begin the first of his two terms of service in the United States Congress. By 1798 the Tredwell family owned 2,754 acres and a barn, assessed in all at $9,179.[5]

Never again in the period before 1850 would any individual comparable in status to either Mooers or Tredwell choose to settle in Beekmantown.

Of the remaining thirteen men who came to live in Beekman Patent before 1790, seven were in what might be called modest circumstances. Silas Pomeroy undertook in 1790 to buy an interior lot of 228 acres and completed the purchase in 1796 by paying the Beekmans £183 principal and £51 interest. Another pre-1790 settler was John Howe (also How), who by 1798 owned 125 acres, a frame barn, and an interest in a sawmill, assessed in all at $1,355. Simon Newcomb, a future supervisor of Plattsburgh, contracted to buy half of a plot of 228 acres but did not complete the purchase until 1819. In 1798 he was listed as owner of 100 acres leased to Anne Hall and valued at $1,000. Abraham and Samuel Beeman fit the general pattern, except that Abraham, a town officer in 1789, was not listed in the assessment of 1798. Samuel then owned 100 acres assessed at $700. Another early purchaser who soon departed was Zachariah Long. In 1788 he paid £182 cash for 228 acres. Although he contracted to buy an adjoining lot of the same

*General Mooers' home, Cumberland Head, to which he moved
in 1794 from Point au Roche in Beekman Patent*

size in 1793, he was not present in 1798. Finally, Captain John
Jersey arranged in 1790 to buy a lot of 228 acres. By 1798 he owned
several plots assessed in all at $1,847.[6]

Only six of the first fifteen settlers in Beekman Patent were
not clearly of rather high status or in moderate circumstances. One
was John Maybee, who apparently cleared an acre or two along
the lake in 1787 and then leased an eighty-seven-acre lot in 1788.
He left before the 1790 census. Another short-term settler was
John Ward, who contracted to buy a lakefront lot of eighty-seven
acres in 1790; he sold his "improvements" to Nathaniel Platt at
three dollars per acre within a few years and "ran off." In the
same category, was Joshua Chamberlain of Vermont. In 1787
Chamberlain agreed with Benjamin Mooers, acting for Hazen, to
lease a part of the Point au Roche property and to "keep a House
of Entertainment," that is, a tavern. In 1790 he committed himself
to buy a lakefront lot of eighty-seven acres. But, he too "ran off"
soon, leaving behind a "small plank house," which Woolsey (then
acting as agent for the Beekmans) deemed sufficient compensation

for use of the property. Two other "birds of passage" were Robert Morris and Isaac Webb. Morris sought to purchase an interior lot jointly with Stephen Mix, while Webb still more ambitiously sought two. Neither was present for the tax assessment of 1798.[7]

Of the six presumably poor pioneer settlers, Stephen Mix was the only one still present in 1798. From his attempted purchase of 228 acres in conjunction with Robert Morris, Mix had salvaged 53 acres and a log house, which were assessed in 1798 at $318. Mix may have been poor, but he was quite respectable. In 1798 he had gained admission to the very selective Presbyterian church by "profession of faith."[8]

Were there additional low-status people whose names do not appear in the records? Probably not many. Mooers—and probably the Platts as well—employed many French Canadian men, but they appear to have lived elsewhere. There is, for example, a high incidence of French names in the 1790 census for Champlain. Only two or three of the eighty-six heads of families listed in the 1790 census for Plattsburgh could possibly have been French Canadian laborers. Plattsburgh's highway assessment records beginning in 1798 show only a sprinkling of French names. They include also an ignominious reference to "Judge Platt's frenchman."[9] Letters to the Beekmans from their agents make no reference to French Canadian squatters, lessors, or purchasers.

A few Negro slaves were present. Plattsburgh had thirteen in 1790 but none belonged to residents of Beekman Patent. By 1798, when the slave population had risen to thirty-five, there were three in Beekman Patent, all belonging to Thomas Tredwell. Three, presumably free, Negro neighbors of Tredwell received a highway labor assessment of one day each in 1799.[10] That the assessors of highway labor, the property tax assessors, the agents of the Beekmans, and the census takers should all have overlooked a significant number of additional poor people residing in Beekman Patent seems highly unlikely.

Evidence supporting the affirmation that the thirty-one settlers living in or near Beekman Patent in 1798 could not properly be characterized as an impoverished lot can be summarized quickly. Eight had property assessments of $1,000 or more and landholdings ranging from 125 acres to 687 or, in the case of the Tredwell clan, to 2,754. Eleven settlers had property valued at from $500 to $1,000 and landholdings of from 69 to 228 acres. Except for George Marsh's 69 acres, all the holdings in this category were above the 75-acre size, which might be considered the minimum required to support a family. George Marsh, incidentally, did not depend only on his farm for his livelihood. He also rented a one-acre tract in town, where he presumably kept a shop. Eight early settlers had assessments ranging from $250 to $500 and landholdings, with the exception of one 87-acre tract, of 40 to 53 acres. Some of these small holdings may have belonged to artisans. Several belonged to men living near larger farms whose owners had the same surname and may well have been their fathers.[11]

Oddly enough, the one seemingly very poor resident of Beekman Patent in 1798 was John Wilson, who appeared in chapter 2 as the agent dismissed by the Beekmans in 1807 as a suspected timber thief. He bore an assessment of only ninety dollars on one acre in Beekman Patent, a log house valued at eighteen dollars, and eight acres "owner not known."[12] Wilson was probably not a farmer.

Comparing data from the 1798 tax list with that from the 1850 census reinforces the argument that the socioeconomic status of the first generation of settlers was probably higher than that of the second. Statistically, the two data sources are not really comparable for a variety of reasons, but it is striking that the largest landholding in Beekmantown in 1855 (447 acres) would have ranked fifth in the patent in 1798. The average landholding of the ten richest men listed in the 1798 assessment was 590 acres, more than double that (255) of the ten largest landholders in Beekmantown in 1850. In fact, it seems clear that the large landholders of 1798 were essentially speculators, while those of 1850 were merely substantial farmers.

Dutchess County was the origin of a substantial proportion of the early settlers of both Beekmantown and Plattsburgh, especially of the elite, but several other areas were well represented. Among those who followed the Platts from Dutchess County were Melanchton L. Woolsey, several Palmers, Baileys, Dr. John Miller, and the Newcombs. From Long Island came Thomas Tredwell, the Reverend Frederick Halsey, numerous Smiths, Parsons, and Dominys. From Connecticut came Dr. Baruch Beckwith, John How, George Marsh, and William Swetland. From Vermont came not only the settlers who took Long Island (present North Hero) from the Beekman Patent proprietors but probably a high proportion of the less prosperous settlers. There were, of course, a few French Canadians among the early settlers.[13]

From the mid-1820s onward, there was something of a "new" immigration into Beekmantown and Plattsburgh. In the same way that immigrants from southern and eastern Europe began to outnumber those from northwestern Europe in late nineteenth-century America, French Canadian and Irish immigrants began in the 1820s to outnumber the immigrants into Clinton County from New England and other areas of New York. Had migrants from New England and New York wished to outbid the new immigrants for Clinton County farmland, they almost certainly could have. But, on the whole, they preferred the more rewarding opportunities farther west, where land was cheaper, more likely to rise in value, and more productive. Fertile farms well situated in terms of water transportation were still available at low prices, and new communities were growing. The new immigrants, however, usually lacked capital for the long trek westward or the experience necessary to take advantage of frontier opportunities. French Canadians may have preferred to remain relatively close to their homeland.[14]

The French Canadians were not eager migrants. "Few," wrote John Lambert from his observations between 1806 and 1808, "ever think of emigrating from their paternal abode. The farm is separated by the father among his children, as long as it will last, and when its divisions can be no longer sub-divided, they reluctantly part." But the French Canadians, Lambert also observed, were "miserable farmers" who got very little production from their land, and they tended to "marry young and are seldom without a numerous family."[15] The pressure of population upon the means of subsistence was forcing many into emigration.

In the 1820s French Canadians were apparently rather few in Beekmantown, but by 1855 they were 10 percent of the population.[16] In the county as a whole, they were twice that. Elsewhere in the county, most of them probably worked in the lumber industry, but in Beekmantown many were farm workers. Lord Durham's report to the British Parliament in 1838 affirmed that "from the French portion of Lower Canada there has, for a long time, been a large annual emigration of young men to the northern states of the American Union, in which they are highly valued as labourers, and gain good wages." Although in the past they had normally returned in a few months or years, the writer believed "a great many now take up their permanent residence in the United States."[17] Farms operated by French Canadians in Beekmantown were remarkably few in 1850 compared with the number run by the Irish. None of the twenty poorest farms in Beekmantown belonged to a French Canadian, although one of the richest twenty farms was owned by John Bertrand, who had left his birthplace in Quebec in 1829. Two other French Canadians owned relatively valuable farms.[18]

In general, French Canadians remained low in status and remarkably isolated. Illiteracy among French Canadians in Clinton County was 38 percent as compared to 21 percent for the Irish immigrants and 2 percent for native Americans.[19] In 1848 37 percent of those assisted by the county welfare authorities were French Canadian, although their representation in the total population was about half that. In criminal convictions, however, French Canadians seem to have been relatively underrepresented, at least in comparison with the Irish.[20] No French Canadians appear to have held any office of consequence either in the town government or in the Democratic party in Beekmantown before 1850.

The Irish had essentially similar but still more compelling reasons to emigrate. In 1841 a census of Ireland found that many of the rural families lived in one-room, windowless mud huts. Farms were generally very small, and many held them as tenants-at-will, subject to expulsion at the whim of an absentee landlord.[21] Ships which carried timber from Quebec to Britain afforded them an opportunity for emigration which thousands chose to take from the later 1820s onward. Indeed, immigrant arrivals in Quebec both in 1830 and 1831 exceeded fifty thousand. Some of those, however, were from England and Scotland, and the numbers did drop after the cholera epidemic of 1832, the Papineau rebellion, and the American depression which came later in the decade.[22]

The hardships of such immigrants were great. Lord Durham's report stated with specific reference to the period from 1826 to 1832 that immigrant ships were usually distinguishable by their odor at "gun-shot" distance. Mortality on the voyage was sometimes 6 percent, chiefly from typhus. Along the crowded shores where they landed at Quebec, there were "daily drafts of from 10 to 30 taken to the hospital with infectious diseases." Those who were not sick often lacked even the price of a night's lodging, and there were "very few of them with the means of subsistence for more than a very short period."[23] Catharine Parr Traill, an upper-class Englishwoman who emigrated at the time of the cholera epidemic in 1832, described the arriving immigrants of lower station as "debilitated by the privations and fatigues" of the voyage and bearing "haggard, careworn faces." [24]

By 1855 14 percent of Beekmantown's population was Irish, although for the county as a whole, the figure was a little lower. In contrast to the French Canadians, they were in that period only about the same percent of the county welfare clients. However, they were somewhat overrepresented among convicted criminals. In 1850 quite a number of the twenty poorest farmers in Beekmantown, those whose land was valued at from $100 to $500, were Irish; but several had farms valued at $4,000 or more. Only twenty farmers in Beekmantown possessed farms with a value of $5,000 or more. By the 1840s, the Irish were participating in the leadership of the Democratic party and holding important town offices. [25]

Emigration in the early years was high. Nine of the first fifteen arrivals in Beekman Patent had departed by 1798. Of the eighty-six heads of families in Plattsburgh as a whole in 1790, only forty-seven appear on the tax list of 1798. Thus, the annual rate of emigration among the settlers of 1790 was about 5.77 percent. [26] Tax lists and census data are of course not strictly comparable in that the former omit the poorest people. However, considering the economic vitality reflected, for example, in the careers of Woolsey, Sailly, and Mooers, it appears unlikely that many of the poor settlers of 1790 were still poor enough in 1798 to have escaped assessment. Judging by John Wilson's case, local residents would have had to be extremely poor to have done so.

Emigration in the early years was clearly higher among the poor than among the wealthy. [27] Except for Colonel Josiah Throop, none of the high-status settlers of the early years left the community before 1798. Mooers had moved from Point au Roche to Cumberland Head, but that was only a few miles and still within the town of Plattsburgh. All the emigrants noted previously were of either low or moderate status.

Later emigration, while it cannot be enumerated because of inadequate records, seemed quite high according to literary evidence and drew substantially from the elite. A few examples may illustrate the point. Thomas Tredwell's grandson, Charles Platt Treadwell (he added an "a" which his grandfather had not used), moved to Canada. Attracted by a government policy which awarded immigrants one hundred acres and sold even the best land at sixty cents per acre, he chose to follow the "land selling" business in L'Orignal, Ontario. He became a leading citizen there but returned often in the later 1820s to visit his relatives in Beekmantown and Plattsburgh.[28]

Dr. B. H. Mooers, son of Benjamin, emigrated under conditions which suggest that frustrated political ambition was a major motivating factor. He had served as supervisor of Plattsburgh but, when Republicans denied him the nomination for county clerk, he went over to the opposition which did give him the desired nomination. He lost the election, however, and subsequently, despite restoration to good standing in the party, moved to Wisconsin. The *Republican* announced (November 16, 1844) that *Colonel* B. H. Mooers had won election to the Wisconsin legislature from the city of Milwaukee.

Political frustration seems also to have figured in the emigration of one of the Sperry brothers. Anson Sperry was one of Beekmantown's original highway overseers in 1820; his brother Gilead had practiced law in Plattsburgh since 1808. They operated a large tavern, Sperry House, and defeated Levi Platt in a battle for control of the Federalist-Clintonian party. They had also established an opposition newspaper, the *Northern Intelligencer*, and intrigued successfully for major offices in the local militia. One died, and the other apparently departed after suffering defeat at the hands of local Republicans in the late 1820s.[29]

Some of the emigrants from Beekmantown went to quite distant points. I. W. R. Bromley, for example, became a district attorney in Oregon in 1848. He had owned much property and had held many local offices earlier in Beekmantown. A son of Henry McFadden, Beekmantown's supervisor of 1849, was a doctor in Kansas. Pioneer settler John How moved to Wisconsin with his son. Two sons of the successful French Canadian farmer, John Bertrand, moved to the Dakotas.[30]

For some of Beekmantown's abler residents, opportunity lay as close as Plattsburgh. George M. Beckwith, son of Dr. Baruch Beckwith, Beekmantown's first supervisor, became a Plattsburgh lawyer, assemblyman, and judge. George Marsh, son of another early supervisor of Beekmantown, was also a promising Plattsburgh lawyer when he died during the cholera epidemic of 1832.

Bigger cities also attracted the ambitious. William Swetland's son-in-law became a merchant in New York.[31] One of the numerous Bromleys went there also. More remarkable is the story of Susan F. Cook. She taught a common school—summer only—elsewhere in the county at age fourteen and then, after moving to Plattsburgh, worked her way through the new academy as a seamstress during the War of 1812. She made an outstanding record there and then managed to attend a finishing school at Burlington. In 1817 she was conducting her own "school for young ladies" at the Plattsburgh Academy but left shortly to head the "female department" at a Vermont academy for two years. From there she moved to Boston, where she operated her own school until she married a clergyman. She was living in Providence at the age of ninety-four in 1888.[32]

A Plattsburgh resident who had attended the academy between 1846 and 1850 compiled a record in 1891 of the doings of his classmates. Less than half had remained in the Plattsburgh area. Most seem to have gone to the Middle West, but many had gone to other parts of the East, the Far West, and even the South.[33] Had Yankees and Yorkers who had not attended the academy migrated in the same proportion, the French Canadians and Irish would have constituted a much larger proportion of the remaining population in 1850.

Relations among the various ethnic groups in Beekmantown and Clinton County, while far from meeting present standards of mutual respect, at least did not include violence on any significant scale. The major groups represented in the community were Yorkers (people descended from residents of colonial New York), Yankees (migrants from New England), Negroes, plus French Canadians and Irish immigrants. It is important to recognize at the outset that the first two groups, the Yankees and Yorkers, were only one group in the perspective of the other three. To Negroes, French Canadians, and Irish, the dominant element in the community was composed of native white Protestants. Whether they descended from New Englanders or New Yorkers made little discernible difference. It is significant too that little evidence survives concerning relations among the three minority groups.[34]

Before examining the treatment accorded each of the minorities by the dominant Yankees and Yorkers, it may be worthwhile to say something more about the relations between those two groups. James Fenimore Cooper in many of his novels and Dixon Ryan Fox in his book, *Yankees and Yorkers* (New York, 1940), make much of the animosity which these two groups felt for each other. Yankees tended to see Yorkers as relatively indolent and slovenly, insufficiently zealous in doing God's work, and distressingly heterodox in the religious views. Yorkers saw Yankees, on the other hand, as brazenly ambitious and as censorious but hypocritical bigots. Neither view was without foundation. Political parties in Clinton County reflected this cleavage. The Federalist-Whig opposition almost certainly included a higher proportion of Yankees than did the Republican-Democratic party. Yorkers, on the other hand, gave their allegiance in greater proportion to the Republican-Democratic party. Yet, neither party ever tried to make the Yankee-Yorker division the basis of an appeal, either positive or negative, for votes. Nor indeed were slurring remarks or other evidences of real hostility or contempt recorded in the pages of the *Republican*. Whatever private opinions may have been, animosity between Yankees and Yorkers in Clinton County, except in the very early days of contention for physical possession of Long Island, was not sufficient to prevent their working together harmoniously in businesses, in political parties, and in religious, fraternal, reform, and other organizations.

How to regard Negroes was a matter of growing disagreement among the Yorker-Yankee majority in the Beekmantown-Plattsburgh community. Some of the initial ambivalence is quite evident in the bewildering record of Thomas Tredwell in relation to blacks. In the debates over ratification of the Constitution, he execrated the institution of slavery. But, he himself owned twelve slaves in 1790 and in fact brought at least three with him to Beekman Patent in 1794. In 1799, while the issue of abolition was agitating the state, he freed Hick and his wife, Jane, but he did not free their daughter, Cynthia. Instead he reportedly sold her to them for $42.50. Three families of free Negroes were living near Tredwell's home in 1799 and, according to local tradition, a female former slave was buried in the Tredwell family plot.[35]

Differing attitudes toward slavery and toward blacks found expression in Clinton County, as elsewhere in the nation, through political activity. Federalists tended to be both antislavery and problack, at least as related to voting rights, but they were normally the opposition party in Plattsburgh and Beekmantown. The usually dominant Republicans, on the other hand, were for many years quite anti-Negro and in some respects seemingly proslavery. The Plattsburgh *Republican*, always the voice of party orthodoxy and usually reflecting majority sentiment, denounced abolitionism steadily throughout the 1830s and 1840s. It did so partly in order to help preserve the unity of the national party and out of basic dedication to state rights. The *Republican* also expressed anti-Negro feelings quite frequently. It implicitly endorsed segregated schools; it praised a minister who "of course" refused to sanction the "unnatural union" of a white man and a black woman. The paper also denounced Whig Francis Granger as a "pretended Negro-loving personage" and affirmed that a plan for educating Negro girls "smells badly." [36]

By the end of the period, sentiment in Beekmantown was becoming more sympathetic to blacks. In 1838 an abolitionist received 102 votes, as opposed to 153 for his Democratic opponent, and 42 for another candidate. By 1843 longtime Democratic leader Philip B. Roberts had deserted the party to become an abolitionist. Three years later the town voted 151 to 50 in favor of equal voting rights for Negroes. In 1848 Martin Van Buren's Free-Soil ticket got 21 percent of Beekmantown's vote, and in 1851 Assemblyman George M. Beckwith, a Plattsburgh lawyer who had grown up in Beekmantown, voted against requiring segregation in the gallery of the legislature. [37]

How the most fortunate Negroes actually fared in Plattsburgh is best revealed by the story of "Black Maria" Haynes. She was the wife of Tom Haynes, a barber. The town thought it a good joke on the British when her son, born not long after the battle of Plattsburgh, was named "Sir George Prevost" after the vanquished British general. Mrs. Haynes, a devout Methodist, sat segregated at services and came forward segregated to receive communion. Rarely did any other Negro join her. She baked cakes for fashionable parties and gave such affairs her "general superintendence," while her daughter, Caroline, served as "lady's maid in the dressing room." When Caroline died, several white persons joined Mrs. Haynes and her son, George, in the funeral procession. [38]

Anti-Irish feeling, in contrast to that against Negroes, was far more prevalent among the Federalist-Whigs than among the Republican-Democrats. Republican-Democratic predominance in Beekmantown and earlier in Plattsburgh helped to keep overt discrimination against Irish Catholics to a minimum. Irish names began to appear in the list of Democratic county convention delegates from Beekmantown before the end of the 1830s. The Plattsburgh *Republican*, recovering from an early inclination to castigate all foreigners and to print purportedly humorous stories of a derogatory nature about the Irish, defended the Irish and "their religion" against Whig attacks. The somewhat Whiggish lyceum showed at least a willingness to listen to arguments on questions related to anti-Irish feeling. Among its topics were whether or not the "policy" of Roman Catholics is consistent with republican institutions (1834) and whether or not a longer residence should be required for naturalization (1835). The similar Literary Club considered in 1837 whether or not the government should permit immigration. On the whole, however, Republican-Democratic dominance and their assiduous courting of Irish votes seems to have protected the Irish against discrimination which deserves comparison with that inflicted upon the Negro.[39]

French Canadians, although present from earliest settlement onward, were of lower "visibility" than the other minority groups. By reputation the French Canadians were intelligent and good-natured, but parsimonious, highly resistant to any innovation, extremely opposed to taxation for virtually any purpose, and indifferent to prospects for betterment. Most men were inveterate pipe smokers and none too temperate rum drinkers. The language problem undoubtedly contributed to the high rate of illiteracy among them, but there is abundant testimony to the inadequacy of schools in Quebec.[40] The *Republican* in 1835 printed a letter defending French Canadians against the imputation of ubiquitous ignorance. In the exigencies of the 1840 campaign, it published in French a lengthy appeal for their votes.[41] The absence of subsequent appeals to French Canadians contrasts, however, with continuous appeals for the votes of the Irish. Such evidence suggests strongly that the French Canadians were largely isolated from the community. Undoubtedly, as Lord Durham's report explained, a large number of them were single men who intended to return to Canada after earning some money as laborers.

Language and cultural traditions seem to have isolated the French Canadians even from the Irish despite their common religion and their shared minority status. Such considerations help explain why French Canadians in the 1850s built their own church instead of attending that which the Irish had created in the early 1840s. The temperance movement manifested the same tendency. What was characterized as a Roman Catholic temperance society operated among the Clinton County Irish from 1841 under the leadership of an Irish priest. The French Canadians apparently remained aloof until 1845, when an itinerant French Canadian priest began soliciting total abstinence pledges. On his second visit (1850), the *Republican* congratulated him on securing fifteen hundred pledges.

That French Canadians had been largely untouched until 1849 by the temperance efforts of the preceding decades was implicit in the observation of the *Republican*: "The good resulting from this great man's labor among us is already manifest. The change in the character and habits of our Canadian friends since his visit one year ago has attracted the admiration of all our citizens and it is hoped that the results of his second visit may not be less lasting and beneficial."[42]

Attitudes concerning sex are largely obscure except in Pliny Moore's correspondence for the revolutionary war years, when he was young and a soldier. In 1776 a friend wrote him that there was "not much Corting in Spensertown [Massachusetts]. I have not Staid with wone Since you left the Place but I will a Sabaday-night and will hump them for you." A young woman had told Moore's correspondent that she had entertained three different men on successive nights, two preceding him, and then inquired, "Wont that damn Smart?" Another friend asked Moore to convey his compliments to the girls with "best wishes for a Continuance of their Virginity till I return." Humorous stories of a similarly earthy nature but in more circumspect language appeared occasionally in the *Republican* in the early days. However, for the most part newspapers and private correspondence, as well as church records of disciplinary proceedings, are almost devoid of references to sexual activities. Thus, the sex mores of Beekmantown remain largely unknown.[43]

Family relationships seem to have conformed largely to the pattern characteristic of communities with a high rate of mobility. Clustering of related families was much lower than in more stable New England towns. In 1790 Plattsburgh's 86 families bore 68 surnames, an incidence of 1.25 families per surname. The figure for highly mobile Germantown, Pennsylvania, was 1.47 in 1766 and 1.7 for 1790, while for much more stable Chatham, Massachusetts, in 1755 the rate was 4.56. By 1798 there were 107 surnames on the Plattsburgh tax list of 145 or 1.35 listings per surname. The wealthier families seem to have had some success in holding children together, at least in the early years. There were, for example, five Platt families in Plattsburgh in 1798, although that number did not include the Dutchess County "patriarch" Zephaniah, who had led the proprietors in securing the patent. The Tredwell home in Beekmantown included four single women, each of whom appeared on the tax list as owner of 228 acres.

Among the 60 households which shared a surname with another family or more in 1798, nearly all appear to reflect the desire of relatives to live close to each other. Champions in this respect were the Allens, of whom there were six families in 1798.[44] For the later years, it appears that dispersion of families became still more widespread.

Wills and church records which have permitted much detailed analysis of demographic trends elsewhere were not available for Plattsburgh or Beekmantown. Thus, information on such aspects of the community history as age at marriage, proportion of adults remaining unmarried, number of children per family, longevity, and the incidence of premarital pregnancy remain largely unknown. Even if such records were available, it is quite possible that the high rate of mobility would greatly limit their utility.

An impressive number of doctors and a still greater number of patent medicine purveyors catered to the health needs of the people of Beekmantown and Plattsburgh. Dr. John Miller, then thirty-eight, arrived in Plattsburgh from Dutchess County in 1798 and remained there until his death at eighty-two in 1842. Dr. Baruch Beckwith from Connecticut took up residence in what was to become Beekmantown in 1810. About the same time, Benjamin Mooers' son, B. H. Mooers, completed his training at the hands of Dr. Miller and began practice in Plattsburgh. Still another doctor had arrived before 1812. That doctors were not completely dependent upon service fees for their income is evident from an advertisement of 1815 (December 30) in which two doctors served notice that they also sold drugs, medicines, groceries, and dye woods. The Clinton County Medical Society, according to historian Peter Sailly Palmer, came into being in 1807. While there may be some doubt concerning the early date, the *Republican* listed nine officers for the apparently flourishing society at its annual convention in 1827. Medical research received a subsidy of sorts from the community, which turned over to the society the cadavers of those executed for criminal offenses.[45] In addition to engaging in research and perhaps in retail shopkeeping, doctors also had time for politics. Dr. Beckwith, a Federalist, was a frequent supervisor of Beekmantown. Dr. Miller, a Republican, quite often served his party in Plattsburgh. Dr. Mooers, as noted previously, may even have migrated to further his political career.

Patent medicines, then as now, were conspicuously available. Quite often the largest advertisements to appear in the Plattsburgh

Republican were those for patent medicines, often in later years with illustrations.

Dentists were harder to find than doctors and not always well trained. As late as 1838, a Burlington dentist advertised in the Plattsburgh *Republican* (March 3) that a man who had served him incompetently as an apprentice had run away and was passing himself off as a qualified practitioner. In 1848 an itinerant dentist from Connecticut advertised (September 30) that he would be at the United States Hotel in Plattsburgh for a few days during which he could make gold fillings, dentures, and extractions. Apparently, Beekmantown settlers with dental difficulties relied for the most part on totally untrained help or suffered until an itinerant came by.

Epidemics were never a serious problem in rural Beekmantown and only rarely gave trouble in the larger community of Plattsburgh. In the spring of 1813, "the prevailing epidemic" was the cause of death given for a number of individuals who had "died in this town." Presumably, the epidemic was of spotted fever, which killed thousands in Vermont that same year.[46] When smallpox ravaged the army forces at Plattsburgh in 1814, advertisements for "kine pock inoculation" appeared in the *Republican* (June 18). Apparently because of inoculation, the community did not suffer as extensively as the army. In 1822 John Parce of Beekmantown contracted smallpox in Montreal and brought it back. His wife and one child died of the disease, but inoculation prevented its further spread.[47]

Cholera posed a more serious threat in 1832. On May 19 the *Republican* reprinted a piece from the Albany *Daily Advertiser* anticipating that the cholera then prevalent in Europe would spread to America. Less than one month later, June 16, somber headlines in the *Republican* proclaimed: "CHOLERA IN MONTREAL." The editor cited a letter from Montreal which asserted that none of the forty who contracted the disease there had lived more than six hours. Quebec had fifty-three cases, the informant added, and many immigrants came down with the disease en route from Quebec to Montreal. The recommended treatment, prophetically printed, was to keep the patient warm and to rub him with a mixture of wine, vinegar, camphor, mustard, pepper, garlic, and cantharides. The last ingredient, prepared from beetles, has the effect of raising blisters on the skin.

The next week's issue of the *Republican* printed in bold type the report of the local Board of Health to the effect that there had been no new cases for several days. In all there had been seven cases and six deaths. The *Republican* reassured its readers, however, that "all the deaths have been of persons who lived in intemperance and in filthy places." The disease had struck first a group of French Canadian fishermen who lived in cabins at the mouth of the Saranac surrounded by "reeking and festering heaps" of the "offal incident to their occupation." They had had no known contact with Montreal. Early in July the board of health imposed a fifteen-day quarantine on all persons entering the area from Canada after June 22. The *Republican* regarded this as an absurdity. The disease, the editor asserted, was not carried by people but was carried in the air or generated from the soil. To prevent it, however, he urged "cleanliness, temperance, calmness and steady habits."[48] For whatever reasons, the epidemic subsided quickly, and the *Republican* happily returned its attention to the reelection of Andrew Jackson.

Cleanliness apparently required repeated endorsement. R. A. Gilman had opened a "bathing establishment" next to his coffeehouse in 1824. He offered "warm, vapour, cold or shower baths" for twenty-five cents.[49] How long he kept the establishment, however, is uncertain. Even as late as 1849, the *Republican* editor observed that many persons of sense neglected for years to bathe themselves more than two or three times yearly. He strongly recommended more frequent bathing as "perhaps one of the most necessary aids for the enjoyment of good health." He had made the same point, possibly more effectively, a few months earlier with the story of a mother who had taken her sickly child to the doctor. When the doctor replied affirmatively to her query as to whether or not it would help to take her child to the "springs" (one of the health resorts located at mineral springs), she asked which he would recommend. "Any will do, madam," the doctor replied, "where you can get plenty of *soap and water*."[50]

Mortality figures are unavailable for the early years, but those for Beekmantown in the census of 1850 are revealing. Of the twenty-two persons who had died in Beekmantown during the previous year, six died from consumption. In four cases the cause was officially "unknown." Two died from diarrhea; two from "debility," presumably old age. Causes of only one death each were Asiatic cholera, childbed fever, "canker," rheumatism, dropsy, "brain fever," drowning, and "lung fever." Four of those who died had been inmates of Clinton Prison, then included in Beekmantown; four were women between twenty and thirty; five were infants under two. Six were New Englanders; twelve, New Yorkers; two, Irish; and two, Canadian. Physical safety was never so much a problem in Beekmantown as it was in many frontier communities. Indians on hunting expeditions caused some uneasiness in the early days. Consequently, the settlers built a blockhouse for protection but never had occasion to use it for that purpose. Brawling was frequent among drunken lumbermen. There were infrequent murders, generally crimes of passion rather than premeditation. Apprehension usually came quickly, as did what was at times a highly ceremonial execution of the guilty before a large and intently interested audience. Public executions became controversial in the 1830s and ceased thereafter.

Accidents involving loss of life were uncommon but did occur. For example, the family of Nathaniel Chittenden, a prominent Beekmantown farmer, was returning from church on October 19, 1845, when four young ladies in a wagon attempted to pass them. Chittenden's spirited horses, inadequately restrained by his young son who was driving, made it a race. When the wagon overturned at a bridge, one of Chittenden's daughters was killed and their grandmother so severely injured that she was not expected to survive.[51]

Fire, however, was the most common danger and the most serious threat to property. Plattsburgh experienced several major fires in its business district, culminating in 1849 with a conflagration which destroyed virtually all of the business establishments in the center of the town. In less crowded Beekmantown, fires did not spread so widely but could be devastating to individuals. On a Saturday in November 1818, for example, fire destroyed the home of James Mix in what was then called Beekman Patent. Next day, even though it was Sunday, his neighbors hewed timbers for a house twenty by twenty-four feet, framed, and raised them. By Tuesday the house was "so far finished" that the family could move in.[52]

Prison sentences were relatively rare in Clinton County and, in the early years, they involved crimes against property far more often than crimes of physical injury. Between 1796 and 1806, the county sentenced only two persons to the new state prison at Auburn, both for larceny. From then into the early 1820s, larceny continued to be by far the most common crime for which prison sentences were imposed. While the figures are probably not precise, it appears that larceny convictions were more than double the number for the combined total of the next two most common offenses, forgery and counterfeiting. Among other crimes involving property, there were two convictions for horse stealing between 1799 and 1823, two for burglary, two for swindling, and one for perjury. In the category of crimes against the person in those years, there were three sentences for assault and battery, two for attempted rape, and one each for attempted manslaughter and attempted murder. While prison sentences for crimes of violence were rare, instances of violence were not. J. C. Hubbell, an early lawyer, later recalled that the free flow of liquor at "logging bees" resulted in "brisk" litigation on charges of assault.[53]

In the later 1840s, the pattern of crime, or of arrest and conviction, had changed. Then sentences for assault and battery exceeded those for larceny. Still more common at that time, however, were convictions for selling liquor without a license. Burglary and forgery were still represented, but counterfeiting, the third most common crime in the early years, was not. Murder and rape seem to have continued to be infrequent. Morals convictions appeared for the first time. There was one conviction for keeping a "bawdy-house" and another for incest. Among those receiving sentences only to the county jail, assault and battery was by far the most common charge, although there were numerous convictions also of "disorderly" persons, presumably drunks. While there are no references to drug addiction, it may be significant that an intemperate Beekmantown resident, Isaac Lewis, apparently committed suicide by eating opium in a shanty left by an earlier Methodist camp meeting.[54]

Conditions for those incarcerated locally were unpleasant but not unbearable. Those jailed for nonpayment of debts in the early years were permitted by state law to wander freely within a fixed periphery around the jail. The tavern of Caleb Nichols was within the prescribed limits in Plattsburgh. As Caleb Nichols was also an attorney, this was perhaps doubly convenient. Solitary confinement for six days was the sentence of a man who stole twelve hats in 1817. Bread and water were to be his only sustenance. A similar sentence for two days was the punishment of an individual who stole a bushel of wheat. The place of confinement originally was the blockhouse by the lake; it also served as a courthouse, a church, and for various other purposes. A state report in 1849 indicated that the jail then had six cells, inadequately cleaned and ventilated, furnished with iron cots and blankets for as many as four inmates each. A new jail was recommended.[55] Log cabins, referred to locally as log houses, were the most common type of residence for many years. In 1798, 91 of the 145 people listed in the assessment roll were assessed for log houses. Precisely how many lived in frame or other kinds of houses is not evident because the assessment register does not differentiate clearly between properties which had frame or other type houses and those which had none at all. Log houses usually bore assessments of fifteen to twenty-five dollars. Two of the few frame houses listed had assessments of forty dollars each.

Barns were a reliable clue to status. In 1798 the town had only forty frame barns. Theodorus Platt had three; Nathaniel and Charles Platt each had two. No one else had more than one. Ten residents had less prestigious log barns. Most had none at all.[56]

The Beekmans often required tenants to build blockhouses, a type of residence which continued to be popular in the 1840s. In 1842 (December) the current agents advised James W. Beekman: "No house has yet been built on [lot] No 64 as was proposed when you was here. We are inclined to advise the building of what is termed a block house, that is, timber or logs hewed on both sides and laid up in that manner. It can be so placed that a front can hereafter be added in case the owner chooses to make an addition in front, and can hereafter also be clapboarded if desired. A house of that kind is very common and comfortable, and can be built, we think with the sum you proposed to expend ($250). . . . We cannot for that sum build a frame house of sufficient size, with the necessary cellar, chimney, etc."

Two and a half months later, after consulting with contractors, the agents revised their estimates. Now (March 15, 1843), they concluded that "no decent and comfortable building, such as it would be expedient to put upon that farm, can be built for $250." For $330 they could secure a blockhouse twenty-six by twenty-two feet with plank partitions, full cellar, and chimney, but no clapboards. Its kitchen would measure sixteen by sixteen, parlor sixteen by twelve, pantry seven by eight, one bedroom eight by ten, and another eight by eleven.

A similar building, twenty-eight by twenty-four, would cost $350 if frame or $400 if brick. Its kitchen would be fourteen by fourteen, hall eight by thirteen, parlor fourteen by twelve, and bedroom eight by eight. However, the agents soon decided that the dimensions were too small. They recommended increasing it to twenty-four by thirty with a corresponding increase in the size of rooms. They reported further that the contractor would make such a building for $400 if the agents arranged to make the cellar—for $450 if the contractor made the cellar. Late in the year, the agents reported that the contractor had lost money on the house. Presumably, it was frame rather than brick, since the agents now charged an additional $35 for having the house painted. Additional expenses (agents' fees and fencing) came later.[57]

Log houses apparently deteriorated rather quickly. Supporting the claim of one tenant to reimbursement for improvement to the property, the agents stated that he had built his log house about ten years before at a cost of thirty dollars and since had added an outside stone chimney. But he valued the one-room dwelling in 1839 at only twenty dollars, a fair price, according to the agents. The depression following 1837 may have had some bearing on the reduction in value, although the agents also reported that its board roof was "rather poor." The agents' reports on the condition of log houses on other rental properties were similar.[58]

The housing situation in Beekmantown in 1855 is summarized in the state census of that year. Of the 468 dwellings in the town 17 percent (78) were of stone or brick, 53 percent (247) were frame structures, while a surprising 30 percent (143) were classified as log houses. Houses of brick or stone averaged $793 in value; frame dwellings, $380; and log houses, a mere $55. Presumably block-houses were included in the log house category. If so, the average value of $55 for log houses must have represented a relatively large number of log houses of the primitive variety worth $20 or $30 and a lesser number of blockhouses worth something more nearly approximating the $330 construction cost cited in 1843.

In conclusion, several points concerning the social characteristics of Beekmantown's settlers seem clear. Most important is the observation that the earliest settlers were relatively high in socioeconomic status, while those of the second generation tended to be comparatively low. It is quite clear also that in the second generation emigration drew disproportionately from high-status people. In intergroup relations, the conspicuous prejudices were those of the Jeffersonian-Jacksonian Democrats against blacks and of the Federalist-Whig leaders against Catholics, especially the Irish. Contrary to the idea fostered by James Fenimore Cooper, there appeared to be little friction between Yankees and Yorkers. Crimes involving property were more likely to draw legal punishment in the early period than those involving physical harm. Consumption was apparently the leading cause of death among adults. Even at the end of the period, nearly a third of the houses were either log cabins or blockhouses.

6

Religion

Religion was less than central to the lives of the earliest settlers in the Beekmantown-Plattsburgh area. Presbyterians dominated the religious life of the community in the early years, although there were some Baptists present and, elsewhere in the county, Congregationalists prevailed. By 1850 Methodists were far ahead of other denominations in Beekmantown. Numerous Catholics and the few Episcopalians and Universalists, if any, had to travel to Plattsburgh to attend their churches.

Plattsburgh's first settlers took a long time to organize a congregation and secure a minister. The proprietors began building mills in Plattsburgh in 1785. A town government took shape in the same year and a new county government was created in 1788. Precisely when the first school opened is not clear, but there were five by 1795. Organizing for religious purposes proceeded much more slowly. The first step was a meeting at the "Block House," on November 10, 1792. Its purpose was to choose trustees whose first responsibility would be to take charge of the "temporalities" of the town's congregation, essentially administration of the "gospel" lot secured from the proprietors as a subsidy to religion. Their second function was to "call" a minister. The meeting did choose trustees, mostly Federalists, but they did not secure a minister.

A fresh start occurred in 1794. Not the original trustees but a "number of People," mostly of Republican persuasion, met to make arrangements for finding a man who would serve both as a "settled Minister" and as an academy (secondary school) teacher.

The meeting authorized Thomas Tredwell, a staunch Republican, to act in the town's behalf. Accordingly, he invited the Reverend Frederick Halsey of Long Island, also a Republican, to come and discuss the situation. Tredwell suggested that Halsey come to Plattsburgh without replying to his letter "for it is not very likely a letter could reach this place unless you could light on some one coming directly here."

The minister's educational services loomed larger, at least in Tredwell's letters, than did purely religious functions. The same man could easily serve both religious and educational needs, Tredwell wrote, as "the number of Scholars will not probably be great for some time." He made clear that the community would be "contented" with only one sermon weekly, instead of the usual two, as it would be "laborious" for a young man to give two while also conducting an academy. Because the community was so distant from other settled areas of the state, Tredwell continued, its residents "think it absolutely necessary to provide for ourselves a place of education." Concerning religion, he was rather less emphatic: "The People in general appear to be anxious to have a Minister."

Finally, Tredwell indicated that financial support would have relatively low priority. His explanation was that "we have so much to do upon roads and shall want money for so many other public uses, that we are willing to use as much economy in these matters [religion and education] as we can with propriety, at least until we get over some of the heavy expenses attending a New Settlement." As fringe benefits, however, Tredwell listed "a good settlement, in as beautiful a part of the Country as I ever saw; and in a place where your labors are as likely to be useful as anywhere at all." He indicated also that if Halsey did not stay, "we shall doubtless think ourselves under obligation to pay at least the expense of your Journey."[1]

The Reverend Frederick Halsey, aged about thirty, arrived in Plattsburgh in response to Tredwell's invitation in 1794. A native of South Hampton, Long Island, Halsey had graduated from Columbia College in 1790. He then taught at Clinton Academy in East Hampton and studied divinity, apparently with a local minister. He had also done some preaching on Long Island and in New Jersey before he received Tredwell's invitation to come to Plattsburgh.[2]

Upon arriving Halsey preached acceptably "from house to house" and was invited to remain at a salary of $250 yearly plus $125 as "settlement." Part of this payment came in cash, but he also took "one swine," fourteen bushels of wheat at eighty-three cents a bushel, plus payments of corn, salt, pigeons, beef, flax, and a yoke of oxen. Seven years later Halsey had actually received payments averaging only $195 yearly instead of the promised $250.

The presbytery of Albany made Halsey a pastor in 1796, but his formal installation did not occur until October 1797. The ceremony took place at the blockhouse, which also served as schoolhouse, courthouse, jail, and fort. Attending the ceremony were a minister and an elder from each of three Hudson valley towns, Salem, Cambridge, and Troy, the nearest organized Presbyterian churches. For many years Halsey would remain the only settled minister north of Salem in the state of New York.[3]

The membership of the church at the outset was small. To be a full member, each individual had to present a letter affirming earlier admission to membership in another church or to describe the conversion experience satisfactorily. At the first formal observation of the Lord's Supper in 1797, there were only eighteen full members. Fifteen had transferred membership from other churches; only three gained admission by narration of their experience. Ten of the eighteen members were women. Not one of the original trustees of 1792 was a member. Neither was Thomas Tredwell, who had extended the invitation to Halsey, nor most of the fifty-nine who had originally pledged contributions to his salary.

Such persons, those who attended the church but were not full members, were called "attendants." If they contributed to the expenses of the church, male attendants were entitled to vote along with members for trustees who would manage the temporal affairs of the congregation. They might also become trustees. Clearly, the attendants in Plattsburgh included a high proportion of community and church leaders.[4]

The elders of the church, in contrast to the trustees, assisted the minister in the management of more narrowly religious matters. While some churches chose elders for life, the Plattsburgh congregation elected them for fixed terms. Only members could vote in such elections or serve as elders. Sitting with the minister at the session, the elders made decisions concerning admission to membership, administration of discipline, the selection of one of their number to represent the church in the presbytery or district organization, and in drafting the covenant to be pledged by all members.[5]

Like most New York churches at the time, Plattsburgh's was an amalgam of Presbyterian and Congregational features. David Dobie, the Scottish immigrant who served the church as pastor in the 1840s, believed that the New England Puritans predominated among the early members and assumed that the church was essentially Puritan, or Congregational, in nature. The evidence, however, indicates clearly that the Presbyterian elements were stronger. Tredwell affirmed in one of his letters to Halsey that "the Presbyterians here, . . . compose a great majority of the people." At Halsey's installation, three New York Presbyterian churches were represented, but no New England church. Had the Puritans predominated, they probably would have selected as their minister a New Englander, most likely a Congregationalist and a Federalist, as did the town of Champlain in 1803.[6]

Congregationalism, however, was visible in at least one feature of the Plattsburgh church. According to Robert H. Nichols, "the custom of having every member adopt a congregational 'covenant'" was a "Congregational practice widespread in New York Presbyterianism. . . . These covenants usually included a doctrinal statement, and there was some variation among them." More orthodox Presbyterians took their faith "without change from Westminster Standards."[7] The Plattsburgh church had such a covenant, but in no other respects did the original Plattsburgh church show clearly any Congregational features.

The intensity of religious feeling remained relatively low in Plattsburgh for some time. "Religion," wrote Dobie, "was not so much in fashion as it is now; . . . the blasphemous sentiments of the French Revolutionists . . . poisoned the minds and corrupted the morals of thousands, even in this Northern wilderness of the new world." Church memberships did increase from eighteen in 1797 to eighty-five in 1810, when Halsey was dismissed. But, it seems likely that most of these new members were migrants who qualified "by letter" from churches in other areas rather than "by experience" or conversion at the instigation of the Reverend Halsey. There were significant revivals in the state around 1800 and in 1807–1808, usually conducted by "settled" ministers. However, there is little indication that revivalism had much effect in Plattsburgh in those years.[8]

Under Halsey's leadership, church discipline was lax, and there was little effort to erect a church. When a new minister was secured in 1812, "ten members of the Church were called publicly to account for their conduct in violating the Sabbath, and joining in worldly amusements, among whom were some of the most prominent men in the Church." Halsey had apparently taken no step whatever to bring about the erection of a church building. Rather, he was content to teach at a school near his home, to preach at the blockhouse (and later the new courthouse), to baptize, and to solemnize marriages—over six hundred to Dobie.[9]

Halsey's leadership apparently satisfied the townspeople quite well. He did resign in 1810, forced out, it appears, by the organized opposition of certain community leaders who apparently disliked his Republicanism as much as his lack of zeal. However, Halsey's tenure (1796–1810 officially) was far longer than that of any of his more zealous successors. He remained in Plattsburgh until his death many years later; in fact, he was called upon to conduct the academy on an interim basis in 1817–1818. Those who characterized him later used such terms as "inoffensive," "a friend of youth," "a peacemaker," and "a man who never made an enemy."[10]

The new minister, selected by the same Federalists who had forced Halsey's resignation, was William R. Weeks.[11] Affronted by the extent of intemperance, profanity, and Sabbath breaking in the community, Weeks and the elders determined "that the discipline of Christ's house should be maintained, let the opposition from without be what it might." They also "resolved—that we consider a participation in fashionable amusements to be utterly inconsistent with the spirit of the Gospel, a criminal waste of precious time, and a sinful conformity to the world, having a very pernicious tendency, and therefore, highly improper and inconsistent with a Christian profession." The "neglect of family prayer" they branded "highly criminal." They considered the children of "professing parents in connection with the Church, and . . . proper subjects of our watch and discipline." In the spirit of the apocryphal Puritan who was haunted by the gnawing fear that somehow someone somewhere might be happy, they determined to "visit from house to house" to seek those who had "brought reproach upon the cause of Christ" so that they might be brought to "evidence their repentance" by public confession.[12]

In contrast to Halsey's long tenure, Weeks departed after two

years (1814) "much discouraged through the obstructions which
the war threw in his way" and by the usual "deficiency of support." Three other ministers in the county also resigned, osten-
sibly because of the war. In 1815 the five towns in Clinton County
had four congregations but had only one ordained minister. The
people, concluded a report of the Champlain presbytery, "are
perishing for lack of vision." [13]

The end of the war brought a dramatic change. Its chief instru-
ment was the Reverend Nathaniel Hewit, who was installed as
minister on July 5, 1815. Hewit, then only twenty-six, was just
beginning what would be a prominent career, chiefly as national
organizer for the temperance cause. In the two years which he
spent in Plattsburgh, he helped to organize the Clinton County
Moral Society, a precursor to the local temperance movement,
and conducted a successful revival. During his stay eighty-five new
members joined the church, seventy-nine by conversion and only
five by letter. It had taken Halsey sixteen years to gain an identical
number of members, most of them apparently by letter.

Yet, zeal was also the cause of Hewit's undoing in Plattsburgh.
He brought disciplinary charges of a serious nature (unspecified
in the surviving account) against William Pitt Platt, an elder who
had been the leading spirit in the movement to secure the erection
of the church, which was completed in 1816. While Platt's church
trial exonerated both accuser and accused from any blame, "it also
resulted in the rupture of one of the most promising and useful
pastorates the Church has enjoyed, [and] in the speedy resignation
of Mr. Hewitt." [14]

The building of a church had been long delayed. From 1794
onward, religious assemblies had taken place successively in private
homes, in the blockhouse, the new courthouse, in the "ballroom"
of Israel Green's tavern, and finally in the "large hall" of Sperry
House, another tavern. When Plattsburgh finally erected a church,
however, the resulting edifice was indeed impressive. The academy, begun a little earlier and completed in 1812, was sixty by
twenty-seven feet and "the largest and most imposing public edifice in Northern New York." Platt's church, begun in 1812, was
to be eighty by sixty feet, almost three times the floor area of the
academy. The war interrupted construction of the church but,
finally on Christmas Day 1816, the structure was completed at a
cost of some $10,000. Late as it was, Plattsburgh's church was

the first for either Presbyterians or Congregationalists in the four-county area of northeastern New York.[15]

The financing of the construction was of course a serious problem for the community. William Pitt Platt's sister donated the land, and Platt mortgaged his home to secure funds for the work. In 1815 those who had purchased pews in advance surrendered them to the trustees to be resold. When the meetinghouse was completed, an auction of pews brought $12,000—enough to pay the remaining construction costs and have some money left for a parsonage and to pay the "deficiency" owed the Reverend Halsey. Platt and his associates were justifiably proud that "we do not owe one cent out of our own community" for the work done. The fact that there was at that time no lighting, stove, or bell was of only minor significance.[16]

The provisions governing the sale or rental of pews to pay construction costs were significant. In advertising the auction of pews, the congregational leaders offered four years to pay and of course accepted promissory notes. They warned against delaying purchase because the expectation was that pews would rise in value—there might be some speculative investment in them. They made clear also that purchase was preferable to rental because the annual rental charge would be 10 percent of the respective value of the pews. They assured purchasers in addition that "no man, however rich, or however large a stockholder he may be, can have any preference over the poorest in the community, who is able to purchase at all."[17] The results of the auction testify to the success of these appeals.

On New Year's Eve, the authorities announced the regulations to be observed in the new church. The sexton would ring the bell at 9:00 A.M. on Sunday mornings and again at 10:00. Services would begin promptly when the bell ringing ceased at 10:10. Persons planning to attend were urged to be prompt, to prevent children and servants from "running in and out" during the service, and to see that their dogs did not follow them to church. "Persons using tobacco are requested to have spit boxes in their pews; and not to spit on the floors of the aisles." They reserved several pews for soldiers from the garrison and one each for black men and women. Some front seats in the side galleries were to be free. Intermission would last one hour in summer but only half an hour in winter.[18]

Those who could afford to do so attempted to make their accommodations comfortable. When Melanchton L. Woolsey's bankruptcy forced him to sell his pews in 1817, he described them in an advertisement as two of the best pews in the church, painted, lined with green cloth, cushioned and carpeted, with spit boxes and footstools. The daughter of Melanchton Smith, Jr., recalled her family pews as "painted white, with a rim of dark wood atop as relief to the eye . . . broad seats . . . upholstered in faded green moreen cloth, a contracted bit of carpet . . . , a square tin footstool encased in a wooden frame, that held a modicum of lighted charcoal during the winter . . . , a huge box lined with lambs wool to slip one's half frozen feet within." There were also three "low wooden benches uncarpeted, and unpainted . . . where the juveniles oft found rest from their weary perch above" but were still under the watchful eyes of a "solemn line" of "august elders . . . [who] sat in large respectable looking armchairs, under the shadow of the bird cage pulpit hoisted so high aloft."[19]

Meanwhile, residents of Beekman Patent had decided to form a Second Presbyterian Church of Plattsburgh. "Living in a part of the town [of Plattsburgh] commonly called Beekmantown at a distance of 6 miles from the stated place of worship, it was found impossible for most of the members statedly to attend the ordinances and preaching of the gospel in the mother church. Feeling themselves able and willing to support the gospel among themselves, and regarding with compassion the numbers around them who were in a great measure deprived of the means of salvation, they unanimously applied to the session of the First Church, to be set off and organized into [a] distinct church." The session of the first church gave unanimous approval on August 10, 1816, and the presbytery of Champlain gave its consent in February 1817. The first official meeting of the new church took place on February 27. The ordination of elders and deacons and the first observance of the Lord's Supper occurred at the Plattsburgh church on March 13.[20]

The membership records of the Beekmantown church, while perhaps not wholly reliable, afford more understanding of its inception. They show that at the beginning there were fifty-nine members. Of these, only six had belonged to the Plattsburgh church before 1816, while fifty-two had never before belonged to any church. Thus, it would appear that the Reverend Nathaniel Hewit's revival (1815–1816), which secured a total of seventy-nine converts in Plattsburgh, must have concentrated to a large extent in Beekmantown, possibly with the specific goal of founding a new church.

Were there only six church members in Beekmantown prior to Hewit's revival? The evidence suggests there were more but not a great many. John Stratton was one. Highway assessments indicate that Stratton lived in Beekmantown, but he remained a member of the Plattsburgh church of which he had been one of the original elders. A few Beekmantown residents had belonged to the church at Chazy. A number, like Dr. Baruch Beckwith, had belonged to churches elsewhere before settling in Beekmantown, but they did not join a local church until Beekmantown secured one.

Beekmantown set about building a church rather more speedily than had Plattsburgh. The members brought timber for the frame and celebrated its raising (1820) with a dinner in Dr. Beckwith's front yard. Energies flagged after the frame raising, and not until 1826 were the walls and roof completed. Meanwhile, the edifice served as a fair weather church. On less balmy days, the congregation met in one of the several schools, as they had before. Apparently, they did not ever meet from "house to house" or in taverns.

Concerning beliefs, the Beekmantown church voted to employ the same confession of faith and covenant as the Plattsburgh church. They recorded both confession of faith and covenant in order to preserve "a lasting testimony of the faith and practice of this church" and to afford "swift witness against any . . . who shall bring in another gospel." The confession affirmed belief in the trinity, in the "total moral depravity of human nature," in salvation by God's grace and mercy, and that all who "live and die in impenitence and unbelief will perish forever." Originally, members affirmed that the "shorter catechism agreed upon by the Assembly of divines at Westminster" [1643] was "a just summary of the Christian religion," but in 1831 this was weakened to read "in General a Good summary."

The covenant requirement dictated an affirmative reply to the query, "Do you desire to enter into covenant with God and his people?" Its principal effect originally was to bind the members to pray "with and for" their children and to "train them up in the nurture and admonition of the Lord." In 1831 the temperance pledge was added. It bound members to refrain from any but medicinal use of ardent (distilled) spirits, but it did not apply to fermented beverages.

The succession of ministers in Beekmantown's church, as in Plattsburgh, was relatively rapid. The first minister of the church was the Reverend Stephen Kinsley, who served from 1818 to 1823. For the next two years, the Reverend Joel Byington of Chazy "was imployed to Labour with us one Third part of the Time," and the Lord's Supper was observed generally every three months. In 1825 the Reverend James Gilbert was "imployed" half-time, but soon (December 19, 1826) the church resolved to offer him full-time employment at $300 per year. The Reverend Phineas Bailey replaced Gilbert briefly, but by 1838 Gilbert was back at his old salary of $300 yearly plus use of the parsonage and "fire wood drawn to his door." As a final installment on his salary in 1841, the church trustees agreed to pay his debt of fifty-five dollars to Brother Benjamin Simonds, the storekeeper. Z. M. P. Luther took up the burden then and served through the rest of the decade.

Discipline was a matter of importance in the Beekmantown church from the outset. The offenses upon which the session acted were of some variety. Nonattendance at services was the most common (four accusations), but actions against other narrowly religious infractions were infrequent. There was only one instance of action against heresy and two for Sabbath breaking. Three individuals got into trouble by drinking excessively, one by dancing, two allegedly by lying, and one by slander. In none of the cases was there overt accusation of sexual immorality. Three instances involved larcenous offenses in which there either had been or could have been criminal prosecution as well.

The larcenous offenses were altering the consideration in a deed, stealing fifty dollars, and selling logs which belonged to someone else. Hiram Allen, accused of the first offense, ultimately confessed in private and agreed to do so publicly but never did. Some six or seven years later, he was excommunicated. Thaddeous K. DeWolf was accused of stealing fifty dollars and in fact had been convicted of that crime in the civil courts. DeWolf still protested innocence and appealed to the presbytery the adverse decision of the session. Before the presbytery could act, DeWolf jumped bail, which had been required of him by the civil courts for "other misdemeanors," and fled to Canada. He, too, was excommunicated. The records terminate before any conclusion had been reached in the case of Ira Robinson, who allegedly sold logs belonging to another.

The more interesting of the two slander accusations involved
Abraham Scribner, former tax collector for Plattsburgh (1820) and
future Baptist trustee. Earlier citations had accused Scribner of
"Profane Swearing and Sabbath breaking," disorderly conduct,
and drunkenness (twice). He had restored himself to good standing, however, by making public confession and asking forgiveness
of those whom he had offended. His allegedly slanderous remarks,
probably made after more imbibing, were that the Reverend Gilbert "was no more fit to preach than . . . that Dog and that he
would Lye." To these he added the accusation that his brethren
of the congregation, despite the temperance pledge in their covenant, "would go to the Store [presumably that of Brother Simonds]
and Drink." This time, too, Scribner was forgiven after public
confession.

The accusations of lying were against Hiram Allen, Minor Lewis,
and Benjamin Simonds. Allen confessed that he had been "wrong
in Stating in strong terms that a thing was so when he had not the
posetive evidence that it was so." The accusation against Lewis was
forgotten due to preoccupation with the more serious charge of
drunkenness. Simonds was the only accused individual in the record
to gain exoneration.

The attention given instances of drunkenness makes it clear that
this was the offense which was considered the most serious. Lewis,
"an immoderate drinking man" who had confessed drunkenness
three or four times, was at last excommunicated—"we discovering
no human probability of reclaiming him." Luther Drury, school
commissioner and overseer of the poor, twice confessed drunkenness, as did Scribner. The church had not yet given up hope for
Drury in 1834. Scribner had become a Baptist.

Nonattendance at services was also a serious matter. In 1822 John
Hubbard was charged "with a breach of Covenant in that for years
he had absented himSelf from the worship of God." Despite the
best efforts of pastor and elders, Hubbard "manifested no desire
to become reconsiled to the Church." He escaped excommunication by moving to "lower Canaday." Ebenezar Allen was equally
intransigent. Charged with "neglect of Christian Duty in attending
to the regular preaching of the Gospel," Allen refused to attend
a formal investigation or "to make a satisfactory confession." Accordingly, he was excommunicated.

Sabbath violation was not a major target of disciplinary actions.
Only two citations of Sabbath violation appear in the record and,
in each instance, it is evident that the charge was an afterthought

in the case of offenders accused of other more significant wrong-doing. For example, in 1826 the charges against Abraham Scribner were "Disorderly conduct in Drinking, Profane Swearing and Sabbath breaking." Sabbath violation came to be taken more seriously in Beekmantown and in the county as a whole in the later 1830s and 1840s after the termination of these records (1834). A Sabbath Convention in Plattsburgh in 1845 considered the state of Sabbath observance and resolved that traveling, visiting, recreational walking, and even the reading of secular newspapers profaned the sacred day.[21]

Heresy on the other hand was taken very seriously. The only accusation on that score was addressed to Polly Larkin on November 28, 1833. Specifically, the charge against Larkin was "Denying the Bible to be the word of God, Speaking lightly and Disrespectfully of the Church and People of God, not maintaining a Life of Piety and Godliness." At least two delegations visited Larkin to reason with her, but she remained adamant. In accordance with prescribed procedure for excommunication, the church then sent her a communication which stated in part: "The first Presbyterian Church in Beekmantown sendeth Greeting—You are hereby cited to appear at the Presbyterian meeting house . . . to answer the Following charge, Viz. Heresy with its evil consequences." Larkin ignored four such citations to appear, and "there appearing no human probability of redeeming her," she was adjudged guilty on January 25, 1834. In arriving at that decision, the session added to the accusations against her that "she Declares the Church to be only the people of the world, Ministers merely Preach for a living . . . and also that she did not Pray. . . . She has not attended the preaching of the word of God but a very few times in three years, has not been present on a sacramental occasion for some years."

Even though Larkin was adjudged guilty, proper procedure required that letters of admonition be given her before the final step of excommunication. The Reverend Bailey's letter (February 25, 1834) reminded her that her "feelings must be very provoking to a holy and Covenant keeping God. . . . From this vortex of ruin," he continued, "there is no escape but by immediate repentance."

She remained adamant. The session voted to send her a second admonition which was considerably stronger in tone. "We are . . . constrained to extend to you this last act of brotherly love, after which if you cannot be reclaimed, you must be forever excluded from the company of saints. Now, therefore, dear sister, . . . break your alegiance with Satan, and come back to Christ. Confess your sins, Pray for pardon. . . . . If you refuse this last Admonition, we must leave you in the hands of God, Praying that He will glorify Himself and build up his cause, whatever becomes of your poor soul." Larkin had given no reply nor yet been formally excommunicated when the record ended.

An earlier application of pressure against Polly Winters had been more successful. Winters' offenses, committed in 1820, were absence from meetings and "attending balls and places of carnal mirth contrary to the express rules of our church and the duties of a Christian." The proceedings had progressed as far as the letter of admonition before she repented and rendered the desired confession on October 28, 1821: I Polly Winters, being senceable of my wrong and the dishonour I have done to religion and that I have wounded My dear Jesus in the house of his friends and grieved the hearts of all gods people and laid great stumbling blocks before the world do take this opportunity to humble mySelf before God and the Church and all gods people and the world and confess that I have let down my watch and run into many sins and that I have broken my solemn covenant that I made with god and his church and have neglected to worship and commune with the church and have attended balls and assemblies appointed for carnal mirth, and when admonished by the Pastor and other faithfull brethren I have for a long time been deef to their admonisions for which I desire . . . to humble myself and ask their forgivness." Thus appeased, the church voted unanimously "to forgive and restore (this our once wandering but now returned and dear sister) to the fellowship and communion of this Church."

The attitude of the church on matters of discipline did not soften over the years of the record. In 1834, for example, the Reverend Bailey and the elders were deeply "grieved with the young in this Church for mingling with the world in vain company and unproffitable recreation." They consequently resolved to "defer Communion for the present." They also resolved that "Dancing and frolicing shall be considered a disciplinable offence, . . . that playing ball is an unproffitable waist of time and ought to be reproved, . . . that horse raising [racing] shall be a disciplinable offence."

These resolutions closely paralleled those adopted by the church at Plattsburgh about the same time. There the elders were to visit from house to house to find out whether family heads prayed twice daily with their families, read scriptures daily, attended services, kept the Sabbath, contributed money, and so forth. The elders were also to inquire what company the children kept, especially if boarding out or "engaged in stores or shops," what books they read, and "whether any . . . are indulging hopes." Those who might be indulging hopes or otherwise on a course of error the elders were to "admonish . . . of their duty," which apparently included being properly pessimistic.[22]

Most new members gained admission by "experience," that is, by conversion in revival movements. But, after the original revival of 1816, there was a long quiescent period. From 1818 through 1827, the number of new members in any year never exceeded four. In 1828, however, there began a six-year revivalist ferment which added a total of 116 members to the church (18 in 1828, 11 in 1829, 30 in 1830, 39 in 1831, and 18 in 1832). Some new members gained admission by letter rather than by experience— but never more than about five per year and usually fewer than that.

Several factors may have contributed to touch off the new revival. Charles Finney, one of the greatest evangelists of the day, was then "burning over" central and western New York. A camp meeting took place at neighboring Chazy in September 1828. The temperance movement was then beginning to take on great religious intensity. Still another influence was the Reverend Moses Chase of Plattsburgh. Chase had come to Plattsburgh's church at the age of thirty in 1826. Around 1830 he began a revival whose "influence was very widely felt throughout this region."[23]

Surviving records of the trustees of the Beekmantown church show the variety of their concerns during the period from 1837 through 1849. Securing "subscriptions for the Pastors Salary" was perhaps their most important responsibility. In 1842 such subscriptions ranged in value from a low of two days of work to a high of twenty dollars and one cord of wood. In the later 1840s, the trustees took on responsibility "for Warming and Lighting the house." The low bid was usually about twenty-five dollars and came almost invariably from one of the leading figures in the community, apparently as a form of service to the town. In 1847 the trustees arranged to warm and light the church twenty evenings during the following year "for Singing Schools."

The use of the church for political meetings posed an issue for the trustees in 1844. Rain had interrupted an outdoor Democratic meeting. Rather than confine the visiting leaders from around the county to the cramped quarters of what passed for a hotel, a generous local leader had invited the Democrats to assemble in the church. The trustees subsequently decided, less than unanimously, that "all Political Meetings . . . be Excluded from the Meeting house."[24]

Charitable contributions, handled by the deacons, were of considerable importance to members. Among the major beneficiaries of Beekmantown's charitable contributions were several national societies. The favorite among them was the American Board of Commissioners for Foreign Missions, which supported missionary work abroad. Others which received donations at one time or another included the American Tract Society, which distributed religious literature; the American Home Missionary Society, which financed revivalist-type missionary work in the United States; the American Bible Society, which distributed Bibles, especially among the needy; and the American Education Society.[25]

Another recipient of contributions from Beekmantown's Presbyterians was the Moral Reform Society. This was not among the major national societies, but apparently it was closely associated with them. Its collection agent, L. Myers, to whom Beekmantown's deacons gave contributions, was the same man who received contributions for other national reform societies.

The deacons also utilized the services of some of these organizations, particularly the American Bible Society, the American Tract Society, and the Moral Reform Society. In 1841 the deacons received from the Clinton County Bible Society, probably only the distribution channel for the national society, twenty-five Bibles in English and two in French "to supply the destitute Familys in this town." In 1838 they secured for use as "Sabbath School question books" fifteen Peter Parley primers. Later that same year, the deacons paid Myers assorted sums for "Tract S" and "Morral reform Tracts," as well as for more question books. It was probably Myers from whom the deacons bought two "Testaments" to use as a "reward of meritt to Sabath School Scollars" in 1839.

Beekmantown's reversal of the rule that charity begins at home extended to its support of national reform groups and also to more narrowly charitable gifts. There were none in this category to individuals, to town, or even county organizations. By way of contrast, the church sent $5.00 in 1842 "to assist a feeble Church in Michigan in the Purchase of a Meeting House." The next year the church gave $2.00 to "assist in building a meeting House in Iowa." In later years, a donation of $20.21 was made "to the Suffering poor in Scotland," while the Ojibway Indians received $2.50. As these sums indicate, the income at the disposal of the deacons was never great. Contributions to the society or church for these purposes ranged from about ten cents to $2.00, rarely more. Communion services seem to have been the occasion for special solicitation. For example, the contribution of $20.21 for the poor of Scotland represented the entire amount collected at one communion service in 1847. Yearly expenditures in the early 1840s ran usually to some $30.00 but had increased to over $60.00 by the end of the decade.

In Plattsburgh and Beekmantown, as in the national reform agencies, there existed what one authority has characterized as a somewhat "ethereal" conception of an official church. At the national level, the conception was clearly interdenominational although essentially Calvinist. In Plattsburgh and Beekmantown, it was more narrowly Presbyterian. Despite provisions in the state constitution barring ministers from public office, ministers and lay leaders of the Presbyterian persuasion did exercise certain functions of a civil nature affecting the populace as a whole.

After 1812 a position as one of the inspectors of common schools, for example, went to the Presbyterian minister for some years almost on an ex officio basis. The school inspectors elected by the town meeting of 1814 in conformity with the law of 1812 were Frederick Halsey, William Weeks, Thomas Tredwell, Daniel B. Vaughan, Jonathan Griffin, and Baruch Beckwith. Halsey was the retired Presbyterian minister; Weeks was the incumbent Presbyterian minister; and Tredwell and Beckwith were prominent citizens with Presbyterian affiliations. The religious feelings of the other two are unknown. In 1815 the new Presbyterian minister, Nathaniel Hewit, almost as a matter of course, replaced the departed Weeks among the inspectors. Whether this virtually automatic inclusion of Presbyterian ministers among the school inspectors owed more to their Presbyterianism or to their superior education is an open question. They were college graduates in a community in which few men possessed such a high level of education. The selection of ministers ceased within a few years, however, probably in deference to the sensitivities of those who belonged to less influential denominations and to those arch-Republicans who believed dogmatically in the separation of church and state.

Presbyterian control of the Public Burying Ground also illustrates the overlap of civil and religious authority. In 1818 Benjamin Mooers, president of the trustees of the First Presbyterian Church, printed in the *Republican* a notice of the trustees' resolution "that the small enclosures erected in the Public Burying Ground in this village be removed, and that John G. Frelich and Eleazer Miller be a committee to carry this resolution into effect; and also to lay out and make such regulations relative to the said burying ground as they shall think best; and further, that the above resolution be published in the Republican for two weeks." In 1827 Sexton Samuel Winchell advertised that the trustees had made him caretaker of the cemetery and that no graves could be dug except by him or with his permission.[26]

Participation by ministers and their churches in political controversies came under strong attack but never died out entirely. The *Republican* in 1812 (August 21) vigorously denounced unspecified but presumably Federalist ministers who, on a day fixed by the Presbyterian General Assembly for "Humiliation Fasting and Prayer," preferred "to slander our government, excite sedition—and in some instances (coming little short of) advising to open rebellion." With less than full consistency, however, the *Republican* subsequently published extracts (June 4, 1814) from a prowar sermon given by an army chaplain in Vermont.

Sunday travel involved the Presbyterians of Beekmantown in a bitter quarrel over church participation in politics. At a Sunday evening service in the church on July 23, 1837, a member called attention to a newspaper story which identified "the irreverence of the day" as the cause of the current depression. To avoid such evils, the member continued, the people must elect "holy men" to office. Then, getting to his main point, he stated, "and now brethren here is one of our [civil] officers, that the most of us have voted for, has passed here today, a sabbath breaker: will brethren support a man who breaks the sabbath?" The speaker also sought to secure a pledge of opposition to all candidates who did not observe the Sabbath but, at that point, the pastor arose to express disapproval of political discussion in their meetings. He did suggest, however, that they might hold a meeting on a weekday and there vote to censor "persons of infidel principles, for I agree with the remarks which have been made by my brother."

Then B. J. Simonds, a storekeeper and a Democratic leader, suggested that the matter should be dropped entirely as it had no place in church. To this the pastor replied: "Now brethren you can see how quick it makes a person squirm if you rake an old sore, or touch private interest. Now if we were as anxious for the cause of Christ as some are for Martin Van Buren's election, how soon we might have a reformation here." Simond's reply, as he recalled it in his letter of explanation to the *Republican*, was "that I had my political opinions and political interests—and that the laws of our country gave me the privilege of voting for whom I thought proper, and I should place myself under no pledge."

Superior Presbyterian organizations exerted some authority and a great deal of influence over the Plattsburgh and Beekmantown churches. Affiliation with a district presbytery, the chief distinction betwen Presbyterian and the nonjoining Congregational churches, committed the member churches to send delegates to semiannual meetings of the presbytery and to send certain church records for examination yearly. The Champlain presbytery, to which both Plattsburgh and Beekmantown churches belonged, met in February to examine the "fidelity of Ministers, in preaching, catechizing and visiting their congregations, and of the general state of religion" in the area. In the summer its second meeting of the year examined the session records (chiefly membership and disciplinary matters) and financial accounts of the member churches. The sessional records of the Beekmantown church, however, include only one notation of such an inspection.

The admission of Baptists was a recurrent problem to the presbytery. In 1814 it concluded that a church could keep as a member an individual who denied the efficacy of infant baptism, but it cautioned the churches against "receiving any person hereafter under similar circumstances." In 1821 the presbytery examined the issue again and concluded that a church which had admitted another Baptist could retain him. The presbytery held also that in general Baptists could be admitted if there was satisfactory evidence of their piety and if the individuals provided assurance that they would "be silent on . . . their peculiar sentiments."[27]

The presbytery was important chiefly in registering Presbyterian consensus and transmitting reform impulses. In 1824 it expressed opposition to admitting European immigrants to membership on the basis of letters from their "national churches." In later instances it resolved that Roman Catholic baptism was invalid (1832) and that marriage to a "papist" should constitute a "disciplinable offense" (1833).[28] Temperance, to be discussed in the next chapter, was the most important of many reforms which the presbytery encouraged its member churches to support.

The history of the presbytery of Champlain illustrates several peculiarities of the Presbyterian-Congregational relationship in northeastern New York, as well as the somewhat unusual status of Plattsburgh and of Beekmantown among the communities of that district. As set off from the much larger presbytery of Columbia in 1812, the Champlain presbytery included the four northeastern counties of Clinton, Essex, Franklin, and St. Lawrence. Of the five ministers who were original members of the presbytery, three (Joel Byington of Chazy, Amos Pettengill of Champlain, and Ashbel Parmelee of Malone) served unaffiliated Congregational churches. Both the Malone and Champlain churches did join the presbytery in 1817, but Chazy retained its independent status until 1833. The other two of the original five members were the Reverend Frederick Halsey and his successor, the Reverend William R. Weeks. Thus, Plattsburgh's was the only Presbyterian church represented in the presbytery at the outset.

That Plattsburgh and Beekmantown were Presbyterian islands in a sea of Congregationalism seems apparent from other evidence in the records of the presbytery. None of the four churches which affiliated with the presbytery between 1814 and 1817 was in Clinton County. In fact, the only other Clinton County churches to join the presbytery before 1828 represented Beekmantown and Champlain, both of which joined in 1817. The Keeseville church, organized as Congregational in 1806, remained so until 1845; the church at Mooers was Congregational from 1807 until it joined the presbytery in 1828. Peru organized a Congregational church in 1826. A Congregational church existed in Essex from 1815 until 1833 before it chose to affiliate. The decision occasioned a split with the part of the congregation at Willsboro which remained Congregational. In Franklin County to the west, Chateaugay organized a Congregational church in 1816 and joined the presbytery only in 1827. Thus, the Plattsburgh and Beekmantown churches were the only ones in their vicinity which were Presbyterian from the outset. All other churches which joined the presbytery were originally Congregational churches which affiliated with the presbytery only after varying periods of independence.[29] Probably this is just another indication that New Yorkers were relatively more numerous and influential in Plattsburgh and Beekmantown, while New Englanders predominated generally elsewhere in the region.

Baptists were also among the earliest settlers of Beekmantown and Plattsburgh, but they were always relatively inconspicuous and in the later years virtually died out as an organized group. The "historical department" of the *Republican* (April 1, 1876) asserted without documentation that in 1787 a Baptist named Benjamin Vaughan preached the first sermon to be heard in Clinton County and that about the same time a Baptist society "sprang up" in the Beekmantown area. Meeting at first in homes and then in the schoolhouse at the "Beekmantown corners," the society was reported to have lasted until about 1825.

A historical publication (1918) of the First Baptist Church of Plattsburgh affirms that Baptist organizational effort began there in 1788 and that a society of seventeen members (ten men and seven women) actually organized at the home of Uriah Palmer in 1791, a year before the Presbyterians began their organizing effort. The Baptist minister, Solomon Brown, the account continues, was the first preacher in the area of Clinton and Essex counties. The function of the church was purportedly to "look after the poor, and to promote temperance and to abolish human slavery." So that its pastor and his family "might have work to do and earn a livelihood," the society purchased fifty acres of land. The minister reportedly farmed this land and taught school in addition to preaching. A church was erected, the account concluded, in 1826.[30]

David Benedict's *General History of the Baptist Denomination* (2 vols., Boston, 1813) brings much of the foregoing into question. His appended list of Baptist societies gives the date of the "constitution" of the Plattsburgh organization as 1796. Even in 1813, he reported that it had only thirty-six communicants and no minister. Peru's society, organized in 1794, he identifies as the first in Clinton and Essex counties. Solomon Brown, identified above as Plattsburgh's first minister, was among the subscribers who helped to pay for this work, as were two pioneer settlers of Plattsburgh, Kinner Newcomb and Uriah Palmer.

Whatever the correct chronology of their organization, Baptists were thus among the earliest settlers of Plattsburgh. Newcomb, a revolutionary veteran from Dutchess County, received one of the "gift" lots awarded by the proprietors to stimulate settlement. Indeed, the *Republican* in 1838 identified him as "the" first settler of Plattsburgh. A staunch Republican, he became supervisor, county judge, and assemblyman—the only Republican to win the district's assembly seat between 1806 and 1812. Several of Kinner Newcomb's relatives were also prominent in early Plattsburgh and Beekmantown, but no surviving evidence links them to the Baptist movement. One was apparently a Presbyterian. Uriah Palmer's name appears among those of the eighty-six heads of families in Plattsburgh at the time of the 1790 census. Solomon Brown's does not.

References to Baptists in the *Republican* and other contemporary records which have survived are remarkably few, especially in comparison with the abundance of information on the Presbyterians and even on the late-coming Methodists. Baptists, however, were present and were organized in Beekmantown as well as in Plattsburgh. An undated reference in the records of Beekmantown's Presbyterian church, for example, indicates that one Lucy Taylor had "gone out from us and joined the Baptists." An obituary notice in the *Republican* in 1825 (March 19) concerned a Beekmantown woman who belonged "to the Baptist church of that place." The trustees of a Baptist society in Plattsburgh in 1832 (June 23) announced in the *Republican* their foreclosure of a mortgage. One of the trustees was Kinner Newcomb; the other was A. Scribner, who had experienced repeated disciplinary action in the Beekmantown Presbyterian church for drunkenness and other offenses, most recently in 1831.

By 1850 the Baptist movement was virtually extinct in both Beekmantown and Plattsburgh. Children from a Beekmantown Baptist Sunday school reportedly marched with those from the town's Methodist and Presbyterian Sunday schools at a parade in 1841.[31] But, the state census of 1845 found no Baptist church building in Beekmantown, although there were two Methodist and one Presbyterian churches. The seven clergymen in the town at that date may have included one or more Baptists. If so, they were very poorly paid for the total compensation paid clergymen barely exceeded the total paid the Methodist and Presbyterian ministers. The *American Baptist Register* for 1852 lists six Baptist congregations in Clinton County, but neither Beekmantown nor Plattsburgh is among them. There were, however, Baptist congregations in adjacent Chazy to the north and in West Plattsburgh on the south.[32]

The rise of the Methodists correlates closely with the decline of the Baptists and may, in fact, have accounted for it to some extent. Methodism, although represented in the area from the earliest times, gained relatively few members until after 1820. From then until 1850, Methodist camp meetings were frequent, and their success in gaining new members was great—far greater, however, in rural Beekmantown than in urban Plattsburgh. Circuit-riding Methodist itinerants began to travel through the Plattsburgh area within a decade of the first settlement. Bishop Francis Asbury noted in 1795 that people of Plattsburgh "have often solicited us to send preachers."[33] In the following year, Richard Jacob did preach in the region, but whether he actually visited Plattsburgh or only areas of Essex County is uncertain. A successor named McCall preached throughout the newly organized Plattsburgh circuit in 1799. In 1800 Elijah Hedding, subsequently to become a bishop, reportedly preached his first sermon in a "humble cottage on the west side of Cumberland Head, about two miles [north] from the village of Plattsburgh."[34] There were then 107 members in the Plattsburgh circuit, but it extended from Ticonderoga to Canada. Hedding and his senior associate, Elijah Chichester, visited each of their "charges" once a month and in so doing preached three times every Sunday and once a day on weekdays. The ministers changed every year or two, but the pattern continued for many years. Mob violence, such as Freeborn Garrettson had encountered in his itinerant preaching in the 1780s, apparently never plagued those who rode the Plattsburgh circuit. But, their initial reception was probably chilly.

Methodism grew slowly in Plattsburgh. Until 1817 Methodist meetings were generally in private homes. Then the Methodists began to meet in the courthouse, which the Presbyterians had apparently monopolized until completion of their church at the end of 1816. Camp meetings may have begun as early as 1808, but these outdoor revivals occurred only once a year, usually in August or September. When Bishop Asbury came to Plattsburgh in 1811, he preached in "a very commodious tavern."[35] According to Peter Sailly Palmer, Plattsburgh Methodists did not organize until about 1816, secured a resident minister (James Quinlan) only in 1826, and erected their first church in 1831. Meanwhile, they had continued to meet in the courthouse,[36] except for one occasion on which they met by invitation in the Presbyterian church. Membership, despite revivalist efforts, remained about one hundred through the 1830s.[37]

Methodism grew more rapidly in Beekmantown. In 1818 a Chazy circuit, embracing Beekmantown and the rest of the northern part of the county, was separated from the Plattsburgh circuit.

The Chazy circuit had only 80 members, but by 1823 there were 463. In 1817 they had built a church at Chazy. Beekmantown became a circuit by itself in 1830. Its membership of 217 was more than twice the figure for Plattsburgh at that time. Beekmantown's Methodists had no church as late as 1838. They did provide a satisfactory parsonage for the incumbent minister, however, and they had at least one church building by 1842.[38]

Camp meetings were the most successful proselytizing agency. While they had reportedly been held since 1808,[39] the Plattsburgh *Republican* began to notice them only in 1819. An advertisement (August 19) indicated that a lake steamboat would carry people to the camp meeting at St. Albans, Vermont, on August 31 and return them on September 3 at a cost of one dollar each way. In 1822 a camp meeting with 170 tents some five miles south of Plattsburgh attracted five thousand people and gained one hundred converts. For several years the annual camp meetings returned to the same site, but later they moved to other locations. A splinter group, the Methodist Protestant church, held one at Point au Roche in 1834. There was one at Chazy in 1836 and another in West Plattsburgh in 1838.[40] Camp meetings seem to have lost favor in the 1840s, but Methodist revivalism continued. The *Republican* reported (February 5, 1848) that a revival had been underway at the Methodist Episcopal church for three or four weeks and that many had been "hopefully converted."

A testimonial to the effectiveness of camp meetings appeared in the journal of Beekmantown's Methodist minister of 1837–1838, Luman A. Sanford. He attended such a meeting at West Plattsburgh in 1838 and in fact sat on the stand with the preachers. The speaker, "Brother Wever from Saranac," turned "several times and addressed himself especially to the Preachers, and the Lord attended the Word with such power as to renew its effect. I went from the stand . . . unable to speak for some time. Never had I deeper conviction for entire sanctification." Returning to Beekmantown, he began a series of meetings at various points in his circuit "till between thirty and forty had sought and found redemption from the guilt of sin through the blood of Christ." There were twenty more penitents at the altar when he himself collapsed and had to give up the work.[41]

Abatement of the initial hostility toward Methodists came slowly. Even in 1819 Beekmantown Presbyterians and Baptists apparently held Methodists in some suspicion. According to a local

Methodist who wrote in protest to the *Republican*, the Reverend Stephen Kinsley (Presbyterian) of Beekmantown had won considerable popularity among Presbyterians and Baptists for having found out and revealed the "GREAT SECRET" that the Methodists had a "NEW BIBLE." The writer explained that the work referred to was John Wesley's translation of the New Testament, first published in 1754. He kept a constant supply at the home of the Reverend Daniel Bromley in Beekmantown for sale to interested parties. After a pointed reference to the "small reading and deep-rooted prejudice" of many residents of Beekmantown, including implicitly the Reverend Kinsley and the Baptist preacher, the writer concluded triumphantly: "O ENVY! when wilt thou cease to trouble, and hide thy dethroned head in the dust!"[42]

An indication that hostility was passing appears in *Republican* notices concerning a camp meeting in 1825. At the request of Methodist officials, the *Republican* printed (August 20) sections from the state law prohibiting intentional "noise-making" or other "disturbance . . . intended to interrupt . . . religious services." Editorially, the *Republican* commended these passages "to the attentive perusal and observance of those who have heretofore so far forgotten what was due to themselves—to religion—and to the good order of society, as to attend camp meetings for the purpose of interrupting its members in the free exercise of a privilege, guaranteed by our Constitution and Laws, to every citizen and society, of worshipping God according to the dictates of their own consciences."

Methodists, like Catholics a generation later, were winning general acceptance with the powerful assistance of the Republican-Democratic party to which a high proportion gave wholehearted allegiance. One of the highlights of the Jackson campaign of 1828, W. C. Watson later recalled, was the visit of Methodist Bishop Elijah Hedding to his brother in Beekmantown. Hedding had just visited "Old Hickory" at the Hermitage and gave a glowing account of the hero's virtues. As Watson remembered it, "Methodist minister was [then] almost a synonym for Democrat."[43] Although some of its supporters were Methodists, the Federalist-Whig opposition as late as 1832 publicly censured as a "Methodist quibbler" the local exhorter who had in an excess of zeal for the temperance cause wished every drunkard would die of cholera within twelve hours. The *Republican*, while disavowing the exhorter's view, printed the condemnation with careful identification of the source for the edification of Methodist voters.[44]

Beekmantown's Methodists did not need to go outside their own ranks to find controversy. The Reverend Daniel Bromley, who had apparently presided over the huge Plattsburgh circuit from 1802 to 1804,[45] had sometime thereafter made his home in Beekmantown. Bromley was one of the self-styled reformers who disliked the episcopal government of the Methodist church and sought to replace it with a more representative polity. By 1831 he was a leading figure in the New York and Lower Canada district of the splinter group called the Methodist Protestant church. At a district conference held at the Presbyterian church in Beekmantown in 1831, Bromley's conduct as presiding officer came under severe censure from a number of delegates. They published numerous accusations in the *Republican* and, in so doing, made it appear that the root of the difficulty was Bromley's effort to fix the voting rules in such a way as to insure his own status as leader. He not only failed but found himself denounced in the *Republican* for "mental imbecility and moral deformity." The majority also chastised Bromley for ridiculing the idea that God might burn the world. "What would He do with the ashes," Bromley was reported to have said, "make potash?" With or without Bromley, however, the Methodist Protestant church continued to hold camp meetings in the area through the 1830s.[46] There is no evidence as to the number of adherents the movement had locally, but probably there were not many.

Methodist success in eclipsing the Baptists and overshadowing the Presbyterians in Beekmantown during the 1830s and 1840s invites analysis. Both the camp meetings and the circuit-riding system gave the Methodists advantages in gaining and holding converts. Undoubtedly, their centralized administration also made for more efficient effort than was normally possible among the more loosely organized Baptists. Compared to Presbyterians, Methodists apparently benefited from popular preference for their doctrine that "anyone who willed to do so could choose to be holy rather than sinful."[47] This was an idea which contrasted with the more pessimistic belief of the Presbyterians in the general depravity of mankind and the predestination of most for eternal damnation. Temperance was also a long-time Methodist objective. There was indeed some tendency to regard it as redundant for a Methodist to take a temperance oath.[48] It may be coincidental that the rise of Methodism in Beekmantown closely paralleled that of the temperance movement. It is important to note also that the Methodist gains were not permanent. Their membership soared to a reported 485 in 1844. By the 1850s, it was declining sharply and, before the end of the 1860s, it had shrunk to less than 100.[49]

The Episcopal church, even more than the Federalist party, suffered the twin taints of association with the British and with the elite. Largely for this reason, Episcopalianism came to Plattsburgh only in 1821 and seems never to have reached Beekmantown at all. Clergymen from Vermont and other areas helped organize the society in 1821 and a regular minister, Joel Clapp, was secured in 1822. Both Clapp and his successor, William Shelton, departed quickly, however, and, for a number of years, there was again no resident rector. Some Episcopalians attended Methodist services whenever their own society had no rector, but the majority rejected a proposal for a "union church" to be built jointly with the Methodists.[50] The revival which began in 1828 seems to have breathed new life into the Episcopal society. A legal reorganization occurred in 1830. A church was completed in 1831, and the rector who came in 1832, Joseph Howland Coit, remained until 1844.

Among Catholics, poverty and prejudice impeded organization. Catholics were present in both Beekmantown and Plattsburgh from the earliest times. But, nearly all were French Canadian or Irish immigrants who lived in extreme poverty and to some extent, especially among the French Canadians, in cultural isolation. Prejudice against French Canadians was almost as strong as that against their religion. James Kent, the Federalist jurist, expressed feelings probably shared widely among Plattsburgh's elite (including his sister, the wife of William Pitt Platt) when he denounced French Canadians as "the most stupid and obstinate of all people in America, . . . a most . . . superstitious People . . . [who] submit to all the Impositions and Nonsense and folly of the Roman Worship."[51] The *Republican*, which would later do much to foster a more respectful attitude, concluded a description of the "taking of the veil" at a Montreal convent in 1811 with the observation that many spectators left the ceremony "wearied . . . if not disgusted with what appears, to us puritans, as nearly allied with superstition." Even after the War of 1812, frequent stories in the *Republican*, although usually free from explicit condemnation, pointed out Catholic practices which would strike its Protestant readers as offensive.[52]

The orthodox Republicans began to assume a more respectful attitude toward Catholicism in the 1820s. Catholics were becoming much more numerous and beginning to organize. On September

16, 1826, the *Republican* carried by request the notice that "the Rev. Mr. Barber of the Roman Catholic Church, is in town, and will preach in the court house tomorrow at 5 o'clock P.M." The language has a distinct Protestant flavor, but it is significant that the courthouse was made available. It is even more important that articles even implicitly adverse to Catholicism no longer appeared. The opposition papers, however, continued to cast aspersions upon Catholicism for many years.

A "Bible-burning" incident in 1842 brought latent anti-Catholic feeling surging to the surface, particularly in Beekmantown. The *Republican*'s first notice of the incident (December 24) was in a report concerning a protest meeting held in the Methodist Episcopal church of Beekmantown. The purpose of the meeting was to consider "the late sacrilegious act of the Roman Catholic Priests in committing to the flames the Holy Bible in the town of Champlain." A committee of four ministers and one layman drafted a resolution stating that two Catholic priests in Champlain had publicly burned Bibles given them by the Champlain Bible Society, presumably because they were the King James rather than the Catholic Douay Version. The resolution affirmed also that the priests had refused to return Bibles which they had not yet burned, had threatened "to burn all they could obtain and did so the next day." The Beekmantown assembly denounced their action as "a disgrace to all Protestants, the government and constitution, Philanthropists, and Patriots, and Almighty God."

The next issue of the *Republican* (December 31) featured a mollifying letter from "a Protestant" who evidently resided in Beekmantown. His theme was that "the act of two erring and infatuated French priests . . . should not in all charity be visited upon such men as Fathers Mignault and Rooney, [local] Priests universally esteemed for their piety and good works." He charged specifically that the resolution was intended to foster prejudice. "The enmity, open and disguised of a [Whig?] portion of Protestant professors, against the Catholics, is well understood: it has manifested itself in this village upon more than one occasion."

Subsequent issues of the *Republican* continued to foster harmonious resolution of the question. On January 14 the paper featured the request of Catholic Bishop John Hughes that a committee of two Protestants and two Catholics investigate and report to him. He promised to pay the expenses and to hold the priests liable if they had in fact committed the act. He also condemned the act as it was reported to him. Next week the *Republican* used the ongoing investigation as an excuse to publish no more letters on the subject.

More than six months after the incident, the committee, enlarged from four to six members, reported its findings. Two of its three Catholic members were Michael Hagerty and John Riley. Each had recently served as a delegate from Beekmantown to the Democratic county convention. The report agreed to by all six committee members exonerated Father Dugas, the resident French Canadian priest at Champlain, and placed all the blame on a French [as opposed to French Canadian] missionary priest. He had in fact burned forty-two Bibles over the opposition of Father Dugas. Three weeks later the *Republican* printed a letter calling to the attention of its readers that the Whig paper had not seen fit to publish the report.[53]

French Canadian Catholics had held religious services in Plattsburgh as early as 1827, but the organization of Plattsburgh's first Catholic church was the work of the Irish, including Father Patrick McGilligan and lay leaders Michael Kearny, Patrick Foy, John Hogan, and Michael Ryan. They first organized in 1827, bought a church site in 1834, and completed a church in 1842. French Canadians formed a separate organization in 1853 and built a church within a few years. All these activities, of course, were in Plattsburgh. Beekmantown, although about one-fourth of its population was either Irish or French Canadian and hence presumably Catholic, had no Catholic church or even a Catholic society at the end of the period.[54]

Quakers were numerous in the southern part of Clinton County, but Universalists were the only other religious group to have much influence in the Plattsburgh-Beekmantown area before 1850. The central beliefs of the Universalists were that Christ was human rather than divine and that all would be saved. Congregational autonomy and great latitude for individual differences also characterized the movement. The *Republican*, almost from the outset (1811), seemed sympathetic to such views and indeed in 1817 had published with implicit endorsement a letter written by Benjamin Franklin expressing doubt as to the divinity of Jesus.[55]

Organization of Universalists, however, came only in the late 1820s. A later Presbyterian minister (1897) offered "in extenuation of the fiery elements" of a rigorously Calvinist confession adopted by the Presbyterians under the Reverend Moses Chase (1826–1836) that the community was then "in convulsions" over the inauguration of the Universalist church. The Presbyterians, in fact, excommunicated several for "going after" the Universalists. In 1835 a Universalist promised to renounce his church if an orthodox minister could answer his questions for one hour from the Bible or by reason without at least five contradictions. No one took up his challenge. In 1845 Universalists announced their intention to erect a place of worship and published a statement of their beliefs.[56] There were probably a few Beekmantown farmers who found these ideas appealing but most undoubtedly reacted more in the manner of the Reverend Moses Chase.

The triumph of sectarianism over the presumption of Calvinist predominance is the most conspicuous feature of the religious history of Beekmantown between 1769 and 1849. Even at the outset, the long delay in selecting a minister and the preeminent concern with his qualification in the field of secular education suggest that the level of interest in religion was low. The normal ascendancy of Republican-Democrats over Federalist-Whigs, to be discussed at length in two later chapters, was not at all coincidentally an ascendancy of rationalists, Baptists, Methodists, Catholics, and of moderate Calvinists over the orthodox. The orthodox zealots whom the Federalists brought in as ministers in the period of the War of 1812 did not last long. The disciplinary proceedings in the Beekmantown church also showed more weakness than strength. Several of the accused merely moved elsewhere; one became a Baptist; the girl accused of heresy stubbornly and apparently successfully refused to recant. This record of failure offset by relatively few successes and a suspicious absence of any accusations of sexual immorality suggest strongly that the church was losing its power to regulate conduct. Revivals did occur among the Presbyterians, chiefly the work of settled rather than itinerant preachers, but Methodism with its circuit riders, its camp meetings, and its promise of better prospects for salvation had outdone the Presbyterians decidedly by 1849. Other Protestant groups had also gained footholds by then and the immigration of French Canadian and Irish Catholics had given the community a significant proportion of Catholic residents well beyond the reach of even the most zealous Calvinists.[57]

7

Culture, Recreation, and Identity

Despite their remoteness from the cultural centers of the nation and their usual preoccupation with material matters, some of the residents of Beekmantown and Plattsburgh made significant efforts to enrich their lives both culturally and socially. Isolation, parochialism, and conservatism weighed heavily on the community in early years, but by 1850 the local folk were tightly integrated into the national society and far more receptive to change.

Education, while definitely subordinate to economic development, was often on the minds of the early leaders of Plattsburgh. Their "common" or elementary schools became largely public institutions after the first few years and will be considered in a later chapter. The Plattsburgh Academy, however, remained primarily a private school. Because it had a major role in the intellectual and artistic life of the area, its history deserves to be considered.

Creating an academy was much on the mind of Princeton graduate Thomas Tredwell as he endeavored to recruit a minister for the community in 1794. "Sensible that the cultivation of the mind is as necessary to the happiness and well being of the Country, as the culture of the Soil is to its growth and prosperity," he wrote to the Reverend Frederick Halsey, "we are determined to avoid the error too generally run into by New Settlers, of having their attention so much engrossed by the latter, as to neglect the former." There were already a number of boys in the area "of a proper age for education and whose parents are anxious to give them something more of one, than they can acquire at our common

Schools." A number of others, he thought, would soon be in the same situation and their needs "cannot longer be neglected without injury."[1]

Halsey's acceptance of Tredwell's invitation by no means brought Plattsburgh an instant academy. For seventeen years after his arrival, no academy existed. Halsey did tutor youths whose parents wished them to have a classical education, but apparently he never had a great many pupils. His successor as Presbyterian minister, the Reverend W. R. Weeks, advertised in 1813 (December 25) that he would "take five or six boys to board and instruct in the Latin and Greek languages, mathematics, etc." Halsey probably had done no more.

The creation of the academy began with a public meeting in 1811. A bipartisan group of local notables agreed to serve as a committee to raise money. They also planned and soon constructed "the largest and most imposing public edifice in Northern New York."[2] It provided classrooms on either side of a central hall downstairs and one large meeting room upstairs. This upstairs room long served both for an interdenominational Sunday school and for the meetings of various civic organizations as well.

Precisely when instruction began at the academy is not clear, but it was probably about 1812. The first instructor was Bela Edgerton. In 1813 he advertised in the *Republican*: "Mr. Edgerton, would inform the inhabitants of Plattsburgh, and its vicinity, that he has again opened his SCHOOL in the Academy, for the reception of scholars, and solicits the patronage of the public."[3]

Tuition charges at the academy were relatively modest, at least when compared to the cost of board and room. In 1833 board and room cost from $1.25 to $1.50 weekly, but this had gone up to $2.00 by 1842. Tuition, on the other hand, was only $3.00 per quarter for younger students in 1833 and $4.00 for the older pupils. In 1842 the tuition fees were $3.00 for "common English studies," $4.00 for higher English studies, including mathematics, and $5.00 for classics. In an egalitarian gesture, the trustees permitted one poor student to perform "services" in lieu of any payment.[4]

The curriculum was always broad. Among mathematical subjects taught in 1842 were arithmetic, bookkeeping, plane geometry, and trigonometry. Science courses included botany, chemistry, and geology. In what would now be called the humanities, there were courses in composition, rhetoric, English grammar, orthography, penmanship, Latin, Greek, French, and philosophy (both "natural" and "moral"). There were also courses in geography and history. To instruct the students in these varied courses, there were four teachers.[5]

Teaching techniques probably varied greatly, but one former student recalled ruefully the means by which Principal Alexander H. Prescott had taught spelling. He made no correction during the spelling exercise. But, at its conclusion, he approached each student who had misspelled one or more words and struck the student's outstretched palm repeatedly with a heavy ruler as he carefully enunciated each letter of the correct spelling.[6]

The nadir of the academy came between 1831 and 1845. It seems to have begun with Prescott's dismissal after a twelve-year tenure beginning in 1819. In 1832, the *Republican* accused the trustees of neglecting the institution, and for several years the turnover of principals was rapid. By 1845, the *Republican* would later affirm, the institution was "to all intents and purposes, defunct."[7]

Symptomatic of the academy's problems was the effort to found a rival institution, the Clinton County High School. The tiny rural community of Schuyler Falls was to be the site of the new school in order to safeguard the students "from many of the temptations and dangers to which they would be exposed in villages or places of more crowded population."[8] Plattsburgh, clearly the source of the "temptations and dangers" which the founders feared, then had about five thousand people. It is probably significant both that the founders met in a Methodist church to inaugurate their enterprise in 1833 and that they chose Prescott to lead their new venture. Prescott did not in fact do well. By 1835 he was back in Plattsburgh as a jeweler.[9]

The worst period for the Plattsburgh Academy was the early 1840s. The report of the regents of the university of the state in 1842 indicated that the academy then had only 69 students. It had had 139 in 1833. Nearby Keeseville with a building only half as valuable had 107 students. The Plattsburgh Academy was also running a deficit in 1842, while Keeseville's was in the black. The academy library contained a meager 141 volumes while some such institutions boasted libraries of over 1,000 books; only two in the state had under 100 volumes. The average age of the students was only fourteen, while at several academies it was as high as nineteen.[10]

The revival of the academy between 1845 and 1850 was dramatic. Enrollment in 1849 was double what it had been in 1845. In 1845 the allocation to the academy from the state's Literature Fund had been among the lowest in the senatorial district. As the aid was dispensed on a matching basis, its amount was also an indication of the extent of local support. In 1850, with the same principle in effect, the academy received the largest amount allocated from the Literature Fund to any institution in northern New York. The reason, as the *Republican* proudly proclaimed, was that residents of the village had raised between $1,000 and $1,500 to remodel the building so that it would accommodate an additional 100 students. Its actual enrollment in 1850 was 336.[11]

Two other factors, in addition to the large infusion of local money, helped to revive the academy. One was the "accomplished and gentlemanly principal, Mr. John Taylor." The other was an additional allocation of state funds under a law passed in 1849 to encourage the introduction of special courses of instruction in the "science of common school teaching."[12]

For girls, education beyond the common schools was available in several forms. They could and did attend the academy from the outset. Susan Cook, herself an alumna of the academy, one who had performed services in lieu of payment, conducted a school for young ladies for some time beginning in 1817. Her school probably imitated the finishing school at Burlington which she had also attended. Tuition in 1820 was $2.50 for "small" girls and $3.00 for girls in the "higher branches." The curriculum at that time included "music, French, painting, and dancing." In 1850 there were more girls than boys (172 to 164) attending the academy.[13]

For working boys and girls, an evening school was available at least in 1820. B. Gilman advertised courses in writing, arithmetic, mensuration, trigonometry, surveying, and single or double entry bookkeeping. His classes ran from six to nine in the evening five nights per week at a cost of $2.00 per quarter.[14]

Sunday schools also provided some education of a secular nature to children of the poor. In 1817 a notice in the *Republican* affirmed that a "Sunday free school" would begin every Sunday at eight o'clock in the upper room of the academy and continue until the services began, presumably ten o'clock.[15] The Sunday schools taught the alphabet, reading, and "the Scriptures" to the children who, in many cases, "had never been to school in their lives." Nearly 100 pupils attended at the beginning, and the number went up soon to 220. Included in that number, it was reported, were boys who had previously hovered about street corners "blaspheming at every breath." In general the pupils came from "the most poor and indigent part of the community, some of whom were of color and among that number several adults." One Negro woman of about forty learned to read at the Sunday school. Three Negro boys walked three to four miles—probably from Beekmantown—to attend.[16]

Ten years later, the institution was still going. Charles P. Tredwell, Thomas Tredwell's grandson who had emigrated to Canada, looked in on the Sunday school twice during a brief stay in January and February 1829. He noted in his diary that during the intermission at the Presbyterian service, "I remained to examine the Sunday schools which was not as numerous as last year. There were about 80 Schollars and twenty teachers present." The next Sunday he found one hundred "Schollars" and the same twenty teachers.[17]

Presbyterian domination of the movement apparently evoked some resentment from the other denominations, as it did elsewhere in the state and nation.[18] The *Republican* in 1824 cautiously published an anonymous letter (February 14) urging establishment of a nonsectarian Sunday school in the pattern fixed by the American Sunday School Union. Three years later, the Methodist minister, the Reverend James Quinlan, spoke at the courthouse on the subject. And, the *Republican* printed an appeal from the New York state agent of the American Sunday School Union urging the establishment of a local branch. The next year, however, the Monthly Teachers Concert Meeting of the Sabbath Union Society convened at the Presbyterian parsonage and chose the Presbyterian minister, the Reverend Moses Chase, as president. In 1830 a Methodist Sunday school operated independently with thirteen teachers.[19]

In the 1840s an interdenominational Clinton County Sabbath School Association was quite active, but each denomination maintained its own Sunday schools. Some three thousand Sunday school children from around the county paraded from the Presbyterian to the Methodist church in Peru in a Fourth of July celebration in 1841. Beekmantown was represented by delegations from Baptist, Methodist, and Presbyterian societies. The third anniversary celebration of the association, however, received much less attention and took place at Plattsburgh's Presbyterian church.[20] How much secular education the Sunday schools then imparted to children of poor families is not apparent.

Dancing schools also existed at various times, although the

morality of dancing remained controversial. Mrs. Deshon operated a dancing school in Plattsburgh in 1821, about the same time that the Beekmantown Presbyterian church, after a prolonged struggle, exacted a confession and plea for forgiveness from Polly Winters for having "attended balls and assemblies appointed for carnal mirth."[21] "Quadrilles" occurred regularly in 1827 in Plattsburgh. But, in 1835 an advertisement for a dancing school carried the introductory reminder that "moderation in all things is the rule of the wise," followed by the utilitarian affirmation that dancing "in moderation" imparts "ease and grace." By the 1840s dancing was apparently winning its battle for moral status locally, for in 1844 the still highly political *Republican* gave it a spirited defense against an attack by the presbytery of New York City.[22]

Music suffered no such moral stigma as attached to dancing, but only in the later years did it appear to have much part in the lives of the people. In the fall of 1815 (October 7), the *Republican* notified "persons disposed to encourage a Singing School the ensuing winter . . . that a subscription for that purpose is left at this office." Such a school may have begun, but the absence of further references suggests the probability that subscriptions were insufficient. A "French lady" advertised piano lessons in 1819 (March 6). In 1837 the *Republican* editorially endorsed a teacher of sacred music, a Mr. Prouty. Mr. Prouty staged a successful concert the following February at the Presbyterian church.[23] Thereafter, advertisements for musical instruments appeared. The regular "exercises" at the academy in 1845 included a piano recital by one of the instructors, Monsieur LaJeunesse. For some time after 1843, there was annually a County Musical Convention dedicated to the betterment of church music. Lest even this quasi-religious endeavor smack too much of mere idle enjoyment, the sponsors listed a number of reasons in justification of their meeting. The first was that singing "tends to strengthen the lungs." By 1850 touring musical groups were giving occasional concerts in Plattsburgh.[24]

Entertainment spectacles of a less cultured variety came to Plattsburgh from very early times. One of the earlier ones was a traveling wax museum which came to J. I. Green's tavern in the spring of 1814—while a considerable body of soldiers was stationed at Plattsburgh in anticipation of the British invasion. Among the attractions were replicas of a fat man who weighed 739 pounds, a three-year-old baby who weighed 105 pounds, a woman weeping at the tomb of Washington, Othello murdering Desdemona, a drowning woman, an Old Testament scene, an American prisoner starving among the Algerines, Jerome Bonaparte, a Negro boy, Indians, and, with lowest billing, "Ezra Stiles, late President of Yale College."[25]

"Exhilarating Gas" or laughing gas was the subject of a demonstration offered to the public at Green's tavern in 1822. Admission was twenty-five cents. An unfortunate explosion of hydrogen at one of the early shows somewhat discouraged attendance at later exhibitions until the sponsor advertised the explanation and the reassuring affirmation that "Nitrous Oxid cannot explode."

What was advertised as an Egyptian mummy made a three-day appearance at Gilman's coffeehouse in 1826.

"The Grand Caravan of Living Animals," a circus, arrived later the same year. Thereafter, circuses and horse shows came often. By the later 1840s, the circus included trapeze artists, clowns, and a variety of animals, but the equestrian performance seemed always to be the major attraction.[26]

Painting drew occasional boosts from the *Republican* and met with some favor. A John Trumbull painting of Governor George Clinton adorned Israel Green's tavern until 1814, when a British soldier vandalized it.[27] Two "landscape and portrait" painters resided in Plattsburgh in 1835. The *Republican* endorsed a Mr. Johnson in 1837 as a "promising artist" destined for high rank. He had done several portraits in the village. Accordingly, the editor recommended that those "who wish to see themselves as others see them" should take advantage of his stay. In 1848 a portrait painter named Cook advertised that he would stop for a short time at the Fouquet Hotel. In 1850 the *Republican* recommended the art periodical, the American Art Union.[28]

Architecture as an art form received even less attention if the record of the *Republican* is reliable. Local resident Abel Chamberlain advertised in 1822 a public lecture on "civil architecture" to be given at his office with an admission charge of fifty cents. His title was "Good Music on King David's Cymball." The report to the state agricultural society in 1849 expressed some pride in the "air of neatness, taste and finish" with which the fair grounds at Keeseville had been completed—cheaply—in "rural Gothic style."[29]

Theatrical performances enjoyed some popularity in Clinton County from about 1821. The presumption of immorality which led to the harassment of theatrical groups, even in major cities before the Revolution, was not much in evidence in Plattsburgh. Traveling companies—sometimes from Montreal, sometimes from New York or other northern cities—performed quite often at Green's, McCreedy's, or other taverns. In 1845 one group performed at the courthouse. The academy, however, was not made available for such commercial entertainment. The works offered seem to have run generally to melodrama and farce, usually interspersed with musical numbers.[30]

Literature in the creative category was rather more controversial. Poetry enjoyed high esteem, as it always had among the Puritans. The *Republican* encouraged its subscribers both to read and to write poetry. Local verse appeared in its pages intermittently for many years. Novels, however, were another matter. As late as 1834, the lyceum debated whether or not novel reading was beneficial. Roswell O. Barber of Beekmantown was one of two speakers on the negative side of the question. In the same year, however, the *Republican* carried large advertisements for *Waldie's Library*, a periodical which reprinted novels as well as less controversial forms of literature, such as travel accounts. In 1849 Plattsburgh's postmaster did a good business in a side room selling paperback novels.[31]

Reading was popular from the beginning. Precisely when Heman Cady first opened his bookstore in Plattsburgh is not clear, but he was among the earliest advertisers in the *Republican* when it began to publish in 1811. His offerings ran heavily to travel, especially accounts of exotic places, and to religion. In the latter category, the sermons of local ministers published in pamphlet form took a prominent place. In 1833 O. R. Cook took a full column of regular print to list the books which he had for sale. Included, in addition to the usual travel books, were Catholic and Protestant religious works, history, poetry, *Don Quixote*, Shakespeare, Plutarch, the Federalist papers, the speeches of Irish orators, and Zadock Thompson's *History of Vermont*. Another such listing in 1844 included a number of books in French. In 1848 an advertisement appeared in Latin for such works as Cicero, Horace, and Homer.[32]

Efforts to establish a library, except for those in some Sunday schools and for those subsidized by the state in the school districts, were uniformly unsuccessful. A rental library began in 1814, but its proprietor required a deposit equal to the value of the book in addition to a rental fee of twenty-five cents per day. It apparently did not last long. A village library of some sort apparently existed briefly, but in 1832 it failed. The *Republican* noted that the village library association would meet to decide the disposition of its books. Four years later the *Republican* established a public "reading room and restorateur," which it "furnished with newspapers from every section of the United States and the Canadas, Foreign Magazines, Reviews, etc."[33] There was still no library in 1850.

Periodicals published outside the area enjoyed some circulation in Beekmantown, but how extensive it was is not evident. Probably the most widely circulated were the religious journals, publications of the reform societies, agricultural periodicals, and perhaps the weekly edition of Horace Greeley's New York *Tribune*. In 1834 the *Republican* urged a boycott of the *Saturday Evening Post*, which had supported Nicholas Biddle and the national bank against President Andrew Jackson.[34]

Public lectures and debates on controversial issues assumed a high place in the intellectual life of Clinton County in the 1830s. The Plattsburgh lyceum was the organization of most importance in this respect, although it experienced competition from a Young Men's Association, which it ultimately absorbed, and later from a Literary Club, which it outlasted. In 1841 the lyceum secured incorporation by the legislature. Its speakers were local people rather than traveling lecturers. Most often the speakers were lawyers, principals, or teachers at the academy. Occasionally, there were speakers who lacked such a background as, for example, did the Beekmantown farmer who denied that novel reading could be beneficial. The topics were most often political—should the United States aid the "Texians" to gain independence (1836), should the presidential veto be abolished, should slavery be eliminated in the District of Columbia, should "emigration" [meaning immigration] be permitted? Occasionally, however, topics were more varied— ghosts, the battle of Plattsburgh, chemistry, civil engineering, the common law—to cite only a few examples.[35]

Fraternal organizations were popular from an early time and continued to be so, although at a lower level, after the Anti-Masonic frenzy of the late 1820s and the early 1830s. Masons were clearly the most important fraternal organization in the early period. In 1801 a group headed by Melanchton L. Woolsey, formerly the leader of a Masonic lodge in Poughkeepsie, tried in vain to secure permission from the state organization to form a new lodge in

Plattsburgh. In a new petition in 1806, Republican Melanchton Smith replaced Federalist Woolsey as the prospective head of the Clinton lodge at Plattsburgh. This time the state organization, headed by De Witt Clinton, approved the request. Despite the substitution of Smith for Woolsey as leader, it appears that Federalists still predominated among the principal members.

From 1806 to 1822, the Clinton lodge prospered. Membership grew from twenty-five to seventy-five. Among the members were a very large proportion of the political and religious leaders of the community. The *Republican* carried stories of Masonic activities frequently, particularly on the occasion of the celebration of the festival of St. John the Evangelist just before Christmas. In 1817 the announcement of the celebration indicated that a procession would proceed from the lodge room to the church, where the program would feature a sermon by the Presbyterian minister, an "oration" by a "companion" from the army forces then stationed in Plattsburgh, and "appropriate" music. To conclude the celebration, there was to be a formal dinner at Israel Green's tavern. In reporting similar ceremonies in 1819, the *Republican* scolded the "noisy, ill-bred boys and girls, who were incessantly opening and shutting the doors, changing their seats, and in other respects disturbing the exercises."

The decline of the Clinton lodge, begun apparently as a result of internal difficulties first apparent in 1822, became more precipitous, indeed fatal, during the Anti-Masonic movement (see chapter 14), which began about 1828. In 1832 the Clinton lodge complied with the advice of state leaders to surrender its charter, as in that same period did 420 of the state's 502 Masonic lodges. Not until 1847 did the Clinton lodge reorganize.[36]

The fraternal groups which published notices in the *Republican* in the 1830s were apparently local. The Red Indian Tribe advertised a dance. The Bachelors Club scandalized at least some elements in the community by holding a dinner at 10:00 P.M. and by continuing the tradition of public toasting in defiance of the temperance movement. There was also a social organization called Yangeese, presumably good-humored New Englanders who may have picked up the name from the Dutch-descended characters in the novels of yankee-hating James Fenimore Cooper. Two other societies identified themselves in their published notices only by initials, G.G.H. and A.F.S.[37]

The heyday of voluntary organizations was clearly the 1830s.

"Societies and associations for . . . almost every purpose are being formed in our vicinity," the *Republican* editorialized in 1836. He had heard hints, the editor added, that there was one "in embryo, to be entitled the 'Anti-going-to-see-the-Chazy-girls-so-often-Society.'" In 1844 the editor suggested the organization of an "Anti-taking-babies-into-public-assemblies-Society."[38] By that time, however, the enthusiasm for forming new groups and even for sustaining old ones had apparently begun to abate. There were far fewer notices concerning fraternal organizations than there had been in the preceding decade.

Isolation weighed heavily upon the consciousness of early settlers, but by 1850 the outside world was a constant and conspicuous influence in virtually every aspect of life. "We are all well and pretty Comfortable [here] under the North Pole," Charles Platt wrote back to Poughkeepsie in January 1786.[39] Thomas Tredwell gave less metaphoric expression to the same sense of isolation in his letters to Frederick Halsey in the early 1790s, especially in telling Halsey not to try to get a letter of reply delivered to him.[40] The relatively easy communication with both Vermont and Quebec seemed to afford little consolation to the uprooted New Yorkers. They were cut off from home.

No such feelings of isolation found expression in the 1840s. Canals had tied the area closely to the great commercial center of New York and to the Middle West. Local residents had long been informed and active participants in state and national politics. They read what was fashionable nationally, organized local chapters of the currently fashionable national societies, and in general kept current with national trends. This was hardly less true for the rural community of Beekmantown than for the more cosmopolitan Plattsburgh.

In the first decade or two, people tended to identify strongly with their towns. In 1800 Pliny Moore complained bitterly over Plattsburgh's political predominance. "Champlain," he observed, "can scarcely be in danger of Erring while she has Plattsburgh to dictate." In the same letter, however, he admitted that "although I still think this town neglected, I do not know a person in it ever was qualified to represent the county respectably" in the state assembly. He thought he would vote for Plattsburgh's candidate, Benjamin Mooers, however reluctantly. But, he hoped too that the time would come "ere long" when the people of Champlain "will be at least thought worth consulting."[41] As these remarks suggest, town rivalry was evident chiefly in competition for nominations to political office at the county or district level. However, local leaders tried to see that their own towns compared well with others in organizing support for particular causes—a political party, a temperance society, a religious or other group. Plattsburgh residents demonstrated more identification with their community than was usual in the county. Their town was the metropolis of the North Country. Its only rivals in the Champlain watershed were the Vermont towns of Burlington and St. Albans. Consequently, there was much consciousness in the community of its leadership role and great pride, for example, in its church and academy buildings. Even so, the secession movements of the various towns, such as Beekmantown, which were formed from Plattsburgh evoked no evident emotional outbreak. The people of the seceding towns apparently sought emancipation from concern with the political affairs of the metropolis and opportunity to conduct a government nearer their homes which could concentrate upon their own narrower range of problems. They seem to have suffered no pangs of anguish at the separation nor, on the other hand, did Plattsburghers wail and lament their departure.

Identification with county, state, and nation will receive extended consideration in chapter 14, but it is worth noting here that nationalism or identification with the American people and their government far surpassed feeling for any other group. The Fourth of July was observed yearly with much ceremony, although enthusiasm had diminished considerably by 1850. There was no comparable occasion identified with state or local history, although celebrations of the anniversary of the battle of Plattsburgh mingled national and local pride. Because it carried implications of antinational sentiment, "Hartford Convention Federalist" remained one of the most effective political epithets despite flagrant overuse for a generation after the event.

Proximity to Canada heightened awareness of rivalry with Great Britain and in 1839 evoked from the *Republican* the assertion that "our young Republic has already . . . surpassed the mammoth power of Great Britain." Lamenting the presumed low state of national self-esteem in 1845, the *Republican* argued that the greatest man of the last century "all and all" was Washington, that the leading metaphysician was Jonathan Edwards; natural philosopher, Franklin; poet, William Cullen Bryant; historian, William H. Prescott; ornithologist, John James Audubon; novelist, James Fenimore Cooper; painter, Henry Inman; humorist, Washington Irving; philologist, Noah Webster; inventors, Thomas Godfrey, James Fitch, Robert Fulton, and Eli Whitney—all, of course, Americans.[42] State, county, or town had never evoked any comparable effusion of pride.

Attitudes toward innovation changed considerably between the early and the middle years of the century. Initially, the prevalent spirit was one of fundamental conservatism. "Opposing all innovations" was the phrase which the Republican county convention of 1813 chose to characterize the party program. When horses first came to outnumber oxen in the county (1817), Plattsburgh's tax assessor lamented the development as very bad economy because of the higher maintenance costs for horses.[43] Like many later pieces to appear with implicit or explicit Republican endorsement (see chapter 3), the assessor's letter assumed that self-sufficiency was the natural economic goal for the town. The experience of the agricultural society around 1820 indicated also that ordinary farmers looked with extreme suspicion on innovative methods.

By 1850 Clinton County was far more receptive to innovation than it had been a generation earlier. The *Republican* still counseled, "New fangled things and thoughts at once, my prudent son, reject," but its pages were filled with indications that the advice was not so widely observed as it once had been. The *Republican* reprinted at great length, for example, Thomas B. Watson's speech to the county agricultural society fair in 1849. Watson reminded his hearers of agricultural improvements which had won acceptance within their recollection: improved plows, horse rakes, corn planters, threshers, and better methods of raising livestock and cultivating the soil. Then he explicitly rejected, as noted in chapter 4, the long popular idea of local self-sufficiency by arguing that the making of cloth was "better left to the looms of Lowell, or the manufactures of Manchester." In a similar vein, the president of the agricultural society affirmed in 1852 that "the benefits which science is capable of conferring upon agriculture are generally conceded and it may be safely stated that increased attention is given by many of our farmers to the application of science in the cultivation of their farms." In support of his assertions, it is noteworthy that nearly 1,000 of the county's 2,200 farmers then subscribed to a journal concerned with agricultural improvement.[44]

Clearly, efforts to cultivate the mind and to raise the spirits were much a part of the early history of the Beekmantown-Plattsburgh community. The depressing effects of the community's early isolation had largely disappeared by 1850. The original parochialism was replaced by a strong American identity. As will be demonstrated more fully in the next chapter, an eagerness for betterment had replaced the earlier inclination to oppose all innovations.

8

Social Reform

Social reform stirred little interest in Clinton County during the first generation, but the temperance movement in particular effected profound changes in the lifestyle of the community during the second generation when the reform spirit was galvanizing much of the nation.

Most Clinton County settlers around 1800, like other Americans at the time, consumed alcoholic beverages in awesome quantities. As is still largely true in Europe and may be becoming true again in this country, alcohol had a major role in the life of nearly everyone at every level of society. Employers supplied rum daily to their workers; militia officers "treated" the troops on training days; candidates often provided alcoholic beverages for the voters at election time; formal ceremonial dinners featured toasts numerous enough to intoxicate even the most practiced drinkers. In one form or another, alcohol was standard fare in all farm homes. Taverns licensed to sell liquor abounded. Doctors asserted that alcohol was essential to health and useful to combat fatigue. But, whereas Europeans usually drank wine or beer, Americans, reflecting in some degree the relative affluence of their society, were likely to consume the far stronger distilled liquors, or "ardent spirits," notably rum and whiskey.[1]

Early residents of the Beekmantown-Plattsburgh area probably drank even more per capita than the national average. The basic local industry was lumbering, and lumbermen were long notorious throughout the region for hard drinking and drunkenness. While farmers as a rule did not drink as much as lumbermen, John Lambert's observation (ca. 1807) that few French Canadians returned home sober from their trips to market[2] applied also to many farmers of the Champlain valley. The presence of the army during the War of 1812 and for several years thereafter by no means diminished local consumption. At the conclusion of the war, James L. Woolsey advertised 600 gallons of whiskey for sale, while the army offered 23,000 gallons which it had accumulated to meet the regular ration for the troops.[3] There is no precise information for the early period as to which were the favorite drinks, but the order was probably the same as in 1834. Then, rum still held the lead, followed closely by whiskey, while gin and brandy were also popular.[4] There were no figures on consumption of fermented beverages: wine, beer, and cider. Beer consumption was probably low, but local farmers provided themselves both amply and cheaply with hard cider, and "gentlemen," judging by advertisements in the *Republican*, imbibed significant quantities of wine.

The campaign against drinking in Clinton County began slowly and inauspiciously. In 1812 Plattsburgh's town meeting heard an oath by the excise commissioners that they would license no tavern except "where it shall appear . . . to be absolutely necessary for the benefit of Travellors." Such action, however, was hallowed by generations of usage in both English and American communities. They were attempting merely to combat the diffusion of saloons so that it would be somewhat less convenient for local folk to frequent such establishments.

More significant was the formation in 1815 of the Clinton County Moral Society. The "intemperate use of ardent spirits" was the third in a list of four targets of this society. The others were Sabbath violation, "profane swearing," and gambling. In a bill of particulars against intemperance, the organizers affirmed that drunkenness "undermines the health, wastes the estate, debases the mental faculties, sears the conscience, extinguishes the natural and social affections of the heart, brutalizes the whole man, and buries him unlamented into an ignominious and early grave and unprepared into the eternal world." Drunkards also allegedly allowed their children "to grow up in the ignorance and debasement of abject and disgraceful poverty, idleness, and their kindred vices." The founders also believed that "the example and influence of one drunkard in the neighborhood will soon corrupt five, and these five again many others. There is," the organizers concluded, "an amazingly rapid increase of vicious and profligate men, where one is suffered to perpetrate his vile actions unpunished and uncondemned." To combat all four evils, the members of the society pledged themselves to guard their own conduct, persuade friends to do the same, to publish tracts, and to work for tighter enforcement of existing laws designed to curb immoral behavior.[5]

Clinton County blazed no trail in establishing its moral society in 1815. Affirming that they proposed no "untried and visionary scheme," the organizers observed that similar societies existed in other parts of New York and in neighboring New England. Such societies were part of the reaction to the heightened conspicuousness of vice in the war years, which had also sparked a religious revival at the war's end. In New England, the moral societies were generally Federalist creations in which there was some tendency to include Republicanism among the evils to be combated. Republican zeal for the separation of church and state appeared to many old-line Federalists to weaken the means for enforcing moral behavior—a result which many Federalists inclined to believe was not uncongenial to their opponents.[6] In Clinton County, however, the moral society was by no means anti-Republican. The chairman of the organizing meeting was Benjamin Mooers, then and for many years thereafter, a principal leader of the Republican party. Its organizing committee included one Federalist, one Republican, and the Presbyterian minister.[7]

The effectiveness of the moral society in combating drinking and other "vices" is hard to judge. If the organization did much after its formation, it did so with remarkably little publicity. The *Republican* carried no notice of subsequent meetings. On the other hand, for several years after 1815, the *Republican* did print numerous poems, stories, and articles dealing with intemperance and profanity.

Probably, the Reverend Nathaniel Hewit inspired both the society itself and the newspaper campaign. Hewit was one of the three members on the organizing committee of the moral society in 1815, but he had left Plattsburgh by 1818 for a position in Fairfield, Connecticut. When the American Society for the Promotion of Temperance was formed in Boston in 1826, Hewit became one of the society's two original "missionaries" who toured the nation in very successful support of the cause.[8]

For about a decade following Hewit's departure (ca. 1818), the drinking men of Clinton County encountered little organized opposition. In Beekmantown such opposition as there was seems to have centered in the Presbyterian church. The leaders of the congregation, following a practice common in the denomination, used the dire threat of excommunication (see chapter six) to combat the evil of drunkenness. They had some success in driving drunkards out of the community. One they merely drove out of the Presbyterian church.

Abstinence became an official goal of the Champlain presbytery in 1827 upon recommendation of the church's national assembly. While the Beekmantown church was without a minister at that time, its elders, Thomas Tredwell, Jr., and George McFadden, attended the presbytery meeting. Both signed the pledge as, of course, did the two ministers from Plattsburgh, Frederick Halsey and Moses Chase.[9] The Clinton County Temperance Society took shape in 1829 or 1830 largely under Presbyterian leadership. A state organization headed by Chancellor Reuben H. Walworth, a former Plattsburgh resident, came into being in 1830. Thus, the Beekmantown Presbyterians were hardly pioneering when in 1831 they added to the covenant sworn to by all admitted to membership in their congregation the pledge "to abstain from the use of ardent spirits except as an article of Medicine."[10]

Soon, however, Beekmantown's temperance movement drew commendation from county leaders. Beekmantown, along with four other towns in the county, received praise in the report of the county society which was published in the annual report of the state organization for 1833. The society created in "central" Beekmantown that year had gained 123 members, while the older society in East Beekmantown had held its earlier membership of 80. The report from Beekmantown indicated further that "all kinds of business are performed without the use of spirits, and most of those who use it at all, do it privately. There is but one place where spiritous liquor can be had, and this is kept by professors of religion [i.e., professed Christians], who have been often importuned to refrain from the practice of making men miserable! Our hopes are that they will yet see their error and amend."[11] The culprit was probably B. J. Simonds, a storekeeper, a Presbyterian, and a staunch Democrat.

Beekmantown, like most communities in the state, was unsuccessful in achieving the state society's goal of a temperance society in every school district. There were some twelve or thirteen school districts in the town in 1833 but only two temperance societies.

Nearby Rouses Point drew high praise for having nine such groups. The difficulties of implementing this policy are evident from the records of the society in the Point au Roche district of Beekmantown. The residents, both Presbyterian and Methodist, met at the school on October 15, 1833, to form a temperance society. The fifty-three people present selected a temporary chairman and secretary and then proceeded to choose a large number of permanent officers and to consider motions. Meeting again on December 29, the society chose 5 delegates to the county convention which attracted a total of 172 delegates. Thereafter, the Point au "Roach" society held occasional meetings at the "school House on the Lake shore," usually to hear a "temperance sermon" or a lecture.

From 1836 to 1841, however, the society apparently lapsed. In October 1841, "a Few Inhabitants of Pointauroach" met again "for the purpose of reviving the Temperance Cause." By then, however, a temperance society for the town as a whole existed. Consequently, the revived Point au Roche organization conceived itself as an "auxilary to the Beekmantown Temperance Society." In its revived form, the Point au Roche society heard a sermon by Benjamin Pomeroy early in 1842 and secured sixty-three signatures to the usual abstinence pledge—binding the signers to avoid consumption themselves and also not to provide any distilled liquor to their families, employees, or guests.

Another lapse ensued until 1846, when a meeting at the "stone school Thought best to drop the old society and begin a new." The new society secured more signatures than ever but apparently followed well-established precedent by becoming dormant within a short time.[12] These cycles of action and dormancy coincided closely with those of the county and state societies.

The function of informing and exhorting the members received great emphasis in the town and the county temperance societies also. Ministers held forth on the evils which followed in the train of drinking. Doctors adduced evidence to show that "ardent spirits," far from being beneficial to health, were in fact positively harmful. Public-spirited and often politically ambitious "gentlemen" attempted to demonstrate that most of the costs of public welfare programs and of criminal law enforcement and incarceration stemmed from liquor. When local talent could no longer attract audiences, traveling speakers provided by state and national societies took up the burden. In the 1840s reformed drunkards, not always immune from occasional relapse, enjoyed great success in drawing crowds with colorful narrations of their "experience," analogous to that of religious conversion. In 1847 several leading citizens of Beekmantown wrote a letter to the Plattsburgh *Republican* commending the forthcoming appearance in Plattsburgh of a reformed drunk named Charles D. Church, who had made a favorable impression on the Beekmantown society with his speaking and singing.[13]

The progressively more extreme positions of the state and national temperance movements made education an almost unending process. Originally, the movement had sought to combat only intemperance or drunkenness. By the later 1820s, it was demanding total abstinence from consumption of "ardent spirits," that is, distilled liquors. Beer, wine, and cider were still acceptable. In the later 1830s, however, even these fermented drinks came under attack. The "Manual" for temperance leaders, which appeared in the *Temperance Almanac* for 1842, instructed the faithful to preach that alcohol in such fermented beverages was as much "poison" as that in distilled liquors and was "always injurious to man in health."[14] The proscription of fermented beverages may have had some bearing on the decline of the temperance cause in Point au Roche and elsewhere in the Beekmantown area, but the idea apparently won general acceptance among society members and in the community of Beekmantown.

To keep the movement out of politics was an early aim of leaders at all levels. They wanted merely to persuade individuals to abstain, but the disposition to impose morality upon others soon prevailed. Reinforcing that tendency was the need of the local Federalist-Whig party to find some popular issue with which to overcome the normally prevalent hostility of most voters. In 1832 temperance leader B. H. Mooers, son of the general and an office-seeking defector from the Jacksonian ranks, indignantly denied having said that within two years no one could be elected to any office unless he belonged to a temperance society.[15] Whether he said it or not, it was obvious that many people, some happily and some unhappily, believed it. In fact, two years later the *Republican* editor affirmed that in Beekmantown it was true and that efforts had been made—presumably by Whigs—to elect a slate of "temperance" candidates to local offices at the town meeting.[16]

Prohibition was gaining support. The county temperance convention meeting in January 1834 had witnessed considerable discussion of a proposed resolution favoring an end to the licensing of taverns—practical prohibition—before concluding that "fair

*The United States Hotel, like Sperry House and J. I. Green's
tavern in earlier times, was a focal point for a wide variety of
community activities. In 1839 it began operating on temperance principles "for the purpose of testing whether a Temperance House can be sustained in Plattsburgh." The answer was
no. A new owner began advertising the hotel's "Bar-room"
in April 1843.*

persuasion" was still preferable to statutory prohibition.[17] By
1837, however, the county convention had changed its mind. The
delegates voted unanimously to seek legislation to suppress the
liquor traffic. The convention of 1838 urged the state society to
organize a statewide petition campaign in favor of legislation to
stop the sale of liquor.[18] It may or may not be significant that
attendance at this meeting was less than in the past and that the
society went into decline for several years. This was also the period
when the abstinence pledge was broadened to include fermented
drinks. The place of hard cider in the Whig campaign of 1840
and the prominence of Whigs in the leadership of the temperance
movement may also have engendered some disillusionment with
the movement about that time.

The climax of the temperance movement in Beekmantown and

Clinton County, as in the state as a whole, came in 1846–1847. Yielding to the pressure of temperance societies, the legislature provided for local referendums to determine whether or not licenses for the sale of liquor should be issued in each community. At a special town meeting in Beekmantown on May 19, 1846, the vote was 187 to 29 against licensing or, in effect, in favor of prohibition. Around the state, licensing generally met defeat, but the triumph of the temperance forces was brief. Claiming that more liquor was sold illegally under the no-license system than had been sold before under the licensing regulation, the liquor interests campaigned for a rematch. Again the legislature obliged. This time Beekmantown voted to ban licenses by only 146 to 124. Elsewhere, most communities chose to return to licensing—with the result that the legislature restored it without any provision for local option.[19]

Thus, in Beekmantown as elsewhere, the temperance forces—after nearly half a century of effort—had failed to eliminate drinking or even to make the sale of intoxicants illegal. The Plattsburgh *Republican*, in fact, advertised a positively bewildering array of alcoholic beverages in 1845.[20] Nevertheless, the movement had profoundly affected the customs of the community. The custom of political candidates, militia officers, and employers providing liquor respectively to voters, militiamen, and workers largely died out. Ceremonial dinners, such as those which usually accompanied the Fourth of July celebrations, ceased to feature the succession of toasts which had made the occasion at times resemble a formal public drinking bout for community leaders. Instead, the Fourth of July celebrations in the 1840s were generally "on temperance principles." They seem also to have been less popular.

Tavern keepers, previously among the local elite and often leading political figures, lost caste. In 1837 eighteen Beekmantown Democrats cut their party's nominee for sheriff because he was a tavern keeper. He lost the town by 11 votes (138–127), although his opponent received only 1 vote more than another Whig candidate who lost the town 145 to 137.[21]

In the brief prohibition period begun in 1845, respect for law diminished, as it was to do later during national prohibition. Each year there were several convictions in the county for selling liquor without a license.[22] How many involved Beekmantown people is not clear, but it would be remarkable if some Beekmantown residents were not implicated, at least as purchasers.

Rival religious groups generally cooperated in the temperance movement. As noted in chapter 5, the Irish and French Canadian Catholics were receiving favorable notice in the 1840s for the organization of temperance groups and their participation in temperance parades.[23]

The greatest success of the temperance movement was in persuading a considerable proportion of the residents to convert from regular drinking to total abstinence. Indicative of the magnitude of this switch for individuals was the exhortation in the temperance leaders' manual of 1842 that society members spend for the cause one-fourth as much "as you would have done fifteen years ago" on intoxicating liquors. Some farmers went so far as to cut down their apple orchards to place the temptation of hard cider beyond their easy reach.[24]

The history of drinking in Beekmantown involved finally an apparent paradox. The temperance movement, like most other reform movements of the time, was largely Federalist-Whig in inspiration and leadership. Yet, Beekmantown was at once the most strongly Republican-Democratic town in Clinton County and also apparently one of the greatest strongholds of the temperance movement. A possible explanation is the rise of Methodism. Methodists from Wesley's time onward had been hostile to alcohol. They were, on the other hand, quite favorable toward the Democratic party. Thus, Methodists, more than patrician Whig reformers, may deserve the credit for changing the drinking habits of many Beekmantown farmers.

Sabbath violation, "profane swearing," and gambling, the other targets identified by the moral society in 1815, excited no such campaign as that against intemperance. The newspapers as well as the ministers expounded often on the evils of Sabbath violation and of swearing, but the people seem to have remained insufficiently motivated to launch large-scale attacks.[25] Probably both Sabbath violation and swearing were less common by 1850 than they had been in 1800 simply because proportionately more people were church members, especially Methodist church members.

In the case of gambling, there was apparently less success. During the 1828 election, the *Republican*, with no evident awareness of immorality, featured prominently its offer to take bets that Jackson would carry the county, the state, and the nation. It may be significant that such offers were not being publicized in the 1840s. But, the race track, which lured members of the agricultural society from their annual fair in 1851 (see chapter 3), was almost undoubtedly the scene of at least some wagering. That a race track existed at all was a sign of retrogression among a people whose religious leaders in 1834 had identified horse racing as a disciplinable offense.

Elimination of imprisonment for debt, a major reform objective nationally in the Jacksonian period, aroused far less interest in Beekmantown and Clinton County than the temperance movement. The only political figure to give the matter significant attention was Bela Edgerton. In 1828 he introduced in the assembly a measure to require county sheriffs to provide information concerning prisoners held in county jails for debt.[26] He believed the collection of data, such as he hoped to secure, would show several things: (1) that the number of people imprisoned for debt was greater than most people realized; (2) that three-fourths of those imprisoned were held for sums less than fifteen dollars; (3) that most individuals so incarcerated were poor; and (4) that their families suffered great hardship as a consequence. Castigating the law providing imprisonment for debt as a "vestage of the barbarous ages," Edgerton also attacked the comforting assumption of the complacent that such results were merely the natural consequence of the "lawless depravity of the labouring part of the community."[27]

The *Republican* apparently sympathized with Edgerton's views at that time, but within a few months Edgerton had fallen from grace among the orthodox.[28] When a measure to abolish imprisonment for debt passed the assembly in 1831, Clinton County's Republican representative was not present.[29]

The campaign to abolish slavery, a prominent issue in the national scene from 1830 onward, attracted relatively little attention in Beekmantown and Clinton County until the 1840s. The *Republican* gave almost no attention to the issue in earlier years. When it did so, as indicated in chapter 5, its position was consistently antiabolitionist and anti-Negro. Because the issue became so political, it is appropriate to treat it in those chapters dealing with political history.

Temperance clearly overshadowed all other reform efforts in the early history of Beekmantown. The movement excited great popular discussion, spawned numerous "grass roots" organizations for its support, and in the end profoundly altered the lifestyle of a large proportion of the people. None of the other reform causes, not even the abolitionist movement, stirred the community so deeply or altered its pattern of behavior so markedly.[30]

PART 3
Government

Benjamin Mooers, pioneer settler of Beekmantown, land speculator, merchant, banker, long-time political leader, and militia commander

9

The Constitutional
Framework

The political authority which was most important in the development of Beekmantown was that of New York State. The United States government exerted some influence, but usually in a remote, almost off-stage sense. For most of the period, after all, the men who ran it were sincerely devoted to the limiting principles of state rights and laissez faire. County and town governments, on the other hand, were explicitly the creations of the state government. They could do only what the state authorized or commanded, and the tendency was for the state to authorize little and demand much.

The role of the state government vis-à-vis both national and local authority was in some measure a legacy of the colonial experience. On the one hand, New York's elected assembly, exercising powers analogous to those of the British House of Commons, had been the principal political weapon of the people— their chief reliance for the protection and advancement of what they perceived to be their interests. During the century prior to the ratification of the United States Constitution, this situation had led to a widespread tendency to exalt legislative over executive authority and also to the development of a strong provincial identification essentially similar to nationalism. Neither of these attitudes died suddenly in 1789. In the minds of the residents of Plattsburgh and Beekmantown, they lingered well into the period of this study.

With reference to local government, New York's colonial legislature had tended to assume powers quite similar to those of the sovereign government of Great Britain, including specifically the authority to create local units of government and to fix both the powers and the duties of these governments. Following the British model and that of other royal provinces, New York granted most of the authority in local government to county officials who were appointed by the provincial government and had as their basic function the enforcement of provincial law.

Because state government was so important in the development of Beekmantown, some additional observations on the state's constitutional system are in order. Executive power was to lie with the governor, according to each of the three state constitutions of the period (1777, 1821, and 1846); but in fact the governor's authority was slight. Under the 1777 constitution, for example, the appointive power lay with a Council of Appointment of which the governor was a member, but which legislators dominated. Most of the influence a governor possessed stemmed from his role as leader of his political party, from his personal popularity, and from his constitutional obligation to make recommendations to the legislature on public policy.

The vast authority which the legislature exercised at first declined over the years as the people took more and more power into their own hands. Civil liberties guaranteed against legislative encroachment were few in the constitution of 1777, but they became more numerous in both the later documents. The appointive provisions of the first constitution gave the legislature predominant influence in the appointment of an absolutely staggering number of officials in both state and local government. By 1849, however, the people were choosing most of their local officials as well as a long list of state executive officers. The 1846 document also imposed numerous limits on legislative authority with reference to substantive matters, such as economic policy.

The right to vote was quite restricted in New York's first constitution. Framed at Poughkeepsie in 1777 while the British occupied New York City, it affirmed at the outset that no authority should be exercised over the people of the state "but such as shall be . . . granted by them." The people, however, were by no means to share equally in choosing those to exercise the powers which they granted. To be qualified to vote for governor, lieutenant governor, and state senators, the citizen had to own a freehold worth £100 ($250). To vote for members of the assembly, the wealth requirement was either a freehold worth £20 ($50) or a rented tenement worth forty shillings ($5) and payment of taxes to the state.[1]

Application of these suffrage restrictions brought interesting results in Clinton County. In 1795 the county had 336 £100 freeholders but only 288 in the lower suffrage category. In 1801 there were similarly 444 £100 freeholders to 317 who qualified to vote only for assemblymen. By 1821, however, voters in the lower category outnumbered the £100 freeholders 943 to 822.

In Plattsburgh, for which data become available only in 1807, the trend was similar. In 1807 the town had 234 £100 freeholders to 164 assembly voters, but by 1821 there were 245 assembly voters to 232 £100 freeholders.

Two conclusions of particular importance seem evident from these facts. First, the initial preponderance of £100 freeholders and later of those in the lower suffrage category reinforces the proposition advanced in other chapters that the socioeconomic level of the community was quite high at the outset and declined thereafter. Second, as time went on, the restrictions reduced the proportion of the total electorate qualified to vote for major state offices. In the county as a whole, 54 percent of those entitled to vote at all in state elections could vote for governor, lieutenant governor, and state senators in 1795. By 1821 only 46 percent could do so by the same provisions. In Plattsburgh the decline was from 59 percent in 1807 to 49 percent in 1821.

With reference to Beekmantown itself, several points stand out in the 1821 data. The first is that while in Plattsburgh 49 percent of the total electorate as defined by the constitution of 1777 could vote for the major state offices, only 38 percent could do so in Beekmantown. The second is the obverse, that while 51 percent of Plattsburgh's electorate could vote only for assemblymen, 62 percent of Beekmantown's voters were so restricted.

A third point concerns the effect of extending the right to vote to those who paid taxes on real or personal property, served in the militia (a nearly universal requirement for young men, as will be explained below), or had performed assessed highway labor and been resident for three years instead of the usual one. How any adult male in Beekmantown could have failed to meet these qualifications, which became effective in 1821, is difficult to imagine. However, their application increased the electorate by only twenty-two voters (10 percent). Thus, it would seem that all but about

10 percent of the white adult males in Beekmantown in 1821 were qualified to vote under the provisions of the 1777 constitution, although 62 percent could vote only for assemblymen and not for the major state offices.[2]

In 1826 an amendment to the constitution of 1821 eliminated the complex definition of suffrage requirements and extended the vote to all adult white male citizens.

Not only voting rights but civil rights in general became more extensive in each of the succeeding constitutions. The first, written in the passion of the internecine revolutionary conflict, omitted reference to freedom of speech and the press and to such familiar guarantees as fair trial, habeas corpus, and others. But, it did assure trial by jury and "free exercise . . . of religious profession, without discrimination or preference, . . . within this state to all mankind." In further affirmation of the separation of church and state, the constitution barred all ministers or priests from holding public office, but this provision was eliminated in 1846. Strong guarantees of freedom of speech and press were in force from 1821. Provisions relating to arrest, imprisonment, and seizure of property were added in 1846.

How did the settlers of Beekmantown and Plattsburgh fare with reference to such guarantees? While settlement came late enough to avoid the pressures for persecution which accompanied the Revolution, the exigencies of the War of 1812 were acute in the area. Neither these circumstances nor any other, however, seem to have evoked significant governmental action in violation of the civil liberties of individual residents of Beekmantown or Plattsburgh at any time prior to 1850. Three groups, however, continued to experience in Beekmantown and Plattsburgh, as elsewhere, infringement of their civil liberties by law. These were the poor, aliens, and Negroes.

Even after they won the right to vote, the poor were subject by the poor law to be deprived of their children and to be incarcerated at involuntary labor (see chapter 11) merely because they were poor.

Negro slavery existed legally for many years after the first settlement of Clinton County. The state's slave law of 1788 was in fact similar in fundamentals to those of the southern states. Slaves were such for life, and the condition of children followed that of their mother. Provisions for recovering runaways included fines against those who sheltered them. Slaves were allowed jury trials only in capital cases, and any justice of the peace could commit a slave to prison for striking a white person. Slaves were not permitted to testify in court except in criminal actions against other slaves. In 1799 the state provided emancipation at the age of twenty-eight for males and twenty-one for females who were born as slaves after that date. But, the law provided that the mother's master was entitled to the services of the child in the meantime "in the same manner as if such child had been bound to service by the overseers of the poor."[3]

Discrimination against Negroes in the laws relating to voting was severe. A law of 1811 (*New York Laws*, chap. 201, p. 287 ff.) required prospective Negro or mulatto voters to present a certificate of freedom, which could be secured only by bureaucratic procedures involving the payment of two fees. When property requirements were largely eliminated for other voters in 1821, they were retained for Negroes. Throughout the remainder of the period, Negroes could vote only if they had possessed for at least one year a freehold estate worth $250 above the total of all debts and had paid taxes on it. The value figure was approximately the same as that fixed as a property qualification to vote for governor and state senators in the constitution of 1777—a qualification which only about one in three male residents of the Plattsburgh-Beekmantown area could meet while it was in force. In addition, Negroes were required to have been citizens of the state for three years instead of merely citizens with one-year residence (constitution of 1821) or citizens for ten days with one-year residence (constitution of 1846) as required of other voters. It seems doubtful that many Negroes voted in Plattsburgh or Beekmantown before 1850. However, Plattsburgh's town meeting minutes record a few of the certificates of freedom required as a prerequisite to voting by the law of 1811 (George Tankard, 1819; Martin Tankard, 1821).

Aliens suffered discrimination of a rather different nature. They were not permitted to vote at all until naturalized. Naturalization, however, was not a difficult process. Once naturalized, former aliens suffered no legal discrimination at all in relation to voting. There was no provision for segregated schools for alien children. Laws concerning ownership and inheritance of land, however, did sharply discriminate against aliens. Until 1830 it took a special act of the legislature to permit individually designated aliens to hold title to real estate and, even after that, there were bothersome restrictions which applied to aliens only. To the end of the period, the landed property of deceased aliens in some circumstances reverted by law to the state unless a special act of the legislature permitted the heirs to take title.[4]

Both aliens and Negroes were targets of discrimination in the apportionment of representation in the legislature, which was otherwise quite equitable. Each of the constitutions required reapportionment to secure roughly equal legislative districts after periodic censuses, and such reapportionments took place quite often. For reapportionment purposes, however, both aliens and untaxed Negroes were excluded from the population figures. Thus, counties with a high proportion of aliens, untaxed Negroes, or both in their population were relatively underrepresented. Clinton County had a rather high proportion of aliens and, consequently, did experience underrepresentation.

With reference to religion, the state constitution of 1777 permitted neither preferential nor discriminatory treatment in law. In neighboring Vermont, the "hiring of preaching" was the subject which occupied the town meeting of Peacham more than any other except election of officers.[5] Yet, the minutes of Plattsburgh's town meetings for the same period are devoid of any reference to the subject. The town did possess a landed endowment referred to as the "gospel and school lots," but the record indicates that the income from this property went to schools—never to any religious purpose. The state legislature frequently incorporated religious societies of one kind or another, but it apparently did so on a nondiscriminatory basis for all religious groups which sought incorporation. The major area in which some overlap of public and religious authority occurred was in the schools, as noted in chapter 6.

Laws aimed at suppressing immorality infringed civil liberties in some measure. The law of 1788 (chap. 42) is a good example. It was really a Sabbath law banning Sunday travel, work (except of necessity or charity), schooling, fishing, playing, horse racing, and the frequenting of "tippling houses." In addition, however, it enjoined profanity and drunkenness at any time. Offenders were to be fined three shillings to be allocated for the use of the poor.

Several bits of evidence suggest that enforcement of such laws was less than rigorous. A bill which failed to pass the senate in 1820 would have required overseers of the poor to sue for such penalties, implying obviously that they had often chosen not to do so. Among the senators voting to kill the measure was Clinton

County treasurer, Benjamin Mooers. Furthermore, the Presbyterian church of Beekmantown found it necessary to take disciplinary action against some of its members for such offenses—to supplement, if not to substitute for, civil officers. While rigorous enforcement would undoubtedly have brought considerable income to the poor fund, the records of Beekmantown's overseers of the poor (see chapter 11) show no appreciable receipts from this source. Defense was a governmental responsibility of great concern. In accordance with ancient tradition, New York's revolutionary constitution of 1777 affirmed that it was "the duty of every man who enjoys the protection of society to be prepared and willing to defend it." The constitution of the United States authorized Congress "to provide for calling forth the militia [of the states] to execute the laws of the Union, suppress insurrections and repel invasions" and "for organizing, arming and disciplining the militia." The state retained the power to appoint its officers and conduct the training as prescribed by Congress. In 1792 Congress required that all "free able-bodied white male citizens" between eighteen and forty-five be enrolled in the militia by the commanding officer of the company within whose bounds he resided. Each such individual had to provide his own weapon, ammunition, and other equipment specified. Each company had to rendezvous for training yearly on the first Monday in September. They also met by regiment or battalion for exercises and inspection at the order of the commanding officer of the brigade. The most important of the detailed provisions of New York laws relating to the militia required that most officers be elected. Members of each company chose their officers by written ballot. Lesser officers chose higher officers. The governor as commander in chief designated the top officers, subject to senate confirmation.[6]

The location of Plattsburgh and Beekmantown—along the obvious and most frequently employed invasion route between the older sections of the United States and Canada—gave particular importance to its militia forces, especially in the period of hostility to Britain which culminated in the War of 1812. In 1803 the district militia numbered 1,300 under Brig. Gen. Melanchton L. Woolsey, who had held the command since the organization of the county in 1788. Although Woolsey probably owed his original appointment to the Antifederalist governor, George Clinton, with whom he had served in the Revolution and whom he supported politically

*Battle of Plattsburgh. This view is from the right bank of the
Saranac, at its mouth. Toward the left is the three-storied
stone mill, and Fort Brown is in the distance. A portion of the
lower bridge, from which the planks were torn up, is seen.
Some of the British are attempting to ford the stream. The
courthouse is on fire. The church was saved and survived until
September 1867, when it was destroyed during a great fire in
the village.*

for a time, Woolsey had subsequently become a staunch Federalist.
Probably under Republican pressure, Woolsey resigned in 1803;
he was replaced by the reliably Republican Benjamin Mooers, who
had been his chief subordinate since 1793. By 1812 Mooers was
a major general, and his command had grown to a nominal ten
thousand men organized as a division of infantry.[7]

In the War of 1812, Mooers' militia forces committed themselves, as did militia forces generally. They declined in the early
years of the war to leave American soil to invade Canada. They
conceived their constitutional function as to "repel" invasions—
not to make them. In 1814, however, circumstances put the local
militia in a position to meet their acknowledged constitutional obligation. The British had determined to invade the United States
via the New York shore of Lake Champlain with the aim, at least,
of seizing Plattsburgh.

General Mooers received orders to assemble his troops to as-
sist the minuscule regular army forces under General Alexander
Macomb. As the British neared Beekmantown, Macomb ordered
Mooers with the seven hundred, who had by then responded to

the mobilization call, to advance toward the British, to observe them, annoy them, and obstruct their progress by felling trees across the road and otherwise. The militia by no means distinguished itself in performance of that assignment and did little better later in trying to prevent the enemy from crossing the Saranac. When the British began their retreat following Thomas Macdonough's victory on Lake Champlain, the militia did pursue them and in fact took 250 to 300 captives, mostly deserters.

The militia changed little after the war. Major General Mooers remained in command of district forces and, as always, successful political figures continued to be represented among the officers. Most notable were Azariah C. Flagg and Reuben H. Walworth. In the early 1820s, Flagg was well on the way to becoming a key figure in Martin Van Buren's phenomenal state political machine. He was a major in the Clinton County militia. Walworth had been principal aide to Mooers at the battle of Plattsburgh. While he served in Congress (1821–1823), his correspondence with Flagg gave much attention to militia appointments. The Sperry brothers, politically ambitious members of the opposition, intrigued to wrest the militia from orthodox Republican hands but apparently enjoyed only temporary success.

To the lower ranks of enlisted men, militia service was merely an expensive and time-consuming burden. They were still compelled to arm and equip themselves and to appear for training and inspection. They could be fined or more severely punished for failure to meet any of these obligations. Those who could profess conscientious objection and afford four dollars could gain exemption.[8]

The state was displaying considerable restraint in the exercise of its authority over local government by the 1840s, but that authority had been vast indeed. The constitution of 1777 had blandly guaranteed to the towns the perpetual right to elect their own clerks, supervisors, assessors, constables, collectors, "and all other officials heretofore eligible by the people." But, the towns were to do so "in the manner directed by the present or future acts of the legislature." Furthermore, the legislature could alter the powers and duties of local officers at will, and it frequently willed to do so. The state fixed fees which encouraged local officials of many kinds to perform their duties; it also fixed fines which hung over the heads of many local officers to stimulate attention to duty. Until the 1840s the legislature quite often undertook to resolve problems unique to one town or county. A law of 1834, for example, directed the supervisors of Clinton County to take certain actions in order to settle a long-standing dispute with Levi Platt over payment due him for constructing a bridge over the Saranac in 1819.[9] By the 1840s the legislature was much more willing to leave such matters to local authorities or to the courts. The state was allowing more home rule in other respects as well; some of these are evident in relation to law enforcement, fiscal administration, and economic development.

For law enforcement in the counties, the state relied heavily, as had the English in earlier times, upon justices of the peace. To the state authorities who appointed them prior to 1821, the justices in each community were responsible individuals possessed of sufficient intelligence, forcefulness, and prestige to enforce order and compliance with state law upon their neighbors. The law was generous in awarding them power with which to meet these obligations. With admirable simplicity, a statute of 1787 provided that justices "have power to . . . cause to be kept all laws . . . for the good of the peace and for the quiet . . . government of the . . . inhabitants . . . and [to] punish all persons offending." Specifically, justices were authorized to require individuals who threatened the peace to post bonds to assure good behavior "and if they shall refuse . . . then [to keep] them in prison until they shall find such security."[10] A law of 1801 authorized a majority of any three justices hearing a case to impose fines up to twenty-five dollars and jail terms up to six months without a jury trial upon confession or the oath of one or more credible witnesses. Those found to be "disorderly persons" could be jailed at hard labor for six months; during that time the offender might be "corrected by whipping" at the discretion of the authorities.[11] Quite often statutes on civil matters, such as the wolf bounty (see below) and the poor law (see chapter 11), gave the justices of the peace a crucial role in implementation of their purpose.

Changes in the method by which they were chosen altered the role of the justices during the 1820s. Initially, their selection by the Council of Appointment made them the agents of the state for enforcing law upon their neighbors. The constitution of 1821 changed this by making the justices appointive jointly by the elected county supervisors and the county judges. After 1826, when justices became elected officials, they were even more clearly responsible to the people of their own community rather than to the state. This change was similar in spirit to that which led the legislature in the later years to grant more "home rule" power to local authorities and to interfere less in local affairs.

Constables were important but inconspicuous agents of law enforcement. Their chief function, judging by the payments made them by the Clinton County supervisors, seems to have been the execution of court orders relating to prisoners, witnesses, jurors, and judgments. In a similar vein, they were also required to pursue escaped prisoners and to transport paupers lacking "settlement" out of the town.[12] The records of Beekmantown and Plattsburgh contain no evidence to contradict the usual characterization of the office as one of low prestige—to be avoided rather than sought by ambitious young men.

The sheriff, on the other hand, although he was in effect only a county-level constable, enjoyed relatively high prestige, and the office was much sought after. In addition to his functions as a fee-paid agent of the courts, the sheriff was responsible for keeping the jail and the prisoners therein. Like the justices of the peace, the sheriff was at first a state-appointed officer held accountable in effect to the state—along with the justices—for preservation of order and the general enforcement of law. The constitution of 1821 had subtly fostered local autonomy by making the office elective.

Prosecution of law breakers was the responsibility of district attorneys, who were appointed by the governor until 1847. It is perhaps indicative of the importance which the state attached to the various law enforcement offices in local government that it allowed sheriffs to become elected officials in 1821; justices, in 1826; and district attorneys, only in 1847. Only at that relatively late date was the state willing to trust the people of the various counties to choose their own prosecutor instead of having the state make the choice for them. The means by which district attorneys attained office may also have some bearing on the fact that, on the whole, they did not figure prominently in the political history of Clinton County in the period of this study.

Justifying, or at least explaining in some measure, the reluctance of the state to trust local folk to elect their own law enforcement officials is abundant evidence that in fact the enforcement of many laws was most imperfect. The law required school inspectors, for example, to visit the schools in each district "quarterly or oftener." But, the minutes of the town meetings of Beekmantown for 1828 include affirmations by the trustees of several districts (see chapter 12) that no inspector had visited the schools in their districts during the year. Both Beekmantown and Plattsburgh for many years violated the spirit, if not the letter, of the law, requiring each town to keep a public pound (see below). Provisions of the poor law requiring that strangers be "warned out" of town in certain circumstances were almost certainly ignored on many occasions, as were the injunctions against Sabbath violation, drunkenness, and profanity. The list could be extended.

Raising money, spending it, and accounting for the expenditures were among the most fundamental functions of local government. The pattern of these functions was well established when settlement began in Clinton County and changed very little before 1849. The assessment of real and personal property and the collection of taxes thereon were the responsibilities of town government. The town meeting regularly chose assessors and collectors along with other town officers. From 1788 to 1800, the state allowed towns to choose yearly from three to seven assessors, but a statute of 1800 fixed the number at three. In 1845, apparently in order to insure some continuity and experience, an amendment provided that assessors serve overlapping three-year terms, with one to be chosen each year. It was the duty of the assessors to compile a list of the residents of their district of the town. They were to indicate in one column the total value of the person's real estate and in another the value of the personal property minus debts. Blank columns were to be left beside each of these for the insertion of the tax as determined by the county supervisors. Should any assessor fail to get his list into the hands of the county supervisors by the end of May, he was liable to a considerable fine (twenty-one pounds in the law of 1788).[13]

The county supervisors determined the tax rate for the entire county. Each town chose one supervisor at its annual town meeting; these supervisors, meeting together, were the basic legislative and administrative authority of the county. To determine the tax rate, they first ascertained the amount of money which would be necessary for the year. To do this they were required to consider various claims or accounts submitted and, after disallowing those which were improper, to determine the total amount to be paid. Next they calculated how much was required to be raised in order to meet various duties imposed by state law (e.g., to repay a debt for capital improvement, to pay a bounty on wolves, et cetera).

The total of these two amounts was then apportioned "equitably" among the towns, that is, in proportion to their share of the county's assessed property. To each town's share of the county tax, they then added such sums as were to be raised for the support of the poor and for other purposes specific to that town, as determined by the vote of its town meeting or in some instances by state law. To the final calculation, they added 5 percent as a fee for the collectors. They next determined the tax rate for each town by dividing the total value of the assessed property into the amount to be raised. Finally, the supervisors had to make the calculation of the amount to be collected on the real and personal property of each individual and to record the amounts in the blank columns of the assessors' list. Only then could the supervisors pass the list along to the collectors.

The collector went to work in September, which by no coincidence was also harvest time. If he had trouble collecting from any individual, he could seize and sell as much property as necessary to meet the tax, returning any surplus income to the taxpayer after the sale. If the collector failed to secure the specified amount from any person, he himself became liable for it to the county treasurer. In order to collect from the collector, the county treasurer could seize and sell his property and, if that brought insufficient revenue, could imprison the collector without bail until the deficiency was made up. After paying a predetermined amount to the overseers of the poor, the collector surrendered the balance of his collections to the county treasurer to be expended as the supervisors directed.[14]

Taxation of property was by no means the only source of revenue for local government, although it was the most important single source. Next most important was state aid, which was available, often on a matching basis, for a wide range of purposes— for killing wolves, maintaining schools, building roads, operating an agricultural society, and others. Plattsburgh also secured income by prosecuting for trespass on its gospel and school lots and later from leasing them. Surplus revenue in the poor fund could be lent at interest.

Procedure for the expenditure of the revenue secured from taxation and state aid was uniform except in the case of poor relief. The overseers of the poor, after receiving from the collectors the amount voted by the town for the support of the poor, then spent it as the law directed. The county treasurer, as noted above, received the rest of the money secured by the collectors, except for their own fees. The treasurer made payments from the funds in his hands only by order of the county supervisors. In the expenditure of funds voted by the town meetings for specific purposes, the county supervisors, of course, complied with the will of the voters. If, for example, the town had voted to raise $200 for highways that year, the supervisors approved expenditures made by town officials for that purpose—up to that amount but no more. State law bound the supervisors similarly in approving the expenditure of funds provided in state aid programs. State law often regulated the expenditure of funds raised by taxation for county purposes but, in some instances, the supervisors were free to exercise their own judgment.

The auditing of accounts to make sure that expenditures were legitimate was normally quite rigorous. In the case of expenditures for poor relief, a preaudit was provided in effect by the requirement that overseers of the poor could make no expenditures except of minimal amounts without the approval of a justice of the peace. Furthermore, the new overseers elected each year regularly audited the accounts of their predecessors; so both incoming and outgoing officials were agreed as to the precise amount of the funds on hand and accounts either due or payable when the transfer of power took place.[15]

For the other town and county expenditures, the audit procedures were of course more varied but no less rigorous. The requirement that expenditures, even of town funds for town purposes, be made by the county treasurer on the order of the county supervisors constituted a preaudit. The supervisors also performed a postaudit yearly on the acounts of the treasurer. Intermittently, the town meetings apparently did some auditing. The town meeting of Plattsburgh in 1798 appointed a three-man committee to audit town accounts. In addition, the town clerk in 1811 made a thorough audit and report to the town meeting on the very mixed-up accounts of the highway commissioners for the preceding several years. In 1840 a state law (chap. 238, pp. 251–252) required that a board of town auditors consisting of the supervisor, clerk, and justices of the peace should audit the accounts of all officers of the town. The clerk was to keep one copy of the audit for the inspection of any interested resident, while the supervisor was to present another copy to the county board of supervisors. This reduced an undoubtedly heavy auditing burden on the board of supervisors. But, the burden grew somewhat heavier after 1845, when the law was altered (chap. 180, p. 183) to require the county supervisors to audit the accounts of all town officers who sat on the town board of auditors. Thus, they had been since 1840 in the somewhat anomalous role of auditors of their own accounts. As if these auditing provisions were insufficient, when the state provided funds for specific purposes or even when it merely fixed certain obligations upon the town or county, the law frequently required an audit by state or county officers, such as a county superintendent of the poor, state superintendent of schools, or the state treasurer.[16]

All things considered, the fiscal system worked remarkably well. One local officer was found guilty of "misconduct" in 1788.[17] County Treasurer Benjamin Mooers complained to the legislature in 1798 that funds raised for roads and bridges had been improperly spent. The legislature did refer his complaint to the attorney general for an investigation which apparently failed to uncover evidence sufficient for prosecution. Mooers was "removed" as treasurer in 1830, probably for senility rather than dishonesty; he had held the office for forty-eight years.[18] The only major scandal involving public money to come to the surface in the entire period was the one involving the bounty on wolves. While public officials in this instance may have been less zealous than they should, the major beneficiaries of the frauds were not public officials but private citizens. The available minutes of the town meetings of Plattsburgh (1798–1820) and of Beekmantown (1820–1850) reveal no evidence nor even allegations of fraud. The same is true of the available minutes of the county supervisors (1811–1815 and 1829–1843). While this is of course a tribute to the system, it is also a tribute to the integrity of the officials and of the community residents who chose them.

To foster economic development was an aim to which both state and local governments devoted considerable attention. The state reserved entirely to itself both the allocation of land (see part 1) and the inspection of export products (see chapters 3 and 4). The chartering of corporations the state also reserved to itself and employed in ways calculated—according to the legislative majority—to foster orderly economic development. Corporations of an economic nature based in Clinton County before 1850 were few: two banks, one railroad, and two manufacturing corporations. None had much effect. Both Clinton County banks failed, as observed in chapter 4. The Plattsburgh Manufacturing Company received a charter in 1834 (chap. 293) with authorization to make cotton cloth, woolens, and machinery or any of those. It does not appear to have survived the depression of 1837, if it lasted that long. The Plattsburgh Iron Company, chartered in 1839, had a similarly inconspicuous life. The railroad was the subject of much legislation and dispute, but it did not become operative until after 1849. The legislature also monopolized the franchising of local services, such as ferries and water supply. In 1810, for example, the legislature authorized Russell Ransom to operate a ferry from Cumberland Head to Grand Isle for ten years. It specified that his boat must be large enough to hold four horses and be ready for service "at all reasonable times and seasons." The common pleas court was authorized to fix both the rates and the schedule of service. Anyone operating a competing ferry service was to be fined five dollars per trip. This ten-year franchise was renewed at least twice. Meanwhile, Jeremiah Parsons received a charter of incorporation in 1818 to operate a ferry service from Plattsburgh proper to the south end of North Hero.[19] In 1818 (chap. 151, p. 135) the legislature conferred on John Mallory the exclusive right to supply Plattsburgh village with "pure and wholesome" water by aqueduct. The price was to be regulated by the village trustees. A law of 1827 (chap. 22, p. 16) transferred the privilege to two other individuals. Grants such as these came usually in response to petitions of local residents after investigation by legislative committees. By the end of the period, it is evident that the legislature was backing away from such detailed regulation of the affairs of individual communities and relying instead on more general laws.

While the state did not engage in research as the term is now popularly construed, it did gather and attempt to disseminate enormous amounts of potentially useful information relating to economic development. The major effort along these lines was made by the subsidized agricultural societies, discussed in chapter 3. The state censuses which had originally been narrowly electoral in purpose became more and more economic and social. In 1845 and 1855 they afforded vast amounts of statistical data which enabled individuals as well as localities to measure their own economic performance and plan more wisely.

The economic regulations, which the state either required or permitted localities to enforce, were major concerns of the annual town meetings. Deciding which forms of livestock would be "free commoners," as town meetings were authorized to do under a law of 1788, was a matter which agitated virtually every town meeting in Plattsburgh before 1820 and in Beekmantown thereafter. While the terminology suggested that the towns possessed title to appreciable quantities of land (as had been the custom in early New England), neither town in fact did so, except for Plattsburgh's gospel and school lots. When cattle, for example, were designated "free commoners," it meant simply that they did not have to be confined but could roam the highways and all unfenced land. Perhaps because this was one of the few areas in which the town meetings could exercise any discretionary authority whatever, the regulations varied enormously from year to year. Beekmantown in the 1840s, for example, went to both logical extremes. In 1840 "no beast" was authorized to run at large, but in 1849 full freedom was extended to cattle, sheep, and hogs. It may or may not be coincidental that in 1840 the more progressive Whigs were in power, while in 1849 the more individualistic Democrats ruled. In general, cattle were the most favored. In 1810, for example, Plattsburgh voted to deny free commoner status entirely to horses, sheep, hogs, and geese but to cattle only from November to April.

Fines of considerably greater magnitude (two to ten dollars) were usual for allowing stallions, bulls, boars, or rams to run at large. In the case of rams, the town at times limited the fine to the breeding season (variously specified August or September to November or December). To what extent such fines explain the occasional notations of small receipts by the overseers of the poor remains uncertain.

Detailed fencing legislation was passed to secure effective confinement of livestock denied "free commoner" status and to bar those enjoying such status from cultivated fields. The law required adjacent landowners each to "make and maintain a just proportion" of the fence between them. If one party refused or failed to do his duty in this respect, the other could do it and recover costs from the negligent neighbor. Damages which resulted from such a failure or refusal could also be recovered. To forestall such controversies, the law allowed town meetings to make necessary regulations for "ascertaining the sufficiency" of fences and to choose "fence viewers" to enforce them. Fence viewers fixed the damages resulting from insufficient fences and as compensation received fees fixed by the town meetings.[20]

Initially at least, Plattsburgh's town meeting took these responsibilities quite seriously. In 1799 the town meeting chose two fence viewers in a manner which seemed to accord appreciable prestige to the office. But, thereafter the number tended to increase until 1806, when the voters provided that the "whole Town" should be fence viewers. Soon after its secession from Plattsburgh, Beekmantown voted (1823) to make the district highway overseers ex officio fence viewers. This action fixed the prestige rating of the fence viewers rather lower than that of the numerous highway overseers or "path masters" (twenty-six in 1825) who were in effect foremen responsible for overseeing the performance of assessed highway labor in their respective neighborhoods. In 1828, however, the town meeting voted that there should be only eight fence viewers, two for each of four districts in which pounds for stray stock were to be located. The town gave the office additional dignity by authorizing compensation at fifty cents per day. The townspeople raised the compensation to seventy-five cents in 1831 but lowered it again to fifty cents the following year.

Stray livestock created a problem which defied satisfactory solution throughout the period. A law of 1788 required that each town keep a "good and sufficient" pound and designate a pound master, who was to be allowed fixed fees for keeping various kinds of stray stock. If no one claimed a stray within six months, the pound master was to sell it and surrender the net income to the overseers of the poor.[21] Neither Plattsburgh nor Beekmantown complied very successfully with the portion of this law which required the keeping of a pound. Plattsburgh initially designated the barnyards of one or more individuals as pounds (1799). Then in 1804 the town meeting authorized purchase of a site for a pound, but it made no provision for raising the money necessary for construction until 1818. Only occasionally in the intervening years did the town meeting designate private barnyards as public pounds. When, if ever, Plattsburgh actually constructed a pound, the records do not reveal.

Beekmantown did little better at complying with the law. Until 1823 the town meeting dutifully chose pound masters, but then it gave the job, along with the fence-viewing responsibility, to the district highway overseers. In 1828 the town virtuously voted to raise $100 for the construction of four pounds. Construction apparently occurred at once and at less than the estimated figure, for the next year the town meeting voted to put the surplus from the pound fund into the poor chest and fixed a fine of five dollars for taking a "creature" from the pound without the consent of the keeper. Fourteen years later, the town meeting authorized the sale of "Two Broken Pounds" to the highest "Bider." They brought $2.56. The problem of strays had not abated. Those who apprehended strays in the 1840s were required to confine them in their own barnyards and pay the town clerk a six-cent fee to enter in the town records a description of the stock and a notation of the place where it was to be found. Some farmers made it a practice to brand or earmark their stock and record a description of the designation with the town clerk, but this was less than universally observed. There were still about ten unidentifiable strays per year in the 1840s.

To deal with the problems of sheep-killing wolves, the settlers secured considerable assistance from both state and local governments. The state law of 1790 (chap. 45) which required counties to pay a bounty on wolves exempted Clinton and Ontario counties, but in 1797 it was altered to eliminate any exemptions. Thus, from 1797 to 1799, state law required Clinton County to pay a bounty of ten dollars to anyone who presented a certificate signed by a supervisor or justice of the peace testifying that he had killed a wolf in the county. In 1799 the mandatory feature was eliminated, and it was left to the counties to decide whether to pay such a bounty. In 1801 the state authorized towns to provide such "further encouragement" as they wished.[22] Under this permissive legislation which remained in force until 1815, Plattsburgh's town meeting voted bounties which ranged from a low of fifteen dollars in 1807 to a high of forty dollars in 1815. Occasionally, the town voted bounties for young wolves (whelps) and for crows in planting season. In at least some years, the county board of supervisors supplemented town bounties with its own; for example, it awarded ten dollars for wolves in 1811 and again in 1814.

After 1815 the state paid $20 for a grown wolf and $7.50 for a whelp, but it required the counties to match these sums. Such generous provisions led to large-scale fraud, especially in Franklin County, adjoining Clinton County on the west, but involving Clinton County as well. To secure payment of the bounty a claimant had to present to a justice of the peace the head of the wolf allegedly killed in the county. The justice was to cut off and destroy the ears and, if otherwise satisfied of the validity of the claim, issue a certificate for payment which the county supervisors and treasurer were bound to honor. The most serious of the frauds under the law involved importation of wolf heads from Canada. Bounty payments records suggest strongly that fraudulent claimants were active in Clinton as well as in Franklin County. Prior to 1821 the largest amount which Clinton County paid in bounties was $120 in 1818. In 1821 the figure suddenly shot up to $840, and in 1822 it was $2,160. Under the new law of 1822, it dropped back to $40 in 1823 and only $5 in 1824.[23]

A wolf bounty of $20 voted in 1821 by the tiny Federalist town of Mooers (population 567) affords an excellent illustration of the integral nature of state, county, and town government as well as of local politics. The bounty, passed April 3 and repealed at a special meeting June 28, applied only to full-grown wolves killed in the town by town residents. However, the county supervisors at their October meeting validated certificates for the destruction of wolves in Mooers after the town bounty had been rescinded—for some killed by nonresidents and for two whelps. This required payment of a staggering $2,040 (over $3 for every inhabitant), which the supervisors accordingly levied against the beleaguered property owners of Mooers. The legislature, responding to a petition from the oppressed taxpayers, required by law that certificates not yet approved by the county supervisors be investigated by the first judge of the county. The judge was to establish that the wolf in question in each case was full grown and was killed in the town by a town resident before June 28. Claimants were also required by law to pay a fee of fifty cents to the judge for his examination of their claims. Those which he did validate were to be paid by the town of Mooers. The certificates already validated by the county supervisors were by law required to be paid by general levy on the county as a whole rather than by the town of Mooers. The enormous assessment against the town was to be used to pay only those claims validated by the first judge. The balance of the $2,040 was to be applied by the county supervisors to future assessments against the town.[24] Thus, the legislature rescued the generally Federalist residents of the tiny town of Mooers from the financial oppression which the Republican majority of the county supervisors had sought to fasten on them.

The law of 1822, drafted with much reference to the frauds under the previous bounty laws, remained in force without substantial alteration for the rest of the period. Its success may be attributed to two features in particular. First, the bounty figures (ten dollars for wolves, five dollars for whelps) were not high enough to provide great incentive for fraud. Second, the law authorized anyone in the long chain of officials who participated in authorizing or making payments to reject arbitrarily any claim regarded as "unjust." Clinton County's supervisors appear to have exercised this authority responsibly throughout the 1830s and into the 1840s. The absence of entries concerning wolf bounty payments in their records for certain years makes any generalization hazardous. However, it appears that they were validating claims for killing about five or six wolves per year in the early 1840s. There is no indication that state authorities ever objected to paying their half of the bounty in any case which the supervisors of Clinton County accepted under the law of 1822.

Several changes of importance to the people of Beekmantown and Plattsburgh altered New York's constitutional system between the 1780s and 1849. Originally, power had centered very narrowly in the legislature. Legislative leaders controlled the appointment of major state officers and also of local officeholders, very few of whom were elected. The legislature intervened frequently in the affairs of particular localities. It followed generally a mercantilist policy of large-scale involvement in economic matters. Suffrage restrictions barred about 10 percent of Beekmantown's adult white males from voting for assemblymen and almost two-thirds from voting for senators. By 1849 virtually all white adult male citizens could vote for members of the legislature and also for major state and local officers previously appointed. Furthermore, the legislature was showing much more respect for what would later be called the "home rule" principle in local government and for the precepts of laissez faire, as opposed to those of mercantilism.

Still, the legislature always fixed the framework of local government and even the duties of specific local officers. The system which it prescribed for the imposition of local taxes, their collection, expenditure, and the audit of the expenditures worked remarkably well, and in fact it required no major change. The areas of discretion permitted to the town meeting by the legislature encompassed road maintenance, welfare expenditure, schools, and the persisting problem of which forms of domestic livestock should be allowed to run at large. Except for the last, each of these functions was sufficiently important to deserve a chapter of its own.

10

Roads

Creating roads, as Thomas Tredwell had observed in 1794, was a matter of crucial importance to the pioneer settlers. Roads took priority, Tredwell explained to the Reverend Frederick Halsey, over both religion and education. In fact, throughout the period prior to 1849, the town continued to demand more of its residents for its road program than for any other purpose. Initially, those who administered the road program showed a high level of ability, but by 1849 the conduct of highway matters reflected an appreciably lower level of ability in the community as a whole.

Before 1797 the state had attempted to centralize responsibility for roads, but in that year the legislature abandoned the effort and reverted to the essentials of the road program in force during the colonial period.[1] As reformulated in the law of 1797, that program required the town meeting to choose three commissioners of highways each year. The duties of the commissioners were : (1) to record with the town clerk a description of the course of each of the town's roads; (2) to divide the town into a number of highway districts; (3) to fix a highway labor assessment for each resident; and (4) to supervise district overseers to make sure that the assigned work was, in fact, properly performed. The town meeting chose the district overseers. The commissioners could also recommend to the town meeting the collection and expenditure of money for specific road projects—those deemed beyond the capacity of the district residents but important to the community as a whole.

The obligation of residents as specified in the state law of 1797 was about what it had long been and would remain. All free male inhabitants over twenty-one were liable. The only exemptions were for priests or ministers, paupers, lunatics, and idiots. Assessments were to be "in proportion to the estate and the *ability* [italics added] of each . . . person" with a maximum assessment of thirty days and a minimum of one. Commutation fees of forty cents per day could be paid to the overseers for expenditure within the district. The overseer could require those who possessed oxen or horses and wagons or carts to make them available, but one day's work with a team and a cart or wagon satisfied three days' assessment. The law also required that the total assessment in any town must be no less than four times the number of people liable to assessment or, in other words, that the average assessment be at least four days. The overseer was to collect fines for failure or refusal to meet the assessment and could secure the assistance of a justice of the peace and constable in seizing "goods or chattels" of the offender, if necessary, to satisfy the fine.

No instructions from the commissioners to the overseers of Plattsburgh or Beekmantown have come to light. But, in nearby Peru in 1835, the commissioners used a printed form which set forth very specific requirements. Presumably, the requirements in Plattsburgh and Beekmantown were similar. Peru's commissioners instructed the overseers to assess any new arrivals or any whose names were omitted from the assessment list "in proportion to their real and personal property." Should the roads need additional work after the assessed labor had been performed, the overseer was to make an additional assessment of one-third the original number of days to each resident. Overseers were charged to get a full eight hours of work as a minimum for each day's assessment and to make sure that any substitutes were able-bodied men. They were to permit no labor on roads which had been unworked for as long as six years. The commissioners expressed their disapproval of log causeways and instructed the overseers instead, "if it is practicable, with the work assessed," to make causeways "by ditching deep on each side of the road, and throwing dirt into the middle of the road." Similar forms used in the 1820s had required the overseers to get one-half of the work done by July 1 and the other half by November 1. Instructions of the 1820s also required the overseers to have "noxious weeds" cut twice yearly—by July 1 and September 1—and to remove loose stones monthly from May to December.

Reports from the overseers to the commissioners were the subject of additional and very specific instructions. They were to be in the hands of the commissioners two weeks before the town meeting (usually in early spring). Should the overseer fail to submit a report, the commissioners had to prosecute him to collect a fine of five dollars or become liable for a fine of ten dollars themselves. Failure on the part of an overseer to perform duties other than the submission of a report made him liable to a fine of ten dollars. The commissioners were subject to a fine of ten dollars if they failed to prosecute overseers for such dereliction of duty. The reports were to list the names of all who had worked, the number of days of labor performed by each, the names of those fined, and the names of those who had commuted (i.e., paid money in lieu of performing labor). In addition, the report had to account for all money spent by the overseer. Any amount collected in excess of their expenditures had to be paid to the commissioners.[2]

For undertakings which required more skill, capital, and persistence than could be secured under the labor assessment system, the town could raise *no more* than $250 yearly by taxation. Within that limit, the commissioners of highways could recommend for approval or rejection by the town meeting such levies as they deemed appropriate. If a levy were approved, then the county supervisors added the amount to the tax to be assessed against the town. The town collector did not turn the amount over directly to the commissioners, however, but rather to the county treasurer. The commissioners got the money from him only after their accounts won the approval of the county supervisors at their annual meeting.

Town meetings at Plattsburgh in the early years always gave much attention to roads. They always needed it. Creating a road meant cutting out the underbrush and *small* trees along a defined course. Stumps had to be low enough to permit a cart or wagon to pass over them. Large trees were often merely girdled with a view to ultimate removal. Meanwhile, they had to be circumvented one way or another.[3]

Under these circumstances it is understandable that until 1806 Plattsburgh often called its district overseers "path masters." It is equally understandable that a common cause of controversy in the period of the War of 1812 was uncertainty over the precise course of roads in relation to what remained private property. The legal requirement that the highway commissioners record definitions with the town clerk was a measure designed to minimize this ground for controversy, but it was most imperfectly observed.

The report of the highway commissioners to the town meeting of 1812 stated:

> The Commissioners of highways have Continued to Experience great Inconveniency from the neglect which has hitherto Existed to ascertain Most of the roads Laid out in this Town, the Improper mannor in which they have been generlly Laid out. The Imperfect manner in which they are Described and Recorded is Constantly the Subject of Dispute and an appeal to the Records Seldom affords any satisfaction in Determining the Dispute. They Conceive it therefore of the first Importance that a Sufficient Sum be Immediately Raised to Procure a Large Map of this Town on Parchment or on paper pasted on Linnen or Cotton and to have Such Roads as are or may be hereafter laid out Should be Correctly marked on Such Map.

The records show no endorsement of this proposal.

The pioneer settlers on the whole met their highway labor assessments reasonably well. Figures are not available for every year but, as table 9 indicates, the number of days reported worked was always fairly close to the number assessed except in 1820. The large discrepancy then may be related to the separation of Beekmantown from Plattsburgh which occurred in that year. Quite often at least some of the deficiency was due to the failure of one or more overseers to report. It is possible that substantial work was done in these nonreporting districts. Thus, the figures for days worked are more likely to understate than to overstate the true total.

Bridges required large and recurring expenditures of tax money rather than assessed labor. They were the principal cause for frequent tax levies up to the maximum $250 yearly authorized by state law. Circumstances such as those reported by the highway commissioners in 1812 were typical:

> The bridge over Salmon River is Raised [by ice]. . . . The money appropriated for that purpose has been all Expended. It remains to be Covered and to have a Railing. . . . The Bridge across the Saranac in the Village has been Raised by the Ice and appears Likely to be Carried away in the Spring should there be any freshet of Consequence.

TABLE 9.

Highway Labor in Plattsburgh

Year	Days Assessed	Days Worked
1810	1,996	1,884-1/2
1815	2,796	2,664-1/2
1816	3,042	2,845
1817	3,599	3,376-1/2
1820	3,920	2,351

SOURCE: Minutes of the Plattsburgh town meetings, Clinton County Historian's Office.

They also found that the bridge on the road north through Beekman Patent was "in a verry Bad State and will Shortly have to be rebuilt." As it was on "the only road to Chazy and Champlain and the Post Road and very much Travelled," they urged that the bridge be built of stone "or otherwise that it may become Permanent and not need a yearly Repair."

After the war, bridge expenditures remained both high and recurrent. In 1815 building and repair of bridges cost $509. In 1816 the town built the recommended stone bridge over the Saranac at a cost of $500. How the commissioners circumvented the $250 yearly limit imposed by state law is not evident. In any case, the commissioners were very much embarrassed at having secured so high a tax levy in a year which proved to be one of general crop failure because of unseasonable cold. In extenuation they stated that "much work of permanent utility has however been done and a continuance of the same policy would in a few years put the roads and Bridges in such a repair as afterwards to require but little work on them." They concluded their report for 1816 with the laconic observation that one of the bridges over the Saranac was "rotten and requires to be rebuilt immediately." In 1817 the commissioners sought $250 for bridges with the explanation that two bridges over the Saranac and the bridge over Dead Creek on the post road were all so badly decayed as to be dangerous. In 1820 seven bridges were described as badly in need of repair.

Confusion in the accounts of the highway funds was perhaps

inevitable and certainly occurred between 1806 and 1810. While the full story of the numerous irregularities in those years cannot be determined, it is clear that in 1809 the collector surrendered $250 for the highway levy to the town clerk, George Marsh, instead of to the county treasury. Marsh kept $105 to meet unspecified demands of his own against the town. The town got a judgment against him for that amount in 1811, but it settled for $87 rather than risk a reversal of the judgment on appeal.

Cash expenditures for highways around 1820, even when the $250 limit was exceeded, were much below the $1,000 yearly average for poor relief at that time. However, if cash value is fixed for the labor assessed and performed on the highways, the relative cost of highway and welfare programs becomes quite different. The value of a day's labor was fixed in the law of 1797 at 40¢, but in 1827 the law authorized a tenant who performed such labor to deduct its cost from his rent at 62½¢ per day. The number of days actually worked each year on the roads of Plattsburgh varied greatly, but around 1820 was always well over two thousand and was at times over three thousand. Thus, even the most conservative estimate would rank roads about equal to poor relief in cost to the community. Probably, their cost was greater.

In Beekmantown, after its separation from Plattsburgh, the road program was similar, but the officials were less zealous. Only in 1823 is there a record of the number of days worked. Then, there were 802 days worked compared to an assessment of 1,029— slightly lower than the proportion in Plattsburgh before 1820. Another possible indication of slipping standards was the request of the commissioners in 1826 that the town meeting make a "judicious selection" of path masters for the town's advantage. Beekmantown also took advantage of a change in the law to reduce its average assessment to a little over three days. For the years 1829 through 1834, the minutes of the town meeting make clear that the total assessment of highway labor in Beekmantown was just over three times the number of people liable to service, the minimum fixed in the revised statutes of 1827.[4]

Expenditures for roads in Beekmantown were somewhat erratic. In 1823 the highway commissioners spent $148 but reported the roads still in such bad shape as to require an appropriation of $250 for the next year. Then in 1824 they managed to spend $377.19 but asked again for $250 for 1825 because the roads were still in "verry bad Condition." Expenditures continued at the maximum

*View in Beekmantown, showing one of the town's "high-
ways" and the kind of traffic it bore*

rate through 1833. In 1834 the town voted no funds at all for roads.
The next year it had to raise $147.14 to pay debts accumulated in
the previous year. Thereafter, except for $50 in 1840, the town
meeting did not vote funds for highways until 1845. Then a nonresident landowner, George M. Beckwith of Plattsburgh, urged
the opening of a road to the site of what was soon to become Clinton (now Dannemora) Prison in the western part of town. Compliance with this request brought expenditures to a high of $500
in 1846, but they dropped again to a very modest $85 in 1848.

The county supplemented slightly the funds which the Beekmantown town meeting voted intermittently for the highway
program. The revised statutes of 1827 authorized county supervisors to collect up to $1,000 yearly from the county as a whole
to be expended at their discretion to assist particular towns in meeting the costs of highway bridges. The records of the Clinton County supervisors from 1829 through 1841 indicate that the maximum
sum was imposed in every year except 1835, 1837, 1840, and 1841.
From these assessments to which its taxpayers contributed, Beekmantown received nothing at all in three years and allocations as
high as $75 only in 1829, 1831, and 1839. Beekmantown's alloca-
tion in 1839 was a healthy $209, earmarked, with the exception of
$50, for the "Dead Creek Bridge Road," which ran through a
swamp.

The explanation for Beekmantown's relatively low highway expenditures in comparison with those of Plattsburgh has several facets. For one thing, Beekmantown had no Saranac River and consequently fewer costly bridges. Traffic on the roads of rural Beekmantown was also probably less destructive than in the larger town of Plattsburgh. There was probably also a diminishing need for new roads in the period after Beekmantown's secession, compared to the needs of the earlier years for which Plattsburgh's records were examined. Furthermore, as will be observed more fully below, the state assumed more of the burden of road building after 1820 than it had before, although not much. Finally, after 1838 commutation of labor assessments against nonresident landowners gave Beekmantown for a few years a cash income far in excess of that which Plattsburgh had ever received in commutation of labor assessments.

After 1827 nonresidents could be assessed highway labor at the rate of one-fourth of a day for each $100 of appraised value, if the value of the property would be increased by the work for which the assessment was made. The assessment against nonresidents, however, was never to exceed that against residents. Under earlier legislation of a similar nature, Plattsburgh had never collected more than negligible amounts in commutation of labor assessments, but from 1838 onward Beekmantown did. In that year it assessed nonresidents 439 days or, at 62½¢ per day, $274.37. Similar assessments were made against nonresidents at times thereafter—the highest being 517 days or $323.02 in 1842. In 1845 the commissioners got an additional $105 from nonresidents but thereafter received apparently little or nothing. The utility of this source of income in relation to the need for expenditure is suggested by the fact that in 1845 the commissioners still had on hand $241 of uncommitted nonresident tax money.

Provisions to protect private rights continually plagued highway commissioners in both Plattsburgh and Beekmantown in matters relating to the laying out of new roads, alteration of routes, and the discontinuance of roads no longer needed. In 1811 three common pleas judges upheld Levi Platt's contention that the highway commissioners could not run a road through his garden but must detour around it. The court upheld the commissioners on a similar appeal in 1816.[5]

The law also permitted interested parties to seek action by petition. Such petitions required creation of a special highway jury which could fix awards for damages resulting from improper actions of the highway commissioners. The records of the county supervisors abound with references to the payment of such highway jurors. In 1846 David R. Parsons and Abraham Miller of Beekmantown petitioned the highway commissioners to discontinue a highway in the Treadwell Bay area. Their petition was approved by a highway jury and by the commissioners, only to be overruled in court. The court found that Point au Roche residents would have to travel at least one mile farther to reach Plattsburgh if the road were eliminated and that consequently it should stay.

By the late 1840s, highway administration in Beekmantown was at a much lower level than it had been in pioneer Plattsburgh. The contrast became even sharper in the 1850s. To begin with the commissioners themselves were men of lesser stature. Plattsburgh's highway commissioners in 1798 were Peter Sailly, John Addoms, and Simon Newcomb. Sailly and Addoms should need no introduction. Simon Newcomb, who came from a family perennially represented among the holders of major local offices as well as among the original investors in the mills, was supervisor of Plattsburgh in 1809–1810. Path masters of the first two highway districts in 1798 were Benjamin Mooers and Melanchton L. Woolsey. Beekmantown's original highway commissioners in 1820 included Thomas Crook and Anson J. Sperry, each of whom had taken an important role in the recent organization of the Clinton County Agricultural Society. Sperry was later an assemblyman. Highway commissioners in the later period did not include men of comparable stature.

There are other indications in the highway records of a general decline in the level of ability in the community. In 1847 a state law (chap. 455, pp. 580–581) required towns either to choose a single highway commissioner for a one-year term or to choose three for overlapping three-year terms. Apparently ignorant of the law, Beekmantown did not change its practice to accord with it until 1855. Such lapses did not occur in earlier years. In 1851 three illiterates affixed marks in lieu of signatures to a petition seeking a new road. A highway jury of twelve in 1855 included four illiterates; another in 1859 had five. There is no hint of illiteracy in any of the earlier highway records.

State aid for highways was available generally only for those portions of through routes which traversed sparsely settled areas. A road from Plattsburgh across the Adirondacks to the settled areas of the state along the St. Lawrence met those specifications. In 1805 the legislature chartered a turnpike company authorized to sell stock to secure funds with which to build a road from Plattsburgh across the western part of Beekmantown to the west line of Chateaugay. The company was organized and the route chosen, but in 1808 the company directors had been unable to sell shares "sufficient to make five miles of road, by reason of the great expense in making the same, and the small prospect of immediate remuneration for such expenditures." Accordingly, local leaders sought additional assistance. In support of their petition, they stated that there were just two houses in thirty miles along the most direct and most suitable route and that the ground was "extremely stony."[6] This request to the legislative session of 1808–1809 received extended study by an assembly committee in 1811. A lottery authorized by the legislature raised $5,000, which commission members, including Sailly, promptly expended without extending the road any great distance. After the war the United States army forces at Plattsburgh went to work on the road. They had it completed for twenty-four miles when a federal economy program removed them from the scene. The remaining stretch of fourteen miles lay in the most difficult terrain.[7]

To complete the road, Charles Platt and others petitioned the legislature in 1822 for $9,000. Such an amount, the petitioners stated, would enable them to complete the road from the west end of the "military road" in Mooers to the Franklin County line. They promised to repay half of the $9,000 appropriation with interest in two years. The other half was to be state subsidy. Edward Livingston reported favorably from the senate committee which considered the request. The project, he affirmed, had "considerable public interest." It was in effect an extension of the recently completed Champlain Canal in that it would permit commerce to flow from the growing settlements along the St. Lawrence to the Champlain and Hudson valleys as well as to Canada. There was, he admitted, a road of sorts across the difficult fourteen miles, but it was "almost impassable." Its improvements would not only increase commerce within the state but also enhance the value of state-owned land along its route.[8]

With this endorsement, the legislature approved a scaled-down version of the original request. The total amount appropriated was $7,000 rather than $9,000. While the state agreed to donate half, as originally suggested, it declined to lend the other half as had been proposed. Instead, it merely authorized the two counties to raise equal portions in two years of taxation. The commissioners named to make the expenditure were Benjamin Mooers, Abijah North, and Thomas Smith. By 1823 twice-weekly stage service linked Plattsburgh to Ogdensburgh on the St. Lawrence. Those who used the road had to pay tolls along the less settled portion of the road. In renewing the authorization to collect tolls in 1843, the legislature exercised its prerogative to determine which sections could be repaired with toll revenue and to allocate a portion of the tolls for the building of a bridge over the Chateaugay River.[9] No other road traversing Beekmantown received significant state assistance prior to 1849.

In a general way, the history of governmental effort to provide roads and bridges in the Beekmantown area seems to underscore the thesis stated earlier that the socioeconomic level of the inhabitants was relatively high in the first generation and declined significantly thereafter. In the first generation, men of very considerable ability worked competently within the framework of the town's prescribed political system to create an adequate network of serviceable roads. By the 1840s the level of competence, reflected in some measure in a declining rate of literacy, had fallen, and the system clearly was not working as well as it had earlier. Partly perhaps for this reason, the state was assuming a larger role in the road program, particularly in helping to provide through roads in sparsely populated areas. In any case, road work remained generally the most expensive function of town government throughout the period. The administrative pattern for its performance was little different in 1849 from the traditional practice of colonial times, which the state had prescribed by statute in 1797.

11

Welfare

.

New York's laws concerning public assistance to the unfortunate maintained at the outset the essentials of ancient English practice. The overriding consideration was not how the unfortunate could be helped or rehabilitated with kindness and in dignity but who would pay the bill for the minimum assistance required. If close relatives could be found, responsibility devolved legally on them. If no relatives could be found who were capable of bearing the burden, then the elemental rule was "every . . . town shall support . . . their own poor." From 1788, when a revised poor law (*New York Laws*, chap. 62, pp. 731 ff.) thus restated the old premise, until 1823 New York's poor laws, as in the past, concerned themselves in large measure with determining precisely where one town's responsibility ended and another's began.

Responsibility in such matters followed "settlement." Those who were "settled" according to law in one town became its responsibility in case of misfortune. One gained settlement under the law of 1788 by renting a local tenement with twelve pounds yearly rental for two years, holding public office for one year, paying local taxes for two years, or serving locally as an apprentice or bound servant for two years. A newcomer who gave notice of his arrival to the town's overseers of the poor within forty days also gained settlement at the end of a year if not "warned out" prior to that time.

To prevent prospective public charges from gaining settlement, the town expected the overseers of the poor to bring them before two justices of the peace for examination. If the apprehensions expressed by the overseers could not be allayed to the satisfaction of the justices, they might order "transportation" of the individuals to the constable of the next city or town, "through which such stranger shall have been suffered to wander and stroll unapprehended, and so from constable to constable, . . . to the place of legal settlement of such stranger." Under the original law, a person thus transported was liable to be whipped (thirty-nine lashes for a man, twenty-five for a woman) if he or she returned. Those whose condition precluded transportation could be aided where they were and the cost recovered from the town in which the recipient possessed a settlement.

Affording "shelter" to an unfortunate stranger thus appeared almost an offense to society. Anyone who sheltered a person lacking settlement could be required to post a bond of one hundred pounds and could be jailed indefinitely if he were able but refused to do so. If he could not do so, his guest was transported. An individual who "entertained" a stranger for fifteen days without giving written notice to the overseers of the poor was liable to a fine of forty shillings to be divided equally between the poor fund and the informer.

To secure assistance, a person possessing settlement applied to the overseers of the poor. They presented the case to a justice of the peace, who could order such relief as he deemed proper to be administered by the overseers. If such "temporary" relief afforded to individuals in their own homes proved inexpedient, towns were authorized to establish workhouses (also called poorhouses) and to require relief clients to reside there as a condition of receiving aid. In such houses, work was demanded of all who were able. Towns could also contract with a local resident to care for all the indigent or could auction them to townspeople for support. Neither Beekmantown nor Plattsburgh ever chose either of the last two options.

Children whose relatives were unable to provide for them were to be "bound out" or apprenticed by the overseers of the poor with the consent of two justices of the peace. The individuals who thus relieved the town of immediate responsibility for such children were entitled to their service until they reached twenty-one, if boys, or eighteen, if girls. In return the masters were required to provide subsistence, a minimal amount of "schooling," and vocational training as specified in a contract or "indenture." Any child who refused to be bound out could be jailed until he changed his mind.

These were the essentials of the welfare system in force in New

York before 1823.[1] How did it work in Plattsburgh and Beekmantown? No records of Plattsburgh's overseers of the poor are known to survive, but the town meetings often considered welfare matters. Until 1810 the chief function of the overseers of the poor seems to have been to manage the surplus money in the poor fund. In 1802 the town meeting instructed the overseers to keep back fifty dollars and to invest the rest of the poor funds at interest in call loans. Precisely how the fund had built up is not evident. It is clear that tavern licenses and fines for such offenses as swearing, drunkenness, killing deer, and allowing a ram to run free in breeding season were earmarked for the use of the poor. Probably, as was clearly true in nearby Peru, income from tavern licenses far exceeded that from fines.[2]

In 1810 Plattsburgh's poor fund ran a deficit of $67.35, and from then on the overseers of the poor were welfare administrators more than money managers. In 1811 the town meeting voted to raise $200 for the poor. In 1817, following a bad crop year, and again in 1819, a year of depression, authorizations were for $500. These were the largest expenditures voted by the town meeting for any purpose up to that time. With no county or state aid in prospect, the town naturally began to look for ways of reducing its burden.

The establishment of a town poorhouse or workhouse was the means decided on to reduce welfare costs. As early as 1806, the town had resolved that "the old Block House or Court House So Called Shall be Repaired with a Brick Chimney and Glased and be a Poor House and that the Poor that is able to work Shall be made to work in the Same under the Care and Direction of the Poor Masters [an alternate designation of the overseers of the poor] and Justice[s] of the Town who are Superintendents to the Same." Nothing came of this but, in 1817, the year of the first $500 authorization, a committee consisting of Levi Platt, Louis Ransom, and Melanchton Smith was designated to study the "practicability of establishing a work house for the poor."

In their report the following year the committee stated

> that the number of Poor in the town has gradually increased
> . . . ; since which a greater addition has been made to the
> former number owing in part to emigration from Canada,
> and from the eastern shore of Lake Champlain (immediately
> from Vermont). That they are not informed of any effectual
> remedy against persons so emigrating to be transported out
> of the limits of the County. That the persons alluded to are

generally of idle, loose, dissolute, or dissipated habits; many of them with large families, who are brought here to suffer want among strangers and to avoid the shame which must necessarily attend their conduct near the places where they are Known. To unite usefulness and economy your Committee report that it would be advisable for the town meeting to pass the following Resolutions.

The resolutions were five in number. The first provided that the committee pick a site of at least one acre between one-half mile and one and one-half miles from the courthouse and build a workhouse thereon at a total cost of no more than $1,500. The second stated that the money should be raised by tax. Third, the "said work house and poor house" be supervised by a superintendent who will "direct the mode of gardening." Fourth, all the labor of the paupers should be directed by the poor masters and the superintendent under their supervision. Finally, the proceeds of the labor should be "exclusively applied to the relief of the poor in said poor House and that the Poor Masters be directed not to give relief to any poor persons whatsoever out of the said poor House unless from sickness or other disability they shall be unable to be removed thereto."

The proposed budget for the operation of the poorhouse during its first year was as follows:

Interest on $1,500 at 7%	$105
Pay of supt. and board	150
Medical expenses including doctor	100
Board of the paupers who will average 10 throughout the year at 4 shillings per week "which is believed will be sufficient"	260
Firewood and clothing	155
	$770

The estimated yearly expense of $770 contrasted with the expenditures of recent years, which averaged about $1,000, plus $150 expended yearly by private charity and the Ladies Society. Thus, the committee concluded, the construction of a poorhouse would permit "a Saving to the town per annum [of] $380 dollars." The committee's figures on recent expenditures were somewhat inflated (see below) but not enough to invalidate the conclusion.

In a final recommendation, the committee urged that the legislature be asked to authorize appropriation of part of the glebe land or glebe money of the town to support of the poor. No evidence

TABLE 10.

Cost of Poor Relief in Plattsburgh, 1817–1822

Before Poorhouse	Transition Year	After Poorhouse
1817 $888.85	1819 $883.36	1820 $650.83
1818 $921.09		1821 $586.06
		1822 $720.75

SOURCE: Minutes of the Plattsburgh town meetings, Clinton County Historian's Office.

which has come to light indicates that the town ever received such authority. The town meeting approved the committee report and proceeded to implement its major recommendations. In reply to an official state inquiry in 1824, Plattsburgh's supervisor reported on the success of the system:

> We have a poor-house and three acres of land which was purchased in 1818. There was raised for that purpose the sum of $600 rather than the maximum $1,500, and the poor were removed to the said house in the spring of 1819. The lot is occupied as a garden, and the male paupers are kept at work in the same, as far as they are able. The females are employed in knitting, sewing, and any other work which they are able to do. A female is employed for the purpose of cooking, washing, etc. and is paid wages for the same. The poor masters have the whole under their immediate control and superintendence.

That the poorhouse system had reduced costs, he demonstrated by listing the total annual expenditures for town and county poor from 1817 through 1822 (see table 10).

In each of the three full years of its operation the poorhouse expenses had been appreciably less than the $770, which the committee had estimated as its annual cost. In seventeen other towns which made reports on the operation of poorhouses in 1822, all but one had still lower expenses per pauper than Plattsburgh. In this action of 1818 requiring the poor to accept incarceration as a condition of receiving public assistance, Plattsburgh was in the vanguard of a reform movement which found reflection in New

York's alteration of its basic poor law in 1824 and in the drastic overhaul of England's Elizabethan Poor Law in 1834. The goal at Plattsburgh, however, was reduction of cost—attaining moral regeneration of the inmates was not such an inspiration as it was in the later movements.[3]

The transfer to the poorhouse system in Plattsburgh coincided with the movement for the creation of Beekmantown as a separately governed community. While Beekmantown had rather more than one-fourth as many people as Plattsburgh (1,343 to 3,519 according to the census of 1820), it was agreed that Beekmantown would receive one-fourth of the $549.50 in the Plattsburgh poor chest, plus $73.00 for its "one fourth Part of the Poor house lot and furniture." On the other side of the ledger, Beekmantown agreed to take "one fourth Part of the Present poor . . . to Support." Fortunately, there were not many poor on hand at the time. Mrs. Amen Williams was Beekmantown's "full Quota of the Present Poor," while Plattsburgh took Robert, Otis, and Henry Sinford "for there Quota of the Poor."[4]

Beekmantown was well prepared to meet its responsibilities to Mrs. Williams and to future unfortunates. Its poor masters, Luther Drury and Ira Howe, received $110.10 as the town's share of the Plattsburgh poor chest, $73.00 (not paid until 1823) for its share of the poorhouse, plus $100.00 voted by the first town meeting and paid over by Collector Cromwell Pearce (spellings vary). In addition, the interest on notes of several individuals, "excise money" (tavern license fees), and numerous small sums from named individuals (presumably fines of one kind or another) supplemented the resources available to the poor masters.

The drain on the poor fund of Beekmantown was relatively slight. The audits in February or March of each year continued to show a healthy, often an increasing balance: $151.59 in 1821, $121.81 in 1822, $250.57 in 1823, and $245.83 in 1824. Never after its initial authorization of $100.00 in 1820 did the town meeting vote additional funds for the poor. The gratifying contrast to Plattsburgh's record of increasing welfare costs under the same system was due apparently to the rural character of Beekmantown. The diligence of the poor masters in "warning out" those who might become public charges may also have helped keep welfare expenditures at a low level.

The only such warnings to appear in the surviving minutes of the town meetings of either Plattsburgh or Beekmantown are those recorded in Beekmantown in 1820 and 1821. In the first instance,

Rebecca, Polly, Jane, and David White were given "legal Warning to depart out of the town, . . . as the Law directs." In the second, Poor Master Luther Drury "warned to leave Beekman Town forthwith" the families of William Castor, Henry Lampman, and John Ellis Warren. It seems likely that the major purpose of warning out was to lay a legal foundation for fixing financial responsibility on another town in the event that the persons in question did become public charges. Whether or not those warned out actually left town is open to some question. The absence of transportation expenses from the records plus the fact that warnings to depart occurred only in the first two years of Beekmantown's existence suggest that after 1821 the town tacitly agreed to stop trying to evade responsibility for new arrivals who became indigent.

Transportation of the indigent did occur in a few instances in the nearby town of Peru. In 1818 the town paid one of its residents $8.75 for "carrying back a foolish (i.e., retarded) boy that was left at his house." In 1824, after providing several weeks of assistance (including eight quarts of rum) to an ailing immigrant, the town authorities terminated their obligation by conveying the man to Montreal. The financial pressure underlying such actions is evident in that during 1827 the town of Peru paid more than $1,000 to assist twenty-two indigent "furiners."

Transportation of the indigent was indeed in strong disfavor throughout the state. In the monumental report on poor relief compiled by Secretary of State J. V. N. Yates in 1824, the tradition of transportation came in for frequent criticism. Litigation and other expenses arising from the practice took one-ninth of all funds spent on poor relief, and the system was often cruel to the sick.[5] Accordingly, the law of 1824 (chap. 331) eliminated transportation except among towns within the same county, but the system came creeping back in future years as will be observed in relation to the records of Clinton County's supervisors.

The relative paucity of paupers in Beekmantown (one in 1823 to Plattsburgh's fourteen) apparently enabled the community to deal rather more generously with them than did Plattsburgh, where they had to accept confinement to win aid. The contrast is even sharper when one examines the record of Beekmantown's northern neighbor, Chazy. In reply to Secretary Yates' inquiry, Chazy's supervisor wrote:

There is no poor house or house of industry, but the authorities of the town have for four years past, at the annual town meetings [!], sold at public sale all the poor of the town; this mode of proceeding has been the means of lessening the expenses for the support of the poor, from the year 1817, at least two-thirds. For none, except those that are objects of charity, will apply to the town for assistance, and be exposed for sale and liable for labor. The poor in this way are provided for much better, as the person who bids them in, gives bond for his faithful performance. In this way, there is no expense charged to the town for services, as the poor masters and justices have nothing to do but make out the bonds.[6]

In a less optimistic view of the system, Secretary Yates affirmed that it was "exceptionable in its principle," that under it the poor were "frequently treated with barbarity," and that the education of children was almost totally neglected.[7] It may be only coincidental that the town which employed this system was normally Federalist in its voting, while Beekmantown which did not was normally a bastion of Jeffersonian Republicanism.

The recommendations which accompanied the revelations of the Yates report in 1824 led to many changes. Indeed, some became effective the same year.[8] While no uniform system existed for decades, the laws relating to Clinton County can, at the risk of some distortion, be stated briefly. First, "indoor" relief replaced "outdoor" relief. What that meant was that, except in emergency circumstances, the unfortunate could no longer receive assistance in their own residences but were required to accept virtual confinement in county poorhouses in order to qualify. The great object of this reform was economy. Poorhouses had demonstrated, as in Plattsburgh, that their establishment did materially reduce the costs of poor relief. In part this was due to obvious advantages in supervision and administration. But, as was widely recognized, the economy occurred also because many of those in need chose to suffer unaided rather than experience confinement in the company of derelicts, drunks, prostitutes, idiots, the insane, the senile, and those with perhaps contagious diseases. As one supervisor reported to Secretary Yates: "The bare name of a county work house appears to strike a dread on paupers; and when sent to said house, the overseer informs us that he is not troubled with their company but a short time."[9]

Another fundamental change was to transfer major responsibility from the town to the county. Previously, the town had borne full administrative and financial responsibility for its own poor. Now relief was to be administered as largely as possible through poorhouses built and operated by county officers. The town still had a considerable role, however. The needy were to apply to a town overseer of the poor for assistance. He was to take the applicant before a justice of the peace for examination. The justice, if he believed relief required, was to issue a warrant to a town constable to deliver the person to the keeper of the poorhouse. The keeper was required to afford aid "as . . . necessities shall require," but the county superintendents of the poor decided how long the individual remained. The towns were required to accept at least partial financial responsibility for those with "settlement" who were admitted to the poorhouse. However, in 1828 the legislature authorized counties which chose to do so to abolish the distinction between town and county poor and thus to make the county responsible for all relief expenditures.[10] Clinton County promptly chose to do this.

Construction of a county poorhouse, as encouraged by the law of 1824, had not come quickly in Clinton County. It was not until December 1826 that the supervisors advertised for a site for a poor farm and for construction plans. The following April, they announced the purchase of a ninety-acre farm in Beekmantown from Ebenezer Allen and solicited bids for construction of a hillside building fifty-four by twenty-eight feet; it was to be two stories in front but only one in back.[11] Precisely when the building was completed remains unknown as the records of the supervisors for those particular years were not to be found. But, the expenditures which they approved in 1829 included $726 as the last installment on the poorhouse and lot plus $1,805 for its operation during the year. The supervisors also chose five superintendents for the poorhouse, including Thomas Crook of Beekmantown.

With the opening of the Clinton County poorhouse, probably in 1828, Beekmantown's welfare functions began to alter considerably but not as rapidly as the law provided. The most fundamental change was financial. Under the law of 1824, Beekmantown was to be charged with the cost of relief administered by the county poorhouse to those who had settlement in the town. It was also to bear the cost of relief to those with settlement whom its own overseers of the poor afforded emergency assistance. As noted above, both these obligations ceased in 1828, when (as authorized by state law) the county assumed financial responsibility for all relief expenditures. The law of 1824 also deprived the towns of the income from fines and license fees collected in the town. Revenue from these sources now went to the county. Thus, Beekmantown's overseers of the poor, while still chosen by the town meeting, had become in effect administrative agents of the county program. Under these circumstances, the accounts of the Beekmantown poor fund might be expected to have been closed out soon after 1828. In fact, the overseers of the poor continued to administer the town poor fund until 1835. They were able to do so because payment of principal and interest on loans from the poor fund continued to provide income for some time. Reflecting a desire on the part of the townspeople to take care of their own, even though the county had accepted the obligation to do so, the poor masters also continued to make some expenditures for welfare clients. Like the residents of some other communities, those in Beekmantown apparently considered that the county system was harsh and unsympathetic.

The records of Beekmantown's overseers of the poor after 1828 reflect their dual role as agents of both county and town. Some entries note only that an individual was "taken on the county to support." Presumably this meant that the overseers as county agents took the individual to the poorhouse and turned him over to the county authorities for assistance. A few entries indicate that a specified amount was expended as "temporary" relief to a county pauper. These expenses were charged to the county rather than deducted from the town poor fund. Numerous entries, however, were clearly charged to the town poor fund with no intention of claiming remuneration from the county. Such entries are common through 1830 but diminish rapidly thereafter. The last was made in 1833.

In closing out the account, the town voted to appropriate $70.00 for schools in 1831 and again in 1832; its final balance, $46.03, went for highways in 1835. Thus, the poor fund of Beekmantown had operated with a chronic surplus.

Beekmantown records rarely specified the nature of the relief afforded or the circumstances which required it. The usual entry in the books was only "for the relief of" a named individual and the amount. An exception was the very first payment made on September 30, 1820. Its recipient, a foreign pauper named Charles Gypson (spellings vary), was supported ten weeks at $1.50 per week and given in addition fifty cents worth of medicine and "1 Pare of overall[s]" costing $1.50. Notations of medical expenses appeared fairly often. A frequent conclusion to a string of entries was a payment for funeral expenses, which most often ran about $5.00 but were at times appreciably lower or higher. In Peru, where records are more complete, the major categories of relief recipients were the ill, especially foreigners newly arrived, the aged, and orphan children.[12]

Recipients of assistance from Beekmantown's overseers were a varied group. Many were French. A few were clearly Irish. None could be identified as members of the Negro community.

With the closing of its poor fund in 1835, Beekmantown ceased to have any role in welfare administration except to choose overseers of the poor, who acted as local agents for what was otherwise entirely a county welfare program. But, Beekmantown property owners paid taxes fixed by the county supervisors to support that program. License fees and fines collected in the town also supported it, and many local residents became relief recipients. For these reasons, as well as because the county poorhouse was situated in Beekmantown, it is appropriate to see how the county system worked from 1828 to 1849.

A quick statistical survey at the outset may afford useful perspective. Between 1830 and 1849, the years for which figures are easily available,[13] the number of persons received annually into the poorhouse varied from a low of 131 in the prosperous year of 1836 to a high of 310 in 1833, the aftermath of the cholera epidemic of 1832. The figure was still under 200 at the end of the period, but by then many people (286 in 1849) were again receiving temporary assistance outside the poorhouse in other than emergency circumstances.

Operating costs of the poorhouse in the years for which records of the supervisors are available (1829–1843) were always the leading county expenditures. They appear to have ranged between $2,000 and $5,000 yearly, while the cost of temporary or outside relief was between $300 and $1,000 during the 1830s and early 1840s. By the end of the 1840s, expenditures for the two forms of relief were nearly equal. In 1848 temporary relief costs were slightly over $2,000, while the poorhouse costs were a little under that figure. Transportation of paupers was never eliminated, although the record of expenditures for that purpose indicates that it was minimal except at the time of the cholera epidemic. The yearly cost per inmate of the poorhouse varied from a low of $18.51 in 1832 to a high of $46.48 during the depression year of 1837. Every year there were births and deaths, but the latter outnumbered the former two or three to one. The proportion of foreign inmates was always high, especially during the cholera scare. There were always a few insane, nearly always one or more feebleminded, and quite often one or more deaf mutes.

The only glimpse inside the poorhouse in these years is afforded by Dorothea L. Dix, who visited the institution in the course of her investigations in the campaign to alleviate the lot of the insane. The Clinton County poorhouse, she wrote, in her 1844 memorial to the legislature

> is not a good building, and much out of repair; it is not large enough for the number thronging to it in the winter. It is distinguished by a remarkable neatness throughout. I visited this place on a stormy day, at an unexpected and unseasonable hour; it was doubly gratifying to notice a place of so much comfort and quiet, made so by the uncommon care and capability of the master and mistress of the house. Here the sick were in well arranged apartments, and well attended; the household suitably and neatly clothed; garments well made, and in *good repair*; clean beds, bedsteads, and bedclothing; clean tables, chairs and floors; clean walls and clean windows, showing that neither the application of whitewash, or water and the scrubbing brush were spared. The kitchen in good order.

This contrasted with her frequent findings elsewhere as, for example, in neighboring Essex County, where she found the beds as well as the floors, walls, and woodwork "*greatly* neglected" and all but two apartments of the poor "ill-kept." [14]

The treatment of the insane at the Clinton County poorhouse Miss Dix described as follows:

> There were here at the time of my visit in October, no insane in close confinement. I saw in the house, seated quietly by the fire, an insane man, who formerly, before the present master of the house was appointed, was kept chained to a post in the barn, in a state of complete nudity, "receiving," said my informant, "no other care than to have his food tossed to him like a dog—and not always cooked." The poor wretch had been released for a considerable period; was washed, dressed, and taken into the house, where he partook of his meals with others of the family. He occasionally ren-

dered some little assistance in bringing wood and water. Great care was requisite in managing him: he was subject to outbreaks of violence, and really was an unsafe inmate; a proper subject for hospital treatment, or for an asylum adapted for such cases. This crazy man bore marks of former "lashes of the cow-skin, applied to drive the ——l out him," as was significantly said.

An insane female was assisting about some household work, and though often much excited was still kept pretty tranquil a large part of the time, by patient care. In most families I have found such cases subject to close confinement.

Compassion was deeply moved at seeing a little girl, about nine or ten years of age, who suffered the fourfold calamity of being blind, deaf, dumb and insane. I can conceive no condition so pitiable as that of this unfortunate little creature, the chief movements of whose broken mind, were exhibited in restlessness, and violent efforts to escape, and unnatural screams of terror. No gentleness or kindness seemed to sooth her, or to inspire confidence. Various methods had been tried to promote her comfort, but with little success. She would rend her garments and bed clothing to pieces, and seemed most content when she could bury herself in a heap of straw; when food was presented, she swallowed it with avidity, and seemed indifferent to its kind or quality. It was necessary to watch her with great care. To promote her comfort at one time, she was removed from the cells and placed with other persons in a large room, fastened by a small chain to the floor, to prevent her from falling upon the heated stove. She resists control, and perpetually struggles to escape. If left at large in mild weather, for a few minutes, she gropes her way, and conceals herself beneath a bush or fence; when brought back she resists violently, and utters the most vehement out-cries. I took her hand gently, but she fell into the wildest paroxysm, which passed by, only when she had concealed herself in the straw in her cell. The utmost care was taken to keep her clean, and to do all for her comfort that her unhappy condition permitted.

There is at this house no provision for the insane who are at any time too violent to be permitted at large, except low, dismal cells, fit for no use, and which should never be employed for any persons of this class. The true remedy will be found in State asylums, on a cheap, but comfortable plan for the incurables.[15]

Dix might have strengthened her case had she mentioned that in 1826 a female inmate killed the keeper of the Plattsburgh poorhouse but was found not guilty of murder because of insanity.[16] The number of the insane, feebleminded, and deaf mutes in the Clinton County poorhouse had diminished by the later 1840s, but it is not clear why. It is true that specialized institutions for the care of the blind, the deaf and dumb, the feebleminded, and the insane were being established in New York State, but their effect on the Clinton County poorhouse is uncertain. The county supervisors allocated twenty dollars in 1840 to pay the tuition of Rosetta Crawford to the New York Institute for the Deaf and Dumb, which had been operating since 1817 and had been subsidized by the state since 1822.[17] The next year the supervisors allocated forty dollars to pay tuition at the same institution for any of its inmates "whose tuition the County of Clinton is liable to pay for the year 1841." There is no indication that the county sent anyone to the institute for the blind which opened in New York City in 1831 and to which each senate district was entitled to send a number of blind persons at state expense after 1839. This might have been done, however, without action by the supervisors. The establishment of the first state asylum for the insane in 1843 came just at the end of the period for which there are surviving records of the county supervisors. The first institution for the feebleminded was not set up until shortly after 1850.

Dependent children were always a major welfare problem. The number in the Clinton County poorhouse between 1830 and 1849 varied erratically, but there were never fewer than ten or more than fifty. The legal requirement that these children be afforded education was only imperfectly met. In 1830 there was apparently no instruction at all for the ten children under sixteen years old then in the institution. At the other extreme, a school was reported in operation all twelve months the next year, and in 1836 the number reported instructed was more than double the number of children present. The reported length of the school term also varied suspiciously from year to year. Usually it was six or seven months, but in 1849 it was down to three. In order to secure a better environment for the children as well as to reduce expenses, "binding out" was a common practice. The highest numbers bound out were sixteen in 1834 and twenty-eight in 1843. While the results were no doubt improvement for the child in many cases, it is also likely that those reported in the press as runaways included at least a few who suffered oppression.

Calculations in the annual reports of the secretary of state as to the incidence of pauperism are probably not very reliable, but they seem to suggest that the rate in Clinton County was rather above the state average. In 1830, for example, Clinton County provided assistance outside the poorhouse to one pauper for every 131 inhabitants, while the comparable state ratio was one in 209. One poorhouse inmate was reported as of December 1, 1830, for every 449 county residents, but the state average was one to 622. The probable explanation for the high rate in Clinton County is the heavy traffic of immigrants, both European and Canadian, via Lake Champlain.

Several significant changes relating to the operation of the county poorhouse occurred between 1830 and 1849. Temporary relief, that afforded to the unfortunate in their own homes instead of in the poorhouse, was again in vogue by 1849, indicating that the economy-oriented program of limiting assistance to those willing to accept compulsory residence at the poorhouse had failed. The labor of the inmates toward their own support, which had been valued at over $2,000 annually in 1832 and 1833, had shrunk to sixty-six dollars in 1849. The number of those "absconding" from the poorhouse, which had been 20 of 218 in 1832 and 36 of 164 in 1840, declined to none of 137 in 1848 and one of 183 in 1849.

These changes reflected an alteration in the public conception of the functions which the poorhouse was to serve. The old tradition, reflected in the law of 1824, conceived of the poorhouse both as an institution for the care of the needy and as a workhouse. There, those convicted as disorderly persons could be confined at hard labor for as long as six months, and discipline could be enforced by solitary confinement on bread and water. In fact, the Clinton County poorhouse seems never to have been used for this latter purpose, but the stigma was long-lasting. It was also popular in the early period to perceive those in need of public assistance as evil persons whose misfortunes were brought on by their own vices, especially intemperance and laziness. For such persons, the requirement of labor was deemed desirable to reduce the burden of the taxpayers and as penitence and also to instill industrious habits.

The new attitude, which reduced the emphasis on required labor, won acceptance slowly. By the 1850s it had gained legislative endorsement. A senate investigation committee reported in 1857 that poorhouse inmates were by no means exclusively worthless and vicious persons but included "persons of great worth and respectable character, reduced to extreme poverty, not by any vice or fault of their own, but by some inevitable loss of property, or of friends and relatives who, if living, would have supported them in their age and infirmities." [18] As early as 1849, the Clinton County poorhouse and the welfare program in general were already being administered in this spirit. In contrast to the earlier period, there was much less emphasis on punishment, the correction of vicious habits, and the seeking of lower costs at the expense of unrelieved suffering.

What appears most striking in the history of public welfare in Plattsburgh and Beekmantown is the low level of welfare expenditures prior to the War of 1812 and the much higher level thereafter. This is still another indication that the socioeconomic level of the community had fallen in the second generation. It seems remarkable indeed that the poor fund always enjoyed a substantial surplus, much of which was lent at interest, during the early years. The principal cause of the later increase in welfare expenditures was the high incidence of illness and indigence among immigrants. While the law authorized returning immigrants to the community from which they had come, Plattsburgh apparently made little effort to do so.

Mounting costs led the town in 1818 to try to discourage people from seeking aid by making it available only to those who were willing to take up residence in a town poorhouse, where it was expected that a work program for inmates would greatly reduce the net cost to the town. Initially, the workhouse program did reduce costs, but its harshness toward the poor and unfortunate produced a reaction. By 1850 the old pattern of affording people relief in their own homes had made a considerable recovery. Experience had taught that the ill, the aged, the afflicted, and orphan children were little better able to support themselves inside a poorhouse than they had been outside it. Despite concern over welfare costs, the community preferred to aid the needy in their own homes when it was feasible to do so, rather than subject them to the disruption and demoralization so generally associated with a move to the poorhouse.

12

Schools

Plattsburgh's earliest schools were neighborhood cooperatives. The town government did assist the schools, but it did so with the income from a proprietary land grant rather than by imposing taxes. Local taxation for schools began only when the state required towns to provide such assistance in order to qualify for matching state aid. Basic administrative authority lay not with the town government but with school districts organized on a neighborhood basis to manage the affairs of a single school. Town and county officers provided some administrative supervision. State law, of course, prescribed the basic pattern to be followed. In later years, the state made a strong effort, as it did also in welfare matters, to centralize administration and in particular to confer great power upon county authorities. To an even greater extent than in welfare administration, the end of the period saw a strong resurgence of district and town authority.[1]

Plattsburgh's proprietors, in contrast to those of Beekmantown, had at the outset set aside a "school lot" of 460 acres and a "gospel lot" of 400 acres to provide subsidies respectively for education and religion. There were state laws of 1785 and 1786 requiring that such lots be set aside in newly granted townships, but they apparently did not apply to the Plattsburgh grant. Charles Platt wrote on February 8, 1786, to Zephaniah Platt, who was still in Poughkeepsie, that "Captain Pomeroy claims the school lot and has cut some oak timber on it. If he has the Lot, it will rather discommode the first settlers here as that has been laid out and called the School lot. The people expected it, and are now uneasy as thinking it will be taken from them."[2] It was not. In fact, the schools received the income from the gospel lot as well as that from the school lot. Minutes of Plattsburgh's town meetings indicate that the town regularly chose commissioners to manage these properties, but there is no evidence for the early years as to how much income they provided or how it was spent.

Schools operated in Plattsburgh within a very few years after the pioneer settlement. Thomas Tredwell in 1794 referred casually to the desire of several local parents to give their boys more of an education "than they can acquire at our common Schools."[3] A report to the state legislature indicated that five schools existed in Plattsburgh in 1795, when the legislature made its first provision for state assistance.[4] As was customary elsewhere in the state, parents in various neighborhoods apparently hired teachers and otherwise managed their schools on a cooperative, tuition-payment basis. The town subsidy seemingly paid only a small proportion of the costs.[5]

The state aid program, which began in 1795, included a five-year subsidy plan under which Clinton County received $200 yearly. Authorities apportioned the money among the towns of the county in proportion to the number of taxable inhabitants and among the districts in each town according to the "aggregate number of days instruction during the previous year."[6] To qualify for state aid, each town had to tax its property owners to raise a sum equal to half that to be received from the state. The law also required the towns to choose annually at their town meetings from three to seven school commissioners to discharge the town's responsibilities under the law. School districts within the towns chose two or more trustees to operate their schools under the supervision of the town commissioners. Should the town commissioners find that the "abilities or moral character" of the teacher employed by the trustees were such that he or she ought not to be "intrusted with the education of the youth," they could withdraw all public assistance money, both state and town funds. They could do the same for other shortcomings as well. The state funds lapsed in 1800 and were not renewed until 1812, but the basic features of New York State's common school system had taken shape.[7] The state, it is important to recognize, had not created the common schools; it had merely begun to assure subsidies and to provide public regulation for neighborhood schools established on a voluntary basis.

Plattsburgh's implementation of this law was unstinting. The five commissioners chosen in 1798—John Howe, John Ransom, Isaac Allen, John Stephenson, and Charles Platt—were men of considerable ability, although as a group they were not as impressive as the commissioners of highways or the overseers of the poor. Plattsburgh's share of the $200.00 in state aid allocated to the county was a healthy $126.60, which the town duly supplemented by a tax of $63.30 on town residents to make a total of $189.90. When the law expired in 1800, Plattsburgh ceased choosing school commissioners but continued to name commissioners of its gospel and school lots and to allocate assistance to its school districts from that source.

How schools developed is evident in the brief memoir of Harvey Smith, a native who later emigrated to Wisconsin. Born in 1796 on his father's farm about two miles north of Plattsburgh, Smith reported in his account that there were no schools in the "wilderness" in which he grew up. His mother taught her children to read and "set us to studying the Westminster catechism and the Bible. . . . When I was about ten years old, my father built a barn and the neighbors wanted him to have a school in the barn and hired a young lady to teach the school, and there I first went to school. In a few years the neighbors formed themselves into a school district and built a schoolhouse and we had schools in the winter sometimes two months and sometimes three months in a year. There was no school law at the time and we were obliged to pay our teacher's subscription, each family boarding the teacher according to the number of children sent to school. . . . I think I attended school about one year putting all the time together."[8]

Another memoir, that of Thomas Miller (born 1804), affords some additional information. In the period just before the War of 1812, Miller attended school in Charles Platt's barn. Another school which he attended was in the Reverend Frederick Halsey's front yard. Halsey taught there for some time. He let the children play in the woods for long periods and rolled apples on the floor for the boys to scramble over. One successor, a man named Scott, made an indelible impression by fortifying himself for his work with an occasional nip from a black bottle which he kept in his desk.[9]

The school situation in Plattsburgh in 1811 was probably much like that in Champlain. In replying to a state inquiry seeking information on the schools of the area, Pliny Moore noted then that some of Champlain's five schools were open nearly all year. They closed only "between masters," meaning from the time the male teacher departed in the spring until a female teacher reopened the school in the summer and again between the end of the summer school and the resumption of the winter school. Some schools, however, were open as little as six months. Those who sent children paid the costs. Attendance was between 250 and 300, although many "from want of means attend but little and some none at all." To a question about teaching methods employed, Moore replied that "scarcely any two were alike in their mode of instruction." [10]

Management of the gospel and school lots was a subject of considerable interest at Plattsburgh's town meetings during the years from 1800 to 1812, when there was no state subsidy. In 1800 the townspeople instructed the supervisor to call upon Zephaniah Platt to "ask him for Title to the School and Glebe Lands to be conveyed to the said Supervisor and his Successors in Office in trust for the . . . town." Platt complied. In 1805 the town meeting replaced the previous commissioners of the gospel and school lots and instructed the new commissioners to investigate the accounts of their predecessors and to lease no more of the land. In 1810 a special town meeting discussed the gospel and school lands at length without reaching a decision on guidelines for the commissioners. Finally in 1812, the commissioners reported to the apparent satisfaction of the town meeting that they had had the school lot surveyed into plots of ten acres each and had leased all the lots for ten years at $14.66 apiece. The lessees had agreed to build stone fences along the highway and rail fences on the other sides as well as to leave the land cleared and planted to grass seed at the expiration of their leases.

The basis of the controversy over the leasing of the lots was the timber which stood on them. Both lessees and trespassers, beginning with the Captain Pomeroy to whom Charles Platt had referred in 1786, apparently exploited this resource to the utmost. By suing trespassers, the commissioners of 1812 recovered $1,410.18 for town use. In 1820 the commissioners informed the town meeting that lessees had removed virtually all the pine from the lots and that they would now have no value until improved for agriculture. To that end they had leased to Thomas Tredwell a plot near his mill. The lease terms required him to build a house and barn and "put the land into good state for Cultivation."

The income which the common schools derived from this source was highly significant in the early years. The amount recovered from trespassers in 1812 was very large in relation to the earlier state subsidy and even to town expenditures of a later time. In 1820 the commissioners reported that they had $280.00 for distribution to the town's school districts and payments due amounted to $786.11. As late as 1845, Plattsburgh reported to the state that it had received income of $84.12 for schools from its "town fund." [11]

By 1812 the state was ready to subsidize and to regulate again. Legislation passed at various times since 1801 had created a common school fund, essentially an endowment derived from lotteries, sales of public land, and investment. From 1812 onward, a portion of the annual income of this fund was distributed to the counties for allocation among the towns and school districts in essentially the pattern fixed in 1795. There were, however, some differences of importance. Aid to the towns was now proportional to school-age population instead of taxable inhabitants. Aid to the districts was to be allocated in proportion to the number of children aged five to fifteen rather than to the aggregate number of days of instruction during the previous year. This change sacrificed an incentive to extend school attendance, which was usually very brief, in order to eliminate discrimination in the allocation in favor of wealthy communities. To qualify for public aid, however, districts had to use the public funds only to pay a teacher approved by town inspectors and employed for at least three months. The law required the districts also to report annually the data necessary to qualify for assistance. The towns had to raise a sum at least equal to, but no more than double, the state aid and of course to report.

The law of 1812 made detailed provision also for the operation of school districts.[12] Meetings of district freeholders called by town commissioners could initiate formation of a school district. Such meetings could pick the schoolhouse site and impose a district tax on property to pay for the site and construction of a school, for repairs, fuel, and necessary "appendages." Three trustees chosen by the meeting managed the affairs of the district. They were to hire, fire, and pay the teachers, and to choose a clerk and a collector, if they wished.

In 1814 the trustees received explicit authorization to assess parents in order to make up the usual deficiency between the amount received from town and state as a wage subsidy and the sum due to teachers in wages. The "rate bill" or tuition payment imposed upon parents was based in part on the total days of instruction each of their children received. Thus, if parents sent three children to school, each for fifty days, and if the total of such pupil days for the school was fifteen hundred, then the proportion of the residue of the teachers' wages due from the parents of the three children would be one-tenth. Parents of large families bore a heavy burden if all children of school age attended regularly. The district trustees could exempt parents whom they believed unable to pay. But, such exemptions were relatively few, while absences designed to reduce rate bills were heavy. Teachers had to keep the attendance record upon which rate bills were based and sometimes had to collect the money from parents as well. The law allowed them to exclude from school those children whose parents they considered bad credit risks.

The procedure for certifying teachers under the law of 1812 was somewhat different from that prescribed in 1795. There were still to be school commissioners, now three in number, chosen by the town meeting and vested as before with general supervisory authority, but the town was also to choose from three to six school inspectors as well. These inspectors were to "examine the teachers and approve or disapprove of the same, and . . . also visit the several schools . . . quarterly, or oftener." No person could teach without prior examination and written certification from at least two inspectors that he was "qualified to teach a common school, and . . . of good moral character."

Education in Clinton County was in a relatively backward state when the law of 1812 went into effect, but it improved within a few years. The state superintendent affirmed in his report for 1819 that when the law first went into effect four of every five children (80 percent) in the state between the ages of five and fifteen attended school. Under the new program, however, the ratio had risen in 1819 to seven out of eight (87½ percent). The same report showed that in Plattsburgh in 1818 only 72 percent of the children aged five to fifteen attended school. By 1819 Plattsburgh had raised the figure to 86 percent, and in 1820 it went over 100 percent, probably due to attendance by pupils over fifteen. There were then 1,093 children who attended school, while the five to fifteen age group numbered only 1,031. The state average did not top 100 percent until 1823.[13]

Plattsburgh's enthusiasm for supporting its schools with local tax funds was low at first but increased later, especially in years of prosperity. In the war years, 1813 and 1814, the town meeting voted merely to equal the state subsidy or, in other words, to do as little as possible without forfeiting the state grant. The records do not show what action the town took in 1815, but in 1816 it voted to raise twice as much as the state provided. The level of support dropped back again to the minimum in 1817, probably because of the economic strain resulting from the crop damage during the abnormally cold growing season of 1816. In 1818 and 1819, prosperity, enthusiasm for education, and a change in the law led Plattsburgh to raise triple the amount of state aid. In 1820 the vote was to raise "the sum allowed by law for the support of common schools." Presumably, that meant the minimum figure. Plattsburgh had by then brought the maximum number of children into its schools; a depression had begun in 1819; and Plattsburgh's state aid allocation for 1820 ($785.37) was more than double the figure for 1819 ($343.43). In 1821 the vote was to raise double the state allocation.

Beekmantown, after separating from Plattsburgh in 1820, reflected concern for education similar to that which had been evident in Plattsburgh. Its school officials included several of the ablest men in the community. Records of school matters occupied a prominent place in the minutes of the town meetings, and the tax levies voted were consistently double the amount of state aid until 1828. From then through 1831, the town preferred to make its school expenses the absolute minimum. But, from 1832 to 1849, the levies voted were nearly always double the amount of the state allocation.

The available statistics on Beekmantown's schools, however, show a rather less favorable situation. The length of time the schools were in operation averaged a steady seven months, but the range in the reports of the district trustees during the 1820s was from three to ten. In the state as a whole, eight months was more nearly average as early as 1824. Seven months was a little low even within Clinton County. As in Plattsburgh at the time of the separation, the proportion of school-age children who actually attended school in Beekmantown in the early 1820s was very high. The lowest figure was 84 percent in 1822. The next year, however, it went over 100 percent and remained above or very near 100 percent until 1831. Prompted only in part by a change in the definition of school-age from five to fifteen to five to sixteen, which occurred in 1830, the percentage of school-age children attending school in Beekmantown declined thereafter to a low of

76 percent in 1840, the next to last year for which figures are available. While no figures are available on the number of months per year during which Beekmantown children actually attended school, the figures for the county as a whole may be highly suggestive (see table 11).

These figures point up an apparent paradox. Schools were open about seven months per year and virtually all school-age children actually attended in the 1820s and 1830s; yet, the average length of time which children spent in school was under four months as late as the 1840s. Why did children actually attend school for such a short time? Part of the answer lies in the customary distinction between winter and summer school. Older children and perhaps their teachers as well spent much of their summer in farm labor. They could afford the luxury of time off for school only in the winter, when there was relatively little farm work to do. Accordingly, the winter school focused on older children. The winter school teacher was customarily a man. The summer school, on the other hand, seems to have been designed largely for younger children who were not needed for farm labor. The summer school teacher was traditionally a woman, who received much less money for her efforts than did the winter teacher. Thus, it appears probable that most children attended either the winter or the summer school, each lasting roughly three months or a little longer, but not both.

Powerful financial considerations tended to keep the period of attendance at school relatively low. Public money, including the state subsidy and the town tax payment, sufficed in the early years to pay only a small proportion of the total cost of teachers' wages. In 1825 in the state as a whole, public money paid for only about 16 percent of the aggregate payment to teachers. The remaining 84 percent was assessed by district trustees against the parents in "rate bills" (tuition payments) collected as were other taxes on property. Because rate bills reflected the number of days of attendance, poor parents had the strongest incentive to keep their children at home in order to avoid or to minimize the charge.

Keeping children at home also reduced or eliminated the obligation to share in paying the cost of providing board (presumably including sleeping accommodation) to the teacher. Sometimes teachers boarded in turn with a number of families. More often during the 1830s in Chazy's second district, a leading citizen, probably one whose house was near the school, boarded the teacher

TABLE II.

Months of Attendance by Pupils in Clinton County Schools

Year	Under 2 Months	2–4 Months	4–6 Months	6–8 Months	8–10 Months
1843	1,793	1,414	1,216	766	257
1844	2,916	2,352	1,649	654	295
1848	2,191	2,505	1,896	1,291	475
1849	2,679	2,590	2,106	1,403	460

SOURCE: Annual Reports of the State Superintendent of Common Schools.

and received compensation at the rate of eight shillings ($1.00) weekly for a woman teacher or ten shillings ($1.25) for a man. Like the cost of teachers' wages in excess of the public money, the expenses for board were assessed in the rate bill against the parents. The more children a family sent to school and the longer they attended, the higher the family's share of the cost of the teacher's board. In the case of summer teachers in the 1830s, board costs of about $4.00 per month were often not much less than those of wages. For the more highly paid winter teacher, board costs, while greater on an absolute scale, were smaller in relation to wages ($5.00 per month as opposed to wages which in one case ran as high as $20.00 per month). Public money, however, could not be used for board costs—only for wages. Thus, to the parents the board bill was an important consideration.

The cost of providing firewood for heating the school during the winter might also be charged against the parents on the same basis as were wage and board costs. Sometimes school districts required each family to provide a specified amount of wood. More often in the later years, however, they contracted with a low bidder to provide the needed wood at a cost not much below that of the teacher's board. In such cases, the district might either prorate the charge among the parents on the usual formula or assess it against the property owners of the district as part of their tax payment to support the school. Chazy's second district vacillated on this point. Presumably, the decision depended upon the relative numbers at a particular meeting—on the one hand, of property-owners without children and, on the other, of parents who owned no property. In 1830 fourteen families sent children to school but owned no property, while twenty-three families owned property but sent no children to school. Thirty-one families both owned property and sent children to school.

Which of the two schools, winter and summer, was more expensive to the parents is not clear. On the one hand, the expenses of the winter school, specifically the higher wage costs of the teacher and the cost of fuel, were greater than for the summer school. However, the districts normally allocated all or at least most of the public money to meet the costs of the winter school. The summer school was far less expensive due to lower teachers' wages and the lack of heating costs, but the parents normally had to bear all of the cost themselves. Initially, such considerations tended to keep the wages of summer school teachers very low. In the 1820s Beekmantown's fifth district, for example, paid the summer school teacher seventy-five cents weekly or three dollars per month. Compared to the twelve dollars, more or less, which the district paid winter school teachers at the time, that was scarcely more than a baby-sitting wage. In the 1830s, however, when public subsidies had increased appreciably, Chazy's second district chose to allocate one-fourth of the amount received to meeting summer school costs. Thus, in one way or another, the districts apparently tried to keep what they regarded as a reasonable balance between the costs to the parents for summer and winter schools.[14]

School authorities in the state government recognized clearly that high rate bills were a major cause of poor attendance. The obvious way to improve the situation was to increase the public money. Without going into detail on how this was done, the extent can be noted. By 1835 the percentage of teachers' wages paid from rate bills in the state as a whole was down to 62 percent. This was still high, but it was an improvement over 1824, when the corresponding figure was 84 percent. By 1844 the figure for Clinton County was down to 28 percent.[15]

Another obvious means of economizing on school costs was to hire women rather than men for the winter school. Azariah C. Flagg, the former Plattsburgh *Republican* editor who served several years as state superintendent of common schools, came very close to recommending such a measure in his report for 1827 (p. 6). While arguing explicitly that "female education should be improved," he seemed to suggest obliquely that in Boston, "where school education is well understood," the authorities quite regular-ly employed women to teach older as well as younger children. Not until 1843 did a superintendent make this argument more explicit. In the superintendent's report for that year, much testimony was adduced to demonstrate that women teachers had no great disciplinary problems with older boys and were often superior to men in knowledge and capacity to teach.

The argument indicated that many districts had already begun to employ women for the winter school, and indeed this was true in Beekmantown district five.[16] In 1837 a Miss Child conducted the winter school for a wage which appears to have been about seven dollars monthly. A male teacher in 1833 had received thirteen dollars; another man had been paid ten dollars in 1834. The innovation seems to have met with less than immediate acceptance. A male teacher was employed for the winter term in at least some of the next few years, but in 1842 the winter school teacher was again a woman, Miss E. Hull, who was paid eight dollars.

Reservations as to the competence of female teachers were widespread. For example, Superintendent Christopher Morgan in 1850 acknowledged that in "weaker districts" hiring "well qualified female teachers" might be the best policy. But, he thought that in such instances "the more advanced scholars" would wish to seek "the more extended advantages of a central town school.[17]

The effect of increased public money and the hiring of women teachers for the winter school is evident in Beekmantown records. Always in the years before 1842, district five appears to have closed down its winter school promptly at the expiration of the three months required to qualify for state and town money. The record of public money received by other districts in Beekmantown in the 1820s indicates that only about half received enough public money to hire a qualified male teacher for three months. Very few would have any appreciable amount left over after meeting that obligation. Thus, in those districts also, the tendency was probably to shut down the winter school as soon as the district had qualified for a share of public money. As late as 1833, the $26.23 in public money received by district five fell short by $12.77 of the $39.00 needed to pay for the three months of winter school "Cept by John D. Marvin." The next year, by hiring Oscar Barber at $10.00 monthly, instead of the $13.00 paid Marvin, the district was able to salvage $1.60 from its $31.60 in public money to apply to summer school. By the 1840s the public money available to the district was often over $50.00. But, by employing women instead of men for the winter school, it had reduced its winter school wage bill from the previous $10.00 to $13.00 monthly to $8.00. Under these circumstances, parents could send their children to school for considerably longer periods before they began to incur rate bills for teachers' wages.

Presumably, these changes should have improved the attendance situation, but the record is not clear. The figures on the duration of attendance unfortunately begin only after both changes had begun to be effective. They show relatively little improvement between 1843 and 1849. The figures on the percentage of school-age children attending school for any period at all register a considerable decline in the years during which these beneficial changes were coming into effect. This should probably be attributed, however, to another change which was occurring in the 1840s—the influx of French Canadian and Irish immigrants.

Exemptions from rate bills in district five in Beekmantown were infrequent after the first few years. In 1828, the second year of its existence, district trustees voted several exemptions. One of those exempted was Elisha "Ostin," probably a relative of the Palmer Austin, who had been "taken on the county to support" in 1826. Among the others exempted were Worcester Eaton, Mary McDavid, and Jane Larkin. Eaton was a highly literate individual who had served as first clerk of the district. Whether his exemption was because of poverty or in recognition of services could not be determined. Notices of exemptions were fewer in later years prior to 1850. Whether this was because they simply were not recorded or because the residents became less disposed to bear their neighbors' burdens is uncertain. To many parents, assuming a share of a pauper's rate bill might require some reduction in the time which they could afford to send their own children to school. Thus, perhaps there would be some pressure to resist exemptions. The stigma of charity may have kept some poor people from seeking exemption.

Chazy's second district quite often voted to add the amount of rate bills which had not been paid to the taxes assessed against the property owners in the district for the next year. Such a system perhaps enabled the children of the parents who were unable to pay to attend school regularly without being stigmatized as paupers. Exemption in advance, as was apparently the rule in Beekmantown's second district, would have carried such a stigma.

The size of the district was of course a factor which affected the disposition to grant exemptions and also the ability to support a good school. The annual reports of the state superintendents abound in complaints over the proliferation of districts. People understandably wanted a school near their homes. Perhaps some also desired a greater voice in school affairs than they could secure in a large district. They often failed to realize how limited would be the resources of a small district when it came to building, repairing, and supplying a school. No public money could be used for those purposes; it was all earmarked for the payment of "qualified" teachers. Thus, the entire burden of these costs was on the property owners of the district.

Forty pupils per school, according to the state superintendent in 1839, was the minimum number which would enable a district to meet these obligations. To this minimum standard, Beekmantown conformed fairly well. Of fifty-four district reports between 1821 and 1829, only twelve recorded fewer than forty pupils. The largest had ninety-one. The average was fifty-one, which compared well with the state average of fifty-seven in 1830.[18] The number of districts in Beekmantown increased to a maximum of sixteen in 1839 but declined the next year to eleven and held there into the early 1840s.

The nature of the expenses which the districts had to meet, in addition to the cost of teachers' wages, is evident in the records of Beekmantown's district five. In 1829 the district voted to "rase saven Dollars and seventy five Cents to pay Jacob Eaton for a stove Elbow and stove pot." In 1830 the residents "resolved that the Trustees Levvy a tax of $1.68 . . . to repare the school house and purchase a pal and cup." The "chimny" had to be repaired for $1.50 in 1833, and another forty-five cents was voted to fix windows. Competitive bidding occurred often, as in 1836, when Cyrus Randle, with a bid of fifty cents, won a job described as "four bits of glass to be putteyed in and seats and desks nailed up strong." In 1847 it was "Moshunted and Second that their be a Tax Raised of $21.50 to pay for one Stove and Elbo . . . , Pail and Cup."

The most nagging problem which the fifth district experienced in supporting its school was supplying it with fuel. The initial policy was that "each man in said district assist in getting wood for the use of the school." The men were to meet together and get the wood as a group, with the proviso that "whosoever shall neglect so to do shall pay in proportion to the number of scholars he shall send . . . at the rate of one dollar for each and every cord." This application of the rate bill principle seems to have worked until 1832, when it was resolved that the parents had until November 15 to get in their share of wood. Thereafter, the trustees would take bids for securing the wood and assess those in default six shillings (seventy-five cents). The next year the district residents resolved to tax themselves $4.80 so that they could hire someone to deliver the necessary amount of wood "corded up, stove length" at the school. This contracting system was followed for three years, but in 1836 the annual meeting voted to return to the earlier system. By 1849 the district had gone back to taxing itself and contracting for the delivery of fuel.

When Chazy's second district took bids on supplying the school with wood, the lowest bidder was almost invariably one of the wealthiest members or most prominent citizens of the district. Apparently, such individuals did not expect to make a profit from such an enterprise but regarded it as a form of public service.

The incompetence of common school teachers was a major problem of the system. "And every Citizen . . . knows," wrote John C. Spencer in an 1827 report to the state senate, "that the incompetency of the great mass of teachers, is a radical defect, which impedes the whole system, frustrates the benevolent designs of the legislature, and defeats the hopes and wishes of all who feel an interest in disseminating the blessings of education." [19] Only about one male teacher in eight, it was estimated in 1831, had been trained at either a university or an academy; seven in eight had no training beyond that afforded in the elementary or common schools, such as they themselves taught. Reports from county superintendents in 1843 showed that "many of the self-styled teachers, who lash and dogmatize in these miserable tenements of suffering humanity [country schools], are . . . low, vulgar, obscene, intemperate, ignorant and profane, utterly incompetent to teach anything that is good." [20] While these complaints applied to the entire state, there is no reason to believe that the teachers of Clinton County in general or of Beekmantown in particular were any better. The concept of teacher training then prevalent in the county is reflected in a notice which appeared in the *Republican* on September 18, 1824, advising young men who intended to prepare for teaching in the *ensuing winter* to attend the academy at the quarter then beginning.

TABLE 12.

*Age and Sex of Winter and Summer School Teachers
in Clinton County, 1843*

	Total*		Under 18		Age						Over 30	
					18–21		21–25		25–30			
	M	F	M	F	M	F	M	F	M	F	M	F
Winter	66	34	4	2	5	4	22	14	20	7	11	2
Summer	9	98	—	35	1	27	4	32	2	9	2	6

★ Except for male teachers of summer school (9), the figures in this category do not agree with the sums of the figures in the age brackets to the right. Those figures show 62 instead of 66 male teachers in the winter school and 29 instead of 34 female teachers. For the summer school they show 109 female teachers instead of 98.

Experience and Pay of Clinton County Teachers, 1843★

	Years Experience						Years in Same School						Pay	
	Under 1		Over 1		Under 1		One		Two		Three			
	M	F	M	F	M	F	M	F	M	F	M	F	M	F
Winter	19	4	41	—	39	14	9	8	4	3	6	—	$15.00	6
Summer	2	41	6	30	3	62	3	24	1	4	1	—	$15.50	5

★ The totals in the two categories, years experience and years in the same school, do not agree except as to the number of male teachers of summer school (8). The former category shows 60 male teachers in the winter schools, while the latter shows 58. For female teachers of winter schools, the former category shows only 4 while the latter shows 25. For female teachers of summer school, the former category shows 71 and the latter 90. SOURCE: Annual Report, Superintendent of Common Schools, Assembly Document 34, 1844.

Statistics on the age and experience of common school teachers in Clinton County help to explain the problem of competence (see table 12).

In the winter school, more than three-fourths of the teachers were twenty-one or under. Among the young women who taught summer school the percentage under twenty-one was not quite so high. But, only a few teachers, winter or summer, were over twenty-five. While most of the teachers seem to have had more than one year of experience, it is evident from their ages that their experience could not have been prolonged. Over 70 percent, winter and summer, were teaching for the first time in that district; none had taught as long as three years in the same school.

The basic problem, as had long been recognized, was pay. "One of the principal reasons why the standard of education in the common schools had not been more elevated," wrote Superintendent Flagg in his 1827 report, "is to be found in the unwillingness on the part of the school districts, to make adequate compensation to teachers of approved talents and qualifications. . . . The monthly wages of the teachers of district schools," he continued, "are frequently one-third less than the amount paid to experienced clerks, or journeymen mechanics, in the same vicinity; and what is still more discouraging to the teacher, he finds employment not more than half the year." The average pay for men teaching winter school and for women teaching summer school in Clinton County was still below the state averages in 1843.[21]

The custom of hiring one teacher for winter and another for summer also impeded the growth of professionalism. A man could not plan a professional career in teaching on the basis of prospective employment for perhaps as few as three months per year and even those at substandard wages. It is true that the period in which schools were operated was lengthening and that pay was increasing. But, if Beekmantown's fifth district was at all representative, the distinction between winter and summer school continued down to 1850. So also did the tendency to hire cheaper teachers to instruct smaller children in the summer, when the district still bore some or all of the bill for wages. The fifth district continued this practice even after beginning to employ women, rather than men, for the winter term. Specifically, the district hired one woman for the winter term, at a rate appreciably below what a man would have required, and another woman for the summer at a still lower rate of pay. Thus, for a woman as well as for a man, planning a professional career as a teacher in Clinton County would have been difficult from the standpoint of securing continuous employment. For men, the very infrequent opportunity for employment in the half or more of the school year which was allocated to summer school would have been even more discouraging. It is perhaps significant, however, that two men in Clinton County in the 1840s seem to have broken the barrier by achieving employment both winter and summer and by remaining teachers past the age of thirty.

Low pay and less than year-round employment complicated the problem of providing professional training for teachers. On the one hand, people could not be expected to spend their own time and money to train themselves for an occupation in which they could not make a living. On the other hand, if the state subsidized the training of teachers, it was reasonably certain that those so trained would necessarily abandon teaching sooner or later for some occupation which afforded more nearly year-round employment and higher income.

Flagg's solution to the problem, borrowed perhaps from Governor De Witt Clinton, was to establish teacher training schools in each county to be operated by "mutual instruction" in the Lancastrian pattern. But, he also urged effort to improve "female education." He pointed to the tradition of employing women for the summer schools and to the economic conditions which seemed to assure its continuance. He suggested obliquely that winter schools too would be hiring more and more women teachers, as in fact they did.[22] Several private institutions for "female education" existed and more were founded, but the legislature did not choose to aid them specifically for the purpose of training "cheap teachers."

The means which the legislature first endorsed to subsidize teacher training was assistance to existing academies, or private schools. There was no doubt that academies subsidized by the state were "fully adequate" to train the requisite number of teachers.[23] In 1827, while ignoring Flagg's suggestion concerning "female education," the legislature had adopted a law designed to secure the addition of teacher training to the curriculum of cooperating academies. In 1834 the legislature revised the program to designate one academy in each of the eight senatorial districts of the state to participate in the subsidized teacher training program. These three-year programs were to run eight months per year on the assumption that the students would wish to leave four months every winter "to teach a district school," thus earning something to support themselves in completing their course of preparation.[24]

The effect of this program on the level of competence among Beekmantown and Clinton County teachers was probably very slight. The Plattsburgh Academy had applied for economic assistance in 1827 and, apparently after its incorporation in 1828, was among those receiving a subsidy under the law of 1827.[25] It was not, however, one of the eight designated under the law of 1834 to develop an expanded teacher training program. The number of students in the academy was usually such that they could have filled all or nearly all of the district schools in the county, but the available evidence does not reveal how many schools hired academy students. That Clinton County received many graduates from the subsidized teacher training program in other academies is unlikely. The number of graduates had increased from 108 in 1835 to 284 in 1837. But, throughout the state, the number of school districts seeking teachers, too often doing so twice each year, was about ten thousand.[26]

In 1841 the state required county supervisors in each county to appoint a county superintendent of schools to serve a two-year term. The law further required that county superintendents offer advice and training to teachers in conjunction with their "inspections" of the various schools, but this was not very practical. Clinton County Superintendent Daniel S. McMaster, in his report for 1844, acknowledged that "a large portion of the teachers in this county are young, inexperienced persons . . . deficient in . . . a knowledge of practical school keeping," but he found that he could do little to help them during "inspection" visits. The large number of districts dictated that the visits involve only one day and, for many districts, this was inevitably toward the end of the term. Furthermore, he argued, it was not entirely appropriate "to commence instruction of a teacher" in the schoolroom in the presence of pupils. His conclusion was that "more instruction can be given the teachers of the town when assembled together in one day, than in as many days as there are schools, spent with the teachers, amidst the business and confusion of school rooms."

Accordingly, he strongly recommended his own version of the "institute" plan which was then gaining wide support: (1) that the county superintendent "visit each town in his jurisdiction every spring and fall, before the opening of summer and winter schools, and spend a week in the instruction of the teachers"; (2) "that each district should be duly notified and present its teacher at the Institute, and that the teacher should be allowed that time [i.e., paid] by the district, if licensed to teach"; (3) "that all certificates [licenses to teach] should be given on the last day of said Institute, by the county superintendent, with the consent of the board of examiners," composed of two residents appointed by the supervisor and the justices of the peace. Unfortunately for McMaster's plan, the office of county superintendent was abolished in 1847.[27]

Institutes, however, did prove popular. Beginning in 1843, the idea had spread quickly across the state. In 1847 the legislature provided a subsidy (*New York Laws*, chap. 361, pp. 459 ff.) for ten-day institutes in each county if a majority of the town superintendents desired. Clinton County, as usual, was quick to pick up the subsidy and apparently conducted teacher institutes with some enthusiasm. Indeed, there had been a "county convention" of teachers at Plattsburgh called by the county superintendent as early as 1842.[28]

Plattsburgh Academy, reviving in the later 1840s after a period of decay (see chapter 8), provided courses specifically designed for teachers. A notice in the *Republican* (August 24, 1850) stated: "The class for instruction in 'the science of Common School Teaching,' organized pursuant to the instructions of the Regents of the University under Act of the Legislature of March 30, 1849, will resume its studies." The academy then had about enough students to supply the county schools with teachers if *all* enrolled students took time off to teach.

College students would not have helped greatly to alleviate any shortage. In 1845 there were only six county residents attending colleges.[29] There was of course no college in the county.

The philosophy of education accepted in Clinton County and in the state was in some respects what would now be called progressive. Azariah C. Flagg's views, as set forth in his report for 1827, probably met general approval in Beekmantown:

> The course of instruction in the common schools ought to be adapted to the business of life, and to the actual duties which may devolve upon the person instructed. In a government where every citizen has a voice in deciding the most important question, it is not only necessary that every person should be able to read and write, but that he should be well instructed in the rights, privileges, and duties of a citizen. Instruction should be co-extensive with universal suffrage. An unenlightened mind is not recognized by the genius of a republican government.

In particular Flagg believed that the common schools should teach government and history. Each student, he thought, should become acquainted with "the history of his own town, county, state and nation . . . [and] with the laws relating to the 'duties and privileges of towns'—the manner in which the business of the county is transacted." He emphasized even more strongly that the rising generation should be well instructed in the history of its own country. While such an argument has long since become commonplace, even conservative, it was not so in 1827. Flagg went on to note that in 1826 only six towns in all of New York State had "introduced a history of the United States into their schools."[30] Flagg's successor, John A. Dix, stated a position which would prove to have strong support in Beekmantown. Denying that instruction should be coextensive with universal suffrage, Dix defended the existing practice requiring that instruction should be coextensive with ability to pay or to secure charitable exemption. He defended this system as imparting to those who paid "a deep interest in seeing that the affairs of the district are managed with economy and prudence." He was sure that each child should be required also to provide his own textbooks, although he was troubled that there was no provision in this respect for the indigent.[31]

Another point of controversy over educational philosophy concerned morality. Good moral character had long been considered an indispensable qualification for teachers—one which was by no means taken for granted. But how teachers should inculcate moral principles was a more difficult question. Federalists, in particular, inclined to the belief that schools should do this by affording religious instruction with the New Testament as a textbook. Republicans were more likely to consider this an invitation to sectarian controversy. They preferred to separate church and state more rigorously by excluding religious instruction and the Bible. Clinton County's Federalist assemblyman for 1814, Robert Platt, favored a defeated move to require religious instruction in all schools. He also supported a bill to require town inspectors to recommend use of the New Testament as a text; this passed the assembly narrowly.[32] Reports on the textbooks in use indicate that two towns in Clinton County used the New Testament as a text from 1827 into the 1830s. Probably they were Champlain and Chazy, where the Federalist heritage was strong, rather than such Republican strongholds as Beekmantown and Plattsburgh. Like the Federalist cause in general, the use of the New Testament as a textbook was in decline. No towns in Clinton County used it after 1835.

Another point of philosophical controversy concerned centralized control. Gideon Hawley, the first state superintendent, in his 1818 report urged laws "to guard our common schools against the arbitrary changes and innovations which the caprice of different teachers is liable to introduce.[33] Others, most often Republican or Democratic in their politics, took a rather less jaundiced view of local autonomy. In 1832 Flagg represented this position by defending vigorously the right of communities to select their own textbooks instead of having the state prescribe. This view prevailed. Clinton County, even as late as 1845, represented the ultimate in decentralization with reference to textbooks. The county superintendent reported then that pupils and their parents had full freedom in selecting textbooks; the result was that several different texts in each subject could be found in the same school. He prepared a list of approved texts and urged teachers to make recommendations to their pupils from it. He advised the teacher to use in each subject the text which most of his students had.[34]

Advocates of centralization achieved temporary success in relation to school supervision. The original law of 1812 had vested supervisory authority over the district schools and their trustees in the commissioners and inspectors chosen by town meeting. On the whole, these town officers did see to it that public money got into the hands of district trustees and that they paid it to teachers in conformity to the law. Their influence over the quality of education dispensed in the district schools, however, was negligible. Evidence accumulated over the years that they rarely fulfilled their obligation to inspect schools and that their examination of prospective teachers to certify their qualification was most often a farce. Between these thousands of town officers and the state superintendent's office, there was no intermediate level of supervisory authority until 1841. Then, after arranging an investigation which starkly revealed the incompetence of town officials, Superintendent John C. Spencer secured legislation to create county superintendents (called "deputy" superintendents until 1843). Endowed with the inspecting and licensing functions previously vested in town officers, these superintendents appear to have improved the quality of common school education greatly in the few years of their existence. Protests against them were loud and frequent, however, and in 1847 a complaisant legislature abolished the office. Supervision below the level of the state superintendent's office then fell to town superintendents, who in 1843 had replaced the old town commissioners and inspectors.[35]

How Beekmantown felt about centralized administration of the common schools is not on record, but several assumptions seem warranted. In 1845 Clinton County's superintendent acknowledged that political considerations, except in his own case, normally figured in the county supervisors' choice of a superintendent and in the subsequent exercise of his functions. Democratic Beekmantown could not be expected to accept readily control over its previously autonomous schools by appointees of the majority of county supervisors—a majority which was often Whig. Moreover, the superintendent cost money. He was superimposed upon the existing administrative structure. Not only was there no reduction of former expenses but an addition of new ones—an exchange for which the benefits were hard to see. This was the major theme in the chorus of complaint; there is every reason to believe Beekmantown voices swelled the volume. Finally, one may suspect that the educational improvements secured by the superintendents were disquieting to Beekmantown residents, as much because they upset a comfortably familiar pattern as because they sometimes cost money.

What students actually learned in the Beekmantown schools is impossible to discover, but various state reports give some indication of what they were exposed to from the 1820s onward. These reports state the number of towns in each county which used each of the more popular texts in various fields. The freedom accorded pupils in Clinton County to select their own textbooks makes it evident that the state report cannot be taken too literally but, with generous allowance for exceptions, the reports do show some things of interest. Two Clinton County towns, for example, in the later 1820s and the early 1830s used a spelling book by Elihu Marshall, which was distinguished chiefly by the inclusion of a set of temperance rules. In the later 1830s, Noah Webster's much more popular speller achieved a monopoly.

The earlier editions of Webster's speller, beginning in 1783, had been designed to woo Americans away from British spellers, which then commanded the market. By substituting American for British place names, by making the moral lessons less sectarian, by eliminating obscure and useless words, and by adopting American instead of British pronunciation—by these means Webster produced a highly appealing text. As he intended, it sharply reduced American dependence on Britain in this respect. After the appearance of his dictionary in 1828, Webster revised his speller drastically to conform to his differentiation of American from British spelling. The 1828 edition of the speller was also more specifically a spelling book. The instruction in reading, grammar, and morality, which had been included in earlier editions, were by then being put into separate volumes. The monopoly enjoyed by Webster's speller in Clinton County in the 1830s testified to a receptive attitude toward his campaign to Americanize the language. Elsewhere, cultured persons of Anglophilic tendencies were still resisting heatedly through the 1840s. Patriotism was not the only reason for the success of Webster's speller, however. It was also pedagogically superior.[36]

Webster's triumph among the dictionaries came later. As late as 1833, only two towns in Clinton County reported using dictionaries, and both employed Walker's, an English product. By 1836, however, Webster was used in two towns and Walker in only one. Presumably, those towns which used both Walker's dictionary and Webster's speller in the 1830s employed earlier (before 1828) editions of the speller in which English spelling was still accepted.

The early addition of American history to the curriculum also suggests that patriotic sentiment ran high in Clinton County. Three of seven towns in Clinton County used American history texts in 1832. In the state at that time, 547 towns reported using English readers, while only 52 used history texts.[37] That Clinton County adopted history texts earlier than most communities may be due in some measure to the local influence of Azariah C. Flagg, who had urged the innovation strongly in 1827. Probably the battle of Plattsburgh, proximity to Canada, and a considerable immigrant population had more to do with it.

Most schools in Clinton County used an English reader, especially in the early 1830s. By that time the religious selections in such works were far fewer than they had been in earlier times, but a content analysis (1825–1875) shows 30 percent still devoted to religion and morality. Another 27 percent of the selections focused on nature.[38] In addition to inculcating moral values, the readers emphasized oral reading and elocution. The state report does not indicate which reader Clinton County towns had chosen, but it was probably the work of Lindley Murray, an American who wrote in England.

English grammar was a cornerstone of the curriculum in all Clinton County schools of the 1820s and 1830s. Until the late 1830s, Murray's text was used in all towns. It first appeared in England in 1795 and, for a generation, it set the pattern which others imitated. A popular competitor to Murray in New York during the 1830s was Samuel Kirkham. Kirkham's text came to be considered oversimplified, however, and quickly lost its following.

No towns in Clinton County reported using Kirkham in 1836, although it was nearly as widely used then around the state as Murray. The rival grammars which found acceptance in Clinton County from 1838 onward were those of Roswell C. Smith (1830) and Goold Brown (1823). Instead of the deductive or rule-memorizing method so long in vogue, Smith employed an inductive, Pestalozzian approach, which first set forth the material from which the rules or definitions were derived. Four Clinton County towns used Smith in 1838. Brown, a New York City teacher and academy principal, wrote a volume which won wide acceptance in academies because of its extreme thoroughness and superior organization. Three Clinton County towns employed it in their common schools in 1838.

Geography was as important as grammar in the curriculum of Clinton County schools. It had had little place in the schools before the Revolution, but the patriotic appeal in *Geography Made Easy* (1784) by the Reverend Jedidiah Morse helped to popularize the subject. In Clinton County, the geography text by William C. Woodbridge had a virtual monopoly in the late 1820s and early 1830s. Woodbridge had been the first to apply the "home geography" approach—begin with the familiar—which had been advocated by Johann Pestalozzi. His text, less concerned with physical geography than most, dedicated more space to cultural characteristics. One town in 1827 employed a text by J. A. Cummins, which characterized the Irish as "haughty, careless of their lives, . . . greedy of glory, . . . often violent in their passions."[39] It was at least convenient that this text was apparently discarded before the major influx of Irish immigrants got underway in the early 1830s. By 1838 several towns employed the Peter Parley (S. G. Goodrich) and Jesse Olney geographies, which were more profusely illustrated and better organized than Woodbridge. But, even at that time, six towns reported continued use of Woodbridge.

In arithmetic, the overwhelming preference of New York State was for the work of Nathan Daboll, *The Schoolmaster's Assistant*, which appeared in 1800. From 1827 until 1838, the towns of Clinton County, however, uniformly rejected Daboll in favor of *The Scholar's Arithmetic* by Daniel Adams; the first edition was printed in 1801. It may be coincidental that Daboll included many problems dealing with gambling and assumed that "gentlemen" bought rum. Neither drinking nor gambling nor "gentlemen," for that matter, enjoyed general acceptance in Clinton County at that time.

Adams' text, on the other hand, was distinguished in the early editions by space in which to work problems and after 1827 by an attempt to employ both inductive and deductive methods.[40]

The schoolhouses of Beekmantown were not imposing edifices. When the residents of district five reconsidered their rash commitment of 1827 to build a stone schoolhouse, they resolved instead

> that we build a school house twenty four feet long and twenty two feet wide. It is to have a good and sufficient stone wall as a foundation to be laid below the frost and the wall above the surface to be laid in line. It is to be built of planks three inches thick . . . to have a teachers desk raised two feet above the floor. Fore tiers of writing desks with six desks in a line. To have a square roof with a good and sufficient stove chimney. To be oiled up to the windows and lathed and plastered also.

The structure was completed and put into service in 1828 at a cost of $170.00 plus $3.80 for the site. It needed repairs often but was never enlarged. In 1836 the district "resolved that a wood shed and back house be built this fall," but a month later a special meeting "resolved that the vote at the Annual meeting be Recawled for Building the Shed and Back house." Neither was added before 1850. The number of pupils which the building served—perhaps divided between winter and summer school—reached fifty-three in 1835 and sixty-five in 1839.

By 1847, and probably earlier, Clinton County schoolhouses compared reasonably well with those of the state as a whole (see table 13). The percentage of frame schools was appreciably lower and those for both stone and brick appreciably higher. Some of the log schools still in use in the 1840s, however, were "half a century" old.[41] The somewhat higher percentage of schools without privies is perhaps attributable in part to lesser population density than in some other areas as well as to poverty. In many counties the percentage without privies was much higher.

How minority groups fared in Beekmantown's schools is difficult to discern. In some areas of the state, district trustees excluded Negro children, and from 1841 onward the law authorized segregated schools. No segregated schools existed in Clinton County, however, and there is no indication that trustees excluded Negro children. Neither, on the other hand, is there evidence to suggest

TABLE 13.

Clinton County Schoolhouses Compared with Those of the State in General, 1847

	Clinton	State
Frame	61%	83%
Stone	13%	6%
Brick	11%	6%
Log	16%	6%
Bad repair	28%	29%
No privy	68%	56%
Poor desks	33%	54%

SOURCE: New York Assembly Documents, 1847, document 10.

that Negro children attended district schools, either by paying rate bills or by securing exemption. Surely there were appreciable numbers of Negro children in Beekmantown's Negro community. Probably like other children of the very poor among minority groups, they attended schools rarely if at all. Some children of French Canadian and Irish immigrants undoubtedly attended common schools. Indeed, County Superintendent Daniel McMaster affirmed in 1845 that children of the Irish and French Canadian parents, who together included nearly all of the 2,761 adult illiterates in the county, were "the most punctual in attendance, most obedient and studious at school, and make commendable improvement."[42] Still, it seems highly probable that the increasing percentage of school-age children not attending school during the 1840s has some relationship to the increasing proportion of poor French Canadian and Irish Catholics in the population. The explanation for the failure of such immigrant children to attend school is probably a combination of poverty, lack of parental concern for educating children, and disinclination to subject children to possible ridicule, condescension, and Protestant indoctrination.

School district libraries became a significant part of the state education program and, consequently, of Beekmantown's school system in the late 1830s and 1840s. Beekmantown's fifth district received yearly about eight or nine dollars from the sum of about one hundred dollars secured by the town from a state subsidy and its matching tax revenue. There are no figures on how many volumes the district secured, but probably it was close to the county and state averages. In the county there were about 60 books per district in 1843. About one-third to one-half were always in circulation. By 1849 successive yearly expenditures had made the state average 125 volumes per district. By that time many districts had long since decided they had enough. The state superintendent, Christopher Morgan, reported strong pressure from 1847 onward to permit the library money to be used to pay teachers' wages instead of to buy books. He resisted, asserting that "the people are in no danger of learning too much," but in 1847 the legislature authorized districts which had more than 125 books and sufficient maps, globes, blackboards, and scientific apparatus to allocate the library money to teachers' wages if the superintendent approved. District five had shown no great aversion to the library system before 1850, but in that year the residents voted to apply the library money to teachers' wages and "not to raise no money for book case." In so doing they validated a longstanding fear that pressure to apply the library money to teachers' wages would be irresistible.[43]

On the "free school" question which convulsed the state between 1849 and 1851, Beekmantown was strongly conservative. The issue was whether to shift the portion of the cost of teachers' wages previously borne by parents under the rate bill system to district property owners in general. Reformers had long recognized that the tuition or rate bill requirement was the principal reason why less than half of the children in the state normally attended school as much as four months per year. Their "free school" law of 1849, which eliminated rate bills, won approval in a state-wide referendum by more than two and one half to one, but in Beekmantown the result was not so favorable. The first election district, including the area of the present town, voted favorably by the narrow margin of 162 to 156. In the second district, the favorable vote was 52 to 3. In the county as a whole, the favorable margin was almost four to one.[44]

When rural property holders realized what had happened, sentiment changed. In Clinton County the average district had been receiving between forty and fifty dollars in public money. That was not sufficient at the prevailing wage rate of about fourteen dollars per month to employ a male teacher for the four-month period then required to qualify for public money. Thus, if a man were employed for the winter school under the "free school" law, the property owners of the district would have to pay part of his salary plus all of the wages for a summer school teacher. If a woman were employed for the winter school, the public money would probably suffice for the winter term and perhaps leave a little to apply against the wage cost of summer school. In either case, however, under the new system, owners of property, whether or not they sent children to the district school, were to bear an increased tax burden to pay its costs. Many protested. In Beekmantown's fifth district, aroused property owners first voted to divert the share of public money earmarked for the library to the payment of the teacher's salary. Then, utterly defeating the intent of the reformers, they resolved most ungrammatically "not to raise no money for teacher's wages." Thus, instead of shifting the district's portion of the cost of the teacher's wages from the parents to the owners of property, the effect of the free school law in Beekmantown's fifth district was to eliminate any district contribution to wage costs. Therefore, school would last only as long as public funds remained sufficient to pay the teacher. Fortunately, the diversion of the library money and perhaps the economy secured by employing women instead of men for the winter term apparently made it possible to keep the school in operation about as long as usual. The average length of the school term reported for the county districts fell only to six and a half months for 1850 and was back at seven for 1851.[45]

The arguments of those who opposed the free school system boiled down to three points. Parents, not government, were morally obligated to bear the cost of educating children. It was unjust to require the childless and the elderly, whose children were grown, to pay for educating the children of others. It was unjust to tax those who had been frugal to aid the indigent and vicious. Catholic spokesmen opposed the measure both because they accepted the first argument and because it tended to undermine Catholicism itself.[46]

Beekmantown's second thoughts on the free school law found expression in another referendum which took place in 1850. The county voted narrowly for repeal, 1,963 to 1,893. In Beekmantown's first electoral district the vote was 228 to 81, or nearly three to one for repeal. The second district cast no votes for repeal but 62 against it.[47] The difference of opinion between the two districts in Beekmantown apparently corresponded to party affiliation. The second district, soon to be separated as the town of Dannemora, was strongly Whig. The first district, the older and much larger portion of the town in population, had long ago given Beekmantown a well-deserved reputation as the most Democratic town in the county.

The resolution of the conflict served Beekmantown's interest quite satisfactorily. The new school law of 1851 restored the rate bill system, but it also imposed a new state tax in order to increase the amount of public money. Under the new law, Beekmantown's twelve school districts in 1852 averaged about one hundred dollars in public money received. That was sufficient to hire a relatively well paid male teacher for four months of winter school and still have forty dollars or more left over to apply to paying a summer teacher. Under these circumstances, one might expect that the Clinton County districts would have hired "cheap" teachers, shut down their schools when the public money expired, and thus avoided entirely the offensive rate bills for wages. Instead, the districts raised the *average* wage for teachers to fourteen dollars, kept their schools open an average of nine months, and to do so assessed rate bills averaging $26.62 per district in 1852.[48] Thus, it seems warranted to conclude that while the *owners of property* were determined that there would be no school improvement if they had to pay the costs, *parents* on the other hand were willing to foot part of the bill in order to secure better schools under the old rate bill system. The schools continued on a rate bill basis until 1867.

In summary, the earliest schools in the Beekmantown-Plattsburgh area were cooperative ventures supported by parents on a neighborhood basis. In Plattsburgh a proprietary land grant administered by town officials subsidized them from the first, but to what extent is not clear. The state subsidy program, initiated on a permanent basis only in 1812, focused on teachers' "wages" and required supplemental town subsidies for the same purpose. Neighborhood school districts had to make up the deficiency in their teachers' wages and to pay all costs of building and maintaining their schools. Initially, state and town subsidies paid only a small percentage of the wage bill, but by the 1840s they paid over 70 percent. Rate bills, essentially tuition payments, made up the difference. To minimize their liability in this respect, poor parents were quite prone to take their children out of school when the subsidy money ran out. In the 1820s virtually all school-age children in Beekmantown attended school, although most of them did so for less than four months per year. In the 1840s the proportion of school-age children actually attending school dropped considerably, apparently because of the influx of poor French Canadian and Irish Catholic families.

Teachers tended to be seasonal workers, very young, poorly trained, and very poorly paid. Each district tended to hire one teacher for the older children in a "winter school" and another for the younger children in a "summer school." The winter school teachers were at first almost invariably male and better paid. Financial pressure and diminishing prejudice against women teachers were beginning to alter that situation by 1849. Because the work was seasonal and the pay so low, nearly all teachers were young—in their early twenties or even younger. Some were academy (i.e., secondary school) students, but many had only a "common school" education themselves. A state program to subsidize teacher training in the academies was just getting underway in the Plattsburgh Academy at the end of the period.

The "free school" law of 1849 aroused Beekmantown's farmers as had few other political issues. In a referendum they voted overwhelmingly against the idea that property owners should bear the proportion of school costs previously paid by parents under the rate bill system. Although the evidence is less clear, it seems likely also that Beekmantown farmers helped to defeat the centralization program which for a time had given county superintendents great authority over their schools. At the end of the period, as at its beginning, trustees chosen by the neighborhood school district held basic authority for managing its affairs. The principal change between the 1780s and 1849 was that the local folk had graciously allowed the state and the town to provide more and more of the money required to pay the teachers of their schools.

13

Republicans and Federalists

The dominant political loyalty in the Beekmantown-Plattsburgh area was at first Antifederalist, then Jeffersonian Republican, and finally, in this period, Jacksonian Democratic. Deviations in support of Federalists or Whigs occurred, but they were relatively short. Clinton County, however, went Federalist or later Whig with far more frequency than either Plattsburgh or Beekmantown. Champlain and Chazy were early Federalist strongholds and newer towns in the interior, such as Mooers, showed strong Federalist-Whig proclivities. Beekmantown itself in the period after its independence became the darling of the partisan Plattsburgh *Republican* by frequently returning the highest proportion of Republican or later Democratic votes of any town in the county. Why this voting pattern developed is difficult to explain, but clearly the heritage from the pioneer settlers had something to do with it.

Leadership in politics, as in other matters, in the early history of the Beekmantown-Plattsburgh area fell quite naturally to the very able proprietors of Plattsburgh and those associated with them. The proprietors of Beekman Patent might have offered some leadership had they chosen to do so, but they did not. The explanation for this contrast lies in the differing backgrounds of the two groups. The Beekmans were urbanites. Their major interests for generations had been in commerce and in New York City real estate. They knew little of rural life. To them and to their friends and relatives, the idea of settling in the wilderness was probably utterly abhorrent. The Plattsburgh proprietors, on the other hand, were men of rural or small-town backgrounds. Except for Melanchton Smith, they knew little of foreign commerce or urban life, but they did know about investment in farmland and in village enterprises. To them Plattsburgh offered real, comprehensible opportunity.

The rural and small-town background of the Plattsburgh proprietors affords clues not only to their interest in the community but also to their political views. While the Plattsburgh proprietors and the Beekmans had shared a strong dedication to the revolutionary movement, they held very different ideas concerning the nature of the government which should replace that of the British. The Beekmans, like most sophisticated urbanites, favored a strong national government. They saw quite correctly that such a government could be very useful, if not indispensable, to increase respect for Americans abroad, to forestall imperialist intervention in American affairs, to promote the foreign and domestic commerce of the United States and, in general, to foster the growth of the domestic economy, as well as to repay the loans which had helped to finance the Revolution. Furthermore, the Beekmans had every confidence that "gentlemen" who shared their beliefs could and would manage such a government effectively for these purposes.

Less cosmopolitan small-town folk, such as the Plattsburgh proprietors, perceived the advantages of a strong national government less clearly, if at all. What occupied their minds was fear that, having banished one distant and aristocratic government from control over their lives, they should see it supplanted by another too similar in nature. They wanted to retain maximum power in state and local governments, which "middling" people like themselves would be more likely to control and to keep responsive to the often disparate wishes of ordinary people in their differing communities.[1]

The best surviving record of the political philosophies held by early settlers of the Plattsburgh-Beekmantown area is in the debates at the state convention of 1788 which ratified the federal Constitution. Three of Plattsburgh's proprietors attended the convention as delegates; they were Melanchton Smith, Zephaniah Platt, and Thomas Tredwell.

Smith, who had been successful as a merchant in New York City after moving there from Dutchess County, was the principal spokesman for the majority, which originally opposed ratification. Far from defending the existing constitutional system under the Articles of Confederation, he frankly acknowledged the need for change. Far from professing principal loyalty to the state rather than to the federal union, Smith expressed strong feelings of American patriotism. Like the majority for which he spoke, however, Smith opposed ratification of the Constitution because, in his judgment, the government which it provided would be insufficiently representative of "middling" people and without adequate safeguards for their liberties. None of the arguments advanced by Alexander Hamilton, John Jay, Chancellor Robert R. Livingston, or others in the debates seem to have altered his views on these matters appreciably. What did persuade him to vote in the end for ratification, even without the restrictive conditions which he had at first proposed, was an eminently practical consideration. More than the necessary nine states had already ratified the document, and a federal government would be established under its terms. Argument over altering the Constitution before it became effective had become academic. The real question remaining was would New York join the American union under that Constitution in the hope that it could be modified to meet some of his objections? To this Melanchton Smith's answer was a reluctant yes.[2]

Zephaniah Platt, like Smith a delegate from Dutchess County, took no significant part in the debates of the convention. He voted, however, as Smith did and apparently held similar views.

Thomas Tredwell, a delegate from Suffolk County on Long Island, was a more adamant opponent. His views deserve consideration for two reasons. First, the extreme Antifederalist position which he represented had great appeal to many of the early settlers of Plattsburgh. Second, unlike his fellow Plattsburgh proprietors, Smith and Platt, Tredwell later chose to make his home in Plattsburgh, specifically in Beekman Patent. After retiring from his Long Island congressional seat and moving to Plattsburgh in 1794, Tredwell became a major influence on the political history of the community. He represented the district in the New York state senate from 1803 to 1807 and remained a locally venerated political figure until his death at the age of ninety in 1832.[3]

Individual liberty was, without any question, Tredwell's overriding interest. He expressed it with passion in the published records of the ratifying convention:

> Can we not, ought we not to speak like freemen on this occasion (this perhaps may be the last time when we shall dare to do it), and declare, in as positive terms, that we can-

not, we will not, give up our liberties; that, if we cannot be admitted into the Union as freemen [under an amended constitution], we will not come in as slaves? This I fully believe to be the language of my constituents; this is the language of my conscience; and, though I may not dare longer to make it the language of my tongue, yet I trust it will ever be the language of my heart. . . . This government is founded in sin, and reared up in iniquity; . . . if it goes into operation, we shall be justly punished with the total extinction of our civil liberties.[4]

The foundation of this suspicion lay in Tredwell's Calvinist conception of the nature of man in general and of Federalist men in particular. Concerning men's hearts he affirmed (p. 401) "from the best authority, they are deceitful above all things, and desperately wicked."[5] Recalling Federalist assurances that no bill of rights was necessary to assure freedom under the Constitution, Tredwell linked them to other Federalist observations favorable to aristocracy and concluded (p. 401): "But notwithstanding the strongest assertions that there are no wolves in our country, if we see their footsteps in every public path, we should be very credulous and unwise to trust our flocks abroad, and to believe that those who advised us to do it were very anxious for their preservation."

Tredwell did not explain fully the basis for his mistrust of Federalists, but Melanchton Smith had done so earlier in a way which Tredwell would almost certainly have endorsed. "Every society," Smith noted (p. 246), "naturally divides itself into classes. The Author of nature has bestowed on some greater capacities than others; birth, education, talents, and wealth, create distinctions among men as visible, and of as much influence, as titles, stars, and garters." Smith referred initially to men of the "first" class as a "natural aristocracy," but more commonly thereafter he simply called them "the great." Throughout history, he argued (p. 247), "It has been the principal care of free governments to guard against the encroachments of the great." His most fundamental objection to the Constitution was that he thought it gave too much representation to "the great" and not enough to those whom he sometimes called yeomen but more often merely the "middling" class.

The unfortunate consequences which Smith feared from this overrepresentation of the great were both economic and social.

First, the great (p. 248) would not "feel for the poor and middling class" because "they are not obliged to use the same pains and labor to procure property. . . . Being in the habit of profuse living, they will be profuse in the public expenses." They would impose high taxes (p. 247) because "they feel not the inconveniences arising from the payment of small sums." Smith did not tie his sociological objection directly to the Constitution. But, he implied that its adoption without change would somehow enhance the tendency of the great to "consider themselves above the common people, entitled to more respect," disdaining to "associate with them," tending "to fancy themselves to have a right of preeminence in every thing." The great, he concluded (p. 247), "possess the same feelings, and are under the influence of the same motives, as an hereditary nobility." Adoption of the Constitution without amendment, he believed, would assist the great in such pretensions.

The assumption common to both Smith and Tredwell that the "great" would control the new federal government under the proposed Constitution requires some examination. Again it was Smith who made the explicit analysis (pp. 246–248) of a point which Tredwell took for granted. His first point was that "in every society, men of this 'first' class will command superior respect; and if the government is so constituted as to admit but few to exercise the power of it, it will, according to the natural course of things, be in their hands." Next, he argued in effect that the social expenses necessarily entailed by a "highly elevated" office would deter plain men from seeking it. He expected "great" men to win elections in large districts not only for these reasons but also because "the great easily form associations; the poor and middling classes form them with difficulty." Even if the latter could unite in support of someone other than a "great" man, Smith believed the object of their support would probably be "some popular demagogue, . . . destitute of principle."

The conclusion of his argument remains to be made explicit. Only by amending the Constitution to increase greatly the number of representatives in Congress, Smith argued, would there be chosen "middling class" men sufficient in number to "control" the great. Such a legislative majority of "respectable yeomanry" was the surest safeguard to the property interests of the poor and the "best possible security to liberty." While such a majority of yeomanry was by his reasoning quite unlikely in the federal Congress under the proposed Constitution, he knew from actual experience that it could often be attained in the legislature of the state. Consequently, he disliked the Constitution for two reasons. It prescribed a governmental system which would be dominated by the great, and it greatly enhanced the power of the federal government and diminished relatively that of the states, thus increasing the political advantages of the great.

Tredwell shared Smith's fear of the great and his assumption that adoption of the Constitution without amendments would assure them control, but he clearly reposed less confidence in the "middling" class. Tredwell was rather disposed to suspect all men and to fear power in any hands. In forming governments, he thought (pp. 397–398), "the design of the people . . . is not so much to give powers to their rulers, as to guard against the abuse of them." It would be "absurd in the highest degree" for the people to "give to their rulers power to destroy them and their property . . . or, in other words, . . . to give unlimited power to their rulers, and not retain in their own hands the means of their own preservation." His emphasis in urging amendments was on limiting governmental power. He wanted provisions to prevent the government from "tyrannizing over our consciences by a religious establishment," to assure trial by jury, freedom of the press, and the freedom of election as well as a "sufficient" representation.

On state rights Tredwell was of two minds. "A union with our sister states," he declared (p. 405), "I as ardently desire as any man, and that upon the most generous principles." Nor was there "the least reference to the clashing interests of the states" in any of the amendments to the Constitution which he suggested (p. 396). "Not one of our objections," Tredwell added (p. 405), "is founded on the motives of particular state interest."

On the other hand, he did accept, whether consciously or not, Smith's belief that a middle-class majority in the legislature, such as New York State then enjoyed, was the best guarantee of liberty. He clearly shared Smith's assumption that "the great" would control the new federal government under the Constitution and that the "middling" group would retain control of the state government. Consequently, he was alarmed at what he perceived to be the balance of power between federal and state governments in the proposed Constitution. "What sovereignty, what power is left to it [the state]," he asked (p. 403), "when the control of every source of revenue, and the total command of the militia, are given to the general government? That power which can command both the property and the persons of the community, is the sovereign and the sole sovereign. . . . I think it is clear that . . . the whole power and sovereignty of our state governments, and with them the liberties of the country is swallowed up by the general government; for . . . they shall be disarmed of all power, and made totally dependent on the bounty of Congress for their support, and consequently for their existence. . . . There are no advantages that can possibly arise from a union," he concluded (p. 406), "which can compensate for the loss of freedom, nor can any evils be apprehended from a disunion which are as much to be dreaded as tyranny." Accordingly, he voted not to ratify the Constitution.

Had Tredwell expressed his political views in the form of a syllogism it would have been something like this:

a. The most important concern with reference to any governmental system in a world of evil men is to assure protection for the liberties and properties of the people.

b. The gravest danger to these liberties and properties is the encroachment of the great, while their greatest bulwark is the political power of the middling class.

c. Ergo, the governmental system to be preferred will minimize the power of the federal government to be dominated by the great and concentrate such minimal authority as is required in the state legislatures which middling-class representatives will control.

This view was the implicit foundation of majority political opinion in Beekmantown and Plattsburgh throughout the period of this study.

Despite the prevalence of Antifederalist views among the Plattsburgh proprietors, it is difficult to discern clearly the political complexion of the town and of Clinton County as the Federalist era, 1788–1800, began. There was no newspaper. Surviving minutes of the Plattsburgh town meetings begin only in 1798. Furthermore, as Jabez D. Hammond noted, "Party lines were not then . . . distinctly marked." Legislators often voted in such a manner as to defy attribution of party loyalty. Appointive positions went often to individuals associated, at least on some occasions, with opposition to the appointing officer.[6]

Such evidence as there is, however, suggests that from the very beginning of settlement Plattsburgh was more "republican" than the county as a whole and that, in contrast to the situation in most frontier areas, it was defections from the Antifederalist-Republican ranks which made the Federalist party viable rather than vice versa.[7] Melanchton L. Woolsey's political career illustrates both points. In 1787 Woolsey expressed views which were definitely in line with Antifederalist thought. Writing from what he called his "mud-walled cottage," Woolsey complained bitterly about high taxes, adding sarcastically that "the expense the public is at in supporting 5 or 600 perhaps 1000 families (genteel families) in opulence Elegance and Ease is done only to secure our property and ought not to be murmured at." In the same vein, he thought nothing more was wanting but a standing army to "secure our persons." Abandoning sarcasm, he expressed a desire to see the government "settle in Republicanism—an Aristocracy however appears to be the aim of those who I fear have too much influence to be baffled in the Attempt."[8] Plattsburgh chose Woolsey its supervisor in 1790.

In 1792, when Federalist John Jay ran a neck-and-neck race with the old Antifederalist George Clinton, who was seeking reelection as governor, Woolsey reported that Clinton received all of the forty-six votes cast in Plattsburgh. He himself, Woolsey noted, had either written or seen every ballot but one. The one which he had not seen belonged to William Pitt Platt, brother-in-law of James Kent and a suspected "Blue Jay," but Platt had later affirmed to Woolsey that "he was an Ostrich," that is, a Clintonian. In Champlain, on the other hand, most of the sixteen to eighteen votes cast went to Jay.[9]

By 1796 Woolsey and a goodly number of his fellow residents of Plattsburgh had become ardent Federalists. They rallied valiantly—but vainly—to try to prevent the "Democrats" from electing Charles Platt to the assembly.[10] To Woolsey it seemed "the highest species of Tyranny" that the Republicans planned to have Benjamin Mooers attend the voting at Champlain and Platt, at Peru. Their intention, he affirmed, was to "overawe or overrule the suffrage of the lowest citizens." He also suspected a Republican postmaster of expediting Republican mail and delaying that of Federalists.[11]

Ideological polarization undoubtedly had something to do with the rapid rise of Federalism in Plattsburgh between 1793 and 1796. As the French Revolution degenerated into the Radical Reign of Terror (1792–1795) and war broke out (1793) between aristocratic Britain and republican France, more and more Americans began to become avid partisans of one side or the other.

Jay's Treaty, a Federalist measure which pulled the nation back from the brink of war with Britain, also became a focal point for political disputation between rival ideological factions. Many New Yorkers gravitated to the Federalist position—partly because of ideological considerations but also in realization that war with Britain would be ruinous both to commerce and to frontier land speculations in New York. Ratification of Jay's Treaty would and in fact did avert these economic disasters.[12]

Woolsey's conversion to Federalism, while probably influenced by both those considerations, may have owed something to his own rise in status and to concern for his appointive positions. He derived income of about six hundred dollars yearly from two patronage positions—one as federal collector of customs and the other as clerk of Clinton County. This income enabled him to send two sons to prestigious Flatbush Academy in Brooklyn and a daughter to boarding school in Montreal. By 1800 he was proudly inviting friends to visit his new house, a vast improvement over his "mud-walled cottage" of 1787.[13] Such advances in status, as will be observed in some later instances as well, could lead to a less jaundiced view than Woolsey had expressed in 1787 of the "aristocratic" party and the "Elegance and Ease" afforded by government jobs. Federalist domination of both the national government and especially of the state Council of Appointment may also have helped persuade him to reconsider his earlier attitude toward that party.

Despite the rise of Federalism between 1793 and 1796, the Republicans clearly dominated Plattsburgh in the last years of the Federalist era. They did so in the face of a strong Federalist tide sparked by the XYZ affair, the undeclared naval war with France, and the widespread fear of Republican radicalism and even of Republican subversion in the interest of France. Plattsburgh's town meeting of 1798 elected Republicans to every major office. In 1799 they rubbed salt in the wounds of the Francophobic Federalists by electing as town supervisor the French immigrant Peter Sailly. They reelected him in 1800.[14]

In the assembly elections, Federalists fared much better. They did so by virtue of maintaining majority positions in some of the other towns of Clinton County and in neighboring Essex County, which then shared an assembly seat with Clinton County. In 1796 the assemblyman was Charles Platt, nominally a Republican, but he cast his vote against the Jeffersonian slate of presidential electors, which included his father, Zephaniah, and in favor of the slate supporting John Adams. He voted Federalist on other occasions as well. Outright Federalists Daniel Ross and William Gilliland held the seat in 1798 and 1800 respectively. Asa Adgate in 1799 had a voting record rather like Platt's.[15]

In the Jeffersonian era (1800–1815), Republicans continued to do much better in Plattsburgh than in the assembly district. Nine of the supervisors whom Plattsburgh chose between 1800 and 1815 were Republicans. Four were Federalists. Three appear to have had no firm allegiance to either party. Dependable Republicans held the assembly seat, however, only four times in the same period.

Political deals designed to gain advantage for Clinton County account for the election of Federalists in some instances. In 1800, for example, a special meeting, held on a night so stormy that even Thomas Tredwell stayed home, agreed to give unanimous support to the assembly aspirant who won a majority of the votes. But, there was an understanding that the victor and his backers would then support the rival candidate the following year. The meeting gave Mooers forty-five votes to twenty-five for William Bailey but, unfortunately for the Republicans, Mooers than suffered defeat at the hands of the Federalist candidate from Essex County. Mooers and his partisans apparently kept their bargain by supporting Bailey, who won the next year. His voting record had a distinct Federalist tinge. In fact, although he had been a Republican in the past, he was in 1800 already well on the way to all-out identification with the Federalist party.[16]

Town jealousies may also have affected political contests. In 1800 Federalist Pliny Moore of Champlain had expressed bitter resentment at Plattsburgh's presumption in arranging the Mooers-Bailey deal without consulting anyone from Champlain. In 1801 conniving Federalists from Essex County encouraged Moore himself to be a candidate, apparently hoping that his candidacy would reduce the Clinton County vote for Bailey and allow another Essex man to win. Plattsburgh Federalists, however, persuaded Moore that there was no chance of success "with a candidate wholly brought forward by our side" and that the lesser "eavil" would be to support Bailey as the "Democrats" had agreed to do.[17] In view of Bailey's subsequent voting record, that was very sound Federalist strategy. It also worked well for Plattsburgh and for Clinton County.

To the avidly partisan Melanchton L. Woolsey, such bipartisan pursuit of advantage for the county or the town was dangerously myopic. Frightened by "an incorrigible spirit of democracy [which] has held good its course in this place for many years," Woolsey feared in 1800 that a Republican assemblyman from the district might help elect a "Jacobinical" president. "Mr. Sailly may preach of Union and Judge Platt respond yes, yes, yes as much as they please [but] when a Jefferson administration stares us in the face it is not time to Unite with them." To him it was more important for Federalists in Essex and Clinton counties to join together in electing a safely Federalist assemblyman than for Clinton County to secure an advantage over Essex through a bipartisan deal uniting the county behind a local Republican one year and a Federalist the next.[18]

Because the state Council of Appointment still filled so many local offices (judges, justices of the peace, sheriff, militia commanders, county clerk, and others), patronage matters were of paramount importance in local politics. The council members, chosen on a partisan basis by the legislature, usually left most incumbents undisturbed, but extreme partisans were likely to face removal if the other party gained dominance of the council.[19] The filling of vacancies, however they arose, always required consultation with the assemblyman of the area, if he was of the same political persuasion as the council majority, or with recognized local leaders of the dominant party if he was not. While Bailey was serving in the assembly in 1802, Pliny Moore urged him to recommend to the council the retention of the justices of the peace for Champlain. He had heard rumors that the council had been urged to appoint several new justices whose principal qualification was recent conversion to republicanism.[20] Bailey replied that he would try but added ominously that he could not "boast of *much* influence with the present Council."[21] By 1805, perhaps because Thomas Tredwell was on the Council of Appointment in 1804, Moore had lost his own judicial office, but he regained it with a promotion in 1807.[22] Woolsey lost command of the regional militia to Benjamin Mooers in 1803. After twenty years in office, he lost his job as county clerk to Charles Platt in 1808. A cautious Federalist council in 1810 declined to return him to that lucrative office.[23]

Patronage appointments, of course, created problems within the majority party as well. In 1802 some Clinton County Republicans sought to have Champlain's Samuel Hicks, an inveterate personal and political enemy of Pliny Moore, appointed sheriff, but Assemblyman Peter Sailly persuaded the council to retain the Federalist incumbent Benjamin Graves. Benjamin Mooers and others were highly displeased. By 1811 Sailly claimed to have lost all influence in his party and gave as part of the explanation that "several persons of the opposite political party were either put or kept into office through my pertinaceous endeavors." Such actions, he continued, led "some of the principle men" with whom he had "joined in politicks" to regard him with "disgust." He did not plan to attend the party meeting which would soon consider nominations because his voice would not be heard.[24]

Federalists, accurately perceiving Sailly's moderation, had in fact schemed successfully to elect him to the assembly in preference to more partisan Republicans. "So low is the state of federalism," Woolsey had concluded in 1802, that the party must "give up all pretensions to a lead in politics or any attempt at securing a [Federalist] candidate for the Legislature. We *know*," he wrote to Pliny Moore, "the Democratic leaders have their eyes on Judge Tredwell and Colonel Mooers [as prospective assembly candidates], either of whom if *they unite in*, will be successful. Our opinions of both these gentlemen are the same: that they are the most rigid and violent in their principles and have the least charity for those in opposition." To forestall the nomination of either, Woolsey urged that Federalists in various towns prompt Republicans in their areas to put forth the name of Peter Sailly. Sailly had agreed to run only if he were nominated before either Mooers or Tredwell. Woolsey insisted that the nomination must be made by Republicans "for I do not conceive a more effective mode can be adopted to defeat his Election than to be brought forward by the federalists." Woolsey suggested further that the Federalists might hint at nominating a Federalist, but that if possible they arrange to have a committee make the "*true* Nomination" [Sailly] before the election. Not even the most rabid Republican, Woolsey concluded, would "dare to attempt to interest him [Sailly] in any thing or measure violent in its nature or distressing in its tendency. He will act on the President's promises [see Jefferson's first inaugural address] and still suffer us to think and speak without persecution."[25]

The strategy worked. Pliny Moore informed Woolsey a few days later that Champlain would be unanimous for Sailly unless the Republicans came to see him as a Federalist choice.[26] Sailly did win the election and did live up to the Federalist expectations albeit, as indicated previously, at the cost of alienation from his own party.

Oddly enough, while Woolsey was scheming with other Federalists to bring about Sailly's election to the assembly, Senator De Witt Clinton was intervening with President Jefferson to dissuade him from firing Woolsey from his lucrative job as customs collector. Presumably in ignorance of Woolsey's conversion to federalism and of his unstinting effort in 1800 to prevent the election of a "Jacobinical president," George Clinton had blandly written to his nephew for transmission to Jefferson the assurance that Woolsey was "a republican in principle and a warm friend and open advocate of our present federal and state administrations." Woolsey, in fact, retained his job until 1809, when President Madison fired him at the behest of Governor Daniel D. Tompkins, to whom he had turned for advice on patronage out of distrust of De Witt Clinton. There is a certain irony in that the man chosen to replace Woolsey was Peter Sailly.[27]

Perhaps to preclude Federalist nomination of Republican candidates in the future, the Republicans began in 1803 to observe a more formal procedure in making nominations. That November party leaders in the towns sent out invitations to "friends of the administration" to meet for the purpose of choosing delegates to a meeting in Plattsburgh in March, which would select an assembly candidate. Nomination was to be by a "plurality of voices." Those who signed the invitation affirmed that the procedure which they proposed was "conformable to the common practice of our Republican friends in all the old Counties of this State."[28]

Commercial restrictions and other aspects of Republican foreign policy designed to force Britain to ease its restrictions on American commerce gradually eroded Republican strength in the years before the War of 1812. Jefferson's embargo was quite unpopular despite its generally favorable impact on the local economy. As Pliny Moore noted without mentioning the smuggling boom specifically, "that ruinous destructive system to our country in general operates favorably to us. Everybody has their hands full of money." Still at the repeal of the embargo in 1809 150 people thronged to a Federalist-sponsored service of thanksgiving. "This town," a Plattsburgh Federalist noted happily, "becomes more federal every day." When Republican Kinner Newcomb lost the assembly contest narrowly to a Federalist, Peter Sailly (by then restored to good standing in the party) lamented that "the Cries of French influence here and of French Torys in Champlain and Chazy coupled with the embargo and supported by every kind of federal

Calumnies have completely deceived the People and we have lost the Election." In 1810 he hoped that "the British faction will be put down throughout," but he was disappointed again.[29]

Somewhat surprisingly the Republican margin of victory was greater among the £100 freeholders qualified to vote for "major" state offices than among those who qualified to vote for the assembly as holders of £20 freeholds or by paying taxes and forty shillings rent (see table 14). One possible explanation is that the agents of the Beekmans influenced the vote of tenants residing in Beekman Patent. The chief among several difficulties with that idea is that the Beekmans' agent in at least the early portion of the period covered by the voting figures was the staunchly Republican Thomas Tredwell. Another possibility is that local Federalists of great wealth, such as Levi Platt, may have exerted influence over numerous employees in their mills and stores and over tenants on their land. There is evidence that Levi Platt was deeply involved as a political organizer behind the scenes in the 1820s. A more plausible explanation is that a high proportion of the £100 freeholders were friends and relatives of the proprietors, still faithful to the Antifederalist and Republican heritage brought with them from Dutchess County and Long Island, while a high proportion of the tenants and small freeholders came from Federalist New England.[30]

The founding of the Plattsburgh *Republican* in 1811 was an event of major political importance. There had been an earlier newspaper in the community, and there would be many others later. But, prior to 1850 all rival papers were of relatively brief duration. The Federalists and later the Whigs were never able, despite repeated attempts, to sustain a newspaper on a really long-term basis. The *Republican*, in contrast, was permanent; it still publishes under the same name. In the period from 1811 until 1850, it was a major influence throughout the "north country" in support of orthodox party principles and candidates.

Accounts of the founding of the *Republican* vary. Piecing them together, it appears that an individual named Samuel Lowell had begun to publish a Republican paper, the *American Monitor*, about 1809. Many Republicans subscribed. Upon Lowell's marriage in 1811, however, he experienced conversion to the Federalist views of his wife's family. His paper then branded the administrations of Jefferson and Madison as "the greatest source of all evils" and contained in general, according to the *Republican*, "the most scandalous hypocrisy, and the most undisguised falsehood."[31]

Meeting at the house of Peter Sailly, the outraged Republicans determined to organize a dependably Republican paper. Chairman of the meeting and of the joint stock enterprise which it initiated was Charles Platt, former assemblyman, then a judge. Secretary of the enterprise and first editor of the paper was Colonel Melanchton Smith, son of the Antifederalist leader of the ratifying convention of 1788. Others who participated were Judge Kinner Newcomb, Isaac C. Platt, Caleb Nichols (lawyer and tavern keeper), Doctor John Miller, Thomas Tredwell, Benjamin Mooers, Judge Nathan Carver of Chazy, and Judge Samuel Hicks of Champlain.[32]

Despite its impressive backing, the *Republican* got off to a shaky start. Smith, as the chief administrative figure in the effort, purchased a press and two or three barrels of type at St. Albans, Vermont, and brought them across the lake in a skiff. He set up shop in one room of the house occupied by Frederick P. Allen's parents, "two doors east of the court house." There on April 12, 1811, Smith, L. J. Reynolds, whose name appears as printer, Luther Marsh, a typesetter, and the youthful Allen brought out "for the Proprietors" the first edition of the Plattsburgh *Republican*.

Observing that it was customary in beginning a newspaper "to declare the sentiments of the editor," Smith served notice bluntly that "his object is to support the present [Republican] Administration of the General and State governments." He pledged to observe a strict regard for *Truth*," to include documentation for assertions likely to be disputed, to publish material relating to improvements in agriculture and manufacturing, and "to select [for publication] such pieces in prose and verse as shall unite amusement with instruction." He expressed his intention also to "espouse the cause of Religion and Morality, against infidelity and vice."

What was the nature of political sentiment in Plattsburgh as reflected in early issues of the *Republican*? On the question of relations with Britain, it was distinctly bellicose. Referring to the impressment of seamen from American ships into the British navy, the *Republican* cited with obvious approval (June 14, 1811) the declaration of the Baltimore *Evening Post*: "It is high time this business of *man stealing* was brought to a head." On October 4 the editor noted that "Great Britain is now at actual War with the United States" and implicitly regretted that all the fighting was "on one side." As Congress moved toward a declaration of war in the spring of 1812, the *Republican* faced the issue squarely. War, the editor affirmed, would cost many lives and require very heavy taxation, but "to suffer many more calls on our patience and forbearance would be pusillanimity; would make us the scorn and derision of nations; would provoke the attack of every power, and would render us unworthy [of] the character . . . of a free, independent, brave, and virtuous People."

The editor did not call for war. Accommodation was still possible, he indicated, if Britain would "speedily alter her conduct with regard to us." But, he urged voters who felt that war was coming if Britain did not so alter its conduct to elect state legislators and congressmen who would support the government in such a war rather than "oppose, divide, perplex, and paralyze" it. In the assembly election which ensued soon after the appearance of this editorial, *Republican* proprietor Kinner Newcomb lost the district to a Federalist, but he carried Plattsburgh with 62 percent of the vote.[33]

The prospect of acquiring Canada did not arouse much interest. Caleb Nichols, one of the *Republican*'s proprietors, used its pages to convey a challenge (February 14, 1812) to any reader to show that it would not be in the interest of Clinton and Franklin counties and of the United States to acquire Canada. There is no indication that anyone took up the challenge, but its wording and the paucity of other stories with the same theme suggest that it was simply not a subject of much interest. The records of the local militia in refusing to cross the border into Canada bears out the impression that expansionism was far less important than "national honor" as a foundation for war settlement in Plattsburgh.

The restrictions on trade with Canada designed to extract concessions from Britain won loyal support from local Republicans in the face of bitter and determined resistance from Federalists. While the *Republican* was not yet in existence at the time of Jefferson's embargo, Kinner Newcomb had given consistent support to it as assemblyman for the district in 1808–1809. Another of the *Republican* proprietors, Peter Sailly, manifested his devotion to party policy at greater risk. Sailly secured appointment as customs collector for the Champlain district when the Federalist incumbent, Melanchton L. Woolsey, began to be suspected of inadequate zeal. One night in January 1812, a group of armed men broke into Sailly's home, which also served as the customs office, in an attempt to recover property which he had confiscated for violation of regulations. Sailly refused to be intimidated. He shot two of the intruders with a pistol and drove off the entire group. The *Republican*'s account of the episode (January 31, 1812) stressed

Sailly's heroism and expressed both outrage and embarrassment that all the "villains" were local residents.

Plattsburgh's Federalists suffer the handicap of being known chiefly through highly biased accounts in the *Republican*. Not only were their own journals short-lived, but relatively few copies of the succession of papers which they instituted have survived. It is clear, however, that in Clinton County as elsewhere the Federalists were attempting to get out from under the onus borne by that designation. As early as 1806, Woolsey was calling for the triumph of "Constitutional Republicans." In 1812 the designations were "Federal Republicans" or the "Friends of Peace, Liberty and Commerce." [34]

In the period of the War of 1812, Republican majorities in Plattsburgh declined to a low of about 60 percent (1813) in assembly contests but recovered sharply on the surge of patriotic feelings aroused in particular by the British invasion. In the spring of 1815, following the battle of Plattsburgh the previous fall, militia commander Benjamin Mooers trounced his Federalist opponent for the assembly with 70 percent of the town's vote. Mooers also carried the district (Clinton and Franklin counties) for the Republicans for the first time since Kinner Newcomb had done so in 1808, the year of the embargo. To do so he had rolled up Republican majorities in Plattsburgh and the southern portion of Clinton County sufficient to overcome the usual Federalist majorities in Chazy, Champlain, and all the towns of more sparsely populated Franklin County to the west. [35]

In the "era of good feelings" which followed the war, Plattsburgh's political course was highly erratic. In 1816 Mooers held his 70 percent over a different Federalist, while Republican Governor Tompkins whipped Federalist Rufus King with 77 percent of the vote. [36] Tompkins resigned, however, to become vice-president of the United States in 1817. Republicans then arranged a state convention to nominate a successor. The informal meeting of Republicans in Plattsburgh, which chose Benjamin Mooers as delegate to that convention, instructed him to support De Witt Clinton. That same week a bipartisan meeting in Plattsburgh, with Republican Melanchton Smith as chairman and Federalist William Swetland as secretary, expressed strong support for the canal program which Clinton had so long advocated and upon which construction was just beginning. Old Republicans in New York tried to stir up support for the more orthodox Republican, Peter B. Porter, even after he lost to Clinton in the state convention. But, the Platts-burgh *Republican* gave him no support whatever and no more than a one-line notice. Only one vote was cast against De Witt Clinton in the town of Plattsburgh in 1817, but partisanship was undimin-ished in other contests. Republican Carver beat Federalist Gates Hoit for the assembly with 67 percent of the Plattsburgh vote, and the Republican senatorial slate of three candidates won by 73 percent.[37]

Republican support of Clinton for governor in 1817 seemingly represented a triumph of expediency over principle. Clinton had opposed the Republican embargo, the Republican war, and had in effect allowed the Federalists to use him as a candidate to oppose the reelection of Republican President James Madison in 1812. He was an inveterate enemy of Republican Governor Tompkins, his one-time protégé. He would have no part of the party loyalty and organizational dedication which were articles of faith to major Republican leaders. His canal program reflected a philosophy of government far more congenial to Federalists than to old-style Republicans.

There were, on the other hand, important political considera-tions which apparently persuaded Plattsburgh Republicans to go along with Clinton's nomination for governor. He had secured nomination by the state convention, which party leaders felt bound to respect. The Champlain Canal promised such obvious advantage to the area that the course of expediency may have demanded eleva-tion of its most effective advocate to the governor's chair, despite the difficulty of reconciling the project and Clinton's views with Republican philosophy. Clintonians also dominated the Council of Appointment, which controlled patronage appointments. High-ly conscious of the importance of such appointments to their or-ganization, Plattsburgh's Republicans perhaps were getting on the Clinton bandwagon in accord with the view that "if you can't lick 'em, join 'em." Clinton's managers helped to palliate the choice by promising that he would "rigidly pursue a republican course."[38]

The easing of the standards of party regularity, however, was soon the occasion for regret among orthodox Republicans. Even while the popular front of 1817 was securing the governorship to De Witt Clinton, the Republicans of Franklin County made a deal with their Federalist opponents. The Franklin County Re-publicans agreed to support the Federalist nominee for the assembly in 1817 in return for a pledge from Franklin County Federalists to support a Franklin County Republican in opposition to a Clinton County Republican in 1818. The arrangement failed to elect the Federalist candidate in 1817. But, it did help Ebenezer Brownson of Franklin County, a Republican follower of De Witt Clinton, to defeat the regular Republican candidate, Melanchton Smith of Plattsburgh, in 1818. Smith, partly because of unexplained but important personal factors and partly because of pro-Clinton feeling in Plattsburgh, received only 38 percent of the town's vote. He carried the county narrowly by virtue of a large Republican vote in Peru, but Federalist support for Brownson in normally Federalist Franklin County assured Smith's overwhelming defeat in the assembly district as a whole.[39]

In 1819 both the Republican split and the weakness of the Federalists became still more apparent. A Republican meeting chaired by Thomas Tredwell affirmed that "political distinctions have not ceased and that the contrary is asserted by designing individuals only to beguile the watchfulness of Republicans." The meeting referred vaguely to the ambitions of a few self-aggrandizing men as the source of disruption in the party.[40] Indeed, the disruption was evident in that three rival delegations appeared at the nominating convention claiming to represent Plattsburgh.

The convention tried to effect a compromise, but it was less than wholly successful. Orthodox Republican Benjamin Mooers received one of the three senate nominations, but he pledged to support Clinton, as did the convention as a whole. Another old-line Republican, Elisha Button, received the assembly nomination, but the Clintonians named former Plattsburgh supervisor, Platt Newcomb, to run against him. With no Federalist candidate in the contest, Newcomb outdid Button 312 (57 percent) to 227 (45 percent). For the three senate positions, the Federalist ran a slate of three candidates, but the Clintonians apparently supported the slate which included Benjamin Mooers. One of the three Federalists received only 13 votes while the tally for the three Republicans ranged from a low of 184 (Mooers) to a high of 212.[41]

In 1820 the old line Republicans suffered ignominious defeat. Mooers, despite having been elected as a Clintonian Republican, quickly moved into opposition and in 1820 accepted nomination for lieutenant governor to run with ex-Governor Tompkins against Clinton. Why he did so is not certain, but a number of factors which may have influenced his decision are evident. By removing

Attorney General Martin Van Buren, leader of the opposition "Bucktail" faction, and many local officers the Clinton Council of Appointments had demonstrated its intention to institute what the *Republican* referred to as a "reign of terror" against its opponents. Thus, appeasement seemed no longer in order. Furthermore, the Van Buren faction did enjoy the support, manifested in federal patronage appointments, of the Monroe administration, which was quite fearful of Clinton.[42] In any case Plattsburgh's old Republicans under the leadership of *Republican* editor Azariah C. Flagg rallied valiantly against Clintonism and for republicanism of the old variety.

The result was disastrous. Tompkins received only 27 percent of the vote in Plattsburgh to Clinton's 73 percent. Mooers did slightly better than Tompkins. Flagg himself as assembly candidate opposing the Clintonian Platt Newcomb secured 40 percent. The town supervisor was an old-line Federalist, Jonathan Griffin, who had held the office once before, in 1806. In Beekmantown, which achieved its independence from Plattsburgh that year, the result was similar. Tompkins got only 25 percent; Mooers 22 percent; Flagg 40 percent. The town's first supervisor was an old-line Connecticut Federalist now calling himself a Republican, Dr. Baruch Beckwith. In the state as a whole, Clinton won by only a narrow margin, which Flagg atributed to the "aristocratical feature in our constitution."[43]

Some of the factors which explain the Republican disaster are evident in the record of the preelection meeting of the inhabitants of Beekmantown. The chairman of the meeting was Charles Marsh, the Federalist supervisor of Plattsburgh in 1819, and its secretary was Dr. Beckwith. The resolutions of the meeting expressed approval of both state and national administrations. More specifically, the inhabitants affirmed that the "whole tenor of his [Clinton's] public measures have been highly republican and calculated for the protection of the interests and equal rights of all classes of the community—that with the federalists as a party we acknowledge no coalition—we support Mr. Clinton still as a Republican." They denied that his administration was any less Republican because of Federalist support. They attacked Tompkins as a defaulter (his wartime expenditure accounts were in bad order) and Mooers as a political turncoat whose "service to this state in the trying time of war and danger was such as reflects on him no *honor*." The

Republican characterized the assembly district nominating convention of the Republican party as including three Republicans and two Federalists.[44]

In 1821 the voters of Beekmantown and Plattsburgh began to switch from the Clintonian-Federalist coalition to the side of the old Republicans. Their senatorial slate got 63 percent of the vote in Plattsburgh and 54 percent in Beekmantown. For the assembly, a regular Republican, Abijah North, defeated old-line Federalist Asa Hascall with 61 percent of the vote in each town. Each town retained its Federalist supervisor for another year, but in Plattsburgh at least the margin of victory was much lower. Only 27 votes had been cast against Jonathan Griffin in 1820, but in 1821 he won reelection by a margin of 7 votes in a total of about 340.[45]

Both recovery from the Panic of 1819 and the elimination of the canal issue aided the Republican revival, but also important was the recognition that the opposition coalition was becoming more Federalist than Clintonian. "Federal Convention" was the heading under which Flagg's *Republican* reported a Clintonian meeting. Observing that the names of those attending were not published, Flagg affirmed that Federalists were up to their old trick of "appearing in disguise and calling themselves *republicans.*" The "federal party," he added, had "never been more purely represented in any meeting within the last ten years." A meeting in Mooers had eleven old Federalists and five Clintonians. He also argued that Clinton's legislative supporters were nearly all Federalists.[46]

Very helpful also to the Republicans was the reappearance of the aristocracy issue. Old-line Republicans had taken the lead in advocating a convention to reform the outmoded constitution of 1777. They wished in particular to eliminate the £100 freehold qualification in voting for governor, lieutenant-governor, and state senators. Clinton had opposed a convention and indeed had cast a tie-breaking vote in the Council of Revision, which vetoed a legislative bill providing for such a convention. Clintonian Assemblyman Platt Newcomb of Plattsburgh had also voted against a convention. The Plattsburgh *Republican* went down the line in favor of the convention and suffrage extension. The Clintonians, Flagg wrote, "well know that an extension of the right of suffrage destroys the hopes of Clintonism forever. And therefore no artifice will be left untried in order to preserve the aristocracy in full vigor, and to prevent those who bear arms and pay taxes from coming into possession of their equitable rights." In the popular referendum of 1821 on the calling of such a convention, Beekmantown voted 192 in favor to none opposed.[47]

Patronage may also have figured in the Republican revival. The Council of Appointment had come under the control of orthodox Republicans again at the beginning of 1821. Following the example set by the Clintonians, the new council majority "removed all, or nearly all the sheriffs, clerks, surrogates, judges of the courts of common pleas, and justices of the peace, who were known or suspected to be politically opposed to them." Before the end of February, virtually all the old-line Republican leaders in Clinton County had secured appointments of one kind or another. In Beekmantown there were four justices of the peace, an equal number of commissioners of deeds, and one coroner.[48] The effect was undoubtedly as good for their morale as it was bad for that of the opposition.

Beekmantown's enthusiasm for the antiaristocratic constitution of 1821 was less than that for the convention. While the vote in favor of a constitutional convention was unanimous, the vote in favor of the resulting constitution was only seventy-four to fourteen, about the same proportion as in the state as a whole. In the Federalist towns, the margin of approval was generally higher.[49]

The suffrage provisions of the new constitution (see chapter 9 for details) nearly tripled the number of Beekmantown residents eligible to vote for major state offices. While Flagg and others on both sides clearly expected the increase in the electorate for major state offices to benefit the orthodox Republicans, the evidence as to the effect is not entirely clear. Plattsburgh's £100 freeholders had, after all, voted consistently more Republican than had assembly voters (see table 14) until the very exceptional election of 1820. They did so again by a slight margin in 1821. In Beekmantown, on the other hand, assembly voters were 14 percent more Republican than were voters in the gubernatorial election of 1820 and still 7 percent more Republican than senatorial voters in 1821. Thus, Beekmantown seemed to warrant Flagg's expectation, but Plattsburgh did not.

The new constitution's provision for popular election of many local officers previously appointed promptly caused trouble in Clinton County. Those chosen by party leaders for such offices as sheriff and coroner had to be presented to voters along with the nominations of the rival party rather than to the Council of

TABLE 14.

Republican Vote by Suffrage Category in Beekmantown and Plattsburgh

Year	£100 Freeholders	Assembly Voters	Difference between Columns 1 and 2
		Plattsburgh	
1807	76%	71%	+ 5%
1811	71%	62%	+ 9%
1812	67%	62%	+ 5%
1815	78%	70%	+ 8%
1816	77%	70%	+ 7%
1817	73%	67%	+ 6%
1819*	94%*	43%*	+51%*
1820*	27%*	40%*	−13%*
1821	63%	61%	+ 2%
		Beekmantown	
1820*	25%*	39%*	−14%*
1821	54%	61%	− 7%

SOURCE: Town Meeting Minutes; Plattsburgh *Republican*.
*In 1819 the senate slate agreed upon by the orthodox and the Clintonian Republicans got from 82 percent to 94 percent of the vote against an old-line Federalist slate, but the orthodox Republican candidate for the assembly got only 43 percent while a Federalist-Clintonian candidate received 57 percent. In 1820 the orthodox Republicans opposed a Clintonian-Federalist coalition in both suffrage categories.

Appointment. The effect was to compel party leaders to give closer attention to the public appeal of their nominees. The kind of difficulties which might arise when nominations were insufficiently considered became apparent quickly in a controversy over the Republican nomination for county clerk.

The incumbent was Charles Platt, who had served as county clerk since the removal of Woolsey in 1808. Republican practice required that a county convention nominate party candidates for county offices. The convention delegates were chosen by meetings held after public notice in each of the towns. In this instance the delegates decided to nominate John Walworth, a local merchant, in place of Platt. While no explanation was published at the time, the major reason apparently was that Platt's advanced age, "nearly 80," had rendered him incapable of performing the duties of the office.[50]

Characteristically, the opposition, consisting of Federalists and Clintonians, promptly endorsed Platt for reelection. Variations of the divide and rule principle similar to this had long been one of the means by which local Federalists secured their infrequent victories. Initially, Platt declined to go along. He published a letter in the *Republican* which made reference to his age, his gratitude to the party for its "liberality" in permitting him to hold the office for over fourteen years, and his disinclination to aid "our political opponents" in creating "divisions" in the party. Soon, however, he changed his mind, and a divisive but revealing contest ensued.

Platt's support came largely, but not entirely, from Federalists and Clintonians. The original nomination which Platt had declined was apparently informal. On the day that Platt announced his willingness to run, however, he was nominated in the old tradition by a "public meeting" at Plattsburgh under the chairmanship of John Addoms, a one-time Republican turned Federalist. When another public meeting at Chazy also "nominated" Platt, the *Republican* claimed that a Plattsburgh Federalist instigated the meeting, that its chairman was a Federalist, and its secretary a Clintonian. A public meeting at Beekmantown in support of Platt, however, had as its presiding officer the venerable surrogate, Thomas Tredwell, still staunchly Republican but related to the Platts through the marriage of his daughter.[51] Also perhaps he was sensitive about the dumping of septagenarian officeholders. Thus, the Federalists had succeeded at least partially with their divide and rule tactics.

There was another issue of importance in this contest in addition to age and party loyalty. The presentation of the issue in the *Republican* was by no means objective, but it does suffice to identify it. Some who supported Platt seemed to feel that it was improper to deprive him of the office which he had held so long. This feeling had the support not only of sentiment but also of tradition. In Anglo-American experience, it had been customary to accord civil servants a kind of prescriptive right to their offices, especially if the office provided income on which the incumbent had come to depend. Occasionally, such offices passed from father to son almost as possessions.[52] The Republicans were bucking this tradition.

In making its case against Platt's reelection, the *Republican* pulled no punches. The reason why Platt changed his mind and decided to run with Federalist support, the *Republican* affirmed, was to accede to the desires of his son, Nathaniel C. Platt. Having failed in business, the son, according to the *Republican*, had been "living on the profits of the office," which amounted to an average of $1,000 yearly. Presumably, the son assisted his father but, again according to the *Republican*, he was usually home in bed so that others had to assist his father at busy times. The county records were also alleged to be in deplorable confusion. With this background, the *Republican* denied the Federalists' imputation that the party was persecuting Platt if it did not permit him to hold the office for life and "to bequeath it to his heirs."[53]

The outcome of the contest was a narrow victory for Walworth, even though he lost Beekmantown to Platt by two votes, while other Republicans carried it.[54] Walworth's triumph was one of party loyalty and also of the principle of popularly controlled rotation in office, as opposed to a preemptive or vested right to office on the part of incumbent civil servants.

By 1823 the Jeffersonian Republicans of Clinton County were in a strong position. They had extended their domination from Plattsburgh so that it normally encompassed the county and the congressional and senatorial districts as well. The major obstacles which they had overcome were association with French radicalism, the unpopularity of Jefferson's commercial restrictions, initially of "Mr. Madison's War," and their own early record of indifference or opposition to Clinton's canals. To overcome these handicaps and reduce federalism and even Clintonism to their low state, they had exploited above all other issues the alleged preference of their opponents for "aristocracy." Their basic appeal would change little in the new political era which was about to begin.

14

Democrats and Whigs

A new political era was beginning for Clinton County as for the nation in 1823. Its precipitating factor was the onset of a presidential election in which the incumbent would not be a candidate, and all of the contenders—and there were many—professed to be Republicans. Most were unwilling to allow the Republican congressional caucus to make the choice for the party, as it had previously. However, no other means existed for avoiding the cumbersome and undemocratic procedure by which the Constitution required the House of Representatives to make the choice in the absence of an electoral majority for any candidate. Amid the rivalrous contention of party leaders, an opportunity arose for the revitalization of the two-party system. Within a few years, Clinton County, like the nation, would have a viable Whig party. Locally, its members would be old Federalists, Clintonians, and important new defectors from the Republican ranks. The Republicans themselves would gain a few old Federalist converts, some transitory in their stay, and transform their organization into the Jacksonian Democratic party.[1]

Prior to 1823 the political contests which aroused most interest in Beekmantown and Clinton County were the annual assembly elections. The names of assembly nominees appeared in the newspaper in much bigger type than those of candidates for other offices. Their qualifications were set forth at greater length and with greater frequency. Among the candidates receiving less attention generally were those for Congress, the state senate, and even governor. In the absence of provision for a popular vote for president, candidates for that office received almost no attention at all.

The explanation for this great focus of attention upon an office which in the twentieth century attracted relatively little interest has several facets. In the first instance, the state had not yet fully abandoned mercantilist intervention in economic affairs in favor of laissez faire; consequently, it had a major role in economic development. At the same time, it was the beneficiary of the state rights philosophy which dominated the federal government. Furthermore, the great authority which the state government exercised tended to be concentrated in the legislative branch. Until the adoption of the constitution of 1821, assemblymen who were of the same party as the majority on the Council of Appointment had considerable influence on the appointments which the council made to major offices in local government. Legislative intervention in the affairs of individual communities, as well as general legislative mandates concerning the functions of town and county government, also heightened local interest in the selection of legislators. The legislature also had a major electoral role in that it cast the state's electoral vote for president, chose United States senators, and filled major state offices as well. Finally, the fact that nearly all adult white males could vote for assemblymen, while only a minority could vote for other officers of state government, tended naturally to make for a wider interest in assembly contests than in the others.

All but the last of the factors just listed would seem to apply also to the election of state senators. There was of course much interest in senate contests, but they clearly drew less attention than those for the assembly. Like the executive in earlier Anglo-American political experience, the members of the upper legislative chamber tended to suffer from their traditionally unrepresentative character. The office was largely hereditary in England, appointed in most of the colonies, and filled by a suffrage restricted to a wealthy minority in New York from 1777 to 1821. Only after 1821 did senators become fully representative of the people.

Assembly contests attracted more attention than did senatorial elections for another reason as well. In Clinton County people identified closely with their county. Like the assembly itself, the county had tradition on its side. In accordance with ancient Anglo-American tradition, the county enjoyed a somewhat autonomous status, possessing its own courts and jail, some law-making and taxing authority, and important administrative functions assigned by the state. To some extent also, the county was a self-conscious economic unit seeking economic advantage in an essentially mercantilist competition with all outsiders. It is quite evident also that voluntary organizations for cultural, religious, or other purposes did not base themselves upon the senatorial district but on the county. Consequently, even when Clinton County shared its assemblyman with another county, as it did much of the time before 1823, the voters tended to look upon the assemblyman as "their" representative—their spokesman, agent, and lobbyist. They were far less likely to look upon their senator in that light.

From 1823 onward, circumstances combined to reduce interest in assembly contests and increase that in presidential elections. The constitution of 1821 diminished the patronage role of the assemblyman by abolishing the Council of Appointment and making many more local offices elective rather than appointive. Furthermore, suffrage reforms, which made major state offices more representative, simultaneously made the assembly contest no longer so nearly the only opportunity for effective expression of local opinion. In 1824 the electoral role of the assemblyman declined also as the legislature surrendered to the people the right to choose the state's presidential electors.

Increased attention to the presidency stemmed from at least two other factors in addition to the provision of a popular vote for president. One was the gradual extension of national feeling—acceptance of the idea that the national government, as well as the state government, might be a "we" rather than a "they."[2] Another arose from the fact that, until the nation had to choose a successor to James Monroe, there had been no spirited contest for the presidency in many years. The free-for-all which began as Monroe's presidency drew to a close attracted particularly great attention in Clinton County because the editor of the Plattsburgh *Republican*, Assemblyman Azariah C. Flagg, was an important participant in the presidential contest.

The best indication of sentiment in Beekmantown concerning the presidential election of 1824 is the assembly contest. There was as yet no provision for a popular vote for president, but Flagg was then running for reelection to the assembly. How he felt about the contest is spread across the record both of the assembly, in which he was a major leader, and in the pages of the Plattsburgh *Republican*, which he still edited. Consequently, his views were quite well known, and the assembly election constituted in effect something of a referendum on them.

Flagg was the assembly spokesman for United States Senator Martin Van Buren's "Albany Regency," the Republican oligarchy which then controlled the state. His views, however, were not necessarily entirely in accord with those of Van Buren on all issues. Van Buren's candidate for president was William H. Crawford of Georgia, Monroe's secretary of the treasury. Van Buren had several reasons for preferring Crawford to the other prospects. Crawford had been runner-up to Monroe in 1816 and thus seemed entitled to succeed him; Crawford commanded more support in Congress than any other. He also had two other qualifications which gave him a unique place in Van Buren's esteem: devotion to the traditional Republican ideology of states' rights and minimum government plus an appreciation for the utility of the Republican party organization and a determination to keep it in good health. Furthermore, the two had long cooperated on federal patronage.

Unfortunately for the Regency's aims, Crawford had numerous enemies. These included nationalists to whom the views of Secretary of State John Quincy Adams and House Speaker Henry Clay had more appeal. There were also enemies of party organization or advocates of nonpartisan government to whom Adams appealed. There were hero-worshiping and opportunistic followers of General Andrew Jackson and northerners who were tired of the succession of southern presidents. Perhaps equally unfortunate, Crawford suffered a stroke which, although it was not widely known at the time, really disqualified him for the presidency.[3]

Flagg's position was extremely difficult. Crawford evoked little enthusiasm in Flagg's constituency but, as the leading prospect, he became the principal target of each of the factions supporting a rival candidate. Thus, it appeared that in Clinton County vast numbers were against Crawford and virtually nobody was for him. Flagg was no less an advocate of traditional republicanism than Van Buren and esteemed party unity fully as much as did the "little magician." Consequently, Crawford must have appealed to him strongly, but perhaps in deference to local opinion Flagg indicated in his public statements that he preferred any of the other contenders to Crawford. His major emphasis, however, was that all were qualified, that the Republican legislative caucus should make the choice, and that all conscientious Republicans should fall in line behind the party nominee.[4]

Circumstances seemed quite favorable indeed to the opposition as the campaign of 1823 developed. One of the succession of opposition newspapers, the *Northern Intelligencer*, was then in operation. The Sperry brothers, Anson J. and Gilead, gave vigorous leadership to the opposition movement. The candidate opposing Flagg's reelection was Robert Platt, former Federalist assemblyman (1814–1815). Platt apparently refrained from endorsing any presidential candidate but ran against Crawford and in favor of a popular vote for president. The town meetings in the spring foretold Republican losses. Both Beekmantown and Plattsburgh chose opposition leaders to replace Republican supervisors elected in 1822.[5]

Flagg's tactics were skillful. Predictably, he raked over both the Federalist war record and the Federalist opposition to extension of the suffrage. He repeatedly endorsed the popular vote for president and disavowed Crawford. Somewhat more subtly, the Republican county convention which nominated him also passed a resolution denouncing "private" or "self-nominated" candidates. The implication that Platt was either self-nominated or chosen by a private meeting of those who would now be called "bosses" apparently had effect. Barely a month before the election, long after the campaign had been in full swing, those whom the *Republican* continued to stigmatize as "Federalists" held a formal convention with delegates representing each of the towns and endowed Platt with a proper nomination.

Flagg also appears to have conducted an effective "get-out-the-vote" drive. After losing the election of town supervisor in the spring, Flagg had identified the cause for the defeat as the fact that too many Republicans stayed home. Accordingly, he made every effort to remedy the deficiency. In Beekmantown, for example, a Republican rally secured the signatures of seventy-five voters on a statement disclaiming all connection with "federalism" and pledging support to Republican nominees. The effect was evident on election day. Platt secured ninety-one votes in Beekmantown, two less than his predecessor had won against Flagg the previous year. Flagg, however, garnered 121 votes compared to 101 in the preceding contest. The result for the district was similar.[6]

As Regency leader in the assembly during the session of 1824, Flagg took a leading role in devising and implementing a Regency program which evoked a statewide protest of disastrous proportions. He helped to block the movement for a popular vote for president, which he had led people to believe he favored. Despite the unpopularity of Crawford in Flagg's district and his own statements to the effect that he preferred any other candidate, when the chips were down Flagg gave his all to put as many New York electoral votes as possible in the Crawford column. Finally, although it did not afford such contrast with previous commitments, Flagg supported the removal of De Witt Clinton from the canal board.

The effect of these actions was rather different in Beekmantown and Clinton County from that in the state as a whole. For the state the effect was to produce a wave of revulsion against the Regency and in favor of De Witt Clinton. Clinton, in fact, rode back from near oblivion to another term as governor on the strength of the tide. The legislature which had been almost all Regency men suddenly became firmly anti-Regency.

In Clinton County the Republican convention strongly supported Flagg and his policies. He himself did not run for reelection, probably in deference to a local two-term tradition. The convention, however, expressed unanimously its high regard for his services, zeal, and "republican integrity." To succeed him the convention nominated Josiah Fisk of Peru. Fisk's opponent was another former assemblyman, the Clintonian Platt Newcomb. The Republican campaign stressed the opposition of both Clinton and Newcomb to the constitutional convention of 1821, equating this with opposing extension of the suffrage. Republicans endeavored also to free their party from the onus of indifference or opposition to Clinton's canal program.

In Beekmantown Clinton lost by a margin of 128 to 106, while Fisk trounced Newcomb 132 to 92. Fisk's margin was actually higher than Flagg's had been the year before.[7]

Why did Beekmantown resist the political current so strongly manifest in the rest of the state? Clearly, local feeling against the Federalists and Clintonians for their role in resisting extension of the suffrage was fundamental. It is also evident, however, that Flagg's conduct in the assembly was not so offensive to his constituents as it appeared to voters elsewhere in the state. Flagg opposed the immediate provision of a popular vote for president because undesirable results would follow. Without provision for a runoff (which seemed impractical), New York's electoral vote would be divided among a number of candidates, thus weakening the state's influence and fragmenting the Republican organization. The probability that the election would be thrown into the House of Representatives would be increased. This would be highly undemocratic (each state delegation casts just one vote regardless of the number of people it represents) and would split the party nationally and greatly enhance the king-making power of House Speaker Henry Clay. Retaining for one more term the legislature's power to cast the state's electoral vote for president would preserve at least an opportunity to work out a compromise which would salvage party unity.

Flagg's support of Crawford thus reflected his overriding concern for party cohesion. In his words it was "a sacred principle in our government that the majority must rule. If the republican party who are a strong majority of the people, wish to maintain the ascendancy, they must be united—to be united, the minority [in the party] must acquiesce in the will of the majority, from whence it follows that *caucus nominations*, are the only bond of union that can save us." While Flagg apparently did not, or could not, conceive of a national presidential nominating convention, he did trust the congressional caucus to perform essentially the same function. He argued that individual Republicans could differ over the choice of the party's nominee but "after the will of a majority of the party is ascertained by a regular [i.e., congressional caucus] nomination, if we belong to the Republican party and wish it well, we shall be bound to hold our peace."[8]

On both these issues, Flagg's thinking was sophisticated, but it was apparently not too difficult for the farmers of Beekmantown and Clinton County. Resolutions of the county nominating convention approved both his support of Crawford and the delay of popular voting for president. That they did so reflected determination to avoid disintegration of their party. This determination which they shared with Van Buren and Flagg probably stemmed mainly from recognition that under a no-party system middle-class farmers and their representatives would stand little chance against the prestige of those whom Melanchton Smith had called "the great," the upper-class leaders of aristocratic and nationalist views. Only in Republican party union could the "middling" sort offset what they regarded as the self-serving, power-grabbing propensities of the great. Accordingly, neither Flagg's desertion of the popular vote for president nor his ardent effort for Crawford struck the majority of his constituents amiss. They were tactical devices which served a more fundamental strategic conception.

The effort of traditional Republicans to put Andrew Jackson in the presidency in place of John Quincy Adams began at the national level soon after the Adams administration took over. In Beekmantown and Clinton County, however, party leaders, perhaps acting under Regency instructions, refrained from beating the drums for Jackson and tried hard to keep the focus in local elections on local issues and candidates.[9] This was probably tactical. The difficulty faced by the leading contender was fresh in the minds of Regency leaders after the Crawford experience. It was true also that many local Republicans still preferred John Quincy Adams to a Southern or Western candidate. Some were probably put off also by Clinton's support of Jackson.

Accordingly, the assembly elections of 1825 and 1826 in Clinton County were largely free from influences relating directly to presidential candidates. What they do reveal is the overriding importance of party. In 1825 Josiah Fisk ran for reelection and defeated former Federalist assemblyman A. R. Moore in Beekmantown 136 to 97.[10] He had gained four votes over his 1824 total. His opponent gained five. In 1826 the "Federalists" first tried to seduce an unidentified "leading Republican" to be their candidate. When that failed, they went to the other end of the social scale to pick Roswell Ransom, whom the *Republican* characterized as "a plain, unlettered man, far below mediocrity; raw and uncouth in his manners, uneducated, ignorant, and superstitious . . . absolutely devoid of every qualification for a member of assembly."[11] By contrast the Republican nominee, Bela Edgerton, as his later record in the assembly amply attests, was a man of considerable erudition and polish. Although each party had a new candidate and the "Federalists" had tried the expedient of nominating a "common man," the result was essentially unchanged. Edgerton exactly duplicated Fisk's vote of 1824, which Fisk had increased by only four votes in 1825. Ransom polled exactly the same vote as Moore in 1825, a scant five votes over Newcomb's total in 1824.[12] Thus, whether the opposition chose a Clintonian Republican (Newcomb, 1824), an old-line Federalist of some distinction (Moore, 1825), or a "common man" (Ransom, 1826), its assembly vote remained essentially the same.

The gubernatorial contest of 1826 also affords striking confirmation of the importance attached locally to party label. De Witt Clinton was seeking reelection and, as an early supporter of Andrew Jackson, might have been expected to attract the votes of some Republican admirers of "the Hero." Furthermore, his opponent, although bearing the endorsement of the orthodox Republicans, was widely known as an "Adams man." This combination of circumstances surely put party loyalty to the test. It passed. Clinton received only one vote more than the opposition's assembly nominee in Beekmantown. His Republican opponent received exactly the same vote as Edgerton, the victorious Republican candidate for the assembly.[13]

In 1827 Van Buren took the wraps off Jackson. He suggested that all Republican candidates in New York that year identify themselves as supporters of Andrew Jackson.[14] The Plattsburgh *Republican*, which had followed assiduously the earlier line isolating local contests as far as possible, was slow to get the message. As late as October 20, it was still stressing that Bela Edgerton's presidential preference was entirely irrelevant to his candidacy for re-election to the assembly. Edgerton was for Jackson, but the *Republican* did not advertise the fact. Presumably, the editor wished to avoid antagonizing the numerous supporters of Adams among local Republicans. The outcome of the contest, in any event, quite clearly hinged on issues other than support of rival presidential candidates.

A major factor in the elections of 1827 in Clinton County was Levi Platt. Platt, as recounted in chapter 4, had been something of an economic colossus in the community. After his ruin in 1827, he sought political prestige to offset what he had lost economically. His object, one observer wrote, was to "build up a personal party in the county, to sustain and aid him in his private difficulties."[15] Once a Federalist, Platt had moved into the Republican ranks after losing a contest with Anson J. Sperry for what the *Republican* referred to (October 27) as "the distinction of leader of the federal party."

Platt's career as a Republican was brief. He wanted local Republicans to recommend his appointment as "first judge" of the county, a prestigious office which may also have been of some economic utility to him in his difficulties. Far from recommending Platt's appointment, Benjamin Mooers wrote Regency member Flagg, then secretary of state: "I should think our County disgraced indeed should he get the appointment." Acknowledging that well-organized Platt forces had controlled a meeting to recommend a person for the appointment, Mooers added that if the state senate "understood the character of the man not only concerning our Bank matters but his morals and Examples otherwise he could never be appointed to office." Platt did not get the appointment.

He blamed Assemblyman Edgerton, at least publicly, for his defeat and made that a principal reason for seeking the defeat of Edgerton for reelection.[16] Platt's campaign against Edgerton began in the Republican nominating convention. There he lost decisively. In reporting on the convention to Flagg, one of the leaders of his "Plattsburgh Sub-Regency" observed that "notwithstanding the exertions of . . . friends of Judge Platt, all was harmonious as could be desired." A secret ballot without previous discussion gave Edgerton fifteen of the total of seventeen votes. Neither Platt nor his stalking horse, John W. Anderson, received a single vote.[17]

Despite this defeat in the nominating convention, Platt put his man Anderson in competition for the assembly seat. The support he sought was from his old associates rather than from the Regency. "Federalists" throughout the county characteristically fell in line behind the returning apostate and his candidate except in Champlain. For unknown but perhaps obvious reasons, the "Federalists" of Champlain declined to support Platt's man.[18]

The campaign was vigorous. The most important attack on Edgerton was that he had committed financial irregularities. While the precise nature of the charge is unknown, it was apparently valid. Two years later Flagg urged Edgerton's removal from the list of potential appointees as federal customs collector, the chief federal patronage job in the area, despite his endorsement by a "strong body of the members of the legislature." Edgerton, Flagg wrote, "has forfeited the confidence of all his friends in relation to money transactions, and his name ought not to be on the list of candidates for collector." He added that he could produce affidavits to that effect, if necessary.

Presidential preferences did not figure in the contest. Republicans made no effort to link Anderson to Adams. Edgerton avoided references to Jackson. "The presidential question," wrote one of Flagg's lieutenants, "was studiously kept out of view in our election." He did note, however, that Edgerton lost some votes in the town of Peru because he became identified there with Jackson.[19]

Two themes dominated the Republican campaign. One was attacks on Platt for his *fancied nobility* and for being a political turncoat.[20] The other featured attacks on Anderson as, for example, an immigrant "Scotchman" with only three years' residence and as self-nominated rather than chosen by a convention.[21]

Beekmantown's vote in this election of 1827 was surprising.

Edgerton secured 132 votes, about par for Regency candidates in that period, but Anderson increased the usual "Federalist" total from 97 to 135.[22] He thus carried Beekmantown by three votes, but he failed to carry the district. Where Platt and Anderson found the extra votes in Beekmantown is not at all clear, but in any case it was a one-shot matter. In the presidential contest of the following year, Beekmantown was again solidly in the Regency's camp.

Despite the great attention given to the candidates' strong personalities and an overlay of smears and emotional claptrap, the campaign of 1828 in Clinton County and in Beekmantown reflected profound political differences. To the aged but unreconstructed Antifederalist, Thomas Tredwell, it appeared that the American people faced another constitutional crisis distressingly similar to that in which they had made the wrong decision in 1788. New York law then required each congressional district to choose one presidential elector. Governor Clinton, in his annual message to the legislature, had urged an amendment to the United States Constitution to require all states to follow a similar policy. In a long and impassioned letter to Senator Martin Van Buren, about to be elected governor on the Jackson ticket, Tredwell expressed and explained his vehement opposition to Clinton's plan.

Tredwell was still fearful of all political authority and concerned above all else with individual freedom—still distrustful of human nature, particularly of the nature of "the great." He affirmed at the outset that the fundamental principle of the Confederation, "to wit, the dependance of the State Sovereignties on the People, and of the general Government on the State Sovereignties, ought never to have been touched or altered. . . . The grand security the People have against oppression from their own state Governments are their frequent Elections by which they have it in their power, whenever they suffer any grievance from their Government, to obtain redress in a peaceable and quiet way by removing the authors of them from office."

Under the Articles of Confederation, he continued, "the state Sovereignties have the same powerful . . . guard against the encroachments or oppressions of the General Government." What he had in mind was the provision of the Articles of Confederation (art. V), which authorized each state to elect its congressional delegation yearly and "to recall its delegates, or any of them, at any time within the year, and to send others in their stead." Accordingly, Tredwell deplored the provision of the Constitution of 1787 which gave the people the right to elect congressmen for two-year terms. He execrated Clinton's proposal as stemming from a characteristically secret scheme of "our Monarchists and Aristocrats" seeking "to make the President also Independent of the State Sovereignties." Their ultimate objective, Tredwell believed, was to "overset our whole system at once by changing it from a confederation of free Republics into one solid Government which would in fact be Monarchy whatever false name it should be called by." [23]

Tredwell's fears may well appear unfounded or even foolish but, to his contemporaries in Beekmantown and Clinton County, they were very real. The *Republican*, always at this time the voice of the local party leaders, identified the major issue of the campaign as the tendency to "consolidate" power in the national government at the expense of the states. In language highly reminiscent of that which Tredwell had used in the ratifying convention of 1788, an editorial of May 3 signed "Daniel" (perhaps Tredwell) urged that the Constitution be amended to "retrace every step which has been taken towards consolidation, and to bring back our government to the original plan of the confederation." Ever since independence, "secret cabals" have worked for "consolidation. . . . Our main . . . object," Daniel continued, "should be to place such men in office as would prefer the character and condition of citizens of a free country, to that of vassals under the greatest monarch on earth." Daniel advocated election of Jackson because as president he would preserve "*freedom*" and combat the threat of consolidation which, "if completed, would certainly and inevitably destroy our freedom." In the "STATE GOVERNMENTS," Daniel concluded, lay the "*great strength* and safety" of the American people.

There was a practical inconvenience in Daniel's position. It did not accord well with the desire of local iron and woolen manufacturers for tariff protection. Regency leader Silas Wright had pushed through Congress that year a tariff measure, the so-called tariff of abominations, which did afford high protection on farm products and on iron. But, it did little for wool manufacturers and apparently did not assuage the feeling that manufacturers could expect far more from an Adams than from a Jackson administration. In any event, the *Republican* found it necessary to try to refute charges that the party's congressional nominee was antitariff. The refutation did not take. The industrial town of Peru, long a solid bastion of Republican strength, returned solid majorities for Adams and his gubernatorial and congressional running mates. Agricultural Beekmantown, however, gave consistent majorities of about fifty-five votes for Jackson, Van Buren (for governor), and other traditionally Republican nominees. Jackson carried the county by twenty-two votes.[24]

Traditional party lines did not disappear in the contest, although there was much shifting of allegiances. The shifts appear to have been largely at the highest socioeconomic level and to have worked both ways. As one of Flagg's lieutenants reported at the end of 1827: "Some of our leading friends in the county . . . are honestly in favor of the administration, and . . . probably will remain so." The Republicans of the county in general were without strong feelings concerning the presidency but were eager to keep the party unified and waiting "for some concentrated, general movement of the republican Party of the Union." He reported also that "some of the leading federalist[s] in this village [Plattsburgh] . . . are already out for Jackson. They are anxious that we shall get up a Jackson Meeting. We shall not be hasty in taking this advice— we dont like such counsellors and we are not anxious of their company, tho their assistance may be welcome." So prominent were old Federalist supporters of Jackson that W. C. Watson, a youthful participant in the campaign, later attributed the defection of traditionally Republican Peru to the mistaken belief that the Jackson movement was just another in the succession of attempted Federalist disguises.[25]

Another indication of the high-level split arose in connection with the editorial policy of the Plattsburgh *Republican*. A report to Flagg, no longer editor of the paper, reminded him in April 1828 that a three-man committee composed of Benjamin Mooers, Levi C. Platt, and John Palmer had the right to fix the paper's political course, if they were all in agreement. In the event of disagreement among them, the stockholders, voting in proportion to the amount of stock held, were to fix the policy. As Flagg's informant put it, "Now General Mooers and L. C. Platt are determined to take the press from us or what is the same to use it to promote the election of Mr. Adams." Mooers and his former enemy, Levi Platt, had in fact joined in organizing an Adams rally. Flagg's correspondent wanted proxies from Flagg and Reuben H. Walworth to help retain control of the paper.[26] Evidently he secured them, for on May 24 the paper announced that seven stockholders with sixty-five of the total of eighty shares favored support of Jackson. Neither Flagg nor Walworth, however, was on the published list of Jacksonian supporters headed by Thomas Tredwell. Whether they had actually sold their stock or were represented by proxies is not evident. They certainly supported Jackson. So did the paper.

The defection of Benjamin Mooers was supplemented by that of his son, Benjamin H. Mooers. The son had been Plattsburgh supervisor—elected as a Republican—several times. At first he intended to support all the Republican ticket except Jackson but, when the "Federalists" offered him the nomination for county clerk—a nomination which the Republicans had denied him—he went all the way into the enemy camp. In Beekmantown he trailed his Republican opponent by only fifteen votes, whereas the rest of the ticket ran about fifty-five votes behind the Republicans.[27]

To explain why some leading "Federalists" supported Jackson, while a number of leading Republicans continued to prefer Adams, is challenging. One explanation came half a century later from a participant in the local campaign, Winslow C. Watson. "Many of the former Federalists in the county," wrote Watson in 1879, "came out earnest and active partizans of Jackson, not actuated by any love to him, but stimulated by a rancorous and inexorable hatred of Adams." Their hatred he blamed, perhaps a little too simply, on Adams' desertion of the Federalist party in the conflict over Jefferson's embargo before the War of 1812.[28]

Among Republicans who preferred Adams, the principal attraction was probably policy. For those interested in national economic development and imbued with deeply nationalist sentiments, the Adams-Clay program for fostering economic growth through protective tariffs, internal improvements, and other nationalist measures was undoubtedly attractive—especially in contrast to the do-nothing attitude of the Republicans. Its attractions may have been particularly great to those, such as Benjamin Mooers, who had risen far enough in socioeconomic and political status to have acquired a different perspective on the Republicans' exaggerated fear of "the great." Banking experience seems in particular to have encouraged defection. Not only did bank president Benjamin Mooers defect from the Republican ranks, but bank cashier F. L. C. Sailly, son of the old Republican congressman, Peter Sailly, also voted for Adams, although he supported the Republican ticket in other contests.[29]

Federalist supporters of Jackson were apparently not so constant as the defecting Republicans. As Watson remembered it: "The Federalists did not find a congenial abiding place in our ranks and soon seceded, while there was a very general reunion of the Democracy, although it cannot be disguised that many high-toned Republicans permanently abandoned the party from an inappeaseable aversion to Jackson." Andrew R. Moore, a "lifelong Federalist" and sometime assemblyman, was one who became "a roaring Jackson man for three or four years" before going back to the opposition.[30]

The Anti-Masonic movement, which convulsed western New York for several years after 1826, came to Clinton County rather late and with quite the opposite of the desired effect. The initial impulse for the movement was the disappearance and presumed murder of a defector whom Masons had been harassing for threatening to "tell all" about the secret society. Indignation over this incident swelled to enormous proportions. It soon became evident that many non-Masons, especially among poorer farmers, perceived the organization as inimical to both Christianity and democracy and offensively exclusive as well. Because many old Republicans in New York were Masons, as was Andrew Jackson, this sentiment afforded an excellent opportunity for the opposition to turn the tide of public indignation to its political purposes. It did so with great success in western New York.[31]

In Clinton County Masonry was both popular and bipartisan. Beekmantown had no Masonic lodge, but there were lodges in Plattsburgh to the south, Chazy to the north, and in Grand Isle, Vermont, on the east.[32] The *Republican* (see chapter 8) had long carried stories about local Masonic matters. Shortly before the Anti-Masonic furor broke, it had trumpeted the news (June 26, 1826) that William F. Haile, a local party stalwart, had won election as "GRAND SWORD BEARER" at the annual "Grand Encampment" of the Knights Templar, a Masonic adjunct, in New York City. A year after the Anti-Masonic movement had begun, the *Republican* was still advertising subscriptions (September 22, 1927) to a Masonic publication. The editor of the opposition newspaper, the *Northern Intelligencer*, was also a Mason. But, even after his paper expired in 1828, the succeeding *Aurora Borealis* showed no disposition to make Masonry an issue.[33] It did not figure at all in the elections of 1828.

By 1830 Anti-Masonry had reached Clinton County. In that year the Anti-Masonic organization was the rallying point for all of the opposition forces in New York State. The only opponent of Republican gubernatorial nominee Enos Throop was the Anti-Masonic candidate. In Beekmantown Throop trounced him 160 (86 percent) to 27 (14 percent).[34]

That the opponents of the old Republicans across the state had put all their eggs into the Anti-Masonic basket became still more evident in 1832. The Anti-Masons fielded a strong slate of candidates for state offices, including the office of presidential elector. The "National Republicans," as many opponents of Jackson called themselves, made no nominations—not even for presidential electors. Instead, they supported the Anti-Masonic slate. For the presidency it was understood that the Anti-Masonic electors, if chosen, would vote in the electoral college for either Anti-Mason William Wirt or Henry Clay, whichever had the better chance of beating Andrew Jackson.

The Clinton County campaign against this peculiar political hybrid was intense. The name of James Kent at the head of the Anti-Masonic list of presidential electors enabled the *Republican* to link the Anti-Masonic ticket to the old Federalists and their support of restricted suffrage, to a pro-British foreign policy, and to other ancient anathemas. Jackson's message, accompanying his veto of the bill to recharter a national bank, was a major campaign document. Its strictures against monopoly, special privilege, and foreign influence struck responsive chords—so responsive that the *Republican* reprinted one thousand extra copies. These issues, supplemented by the unpopularity of the Anti-Masonic theme and by allegations of bribery attested to by a number of Beekmantown residents, enabled the Jackson ticket to increase its margin of 1828 considerably. The Beekmantown vote for president was 207 (72 percent) for Jackson to 80 (28 percent) for the Anti-Masonic slate. All other contests had quite similar outcomes. Jackson carried the county by some 600 votes as against a majority of only 22 in 1828.[35]

Following Jackson's reelection, denunciations of aristocracy became both more frequent and more strident in the columns of the *Republican*. The newly appointed editors, Hugh Moore and Roby G. Stone, declared flatly in their initial statement of policy (August 10, 1833): "The evil of the greatest magnitude with which the people have to contend, is an *aristocracy*." The editors seemed a little uncertain, however, whether the evil was already present or merely anticipated. In economic terms it seemed already to exist. "The hand of wealth rests heavily," the editors averred, "upon the shoulders of the poor," and the "wealth of the country is possessed by a minority of the population." Somewhat more eloquently, they proclaimed, "There is but little sympathy between the pockets of the rich and the wants of poverty." They pictured the rich man continuing to quaff champagne, while the children of the poor cry for bread, their mothers pine in want, the dying man moans, and the prayers of the wretched starveling waken no "thrill of sensibility" in the rich man's soul. Their remedy for this distressing state of affairs was the mild suggestion that "the middling interest—the workingmen of the country—ever be vigilant in the exercise of their duty." They should, in other words, vote.

In political, as opposed to economic terms, the editors saw aristocracy as a potential danger rather than an existing condition. They seemed to acknowledge freely that their government was one of "republican simplicity" and that "free institutions" had brought "blessings." But, to preserve these they warned that "the people should ever be vigilant." Once deprived of their liberties, the people "must struggle in blood to recover them."

Clearly, it was the traditional advantages of wealth with which the *Republican* was most concerned. "Look abroad in our own country," urged the same editorial, "see the rich lordlings hovering, like vultures over a battlefield, around the thatched cottage of the poor and depressed citizen—wringing from him through the channel of the law, the poor pittance of his daily bread! . . . The greater their amount of property, the more extensive their means of carrying their plans of personal aggrandizement into effect. Devoid of sterling talents, they exercise a controlling influence upon political and religious matters *in proportion* to their amount of money!" Grumbling that the man of inherited wealth is accounted a worthy citizen while the poor man is not, the editors concluded that it would accord better with the "spirit of our government, to give every man his deserts without regard to the *weight of his coin.*"

The social as well as the economic and political advantages of wealth came under specific *Republican* editorial attack. Concerning Plattsburgh's "village aristocracy" the editors observed in verse:

> In every country Village, where
> Ten chimney smokes perfume the air,
> Contiguous to a steeple:

Great gentle folks are found, a score,
Who can't associate any more
With common country people.

The editors also chided the village "ladies" for tending to "arro-gate to themselves a great share of gentility," and quoted approv-ingly a perhaps apocryphal farmer who declared: "I go for no ruffle-shirt fellows, such as the federalists always put up: but plain, sound Republicans, who don't feel themselves above shaking hands with a farmer."[36]

Subsequent editorials left no doubt that by "aristocrats" the *Republican* meant the opposition party. They made equally clear that, whatever the name under which it operated at any given time, the opposition consisted of the same men with the same ideas. As this opposition completed what the *Republican* saw as merely another regrouping, this time under the "Whig" label, the editors reprinted (September 6, 1834) with obvious approval an editorial on "The Parallel," which appeared in the Seneca *Observer*. After listing the various names under which the opposition had done battle and identifying the positions taken, it concluded: "The Parallel is complete. Disguise itself as it may, the mark on its brow is there, and . . . the united energies of the democracy [will] over-whelm with signal defeat the lurking but active and embittered spirit of federalism."

Three weeks later the *Republican* itself stated: "Whether as Tories or Federalists, Peace Party men, or Federal Republicans, National Republicans or Whigs, the band of aristocrats, who oppose the rights of the people, and the principles of the constitution, will be met and defeated." A month earlier a Democratic-Republican rally resolved: "That we have no confidence in those politicians who have heretofore assumed the names of Federalists, Peace Party men, National Republicans, and more recently the name of whigs. They have always been, and ever will be found acting with a proud aristocracy, opposed to the free, and pure principles of the Demo-cratic Party." The editors accused the Whigs specifically of favor-ing a "moneyed oligarchy" and believing that "a portion of man-kind were born 'gentlemen,' to ride the 'simplemen, legitimately, by the grace of God!'"[37]

Beekmantown Republicans saw things the same way. The "Jack-son Republicans" of Beekmantown, when they met to express support for Jackson against the Senate majority which had censured him for removing the government's deposits from the United States Bank, evinced neither surprise nor doubt at the report that all surviving members of the Hartford Convention supported the new Whig party.[38]

Beekmantown's voting pattern held firm in this period of intense concern over aristocracy and attempts to brand the Whig party as its new vehicle. In 1833 the Republican assembly nominee received 102 votes to none at all for the able Whig candidate, Luther Bradish, who was branded a "Hartford Convention Federalist" and had been an Anti-Mason as well.[39] In 1834 the Democratic-Republican ticket headed by William L. Marcy for governor outdid the Whig slate led by William H. Seward more than two to one (197 to 89 with minor variations for lower offices). In 1835 the Democratic-Republican candidates for the senate and assembly were unopposed, while Beekmantown's Thomas Crook bested his opponent for county clerk by 126 to 55. In 1836 the vote both for Van Buren over William Henry Harrison for president and for Marcy over Jesse Buel for governor was 138 (69 percent) to 63 (31 percent).[40]

Apparently moribund, the "aristocratic" opposition party sprang back to life dramatically in the later 1830s. Several issues helped to revitalize the opposition. The temperance movement may have been one. The *Republican*, while supporting the popular temperance idea, made every effort to keep it nonpolitical. There may have been an immediate practical reason for that emphasis. Like most other reform movements, the temperance crusade proceeded under leadership which, while bipartisan, was generally more "Federalist" than Republican. In any event Beekmantown came in for some censure from the party because in its town elections "no individual . . . save a member of the temperance society can be elected to an office." The *Republican* also criticized efforts in Beekmantown to "effect the election of a 'Temperance Ticket' of town officers." It did not accuse the opposition of trying to ride this popular tide to power, but it apparently recognized a danger. The danger materialized in 1838, when the party nominee for sheriff lost the county by seven votes, apparently because as a tavern keeper he offended temperance advocates. In Beekmantown he lost 138 to 127, while other Democrats, as Jeffersonians were coming to be known, won.[41]

More important as a difficulty for the Democrats in the long run was their identification as an antiabolitionist party. The local

Whigs were by no means all abolitionists, but Horatio Boardman, editor of the Whig paper, was a leader of the local antislavery society. The *Republican*, on the other hand, was both antiabolitionist and anti-Negro. Consequently, when the opposition made great gains in 1837, the *Republican* cited growing abolitionist sentiment as one explanation. In Beekmantown that year, the assembly candidate, whom the *Republican* still stigmatized as "federalist," lost the town 145 to 137, but this was much closer than the more than two-to-one margins by which they had usually lost in the immediately preceding years.[42]

Another issue helpful to the opposition was the French Canadian insurrection of 1837. Many Americans ardently wished to aid the Canadians, but Democratic administrations at both national and state levels took action to enforce strict neutrality and avoid involvement. The opposition was quick to exploit the opportunity. The *Republican* blamed this issue exclusively for the "federalist" success in electing supervisors in Beekmantown and several other towns in 1838.[43]

Economic issues were probably more fundamental in accounting for the revival of the opposition. The cause of the depression of 1837 is too complex to permit its review here. However, it is evident that the public in general blamed the banking policies of the Democratic administrations, state as well as national, for the economic troubles. In New York a measure enacted by the legislature in 1835 was gradually eliminating from circulation all bank notes under five dollars in value. This, of course, aggravated the depression. In 1837 the Democratic majority in the legislature defeated a popular effort to suspend the law. According to Jabez Hammond, this "more than any other cause . . . carried the multitude against the democratic party at the then ensuing election."[44] A minority of self-styled Conservatives also broke off from the Democratic party in opposition to Van Buren's policy of holding government deposits in the treasury instead of in state banks, which had enjoyed that advantage since 1834. Economic factors, such as these, helped the opposition to narrow the Democratic margin of victory for its assembly nominee in Beekmantown from seventy-six in 1836 to only eight in 1837.[45]

The opposition revival continued into the campaign of 1838, which the *Republican* characterized as without precedent for its zeal. Governor Marcy carried Beekmantown by the narrow margin of 154 to 142, while losing to Seward in the state as a whole. The

Whig assembly nominee, Andrew Moore, however, carried the town by two votes, 149 to 147, over the victorious Democratic Abijah North. Whig editor Boardman, hindered by a third candidate who was apparently an antiabolitionist Whig, won only 102 votes for county clerk as opposed to 153 for the winning Democrat.[46] From 1838 through the 1840s, the issue of "nativism" usually had some place in the elections of Beekmantown and Clinton County. While the *Republican* in the past had printed unkind remarks about the Irish and about "foreigners" in general, especially if they were British and voted "wrong," it now came to the defense of the minorities against Whig nativists. The issue could not be exploited against Seward, a conspicuous friend of the immigrant, but it could be employed against the Whig party in general. In 1838, for example, the *Republican* condemned the following item from the Troy *Whig*: "The Irish, too idle and vicious to clear and cultivate land, crowd the meaner sort of tenements, and fill them with wretchedness, filth and disease—what are they but mere marketable cattle?" After the election of 1839, the *Republican* asked, "Why do the Whigs make it a practice to insult our Irish citizens at the polls by challenging their votes, when they know them to be as good voters as any other men?"[47]

The effort of local Democrats to win Irish votes was not limited to verbal appeals. They also welcomed Irish individuals into the party organization. Precisely when this began is unclear. But, in 1839 Beekmantown's county convention delegation included Patrick Foy; in 1840, Michael Hagerty; and in 1841, John Riley. Hagerty was on the executive committee of the Democratic Association of Beekmantown in 1844.[48] While the evidence of these names is not conclusive, it seems likely that the three individuals were in fact Irish Catholics. There may well have been other Irish Catholics in positions of political leadership in the Democratic party of Beekmantown in years when less information was published.

As if to warm up for the "Log Cabin" campaign of 1840, the Whigs and Democrats of Clinton County waged a titanic struggle in 1839 with Beekmantown a prominent battleground. Beekmantown's prominence was because of the identity of the opposition candidate, George M. Beckwith. Beckwith was the son of Beekmantown's first supervisor and long-time doctor, Baruch Beckwith, a former Connecticut Federalist. Not only had the son grown up in Beekmantown but, as a Plattsburgh lawyer associated with another old Federalist, William Swetland, he was an agent for many of the Beekmans, still the absentee owners of much land in Beekmantown. Beckwith, despite his Federalist associations, had long been a Democratic leader, but he broke with the party on the independent treasury issue and joined the "Conservative" movement. Whig leaders then accepted Beckwith as their nominee for the assembly. Again, a defector from the majority party would attempt to lead into opposition ranks enough voters to put him into office.

To meet this challenge, the *Republican* mounted a vigorous campaign. "The opposition in this state," the paper affirmed (October 21), has made it a practice to take "apostates fresh from our ranks as candidates for elective office, with a view of drawing support from our party; but we do not recollect a single instance in the state where this dishonorable course has been crowned with success." The *Republican* also derided the Whig claim that they would make "great inroads on our ranks in Beekmantown." Beekmantown, the *Republican* avowed, "has always done her duty, and nobly sustained her full share of the fight in all our battles with federalism, and that too whether they fight under their own or false colors."

The *Republican* attempted also to get back to fundamentals. "The country," the editor asserted (October 19), "is divided into two great leading parties; the one denominated the democratic party and the other the federal party. This distinction had its origins at the adoption of the constitution and has been continued down to the present day." The Democratic party he identified as the followers of Jefferson advocating "republican" government, while the Federalist followers of John Adams favored a "consolidated" government.

Beekmantown did not sustain the *Republican*'s confidence. Beckwith carried the town by 168 to 158, although the Whig senatorial candidate lost by an identical margin. As in the case of the earlier apostate, Levi Platt, the party faithful had not been swayed. In fact, the Democratic vote was up slightly over 1838. The opposition's margin of victory came from the organization of people who had not voted previously, perhaps old friends of Beckwith and his family. Whether Beckwith had exploited his agency authority to exert economic pressure on Beekmantown tenants remains uncertain. Probably he did not, for if he had the *Republican* would almost certainly have learned of it and published accusations. When it became clear that the county had defeated Beckwith and returned North, the *Republican* sharply criticized Beckwith's ungentlemanly conduct at the polls in Beekmantown and Platts-burgh. It accused him of possessing a violent temper, a persecuting and cruel spirit, and of having only mediocre talents. While it was not specified that Irish voters were his target, the *Republican*'s complaint about harassment of Irish voters appeared in the same issue.[49] Such complaints were most unusual.

The campaign of 1840 began auspiciously for the Democrats of Clinton County. In Beekmantown the town meeting in the spring returned Democrat Peter Vandevoort to office as supervi-sor. He had held the office from 1834 through 1837, but the Whigs had held it in both 1838 and 1839. The Democrats also regained control by a six to four margin of the county board of supervisors. Among other things this meant that the county's printing business, which had been enjoyed the previous year by the Plattsburgh *Whig*, would now go back to the Plattsburgh *Republican*.

Indications that the outcome would be close helped to make the 1840 campaign the most exciting in local history. For the first time, the *Republican* took notice of the French Canadian voters with an appeal of nearly two columns in French, emphasizing the aristocratic tendencies of the opposition.[50] A Beekmantown farmer charged that a Whig merchant and bank director from Plattsburgh dispatched a cattle buyer into Beekmantown with instructions to offer low prices and to blame Democratic administrations for them. The farmer alleged also that the buyer was to pay higher than market prices to those who would appreciate Whig money properly. On election eve the *Republican*, apparently with Beck-with's tactics of 1839 in mind, urged every effort to see that "bul-lies" did not prevent Democrats from voting and to make sure as well that there were no illegal voters.[51]

Beckwith was again a candidate for the assembly, and this time there were allegations that he attempted to coerce voters through his powers as agent for the Beekman proprietors. According to an unnamed source, Beckwith had stated: "You must know, sir, that I can bring the Beekman Agency to bear with tremendous effect upon my election. I have already, sir, straightened out two . . . tennents within the borders of my agency, and I have another under the screws." That the allegation refers to only three tenants suggests that this presumed power, even if exerted, could hardly have been decisive in the contest.[52]

In temperance-conscious Beekmantown, the "hard cider" portion of the popular Whig slogan and the extensive consumption of that beverage at Whig rallies were real handicaps. It was Whig national strategy to present their presidential candidate, William Henry Harrison, as a frontier leader in the pattern of Jackson— content to live in a log cabin and drink hard cider. Van Buren, seeking reelection on the Democratic ticket, was caricatured as a high-living aristocrat who preferred a mansion and champagne.

Philip B. Roberts, long-time Democratic leader in Beekmantown and frequent local officeholder, wrote a letter of indignant protest to the editor of the *Republican* on the Whig use of cider. Leading Beekmantown Whigs, he asserted, despite "their professions of love to the cause of temperance, . . . have joined with a throng of inebriates, and countenanced by their presence the use of intoxicating drink." Another Beekmantown letter writer reported internal dissension on the question among Whigs. A Whig neighbor, he averred, reported that local Whigs had planned a "log cabin and hard cider" rally but had altered their plan to meet objections raised by temperance advocates. They would make the cabin of slabs rather than logs, apparently to dissociate themselves further from the log cabin and hard cider conjunction, and serve no cider in it. There were assurances, however, that the Plattsburgh Tippecanoe Club would see to it that "those who wanted a taste should be supplied from the music wagon of the Club." Beekmantown Democrats chided one of the organizers of the Whig rally, a Mr. C. (perhaps Samuel Chatterton, a leading farmer), by reminding him that at the temperance society meeting it was he who had introduced a resolution favoring a boycott of all merchants who sold liquor, beer, *or cider*.[53]

Despite the great attention to these peripheral or incidental issues, leading Democrats did not lose sight of what they regarded as major substantive issues. "THE REAL ISSUE," stated the *Republican*, was "whether the few or the many shall govern." As Democratic principles, the editor listed strict construction of the Constitution, frugal government, minimum public debt, no internal improvement system, no connection between government and banks, no exclusive charters for banks, no connection between church and state, no repeal of the naturalization laws and, a more positive note, aid to education. Against Harrison, the editor cited his age (sixty-eight), his youthful membership in an abolition society, and his support of both the Alien and Sedition Acts and a restricted suffrage.[54]

Philip B. Roberts of Beekmantown was still more explicit. "The election of Harrison," he wrote, "appears to be the first step towards their beloved aristocracy, which some three or four of the most enlightened and influential men of the Whig party in Beekmantown have frequently acknowledged was the main object of their zeal." If they succeeded, "our glorious Constitution with all its blessings must be forever abolished, and the chains of tyranny which our venerable fathers broke from themselves in the Revolution, will be riveted on us, their descendants, with double bars, and the government with Harrison at its head, will join hand and glove with the bankers of the petticoat [Queen Victoria's] government of England." More specifically, he alleged that Beekmantown Whigs advocated a $250 property qualification on the right to vote. "Stand to your posts," he concluded, "every man who wishes to entail to your children the blessings purchased by the blood of your ancestors."[55]

The result in Beekmantown was different from that in the nation, the state, and the county. Van Buren led the Democratic ticket with a majority of forty over Harrison. Other Democrats had majorities between thirty and forty, except for the assembly candidate who defeated Beckwith by a majority of only twenty-seven. The *Republican* editor found little consolation in the vote except in Beekmantown: "Democratic Beekmantown has sustained itself nobly, notwithstanding the tremendous efforts made by the federalists to carry it."[56] Reporting a meeting of the victorious Whigs in December, the *Republican* alleged that "an aristocracy, or village Regency which had little influence on the outcome of the election" had taken control of the movement because it was "part of the Federal creed, that the poor should make way for the rich."[57]

For the county the increase in the total vote in 1840 over previous years was about one-third.[58] Presumably, this was true in Beekmantown also, but the absence of any figures other than the majority for each candidate makes it impossible to be sure.

Beekmantown's Whigs, having failed to carry the town despite their prodigious effort of 1840, did not work so hard thereafter. Their ticket lost in 1841 by about the same margin as in 1840, but this time the county "REDEEMED" itself in the eyes of the *Republican* by returning solid Democratic majorities. In 1842 the *Republican* pictured the Whigs as "a self-interest[ed] oligarchy" seeking their own aggrandizement and opposing the "yeomanry of the country." In Beekmantown the "yeomen" won by about

102 votes. To achieve this victory, the Democrats had apparently appropriated an old opposition technique—nomination of an apostate. In this instance, it was J. C. Hubbell, an old-line Federalist—but one who had supported the War of 1812. The results of 1843 were virtually identical.[59]

In the campaign of 1844, the situation changed little. Beekmantown's Democrats organized efficiently and participated in a giant northern New York rally in Plattsburgh. To counterbalance Whig arguments that the Whig tariff program helped the farmer, the *Republican* cited declining farm prices and promised a higher tariff on raw wool. Beekmantown's Democratic majority was 102 votes, the usual figure since 1842. The Liberty party slate of antislavery zealots received a paltry 35 votes, compared to 244 for the Democrats and 142 for the Whigs. Still, the Liberty party did better in Beekmantown than it did in the state as a whole, 8 percent as compared to 3 percent. The Whig candidate for the assembly was a prominent Beekmantown farmer, Samuel Chatterton, but his fellow townsmen gave him only three more votes than they gave the Whig gubernatorial nominee, Millard Fillmore.[60]

In 1845 Beekmantown's vote for elective offices was Democratic as usual, but one aspect of the election could have been construed as foreboding trouble. For assembly and senate, the Democratic majorities averaged 80 votes, but the vote in favor of a state constitutional convention which the party had opposed was 143 to 30.[61]

The year 1846 brought still more forebodings. In the spring elections of town supervisors, all seemed well. The Democrats increased their majority on the eleven-member county board from six to seven. Beekmantown's supervisor, as usual, was among the Democrats. In the fall, however, a number of interesting portents appeared. Democrat Silas Wright carried the town easily against both Whig and third-party gubernatorial nominees. The Democratic nominee for sheriff, however, barely squeaked by, and the assembly nominee met defeat in Beekmantown at the hands of Beckwith. Beckwith did not run so well elsewhere and did not unseat the Democratic incumbent. The referendum on the new constitution of 1846, a strongly Democratic document which included provisions limiting state debt and making many more offices elective, secured approval in Beekmantown by the narrow margin of 140 to 124. Still more interestingly, despite the usual anti-Negro feelings of the Democratic party, Beekmantown voted 151 to 50 in favor of equal voting rights for Negroes. This was far higher than in the rest of the county. The county was the most favorable in the state toward a measure which was soundly defeated.[62] Thus, it seems evident from the high vote for Beckwith, from the high vote for equal suffrage for Negroes, and from the close vote on the constitution that the Whig party was not without issues with which to appeal to Beekmantown farmers.

Whig strength became still more evident in 1847, when the town meeting chose a Whig supervisor. In a special judicial election in June, however, Beckwith lost to his Democratic opponent by almost two to one (102 to 52). In the fall all Democratic candidates received comfortable majorities in Beekmantown, except for the assembly nominee whose winning edge was only 23 votes (161 to 138).[63]

The combination of these circumstances, especially the defeat of Beckwith in 1847, suggests strongly that the high Whig vote for assemblyman in 1846 was not so much a vote for Beckwith as a vote against Democrat Rufus Heaton. Heaton again trailed the Democratic ticket in 1847 as a candidate for reelection against a different opponent. Apparently, Heaton was a "Hunker," a Democrat sympathetic to the southern position on slavery and favorable to state internal improvement projects, while the vote against him came from Beekmantown Democrats with "Barnburner" sympathies. The Barnburners, led in 1846 by the Beekmantown ticket-leader Silas Wright, were strongly antislavery and about as staunchly opposed to increasing the state's debt for internal improvement projects. In Plattsburgh the minority Barnburners did cut the Hunker-dominated Democratic ticket with the result that the Whigs elected their man as supervisor in 1848.[64]

In the presidential election of 1848, the Hunker-Barnburner split of the Democrats was still more ruinous. The Hunkers controlled the Democratic machinery. They supported the regular nominee, Lewis Cass, for president, and ex-Plattsburgh resident Reuben H. Walworth for governor. The Barnburners, supported by other dissidents, organized the Free-Soil party and nominated Van Buren for president with John A. Dix as candidate for governor. The Whig ticket consisted of Mexican War hero Zachary Taylor for president and Hamilton Fish for governor. The Plattsburgh *Republican*, as usual, went down the line in support of the regular ticket. It branded the Whigs as old Hartford Convention Federalists, trying to sneak into office "behind General Taylor's uniform." The Free-Soilers it denounced for abandoning Jefferson's strict construction of the Constitution with reference to state rights. The Democratic principles which the *Republican* defended included equal rights and no special privileges [not applied to Negroes, but to white citizens]; no corporate monopolies; no legislative interference with the business pursuits of the citizen; no bank of the United States ("the chief engine of absolute despotism"); tariff for revenue only; noninterference in the domestic affairs of the states (i.e., slavery); strict construction of the Constitution; freedom of religion, the press, and suffrage; civil and religious liberty to aliens; the independent treasury; and others. The *Republican* made special effort to associate the Democratic party and candidates with friendship for the Irish and to tar both the Whigs and the Free-Soilers with nativism.[65]

The result was a general victory for the Whig candidates in Clinton County as in the state and nation, but Beekmantown resisted the trend. "Always true, always reliable," wrote the *Republican* editor, Beekmantown "has covered herself with glory." See table 15 for the election returns for the two Beekmantown districts which evoked this praise. While some of the Free-Soil vote may have come from erstwhile Whigs, most of it came from Democrats. Yet, with 21 percent of the vote going to that largely Democratic splinter group, the regular Democrats still held a decisive margin over their Whig rivals.[66]

The more Whiggish results in the second district require brief explanation. This recently settled area was soon to be set off as the separate town of Dannemora. The impetus to its settlement came from iron deposits and the decision of the state government to erect a prison at the site so that convicts could be used in mining operations. As a community it already differed strongly in major ways from the old agricultural township of Beekmantown, which comprised the first district.

The strength which a united Democratic party could muster in Beekmantown was quite evident in the elections of 1849. With the Hunker and Barnburner factions temporarily reconciled, Thomas Crook, former supervisor of Beekmantown, swamped his Whig opponent for the senate by 218 to 115, a margin which other Democratic candidates approximated. This was more than sufficient to offset a nearly solid Whig vote (8 for Crook to 48 for his opponent) in the area which became Dannemora. Beekmantown again drew special praise for the size of its Democratic majority.[67]

Between 1823 and 1850, the nature of political contests in Beek-

TABLE 15.

Beekmantown Votes for President and Governor, 1848

| | Whig | | Democratic | | Free-Soil | |
	Taylor	Fish	Cass	Walworth	Van Buren	Dix
District 1	135	132	197	199	90	92
District 2	31	32	16	17	2	2

SOURCE: Plattsburgh *Republican*, November 25, 1848.

mantown and Clinton County had altered profoundly, but a measure of continuity was also clear. Assembly contests lost much of their significance; presidential politics came to dominate the political scene. The temperance question, nativism, the tariff, and the slavery question produced aberrations and disruptions. Party names changed. Yet, throughout the period—as indeed from the beginning of settlement, although with diminishing intensity—the majority of the voters remained fearful of the aristocratic aspirations which they attributed to "the great."

The Jeffersonian-Jacksonian following believed that "great men" controlled the opposition party, whatever its name at any given time, and that those men aimed to strengthen the national government so that it could be used to enhance the social, economic, and political status of the rich at the expense of the common people. To frustrate their opponents, the normal majority believed, however irrationally in view of their usual dominance of the national government, that they must keep maximum authority in the state rather than in the federal government. They believed also that to win the election victories necessary to serve that end, they must give steadfast loyalty to their political party and its chosen leaders.[68] For the most part, Beekmantown's farmers did just that.

Conclusion

Each chapter of this study has offered concluding suggestions on the topic which it considered. But, with the exception of the argument that the socioeconomic status of the first generation of settlers was significantly higher than that of the second, no overall theses have appeared. In concluding this work, it is appropriate to consider what the study of this one community suggests with reference to the history of the American people in the years between 1769 and 1849.

One general hypothesis suggested by the Beekmantown experience concerns the pattern of frontier development in forested regions of the North. The first part of that hypothesis is that the forest frontier offered great economic opportunity which attracted a first generation of settlers with relatively high socioeconomic status. The second part of the hypothesis states that the reduced economic opportunity brought on by the termination of frontier conditions lowered the socioeconomic level of the community by driving the upwardly mobile to migrate and attracting as immigrants primarily people content to be more nearly subsistence farmers.

The foundation of this two-part hypothesis is an analysis of economic changes which needs to be made explicit. The economic attractions of the northern forest frontier were basically twofold. First was the opportunity for capital gain from converting cheap wilderness land into more expensive farmland in a developing community. The advantage was great, but it died with frontier conditions. The second attraction was virgin timber resources. Industries based upon such resources afforded money-making opportunities for entrepreneurs, for workers (including members of farm families working part time), and for farmers who sold fodder crops for the draft animals and food for the workers employed in timber-based industries. This avenue to economic betterment also disappeared with the virgin forests which were its foundation. Pursuing the economic advantages of the forest frontier westward provides the "carrot" aspect of the motivation for westward migration among the upwardly mobile. The "stick" motivation for outmigration was not just the inability of parents to provide ample amounts of land for their children—the feature so emphasized by New England studies—but the reduction of economic opportunity brought on by the nearly simultaneous disappearance of the chance for significant capital gain from sharply rising land values and of the economic advantages afforded by timber industries.

No other hypotheses explain as well the evident change in the socioeconomic level of the community between the first and the second generations, as noted in so many different contexts in the preceding chapters. How widely the hypothesis applies, if at all, to other forested regions of the North perhaps other writers will inform us.

The second hypothesis perhaps ought not to be called that as it merely reaffirms a traditional view which has come in for much questioning in recent years. The experience of the settlers of Beekmantown suggests that the "common man" did indeed make dramatic progress in the period which this study covers.

Part of this progress took place in a political context. In New York State prior to 1821, the common man could not vote for governor, lieutenant governor, or state senators. By the 1840s virtually all adult white males could vote for all elected state officers. At the outset the common man had only an indirect vote (through the influence, if any, of his assemblyman upon the Council of Appointment) in the selection of most county officials of importance. By the end of the period, nearly all such county officials were elected by the wide suffrage just noted. There was a similar increase in the number of state officials chosen directly by the people. Before 1824 New York's common men had had little direct say in the choice of the nation's president. He was nominated by congressional caucus and chosen on the basis of an electoral college vote which was cast by members of the legislature. By the 1840s the voters were both choosing delegates to a convention to pick a presidential candidate and determining by popular vote how the state's electoral ballots would be cast. In his home community, the common man also enjoyed much greater autonomy in that the legislature interfered far less in local affairs than it had at the beginning of the period. Perhaps most fundamental of all the political considerations is that when settlement began in Beekman Patent the common man had only a rudimentary political organization working for him at the state level and none at all nationally. By the end of the period, a party widely (and I think on the whole correctly) perceived to be that of the common man had not only organized at both state and national levels but had wrested control of the national government from the hands of the Federalists, who were widely (and I think correctly) considered to be elitists. The common man's party had made itself the normal majority party of the nation as well as the state. Then, after suffering the defection of its quasi-Federalist wing during the "era of good feelings," it had regained the distinction in the 1830s.

The economic lot of the common people of Beekmantown also improved over the years of this study despite the economic decline which afflicted the community in the later years. Under frontier conditions at the beginning of settlement, great inequalities of wealth existed. The wealthy proprietors, of course, owned all the land at the outset. Even in the 1790s, Thomas Tredwell and others, as well as the Beekmans, had large speculative landholdings. By 1850, when farming had become almost the only way to make a living in the town, virtually all the farmers owned their land and disparities in the size of individual holdings were far less than they had been in the 1790s. Furthermore, improvements in transportation had brought the common people advantages which were perhaps more significant in absolute terms than with specific reference to their relative standing vis-à-vis the wealthy. These improvements both lowered the cost of consumer goods brought into the community and helped them to compete for sales of their products in distant markets. The proliferation of banks had helped to increase the supply of money and to begin the transition from the "bookkeeping barter" system, in which prices were greatly inflated to offset an expected long delay in payment, to cash transactions with far lower prices. Factory production of textiles had so reduced costs for cloth and clothing as to lower greatly the number of farm families finding it necessary to produce their own.

Socially, too, common people were a lot better off in Beekmantown during the 1840s than they had been in the first decades of settlement. Slavery and indentured servitude had ceased. Imprisonment for debt was at least far less common. Handicapped persons were beginning to receive special care in state institutions. The assumption of uniform religious belief enforced by church disciplinary proceedings, weak admittedly even at the outset, had expired almost completely by the 1840s. It was replaced by much greater freedom for the individual to affiliate with any one of a variety of churches or none at all. In educating their children, common people at the outset had had to meet all the expenses themselves, except for the assistance afforded somewhat irregularly and in uncertain amount by the town fund for school support. By the end of the period, state and town taxation were making major contributions to the cost of educating children, while leaving the local people very much in charge of the administration of their neighborhood schools.

Thus, politically, economically, and socially the common people of Beekmantown in the 1840s were enjoying advantages which would have excited the envy of many of their counterparts in Beekman Patent during the 1790s, even though their prospects for significant economic gain were not so good.

A third hypothesis helps in some measure to reconcile the seemingly contradictory aspects of the first two. The first hypothesis, to repeat, affirms that the socioeconomic level was higher in the first generation of settlers than among those who came later. The second hypothesis states that the common people were better off in the second generation than in the first. The third hypothesis is that, quite contrary to Frederick Jackson Turner, the first effect of the northern forest frontier was to foster inequality and that it was the ending of frontier conditions which brought an increased measure of equality. Underlying this hypothesis, in addition to the record of Beekmantown's experience, is the observation that in general it is great economic opportunity which increases economic inequality. Conversely, it is the near absence of major economic opportunities which fosters economic equality such as, for example, generally prevails among very primitive people.

Finally, it may be worth suggesting that the answer to the

controversial question of whether the nation as a whole was becoming more or less egalitarian with reference to the distribution
of wealth in the early decades of the nineteenth century may depend
upon the proportions of the population which lived, on the one
hand, in developing cities and frontier areas and, on the other,
in older, rural communities, which had passed through their frontier period and found no great economic opportunities to replace
those afforded by the frontier.

Woolsey house, Cumberland Head, the residence to which
Melanchton Woolsey moved from his "mud-walled cottage"
in 1800 but lost when he became bankrupt in 1817

Notes

Abbreviations Used in Notes

BFP	Beekman Family Papers, The New-York Historical Society
Doc. Rel.	Edmund B. O'Callaghan (ed.), *Documents Relative to the Colonial History of the State of New York* (11 vols., Albany, 1853–1861)
LC	Library of Congress
NA	National Archives
NYAD	New York Assembly Documents
NYAJ	New York Assembly Journal
NYHS	The New-York Historical Society
NYPL	New York Public Library
NYSAS	New York State Agricultural Society
NYSD	New York Senate Documents
NYSJ	New York Senate Journal
NYSL	New York State Library
PAC	Public Archives of Canada, Ottawa
PRO, CO	Public Records Office, Colonial Office, London
Republican	Plattsburgh *Republican*

Prologue:
No Man's Land

1. Edward G. Bourne, *The Voyages and Explorations of Samuel de Champlain*
   (2 vols., New York, 1922), I, 197.
2. Francis Parkman, *Pioneers of France in the New World* (Boston, 1910),353.
3. Bourne, *Champlain*, 205. See also Guy Omeron Coolidge, "The French
   Occupation of the Champlain Valley from 1609 to 1759," *Proceedings of Vermont Historical Society*, n.s., VI, no. 3 (September 1938),
   146–147; Albert C. Ganley, "Land Grants and Settlement in the
   Champlain Valley of New York, 1664–1800" (M.A. thesis, Cornell
   University, 1940); Nell J. B. Sullivan and David K. Martin, *A History
   of the Town of Chazy* (Burlington, 1970), 10.
4. Frederic Van de Water, *Lake Champlain and Lake George* (Indianapolis,
   1946), chap. 10, passim.
5. Ibid., 130 ff.
6. George S. Bixby, "Peter Sailly," *New York State Library History Bulletin
   No. 12* (Albany, 1919), 66.

1. The Proprietors
and the Land

1. NYSL, Land Papers, XXIV, 126.
2. *Doc. Rel.*, VII, 125.
3. Philip L. White, *The Beekmans of New York* (New York, 1956), passim.
   The complaint of 1768 appears in James Beekman's letter to Peach
   and Pierce of Bristol, February 18, 1768. See Philip L.
   White (ed.), *The Beekman Mercantile Papers* (3 vols., New York,
   1956), II, 867– 868.
4. *Letterbook of John Watts* (New York, 1928), 342.
5. White, *Beekmans of New York*, passim.
6. *Letters and Papers of Cadwallader Colden* (9 vols., New York, 1917–
   1923), II, 112.
7. Guy O. Coolidge, "The French Occupation of the Champlain Valley
   from 1609 to 1759," *Proceedings of the Vermont Historical Society*, n.s.,
   VI, no. 3 (September 1938), chap. 9, passim. See also *Jackson ex
   dem. Winthrop v. Ingraham*, New York Supreme Court of Judicature,
   4 Johnson, 163–183, February 1809; Albert C. Ganley, "Land Grants
   and Settlement in the Champlain Valley of New York, 1664–1800"
   (M.A. thesis, Cornell University, 1940); Ruth L. Higgins, *Expansion
   in New York* (Columbus, 1931), 87 ff. Among many histories of
   Lake Champlain, the best are Peter S. Palmer, *History of Lake Champlain* (Albany, 1866); Winslow C. Watson, *Pioneer History of the
   Champlain Valley* (Albany, 1863); and Frederic Van de Water, *Lake
   Champlain and Lake George* (Indianapolis, 1946).

8. *Doc. Rel.*, VII, 642–643.
9. PRO, CO 5, 1098–209 (Moore to Lords of Trade, January 12, 1767); 215 (Moore to Shelburne, February 22, 1767); 265 (ibid., April 4, 1767).
10. *Doc. Rel.*, VII, 873 ff.
11. PRO, CO 5, 1098–265 (Moore to Shelburne, April 4, 1767).
12. *Doc. Rel.*, VIII, 12.
13. *Doc. Rel.*, VIII, 89.
14. PRO, CO 5, 1099–223 (Moore to Hillsborough, October 19, 1768, with P.S. October 24).
15. NYHS, *Abstracts of Wills*, XV, 134 ff.; *Calendar of Sir William Johnson Manuscripts* (Albany, 1909), 254, 313; Chilton Williamson, *Vermont in Quandary, 1763–1825* (Montpelier, 1949), 186, 187; Wendell E. Tripp, Jr., "Robert Troup" (Ph.D. dissertation, Columbia University, 1973), 144–146; James B. Wilbur, *Ira Allen: Founder of Vermont, 1751–1814* (2 vols., Boston, 1928), II, 86 passim. Allen termed Kelly a "Damned . . . Rascal." Williamson compared him to Talleyrand.
16. Kelly to Lott, May 16, 1768, BFP.
17. NYSL, Land Papers, XXIV, 126.
18. Kelly to Lott, August 22, November 19, 1768; Kelly to William Beekman, December 12, 1768, BFP.
19. Office of the Secretary of State, Deed Book 20, pp. 161, 292. On the general use of dummies, see Higgins, *Expansion*, and Robert J. Rayback (ed.), *Richards Atlas of New York State* (Phoenix, N.Y., 1959).
20. *Doc. Rel.*, VIII, 175, 193; PRO, CO 5, 1100–270 (Colden to Hillsborough, September 13, 1769).
21. Documents dated December 14, 1768, and October 13, 1769, BFP. On the problem of where New York's northeastern border lay, see Philip J. Schwarz, "New York's Provincial Boundaries" (Ph.D. dissertation, Cornell University, 1963); Charles A. Jellison, *Ethan Allen: Frontier Rebel* (Syracuse, 1969); Williamson, *Vermont*; Wilbur, *Ira Allen*; Lawrence H. Gipson, *The British Empire Before the American Revolution*, vol. XI, *The Triumphant Empire: The Rumbling of the Coming Storm, 1766–1770* (15 vols., New York, 1965), 310–330; Matt B. Jones, *Vermont in the Making* (Cambridge, 1939).
22. This undated manuscript appears in the papers of William Beekman in the BFP.
23. Clarence Danhof, *Change in Agriculture: The Northern United States, 1820–1870* (Cambridge, 1969), 114–119. For other estimates, see David M. Ellis, *Landlords and Farmers in the Hudson-Mohawk Region, 1790–1850* (Ithaca, 1946), 74; Martin L. Primack, "Land Clearing under Nineteenth-Century Techniques: Some Preliminary Calculations," *Journal of Economic History*, XXII (1962), 484–497; Paul W. Gates, "Problems of Agriculture, 1790–1840," *Agricultural History*, XLVI (1972), 33–57.
24. See Ian C. C. Graham, *Colonists from Scotland* (Ithaca, 1956); Isabel Frances Grant, *The Macleods: The History of a Clan, 1200–1956* (Lon-

don, 1959); Henry Hamilton, *An Economic History of Scotland in the 18th Century* (Oxford, 1963).

25. Newspaper item quoted in Graham, *Colonists*, 72.
26. Quoted by Hamilton, *History of Scotland*, 381.
27. Graham, *Colonists*, 50.
28. Graham, *Colonists*, 70.
29. William Beekman to Troup et al., May 18, 1795, but see also Tredwell to William Beekman, June 27, 1795, BFP. The latter shows Tredwell assuming a purchase contract originally made by a third party.
30. Memorandum to State Auditor, March 27, 1793, BFP. For details of the agreement with Platt, see below.
31. Quit rent account, January 1, 1787; Cockburn's expenses, in copy of letter to Kelly, November 12, 1785, BFP.
32. *Laws of the State of New York, 1785–1788*, II, chap. 55, 300–301; Cockburn to Kelly, March 5, 1786; William Beekman to Platt, December 28, 1786; Memorandum to State Auditor, March 27, 1793, BFP.
33. Winchester Fitch, "The Throop Family and the Tradition," *New York Genealogical and Biographical Record*, XXXVI (1905), 134; XXXVII (1906), 36, 39, 40. See also Allan S. Everest, *Moses Hazen and the Canadian Refugees in the American Revolution* (Syracuse, 1976), 117–118, 125–127, 139.
34. Melanchton L. Woolsey, *Melanchton Lloyd Woolsey: A Memoir* (Champlain, 1929), passim; Palmer, *Lake Champlain*, 169–170; Hugh Hastings (ed.), *Military Minutes of the Council of Appointment, 1783–1821* (4 vols., Albany, 1901), I, 142, 356, 638.
35. Woolsey, *Memoir*, 18; letter to Woolsey, March 23, 1789, BFP.
36. Sung Bok Kim's *Landlord and Tenant in Colonial New York, 1664–1775* (Chapel Hill, 1978) makes clear that tenants on the large Hudson valley estates were better off than Irving Mark's *Agrarian Conflicts in Colonial New York, 1711–1775* (New York, 1940) had led a generation of historians to believe. But, Kim's work also shows that landlords could and did restrict the actions of their tenants, even in the sale of their improvements, and that settlers from New England in particular strongly preferred to buy rather than to lease.
37. For example, see Paul W. Gates, *The Wisconsin Pine Lands of Cornell University* (Ithaca, 1943), 7–8, 69, passim.
38. Mortgage records, Clinton County Court House, Plattsburgh.
39. Gerard Beekman to Henry and Samuel McFadden, November 1, 1827, BFP.
40. Accounts in BFP.
41. *Proceedings of the Bar of the County of Clinton . . . Commemorative of the Life and Character of William Swetland* (Plattsburgh, 1865); D. H. Hurd, *History of Clinton and Franklin Counties* (Philadelphia, 1880), passim. See also the references to Swetland in chapter 14.
42. Swetland to James W. Beekman, March 15, April 12, 1843; May 6, 1844; December 1, 1849.
43. On the antirent controversy, the best treatment is still Ellis, *Landlords and Farmers*, chap. 7. Other treatments include Eldridge H. Pendleton,

"The New York Anti-Rent Controversy, 1830–1860" (Ph.D. dissertation, University of Virginia, 1974); Henry Christman, *Tin Horns and Calico* (New York, 1945). On New York frontier settlement generally, see, in addition to the works of Mark, Kim, and Tripp cited above, Neil A. McNall, *An Agricultural History of the Genesee Valley, 1790–1860* (Philadelphia, 1952); William Chazanof, *Joseph Ellicott and the Holland Land Company* (Syracuse, 1970); Paul D. Evans, *The Holland Land Company* (Buffalo, 1924); Helen I. Cowan, *Charles Williamson* (Rochester, 1941); Higgins, *Expansion*; Robert W. Silsby, "Frontier Attitudes and Debt Collection in Western New York," and Henry Cohen, "Vicissitudes of an Absentee Landlord: A Case Study," both in David M. Ellis (ed.), *The Frontier in American Development* (Ithaca, 1969); Edward P. Alexander, "The Provincial Aristocracy and the Land," in Alexander C. Flick (ed.), *History of New York State*, III, *Whig and Tory* (New York, 1933); Alexander, *A Revolutionary Conservative: James Duane of New York* (New York, 1938); David M. Ellis, "The Coopers and the New York State Landholding System," *New York History* (special issue on James Fenimore Cooper, 1954), 412–422; Cooper's novels, *The Pioneers*, *The Chainbearer*, and *Satanstoe*; William Cooper, *A Guide in the Wilderness* (Dublin, 1810); Arthur J. Alexander, "Judge John Laurance," *New York History*, XXV (1944), 35–45; Raymond Walters and Philip G. Walters, "David Parish," *New York History*, XXVI (1945), 146–165; Orsamus Turner, *History of the Pioneer Settlement of Phelps and Gorham Purchase* (1851) and *Pioneer History of the Holland Purchase of Western New York* (1849); Rayback (ed.), *Richards Atlas*; William Charles Lahey, "The Influence of David Parish on the Development of Trade and Settlement in Northern New York, 1808–1822" (Ph.D. dissertation, Syracuse University, 1958); Paul V. Lutz, "Land Grants for Service in the Revolution," *New-York Historical Society Quarterly*, XLVIII (1964), 221–235; John Pell, "The Saga of William Gilliland," *New York History*, XIII (1932), 390–403; Barbara A. Chernow, "Robert Morris: Genesee Land Speculator," *New York History*, LVIII (1977), 195–220; William Siles, "Genesee Settlement, Economic Opportunity and the Safety Valve Thesis: A Fresh Look" (paper presented at the second annual conference of the New York State Studies Group, SUNY-Brockport, June 9, 1978).

44. For excellent historiographical perspective on land speculators, see Robert P. Swierenga, "Land Speculation and Its Impact on American Economic Growth and Welfare: A Historiographical Review," *Western Historical Quarterly*, VIII (1977), 283–302.

2. Forest Products

1. Arthur R. M. Lower, "Lumbering in Eastern Canada," (2 vols., Ph.D. dissertation, Harvard University, 1928), I, 34 ff. Lower's dissertation provides the best overall account of the timber industries in the St.

Lawrence area during this period. The first two chapters of volume I are especially good. Lower's published works, including *Settlement and the Forest Frontier of Eastern Canada* (Toronto, 1936), *North American Assault on the Canadian Forest* (Toronto, 1938), and *Great Britain's Woodyard: British America and the Timber Trade* (Montreal, 1973), are much less detailed. Extremely valuable also are Michael S. Cross, "'Dark Druidical Groves': The Lumber Community and the Commercial Frontier in British North America to 1854" (Ph.D. dissertation, University of Toronto, 1968), and two articles by H. N. Muller, "Smuggling into Canada: How the Champlain Valley Defied Jefferson's Embargo," *Vermont History*, XXXVIII (1970), 5–21, and "Floating a Lumber Raft to Quebec City, 1805: The Journal of Guy Catlin of Burlington," *Vermont History*, XXXIX (1971), 116–124. See also his "Canadian-American Trade on Lake Champlain and the Richelieu River, 1789–1815" (Ph.D. dissertation, University of Rochester, 1968). For trans-Atlantic perspective, Robert G. Albion, *Forests and Sea Power* (Cambridge, 1926), is invaluable. See also D. D. Calvin, *A Saga of the St. Lawrence: Timber and Shipping through Three Generations* (Toronto, 1945); Chilton Williamson, *Vermont in Quandary, 1763–1825* (Montpelier, 1949); and James B. Wilbur, *Ira Allen: Founder of Vermont, 1751–1814* (2 vols., Boston, 1928). Ronald Fahl's *North American Forest and Conservation History: A Bibliography* (Santa Barbara, 1977), appeared too late for me to use it.

2. Lower, "Lumbering in Eastern Canada," I, chap. 2.
3. Thomas F. Gordon, *Gazetteer of the State of New York* (Philadelphia, 1836), 395.
4. Ibid., 395 ff.; on Hazen, Allan S. Everest, *Moses Hazen and the Canadian Refugees in the American Revolution* (Syracuse, 1976), chaps. 1 and 2, passim; on the Allens, Wilbur, *Ira Allen*, I, 490–491, 508–523, 525; Williamson, *Vermont in Quandary*, passim; on Gilliland, Winslow C. Watson, *Pioneer History of the Champlain Valley* (Albany, 1863), passim; and John Pell, "The Saga of William Gilliland," *New York History*, XIII (1930), 390–403.
5. Lower, "Lumbering in Eastern Canada," I, 130 ff.
6. The following description derives largely from Lower (I, chap. 8; II, chaps. 12 and 13) but owes something also to the other works cited in note 1.
7. John Lambert, *Travels through Canada and the United States . . . 1806, 1807, and 1808* (2 vols., 2d ed., London, 1813), I, 245 ff. See also Hilda Neatby, *Quebec: The Revolutionary Age, 1760–1791* (Toronto, 1966), 75. For instructions on how to build a timber raft by one who had actually done it, see William Fox, *A History of Lumbering in the State of New York*, Bulletin 34, Bureau of Forestry (Washington, 1902), 19–20.
8. Pliny Moore Papers in the possession of Charles W. McLellan, Champlain, New York.
9. Muller, "Floating a Lumber Raft," 116–124.
10. Agreement with Peter Turner, December 14, 1868, BFP; Adolphus Benzel, "Remarks on Lake Champlain," *The Bulletin of the Fort*

Ticonderoga Museum, XII (1969), 358–364. For perspective on Hazen's role as agent of the British government, see Joseph J. Malone, *Pine Trees and Politics* (Seattle, 1964).

11. Quoted in Everest, *Moses Hazen*, 29. Everest's meticulously researched study is the basic source for my observation on Hazen's career, although I have also examined much manuscript material on Hazen, chiefly at the library of the State University College, Plattsburgh.

12. Everest, *Moses Hazen*, 148, passim.

13. Ibid., 134–135, passim.

14. Ibid., 144, passim. On September 7, 1788, in one of several papers relating to wage payments, Mooers paid wages to fourteen laborers for the preceding twenty-three months. Manuscript account, Bailey Collection, State University College Library, Plattsburgh.

15. Mix to Pliny Moore, July 29, 1787, Pliny Moore Papers.

16. An account of the shipment dated at London, March 25, 1792, appears in the Benjamin Mooers Papers, Bailey Collection, State University College Library, Plattsburgh. References to the timber trade are in Mooers to Pliny Moore, February 1, 1792, Pliny Moore Papers.

17. Adam Shortt and A. G. Doughty, *Documents Relating to the Constitutional History of Canada, 1759–1791* (Ottawa, 1918), 945–946. On exports from the valley after the Revolution, see the accounts in Wilbur, Williamson, and Lower (I, chaps. 3 and 4) and A. L. Burt, *United States, Great Britain, and British North America* (New Haven, 1940), 68.

18. *Republican*, January 26, 1878; Platt Papers, Plattsburgh Public Library, passim.

19. Moore to Assemblyman Cantine, January 14, 1788; Corbin to Moore, August 16, 1788, Pliny Moore Papers.

20. Albion, *Forests and Sea Power*, 344–345, 355; Fernand Ouellet, *Histoire Economique et Sociale du Québec, 1760–1850* (Montreal and Paris, 1966), 189; Lower, "Lumbering in Eastern Canada," I, 130–153; for a discussion of Ouellet and his critics, see T. J. A. LeGoff, "The Agricultural Crisis in Lower Canada, 1802–1812: A Review of a Controversy," *Canadian Historical Review*, LV (1974), 1–31.

21. *Jackson ex dem. Winthrop v. Ingraham*, February 1809, New York Supreme Court of Judicature, reported in 4 Johnson, 163–183. H. Fuller Allen, attorney at Plattsburgh, kindly informed me of this action. The remaining information concerning Schiefflin derives from the Pliny Moore Papers, passim. Brazen trespassing was quite the rule in the timbered areas of Canada also. See Cross, "'Dark Druidical Groves,'" 239, chap. 3, passim.

22. *Republican*, November 10, 1883; February 2, 1894. Customs Collector Peter Sailly estimated to Treasury Secretary Gallatin, March 2, 1810, that "our rafts of Lumber" in the coming season "may fetch in Quebec Six Hundred Thousand Dollars." Comptroller's Letters, Champlain District, Record Group 217, National Archives.

23. Lower, "Lumbering in Eastern Canada," I, 153–156.

24. See Albion, *Forests and Sea Power*, appendix D; Ouellet, *Histoire*, 291 ff.

25. J. E. Defebaugh, *History of the Lumber Industry of America* (2 vols., Chicago, 1906–1907), I, 477 ff.
26. Great Britain, *Sessional Papers* 186, vol. VI, 1821, Report of Select Committee . . . on Foreign Trade; *Statutes at Large*, 3 George IV (1822), chap. 119.
27. NYSJ, 46th Session, 1823, p. 506, Annual Report of the Canal Commissioners; PAC, "Imperial Blue Books Relating to Canada, 1820–1821," no. 66. p. 6.
28. NYAJ, 1824, pt. 1, 548 ff., Report of the Canal Commissioners.
29. United States Census, 1850, *Productions of Industry*, New York, 369.
30. United States Register of the Treasury, Bureau of the Census, *Commerce and Navigation of the United States*, annual publications for the years cited.
31. Defebaugh, *Lumber Industry*, I, 489–490; NYSD, 1836, doc. 70, pp. 2, 8; 1847, doc. 90, statements 3 and 26. Statistics presented in the New York Senate Documents are often not easily comparable. For example, lumber traffic figures are sometimes given as of entry at Whitehall, but sometimes only as entering the Hudson from the Champlain Canal. Only the former truly represents Champlain valley production. Figures for 1835 are my calculations based on price and quantity figures in the documents cited.
32. Malachy Postlethwayt, *Universal Dictionary of Trade and Commerce* (London, 1774); J. R. McCulloch, *Dictionary of Commerce* (London, 1843); Jared Van Wagenen, *Golden Age of Homespun* (Ithaca, 1954), 164–165.
33. William B. Weeden, *Economic and Social History of New England* (2 vols., New York, 1890), I, 168; John MacGregor, *Commercial Statistics* (3 vols., London, 1850), III, 400.
34. United States Bureau of the Census, *Statistical History of the United States* (New York, 1976), 1183–1184.
35. Lower, "Lumbering in Eastern Canada," I, 114; Ouellet, *Histoire*, 88–90.
36. Arthur H. Cole, *The Industrial and Commercial Correspondence of Alexander Hamilton* (Chicago, 1928), 114, 280, 297. Some agricultural historians have declined to accept Hamilton's categorization. Bidwell and Falconer, for example, mention the income which frontier settlers could derive from producing potash, but they regretted that such activities "interfered with farming operations and hindered the development of good agricultural practice." Percy W. Bidwell and John I. Falconer, *History of Agriculture in the Northern United States, 1720–1860* (Washington, 1925), 78–79.
37. *New York Laws*, 1 Greenleaf 100 (1784); 2 Greenleaf 315 (1790); Statutes 1843, chap. 202; Williamson, *Vermont*, 245.
38. Frederick J. Seaver, *Historical Sketches of Franklin County* (Albany, 1918), 27 ff.
39. Sales notes, 1799, BFP; Abby Maria Hemenway, *Vermont Historical Gazetteer* (5 vols., Claremont, Vt., 1877), III, 319–429.
40. Lambert, *Travels*, II, 526. See also the recollections of a Vermont worker in Rebecca Skillin (ed.), "William Cheney (1781–1875): The

Life of a Vermont Woodsman and Farmer," *Vermont History*, XXXIX (1971), 43–50.

41. Neil A. McNall, *An Agricultural History of the Genesee Valley, 1790–1860* (Philadelphia, 1952), 28. See also Paul W. Gates, "Problems of Agriculture, 1790–1840," *Agricultural History*, XLVI (1972), 33–58.

42. Seaver, *Franklin County*, 27–28. For rental terms in Vermont, see Skillin's article cited in note 40.

43. Peter S. Palmer, *History of Plattsburgh* (Plattsburgh, 1877), 30; United States Census of 1850, *Products of Industry*, New York, 369.

44. Seaver, *Franklin County*, 29.

45. See table 3 for imports at St. Johns. See also Muller, "Smuggling into Canada," 5–21.

46. *Republican*, February 24, 1816; December 9, 1820; NYSJ, 1817, 124–125.

47. NYAJ, 1819, pp. 384–385. Governor De Witt Clinton ranked potash with wheat as leading exports of the state in 1822—David M. Ellis, *Landlords and Farmers in the Hudson-Mohawk Region, 1790–1850* (Ithaca, 1946), 113. Muller (see note 45) states that in the period of the War of 1812, potash and pearlash exports were 38 percent of all trade northbound from Lake Champlain, exceeding the value of any other product. Cross identified potash as almost the only forest product of significance in Canada's exports between 1763 and the Napoleonic era—"'Dark Druidical Groves,'" 128.

48. NYSD, 1849, doc. 60.

49. United States Register of the Treasury, *Commerce and Navigation of the United States*, 1824, 1825, and 1826.

50. See Charles F. Carroll, *The Timber Economy of Puritan New England* (Providence, 1973), for an argument supporting this proposition with reference to seventeenth-century New England.

51. David C. Smith, "The Logging Frontier," *Journal of Forest History*, 18 (1974), 96–106, chides frontier historians for neglecting the "logging frontier."

3. Farming

1. Percentage figures are calculations based on census data in the *Republican*, February 3, 1821, and the *United States Census*, 1840 (microfilm at NYSL). Stephanie G. Wolf, *Urban Village* (Princeton, 1976), 68, found only 15 percent of the residents of Germantown, Pennsylvania, in 1773 called themselves farmers.

2. Percy W. Bidwell and John I. Falconer, *History of Agriculture in the Northern United States, 1620–1860* (Washington, 1925), 254. See also Clarence Danhof, *Change in Agriculture: The Northern United States, 1820–1870* (Cambridge, 1969), 16, 17. The classic refutation of the myth of self-sufficiency is Rodney C. Loehr, "Self-Sufficiency on the Farm," *Agricultural History*, XXVI (1952), 37–41, but see also William

Norton, "Frontier Agriculture: Subsistence or Commercial?" *Annals of the Association of American Geographers*, 67 (1977), 463–464; Robert D. Mitchell, *Commercialism and Frontier: Perspectives on the Early Shenandoah Valley* (Charlottesville, 1977); and James T. Lemon, *Best Poor Man's Country* (Baltimore, 1972).

3. NYSAS, *Transactions*, 1851, XI, 486.

4. Peter S. Palmer, *History of Plattsburgh* (Plattsburgh, 1877), 21; idem, *History of Lake Champlain* (Albany, 1866), 151 ff.

5. *Republican*, July 19, 1817; October 14, 1843.

6. Robert Platt to Zephaniah Platt, July 3, 1798, Platt Papers, Plattsburgh Public Library. Estimates as to the time required to clear land vary greatly. That given here is from Danhof, *Change in Agriculture*, 117–119. See Rebecca Skillin (ed.), "William Cheney (1787–1875): The Life of a Vermont Woodsman and Farmer," *Vermont History*, XXXIX (1971), 43–50, for the informative reminiscences of a man who spent much of his life clearing frontier land, sometimes in New York.

7. James Dean to Moore, April 23, 1787, Pliny Moore Papers in the possession of Charles W. McLellan of Champlain.

8. Moore to Assemblyman Cantine, January 14, 1788, Pliny Moore Papers.

9. Charles Platt to Zephaniah Platt, March 13, April 4, 1785, Platt Papers, NYSL.

10. Murdoch McPherson to Moore, January 1, 1789, Pliny Moore Papers. On similar conditions in Vermont, see James B. Wilbur, *Ira Allen: Founder of Vermont, 1751–1814* (2 vols., Boston, 1928), I, 524.

11. William Beaumont to Moore, January 25, 1789, Pliny Moore Papers.

12. *Republican*, January 26, 1878.

13. M. L. Woolsey to William Beekman, July 22, 1789, BFP. I have not seen Elizabeth Cometti (ed.), *The American Journals of Lt. John Enys* (Syracuse, 1976), but *North Country Notes*, no. 137 (February 1978), reports that Enys found great privation in the area in 1785.

14. Royal Corbin to Moore, June 2, 1792, Pliny Moore Papers.

15. Dr. Reuben Garlick to Moore, October 13, 1792; Moore to John Taylor, March 2, 1803, Pliny Moore Papers.

16. James Kent Diary, LC.

17. Charles Platt to Zephaniah Platt, August 12, 1797, Platt Papers, NYSL.

18. Moore to William Logan, December 17, 1801, Pliny Moore Papers. Andrew Hill Clark, "Suggestions for the Geographical Study of Agricultural Change in the United States, 1790–1840," *Agricultural History*, XLVI (1972), 155–172, suggests that supplying new settlers afforded a major commercial market for many pioneer farmers. To what extent this was true in Beekmantown is not clear.

19. Bidwell and Falconer, *History of Agriculture*, 82–83. For a similar observation, see Ernest L. Bogart, *Peacham: The Story of a Vermont Hill Town* (Montpelier, 1948), 36.

20. BFP, passim.

21. See note 18. Evidence supporting this proposition in relation to Beekmantown at a later period will be adduced below. On the general

proposition, see A. R. M. Lower, "Lumbering in Eastern Canada" (2 vols., Ph.D. dissertation, Harvard University, 1928), II, 525, and Michael S. Cross, "'Dark Druidical Groves'" (Ph.D. dissertation, University of Toronto, 1968), 280–281. On western competition, see Russell H. Anderson, "New York Agriculture Meets the West, 1830–1850," *Wisconsin Magazine of History*, 16 (1932–1933), 163–198, 285–296.

22. Edith Van Wagner, *Agricultural Manual of New York State*, Bulletin 133, New York State Department of Farms and Markets (Albany, 1922), 207; Alfred L. Diebolt, "Economic and Social Practices in Clinton County" (undated mimeographed paper, State University College Library, Plattsburgh). Clinton County agricultural agent Merle W. Reese characterized the agricultural resources of Beekmantown for me in an interview.

23. Chester W. Wright, *Wool Growing and the Tariff* (Boston, 1910), 21–22, 25; Bidwell and Falconer, *History of Agriculture*, 217–219; *New York Laws*, 5 Webster 359, 361.

24. Wright, *Wool Growing*, 24–27; Bidwell and Falconer, *History of Agriculture*, 217–219; Paul W. Gates, *Farmers Age* (New York, 1960), 222.

25. Trends in sheep raising after the end of the Merino madness are summarized in Bidwell and Falconer, *History of Agriculture*, 219–223.

26. Donald B. Marti, "Early Agricultural Societies in New York: Foundations of Improvement," *New York History*, XLVIII (1967), 313–331; Hugh M. Flick, "Elkanah Watson: Gentleman Promoter, 1758–1842" (Ph.D. dissertation, Columbia University, 1958); Bidwell and Falconer, *History of Agriculture*, 184–192.

27. *Republican*, October 9, December 4, December 18, 1819.

28. *Republican*, December 11, December 18, 1819.

29. *Republican*, December 25, 1819.

30. *Republican*, October 21, 1820.

31. *Republican*, October 20, 1821.

32. *Northern Intelligencer*, May 14, October 15, 1822.

33. *Republican*, October 11, 1823. Leaders of the society scheduled a one-day fair for October 13, 1824, and fixed prices (*Republican*, October 9, 1824), but the *Republican* carried no notice of the actual event.

34. *Republican*, October 20, 1821.

35. Ibid.; *Northern Intelligencer*, October 15, 1822.

36. United States Bureau of the Census, *Statistical History of the United States* (New York, 1976), 548. Each year from 1852 through 1855, the wholesale price index for lumber was higher than ever before.

37. United States Census, 1850, *Productions of Agriculture*.

38. Percy W. Bidwell, *Rural Economy in New England at the Beginning of the Nineteenth Century* (New Haven, 1916), 337 ff.

39. NYSAS, *Transactions*, 1851, XI, 489. Italics added. Cf. Gates, *Farmers Age*, 226.

40. United States Census, 1850, *Productions of Agriculture*.

41. NYSAS, *Transactions*, 1851, XI, 489.

42. United States Census, 1850, *Productions of Agriculture*.

43. NYSAS, *Transactions*, 1851, XI, 487.
44. United States Census, 1850, *Productions of Agriculture*. The national average, including both beef and dairy cattle, was about twelve in 1860. See Gates, *Farmers Age*, 231, for comparative figures on all major forms of livestock.
45. Ibid. The national average was three per farm in 1860. Gates, *Farmers Age*, 231.
46. NYSAS, *Transactions*, 1851, XI, 481 ff. On the importance of hay in the Genesee country, see Neil A. McNall, *Agricultural History of the Genesee Valley, 1790–1860* (Philadelphia, 1952), 254. For Hinton R. Helper's famous affirmation that the hay crop of the northern states in 1850 exceeded the combined value of all the South's plantation crops, see *The Impending Crisis of the South* (New York, 1857), 50–53.
47. United States Census, 1850, *Productions of Agriculture*.
48. NYSAS, *Transactions*, 1851, XI, 484.
49. My calculations based on United States Census, 1850, *Productions of Agriculture*.
50. NYSAS, *Transactions*, 1851, XI, 484–485.
51. United States Census, 1850, *Productions of Agriculture*.
52. NYSAS, *Transactions*, 1846, VI, 533.
53. Ibid., 1845, V, 116; 1844, IV, 196. Cf. Bidwell and Falconer, *History of Agriculture*, 229, 431, and Gates, *Farmers Age*, chap. 11.
54. Ibid., 1842, XII, 374 ff.
55. On the value of New York farmland, see the state census of 1855. On migration and the value of Vermont farmland, see Lewis D. Stilwell, "Migration from Vermont, 1776–1860," *Proceedings of the Vermont Historical Society*, V (1937), 63–246, especially chap. 7.
56. NYSAS, *Transactions*, 1852, XII, 374 ff.
57. New York State Census, 1855.
58. Cf. Douglass S. North, "Location Theory and Regional Economic Growth," *Journal of Political Economy*, 63 (1955), 243–258. For a more general discussion of this point, see the appended Bibliographical Note.
59. Beekmantown's production of fodder for oxen and horses used in timber and iron operations fits the developmental pattern suggested by North (see note 58). Andrew Hill Clark's "Suggestions for the Geographical Study of Agricultural Change in the United States, 1790–1840," *Agricultural History*, XLVI (1972), 155–172, reconsiders farmers' markets imaginatively.

4. General Economic Development

1. Gertrude Cone, "Studies in the Development of Transportation in the Champlain Valley to 1876" (M.S. thesis, University of Vermont, 1945), 27. On transportation in the valley, see also John E. O'Hara,

"Erie's Junior Partner: The Economic and Social Effects of the Champlain Canal upon the Champlain Valley" (Ph.D. dissertation, Columbia University, 1951); Elsie A. Potter, "The Influence of the Champlain Canal on Eastern New York and Western Vermont (1823–1860)" (M.A. thesis, Cornell University, 1939); Dorothy Kendall Cleaveland, "The Trade and Trade Routes of Northern New York," New York State Historical Association, *Proceedings*, XXI (1923), 205–231; Ogden R. Ross, *The Steamboats of Lake Champlain, 1809–1930* (privately printed, 1930); Benjamin Silliman, *Remarks Made on a Short Tour between Hartford and Quebec . . . 1819* (2d ed., New Haven, 1824); Isaac Weld, *Travels* (4th ed., London, 1800); John Pell, "Saga of William Gilliland," *New York History*, XIII (1932), 390–403; Winslow C. Watson, *Pioneer History of the Champlain Valley* (Albany, 1863).

2. Charles Platt to Zephaniah Platt, March 4, 1785; March 13, 1785, Platt Papers, NYSL.

3. Barent Bleecker to Moore, January 26, 1805, Pliny Moore Papers in the possession of Charles W. McLellan of Champlain.

4. Sailly to Joseph Anderson, February 13, 1817, Comptroller's Letters, Champlain District, Record Group 217, National Archives.

5. Lewis D. Stilwell, *Migration from Vermont (1776–1860)* (Montpelier, 1948), 105. This is a reprint of the work cited in note 55, chap. 3.

6. Moore to James Woolrich, March 17, 1804, Pliny Moore Papers; Sailly to Comptroller Duval, November 25, 1809, Comptroller's Letters, Champlain District, Record Group 217, National Archives; NYAJ, 1821, pp. 179–180; Mooers to A. C. Flagg, April 3, 1822, Flagg Papers, NYPL.

7. Cone, "Transportation," 13, 22. E. L. Jones, "Creative Disruption in American Agriculture, 1620–1820," *Agricultural History*, XLVIII (1974), 510–528, elaborates on the difficulties of sustaining animal life in regions of dense forest.

8. NYAD, 1834, doc. 110; James Kent Diary, LC.

9. John Lambert, *Travels through Canada and the United States . . . 1806, 1807, and 1808* (2 vols., 2d ed., London, 1813), II, 528–529.

10. Pliny Moore Papers, passim.

11. Fernand Ouellet, *Histoire Economique et Sociale du Québec, 1760–1850* (Montreal, 1966), passim; O'Hara, "Erie's Junior Partner," 305.

12. Arthur R. M. Lower, "Lumbering in Eastern Canada" (2 vols., Ph.D. dissertation, Harvard University, 1928), I; 232 ff.; Ouellet, *Histoire*, passim; Chilton Williamson, *Vermont in Quandary, 1763–1825* (Montpelier, 1949), 246 ff.

13. William Torrey expense account, September 26, 1786, Kent-DeLord Papers, State University College Library, Plattsburgh.

14. Cone, "Transportation," 19.

15. Stilwell, *Migration*, chap. 5, passim.

16. Ernest L. Bogart, *Peacham: The Story of a Vermont Hill Town* (Montpelier, 1948), 294; Cone, "Transportation," 45–46.

17. *Republican*, April 27, 1844.

18. Cone, "Transportation," 88.

19. *Republican*, March 1, 1834; Cone, "Transportation," 27.

20. *Republican*, July 29, 1839; O'Hara, "Erie's Junior Partner," 342.

21. Cone, "Transportation," 115–116. The Albany-Montreal stage in
    1815 went via Burlington rather than Plattsburgh. Allan S.
    Everest, "Early Roads and Taverns of the Champlain Valley," *Vermont History*, XXXVII (1969), 247–255. Stage coach service from Plattsburgh
    to Montreal began only in 1815. Nell J. B. Sullivan and David K.
    Martin, *History of the Town of Chazy* (Burlington, 1970), 172.
22. William Pitt Platt to Zephaniah Platt, April 7, 1794, Platt Papers,
    Plattsburgh Public Library.
23. Lambert, *Travels*, II, 4–22.
24. Cone, "Transportation," 35; O'Hara, "Erie's Junior Partner," 127,
    190. Cf. Sullivan and Martin, *Chazy*, 167 and Ross, *Steamboats*,
    passim.
25. *Republican*, May 2, 1896.
26. Swetland to Beekman, December 2, 1848, March 12, 1849, BFP;
    Republican, December 4, 1847; Edward C. Kirkland, *Men, Cities,
    and Transportation: A Study in New England History, 1820–1900* (2
    vols., Cambridge, 1948), I, 169; Sullivan and Martin, *Chazy*, 175.
27. Peter S. Palmer, *History of Plattsburgh* (Plattsburgh, 1877), 32. The
    best general description of how rural storekeepers operated is still
    in Lewis E. Atherton's two works: *The Southern Country Store* (Baton
    Rouge, 1948) and "The Pioneer Merchant in Mid-America," *University of Missouri Studies*, XIV (1939). But, see also Gerald Carson,
    The Old Country Store (New York, 1954); R. E. Gould, *Yankee Storekeeper* (New York, 1946); Carol H. Schwartz, "Retail Trade Development in New York State" (Ph.D. dissertation, Columbia University,
    1963); and William C. Lahey, "The Influence of David Parish on
    the Development of Trade and Settlement in Northern New York,
    1808–1822" (Ph.D. dissertation, Syracuse University, 1958).
28. United States Census, 1840; New York State Census, 1845.
29. *Republican*, January 17, 1846; September 30, 1848, passim. Merchants
    who dealt on a credit basis inflated their prices rather than charge
    interest.
30. NYSJ, 1817, pp. 124–125, 221–222. On banking in New York State,
    see Robert E. Chaddock, *The Safety Fund Banking System in New
    York, 1829–1866* (Washington, 1910); John M. McFaul, *The Politics
    of Jacksonian Finance* (Ithaca, 1972), 48–56, 101–106; James Roger
    Sharp, *The Jacksonians versus the Banks* (New York, 1970), 297–305.
31. NYAJ, 1819, pp. 248–249; 1823, p. 103; 1824, p. 274; 1825, pp.
    752–753; 1826, pp. 418–419; 1827, pp. 442 ff.; *Republican*, July 10,
    1819; May 3, November 1, 1823; November 6, 1824; April 7, 1827;
    June 2, 1827; statement of bank's condition, July 1, 1826, in Mooers
    Papers, Kent-DeLord Collection, State University College Library,
    Plattsburgh.
32. Platt to Mooers, November 8, 1822, statement of bank's condition,
    July 1, 1826, Mooers Papers; NYAJ, 1824, p. 274; Paige's *Chancery
    Reports*, I, 464–466 (*Bank of Plattsburgh and others* v. *Platt and others*,
    May 5, 1829).
33. *Republican*, April 7, June 2, 1827; Mooers to Flagg, February 6, December 24, 1827, Flagg Papers, NYPL.

34. NYSJ, 1819, pp. 67–68; NYAJ, 1830, pp. 304, 338; 1832, pp. 679–680; 1833, pp. 76, 257, 471, 531, 780; 1834, p. 760; 1835, p. 668; 1836, pp. 1082, 1246.

35. NYAD, 1842, vol. 2, doc. 29; 1843, vol. 2, doc. 34.

36. Swetland to Beekman, May 29, 1840, BFP.

37. Swetland's letters to Beekman, 1838 through 1841, BFP.

38. *Republican*, October 7, 1848.

39. *Republican*, January 26, 1878.

40. Quoted in George S. Bixby, *Peter Sailly* (Albany, 1919), 22; James Kent Diary, LC; *Republican*, February 2, 1878.

41. Palmer, *Plattsburgh*, 51; *Republican*, passim.

42. *Northern Intelligencer*, May 14, 1822; *Republican*, July 8, 1820. The only significant work on household manufacture is Rolla M. Tryon, *Household Manufactures in the United States, 1640–1860* (Chicago, 1917). On manufacturing in other areas of New York, see Richard L. Ehrlich, "The Development of Manufacturing in Selected Counties in the Erie Canal Corridor, 1815–1860" (Ph.D. dissertation, State University of New York at Buffalo, 1972). Cf. Margaret Walsh, *The Manufacturing Frontier: Pioneer Industry in Antebellum Wisconsin* (Madison, 1972).

43. *Republican*, October 20, 1821. Caroline F. Ware, *The Early New England Cotton Manufacture* (Boston, 1931), and Arthur H. Cole, *The American Wool Manufacture* (2 vols., Cambridge, 1926), are standard works on the rise of factory production of those two textiles.

44. *Republican*, October 14, 1843.

45. *Republican*, October 20, 1849. Jared Van Wagenen, *The Golden Age of Homespun* (Ithaca, 1953), is excellent on artisans of New York State in this period.

46. United States Census, 1850, *Productions of Agriculture*.

47. United States Census, 1850, *Productions of Industry*.

48. Sailly to Comptroller Anderson, February 3, 1817, Comptrollers' Letters, Champlain District, Record Group 17, National Archives. The "year without a summer," attributed to volcanic eruptions in the South Pacific, is the subject of John D. Post's *The Last Great Subsistence Crisis in the Western World* (Baltimore, 1977).

49. *Republican*, January 26, 1878.

50. Robert Platt to Zephaniah Platt, July 3, 1798, Platt Papers, Plattsburgh Public Library.

51. Lahey, "David Parish," 57.

52. United States Census, 1790. See also Edgar J. McManus, *A History of Negro Slavery in the State of New York* (Syracuse, 1966); Leon Litwack, *North of Slavery: The Negro in the Free States, 1790–1860* (Chicago, 1961); and David Brion Davis, *The Problem of Slavery in the Age of the Revolution, 1770–1823* (Ithaca, 1975).

53. *Republican*, October 9, 1897.

54. Minutes of the town meetings of Plattsburgh for this period are in the Clinton County Historian's Office. Data on the numbers of Negroes in Beekmantown come from the state and federal censuses for the years mentioned.

55. NYSJ, 1824, appendix A, 11. See chapter 11 for more information on binding out.
56. Melanchton L. Woolsey, *Melanchton Lloyd Woolsey: A Memoir* (Champlain, 1929), passim. Most laborers in Clinton County probably spent their lives much as did William Cheney of Vermont. See Rebecca Skillin (ed.), "William Cheney (1787–1875): The Life of a Vermont Woodsman and Farmer," *Vermont History*, XXXIX (1971), 43–50. On the labor of New York farm boys, see Henry Conklin, *"Through Poverty's Vale": A Hardscrabble Boyhood in Upstate New York, 1832–1862*, ed. by Wendell Tripp (Syracuse, 1974).
57. D. A. Hurd, *History of Clinton and Franklin Counties, New York* (Philadelphia, 1880), 236 ff.
58. Swetland to Beekman, 1845–1846, passim, BFP; United States Census, 1850, *Productions of Agriculture*.

5. People

1. The classic statement of the view to which Beekmantown's experience does not conform is in Frederick Jackson Turner, "The Significance of the Frontier in American History," an essay presented to the American Historical Association in 1893, which appears in a book with the same title edited by Turner (New York, 1920). On pages 19–20 Turner approvingly quoted an 1837 western guidebook which affirmed that the "men of capital and enterprise" were the last arrivals, following first the pioneer squatter and then the small farmer. Historians who have found "men of capital and enterprise" among the earliest arrivals are too numerous to list except for three examples. Thomas P. Abernethy, *Three Virginia Frontiers* (Baton Rouge, 1940), 65–67, states that "the Bluegrass country was never a poor man's frontier." John D. Hicks, "The Development of Civilization in the Middle West, 1860–1900," in Dixon Ryan Fox (ed.), *Sources of Culture in the Middle West* (New York, 1934), 78, observed that "there was always a steady drainage (from older areas to the frontier) of fairly well-to-do citizens, who disposed of their property because they hoped that the dollars they would get for it would buy more acres of land, or bigger business opportunities, farther west." Jack M. Sosin, *The Revolutionary Frontier, 1763–1783* (New York, 1967), 181, affirmed that "in every frontier region there lived a small number of leading men from distinguished families." A nearly Turnerian view appears in Ray Allen Billington, *America's Frontier Heritage* (New York, 1966), 43–44: "The small-propertied farmers . . . opened the door to later comers with sufficient capital to require security before migrating." Similarly, John D. Barnhart, *Valley of Democracy* (Bloomington, 1953), 167, argued that the Indiana frontier "was a poor man's home." A call for comparing the first and second generations of settlers appears in Mario S. De Pillis, "Trends in American Social History and the Possibilities of Behavior Approaches," *Journal of Social History*, I (1967), 37–60.

2. United States Census, 1790; Plattsburgh tax assessment list for 1798 printed in *Republican*, December 17, 24, 1898 (cited hereafter as 1798 tax list).
3. M. L. Woolsey, *Melanchton Lloyd Woolsey: A Memoir* (Champlain, 1929), passim; 1798 tax list.
4. George S. Bixby (ed.), *Peter Sailly* (Albany, 1919), passim; 1798 tax list.
5. Billy Bob Lightfoot, "State Delegations in the Congress of the United States, 1789–1801" (2 vols., Ph.D. dissertation, University of Texas, 1958), I, 384–385; 1798 tax list.
6. 1798 tax list; BFP, passim. Biographical sketches of early settlers appear in H. K. Averill, *History of Clinton County* (2d ed., Plattsburgh, 1885); D. H. Hurd, *History of Clinton and Franklin Counties* (Philadelphia, 1880); John H. French, *Gazetteer of the State of New York* (8th ed., Syracuse, 1860).
7. Woolsey to William Beekman, July 22, 1789, February 6, 1791, BFP; BFP, passim; 1798 tax list.
8. 1798 tax list; David Dobie, *Discourses Doctrinal and Practical* (Plattsburgh, 1854), 197.
9. Plattsburgh Town Meeting Minutes, Clinton County Historian's Office, Plattsburgh.
10. United States Census, 1790; *Republican*, October 9, 1897 (slave census of 1798); Plattsburgh Town Meeting Minutes.
11. 1798 tax list; New York farms were usually about one hundred acres, but recent studies have fixed the minimum acreage required for subsistence as low as thirty and as high as seventy-five. Neil A. McNall, *An Agricultural History of the Genesee Valley, 1790–1860* (Philadelphia, 1952), 33; David M. Ellis, *Landlords and Farmers in the Hudson-Mohawk Region, 1790–1850* (Ithaca, 1946), 104; Stephanie G. Wolf, *Urban Village* (Princeton, 1976), 66–68.
12. 1798 tax list.
13. See the works cited in note 6; obituaries in the *Republican*, passim.
14. Cf. McNall, *Genesee Valley*, 66 ff. McNall found that from about 1825 the more affluent migrants were passing through to the West and only the poorer sort stopped to purchase the low quality land remaining available. See also Lewis D. Stilwell, *Migration from Vermont (1776–1860)* (Montpelier, 1948), 171, 232 ff. For an account with less economic emphasis, see Lois K. Mathews, *The Expansion of New England* (Boston, 1909).
15. John Lambert, *Travels through Canada and the United States . . . 1806, 1807, and 1808* (2 vols., 2d ed., London, 1813), I, 136, 131, 165. Mason Wade, *The French Canadians, 1760–1945* (Toronto, 1955), is an insightful overall account. Excellent background on French Canadian emigration appears in Fernand Ouellet, *Le Bas Canada, 1791–1840: Changements structuraux et crise* (Ottawa, 1976), which came into my hands as this book was going to press.
16. Population statistics relating to ethnic groups appear in New York State censuses of 1845 and 1855.
17. C. P. Lucas (ed.), *Lord Durham's Report on the Affairs of British North America* (3 vols., Oxford, 1912), I, 273.

18. Author's calculations from data in the United States Census, 1850.
19. Author's calculations from data in state census of 1855.
20. NYSD, 1849, doc. 83; NYAD, 1850, doc. 169; 1847, doc. 160.
21. Cecil Woodham-Smith, *The Great Hunger: Ireland, 1845–1849* (London, 1962), 20 ff.
22. *Durham Report*, I, 223, 244.
23. Ibid., 244.
24. Catharine Parr Traill, *The Backwoods of Canada* (London, 1846), 32.
25. New York State Census, 1855; NYSD, 1849, doc. 83; 1847, doc. 160; United States Census, 1850, *Productions of Agriculture*. On the role of the Irish in political life, see chapter 14.
26. This figure makes no allowance for deaths, although inconclusive evidence suggests that a few of the 1790 residents had been succeeded by widows or sons. It should be noted also that the town of Peru separated from Plattsburgh in 1792. Consequently, those Plattsburgh residents of 1790 who appear on Peru's tax list of 1798 (*Republican*, January 14 through February 4, 1899) were counted as still in the community. For broader perspective on migration, see especially George W. Pierson, *The Moving American* (New York, 1973). For contrasting evidence on migration rates in different areas, see Kenneth A. Lockridge, *A New England Town* (New York, 1970), 63–64; James T. Lemon, *Best Poor Man's Country* (Baltimore, 1972), 73–75; Linda A. Bissell, "Family, Friends, and Neighbors" (Ph.D. dissertation, Brandeis University, 1973), 59; Roberta G. Miller, "City and Hinterland" (Ph.D. dissertation, University of Minnesota, 1973); Douglas Lamar Jones, "Geographic Mobility and Society in Eighteenth-Century Essex County, Massachusetts" (Ph.D. dissertation, Brandeis University, 1975). Lockridge found very low emigration from Dedham (about 1 percent per year), but Bissell found that almost half of the first settlers of Windsor, Connecticut, left the community. Lemon found migration quite high in southeastern Pennsylvania (about 5 percent yearly), while Miller found great variation in migration rates in upstate New York from one decade to another. Jones found decennial persistence rates averaged 67 percent in seventeenth-century New England, but only 41 percent for rural communities of the nation as a whole in the nineteenth century. The persistence rate for Plattsburgh between 1790 and 1798 (with no allowance for mortality) was 55 percent.
27. In the books cited above, Lemon (p. 84) found the poor contributing disproportionately to the tide of emigration in one township, while Lockridge (143n) found the wealthy doing so.
28. C. Thomas, *History of the Counties of Argenteuil, Quebec, and Prescott, Ontario* (Montreal, 1896), 513 ff.; Charles P. Treadwell's diary, PAC; N. H. Tredwell to Mooers, January 3, May 20, 1821, Mooers Papers, Kent-DeLord Collection, State University College Library, Plattsburgh.
29. *Republican*, passim, especially September 10, October 27, 1827; March 9, April 6, 1822; A. C. Flagg to Mooers, March 19, 1821, Mooers Papers.

30. See the sources cited in note 6.
31. Swetland to J. W. Beekman, April 29, 1841, BFP.
32. *Republican*, November 15, 1817; November 17, 1888. On the Bromleys, see the sources cited in note 6.
33. *Republican*, October 3, 10, 1891.
34. French Canadian and Irish lumbermen fought the "Shiners War" in frontier Ottawa, but there is no evidence of such hostility in Clinton County. See Michael S. Cross, "'Dark Druidical Groves'" (Ph.D. dissertation, University of Toronto, 1968), chap. 6.
35. Jonathan Elliot (ed.), *Debates in the Several State Conventions on the Adoption of the Federal Constitution* (5 vols., Philadelphia, 1861), II, 402; United States Census, 1790 (Smithtown, Suffolk County); *Republican*, October 9, 1897 (reprint of slave census of 1798); Peter S. Palmer, *History of Plattsburgh* (Plattsburgh, 1877), 22; Plattsburgh Town Meeting Minutes; notes of Nell J. B. Sullivan on Chazy.
36. *Republican*, August 29, 1835; November 12, 1842; March 20, 1841; September 21, 1833.
37. *Republican*, October 10, 1838; August 12, 1843; November 14, 1846; November 25, 1848; NYAJ, 1841, p. 442. Material on the distribution of the abolitionist paper in Beekmantown comes from manuscript material in the possession of Marjorie Lansing Porter of Elizabethtown, New York. *North Country Notes*, no. 32 (November 1968), reports that in 1839, when a mob prevented abolitionists from holding an organizational meeting in the courthouse, the organizers met instead at the "Stone Church in Beekmantown."
38. *Republican*, March 15, 1884.
39. Among many issues of the *Republican* which contain such information are the following: April 19, 1834; September 26, 1835; February 18, 1837; August 31, September 14, 28, and November 9, 1839.
40. See in particular appendix D, "Report of the Commissioner of Inquiry into the State of Education in Lower Canada," November 15, 1838, in vol. III of the *Durham Report*.
41. *Republican*, March 7, 1835; October 31, 1840.
42. Palmer, *Plattsburgh*, 76 ff. re churches; *Republican*, January 9, 16, 1841; July 4, 1842; September 21, 1850.
43. Jacob Van Huzan to Moore, July 7, 1776; Elisha Pratt to Moore, May 25, 1782, Pliny Moore Papers in the possession of Charles W. McLellan of Champlain; *Republican*, passim.
44. Calculations from United States Census, 1790, and 1798 tax list. On the comparative data, see Wolf, *Urban Village*, 289–290.
45. *Republican*, January 20, 1827; Palmer, *Plattsburgh*, 43.
46. *Republican*, April 2, 1813; David M. Ludlum, *Social Ferment in Vermont, 1791–1850* (New York, 1939), 49.
47. *Republican*, February 2, 9, 1822.
48. *Republican*, May 19 through July 14, 1832, also October 12, 1878. The basic work on this subject is Charles Rosenberg, *Cholera Years: The United States in 1832, 1849, and 1866* (Chicago, 1962). Rosenberg notes (p. 76) that a Plattsburgh doctor studied the incidence of cholera in Montreal and helped establish the prevailing medical opinion cited

by the Plattsburgh *Republican* editor that contact did not communicate the disease. In fact, it does spread by direct contact with fecal material or by means of contaminated drinking water. See also John Duffy, "The Impact of Asiatic Cholera on Pittsburgh, Wheeling, and Charleston," *Western Pennsylvania Historical Magazine*, 47 (1964), 199–212.

49. *Republican*, November 6, 1824, et seq.
50. *Republican*, November 3, August 11, 1849.
51. *Republican*, October 25, 1845, passim; also Palmer, *Plattsburgh*, passim.
52. *Republican*, November 7, 1818.
53. *Republican*, January 14, 1905. Statistics on convictions by county were reported yearly in legislative journals or documents. On New York prisons, see Walter David Lewis, *From Newgate to Dannemora: The Rise of the Penitentiary in New York State, 1796–1848* (Ithaca, 1965), and Orlando F. Lewis, *The Development of American Prisons and Prison Customs, 1776–1845, with Special Reference to the Early Institutions in the State of New York* (Albany, 1922). Neither analyzes types of offenses for which men received prison sentences.
54. *Republican*, October 12, 1839.
55. Ibid., May 10, 1817; NYAD, 1849, doc. 243, pp. 254–255.
56. 1798 tax list.
57. Swetland and Beckwith to James W. Beekman, March 15, April 12, October 9, 1843; May 6, 1844, BFP.
58. Swetland and Beckwith to A. B. Cox, March 4, 1839. See also letters of February 1, December 21, 1840; March 5, 1842; April 5, 1849, BFP.

6. Religion

1. "Proceedings at the Centennial Anniversary of the Organization of the First Presbyterian Church, Plattsburgh, New York, October 1–3, 1897" (pamphlet [MI 74], Union Theological Seminary, New York), 36, 104–105 (hereafter cited as "Centennial"); *Republican*, October 22, 1836; January 19, 1878.
2. *Republican*, August 11, 1838, reprinted September 2, 1899.
3. "Centennial," 36–37; *Republican*, August 7, 1875; David Dobie, *Discourses Doctrinal and Practical* (Plattsburgh, 1854), 197–198.
4. Dobie, *Discourses*, 197; *Republican*, October 7, 1893.
5. "Centennial," 50 ff., passim.
6. "Centennial," 105–106; Dobie, *Discourses*, 196, 198.
7. Robert Hastings Nichols, *Presbyterianism in New York State* (Philadelphia, 1963), 114; Records of the Beekmantown church in the possession of Addie Lawrence Shields of Beekmantown indicate that the Beekmantown church at its inception took its "Confession of Faith and Covenant" from the mother church in Plattsburgh.
8. Dobie, *Discourses*, 199; "Centennial," 21; Nichols, *Presbyterianism*, 99.
9. Dobie, *Discourses*, 200, 203; "Centennial," 21.

10. M. L. Woolsey to Pliny Moore, January 3, 1810, Pliny Moore Papers, in possession of Charles W. McLellan of Champlain; Dobie, *Discourses*, 200.

11. M. L. Woolsey to Pliny Moore, January 28, 1812, Pliny Moore Papers.

12. Dobie, *Discourses*, 202–203; "Centennial," 106–107.

13. "Centennial," 106–107; Dobie, *Discourses*, 203–204.

14. Dobie, *Discourses*, 204–205; "Centennial," 108.

15. Dobie, *Discourses*, 205–207.

16. Ibid.; "Centennial," 36–56.

17. "Centennial," 55–57.

18. *Republican*, November 4, 1893.

19. *Republican*, June 10, 1899; March 19, 1898.

20. Records of the Beekmantown church from which the above information and much of that in the next few pages derives are in the possession of Addie Lawrence Shields. See also *Republican*, August 14, 1886.

21. *Republican*, February 15, 1845.

22. "Centennial," 59 ff.

23. Whitney R. Cross, *The Burned-over District: The Social and Intellectual History of Enthusiastic Religion in Western New York, 1800–1850* (Ithaca, 1950), chap. 9; *Republican*, August 23, 1828; Dobie, *Discourses*, 208.

24. *Republican*, July 12, 1844; Beekmantown church records in the possession of Addie Lawrence Shields.

25. For discussion of these national organizations, see Nichols, *Presbyterianism*, 108, passim; Cross, *Burned-over District*, chap. 7; Fred J. Hood, "Presbyterianism and the New American Nation" (Ph.D. dissertation, Princeton University, 1968), 276 ff.; Clifford S. Griffin, *Their Brothers' Keepers: Moral Stewardship in the United States, 1800–1865*; C. I. Foster, *An Errand of Mercy* (Chapel Hill, 1960); M. J. Heale, "Humanitarianism in the Early Republic: The Moral Reformers of New York, 1776–1825," *Journal of American Studies*, 21 (1968), 161–175; Lois W. Banner, "Religious Benevolence as Social Control: A Critique of an Interpretation," *Journal of American History*, LX (1973), 23–46.

26. *Republican*, August 22, 1818; February 24, 1827. For a discussion of the "etherealized notion" of a national church, see Nichols, *Presbyterianism*, 146, and Hood, "Presbyterianism," 250 ff.

27. Records of the Champlain Presbytery of the Presbyterian Church, Hancock House, Ticonderoga, New York; E. A. Bulkely, *Historical Sketch of the Presbytery of Champlain* (Plattsburgh, 1877), 3–5.

28. Bulkely, *Historical Sketch*, 5–6.

29. Ibid., 9 ff.

30. *Fortieth Anniversary, 1878–1918, First Baptist Church, Plattsburgh* (pamphlet in the American Baptist Historical Society, Rochester, New York).

31. *Republican*, July 10, 1841.

32. *American Baptist Register*, 1852 (Philadelphia, 1853), 231.

33. Elmer T. Clark (ed.), *The Journal and Letters of Francis Asbury* (3 vols., Nashville, 1958), II, 61. On American Methodism in general, see

E. S. Bucke (ed.), *History of American Methodism* (3 vols., Nashville, 1964).

34. Stephen Parks, *Troy Conference Miscellany . . . a Historical Sketch of Methodism within the Bounds of the Troy Conference* (Albany, 1854), 43. Much of the same information on early Methodism in the Troy Conference appears in Parks and two other sources: Henry Graham, *History of the Troy Conference of the Methodist Episcopal Church* (Albany, 1908), 9 ff., and Samuel Gardiner Ayres, "Historical Materials Relating to the Methodist Episcopal Churches . . . of the Troy Conference" (typescript, 2 vols., Rose Memorial Library, Drew University, Madison, New Jersey).

35. Clark, *Asbury*, II, 676.

36. Peter S. Palmer, *History of Plattsburgh* (Plattsburgh, 1877), 74 ff.

37. Graham, *Troy Conference*, 212-213; *Republican*, June 9, 1883.

38. Ayres, "Historical Materials," I, 173 ff., 55-57; *Republican*, December 24, 1842.

39. Ayres, "Historical Materials," I, 56.

40. *Republican*, August 17, September 14, 1822; August 30, 1834; September 3, 1836.

41. Ayres, "Historical Materials," I, 55.

42. *Republican*, February 20, 1819.

43. *Republican*, February 22, 1879.

44. *Republican*, August 25, September 1, 1832.

45. Ayres, "Historical Materials," I, 55, 59.

46. *Republican*, April 14, 1832. For the history of the Methodist Protestant Church, see Edward J. Drinkhouse, *History of Methodist Reform* (2 vols., Baltimore and Pittsburgh, 1899), and Ancel H. Bassett, *A Concise History of the Methodist Protestant Church* (Pittsburgh, 1887).

47. Cross, *Burned-over District*, 27. Sydney E. Ahlstrom, *A Religious History of the American People* (New Haven, 1972), 438, appears to challenge this rather conventional view, but his statement is quite guarded. Wesley W. Gewehr has an excellent analysis of "Some Factors in the Expansion of Frontier Methodism," *Journal of Religion*, VIII (1928), 98-120.

48. *Republican*, April 7, 1832.

49. Graham, *Troy Conference*, 228.

50. Palmer, *Plattsburgh*, 76 ff.; *Republican*, October 20, 1883.

51. James Kent Diary, LC.

52. *Republican*, May 31, 1811; January 18, 1817.

53. *Republican*, December 24, 31, 1842; January 14, 28, July 1, 22, 1843.

54. Palmer, *Plattsburgh*, 76 ff. See also *Republican*, September 13, 1815, for evidence that nuns were present much earlier.

55. *Republican*, July 12, 1817.

56. "Centennial," 111; *Republican*, August 29, 1835; December 6, 1845. For a record of similar convulsions, see William Griffin, "Vermont's Universalist Controversy of 1824," *Vermont History*, 41 (1973), 82-94.

57. These conclusions contrast in some ways with those of T. Scott Miyakawa, *Protestants and Pioneers: Individualism and Conformity on the*

American Frontier (Chicago, 1964). Cf. also Cross, Nichols, and Judith M. Wellman, "The Burned-over District Revisited: Benevolent Reform and Abolitionism in Mexico, Paris, and Ithaca, New York, 1825–1842" (Ph.D. dissertation, University of Virginia, 1974).

7. Culture, Recreation, and Identity

1. *Republican*, January 19, 1878. On academies in New York, see George F. Miller, *The Academy System of the State of New York* (Albany, 1922); a more recent study of New England secondary education is Robert Middlekauf, *Ancients and Axioms: Secondary Education in Eighteenth-Century New England* (New Haven, 1963).
2. Peter S. Palmer, *History of Plattsburgh* (Plattsburgh, 1877), 33–34.
3. *Republican*, November 20, 1813.
4. *Republican*, October 12, 1833; Regents of the University of the State of New York, *Fifty-fifth Annual Report*, 1842, pp. 86, 112.
5. Regents, *Report*, 1842, pp. 86, 91.
6. *Republican*, December 22, 1833. See also January 12, 1884. The reminiscences of George Stevenson affirm that Prescott became negligent in time from a frequent use of alcohol. See *North Country Notes*, no. 123 (September 1976).
7. *Republican*, May 5, 1832; July 28, 1849.
8. *Republican*, August 17, 1833.
9. *Republican*, November 23, 1833; August 19, 1899 (reprinting a "register" of town businesses of 1835).
10. Regents, *Report*, 1842, pp. 60, 69, 112; *Republican*, January 7, 1882.
11. *Republican*, July 28, 1849; March 9, August 24, December 14, 1850.
12. *Republican*, August 24, December 14, 1850.
13. *Republican*, November 15, 1817; December 30, 1820; December 14, 1850.
14. *Republican*, November 25, 1820. Evening schools were by no means an innovation at this time. See Robert F. Seybolt, *The Evening School in Colonial America* (Urbana, 1925).
15. *Republican*, May 10, 1817; Palmer, *Plattsburgh*, 37. Robert W. Lynn and Elliott Wright, *The Big Little School: Sunday Child of American Protestantism* (New York, 1971), give a very brief history of the Sunday school. Ralph R. Smith, Jr., "'In Every Destitute Place': The Mission Program of the American Sunday School Union, 1817–1834" (Ph.D. dissertation, University of Southern California, 1973), is much more detailed. While the movement in England remained committed to affording secular education to the poor—despite some effort to direct it toward evangelical purposes—the American movement tended from the late 1820s to become both religious in purpose and sectarian, rather than interdenominational in control. The extension of public education (see chapter 12) figured in the shift. See Thomas Walter Laqueur, *Religion and Respectability: Sunday Schools*

and the English Working-Class Culture, 1780–1850 (New Haven, 1976), which I read as a Princeton dissertation; Carl F. Kaestle, *The Evolution of an Urban School System: New York City, 1750–1850* (Cambridge, 1973), 120–126; Judith M. Wellman, "The American Sunday School Union: Upstate New York, 1820–1840" (paper presented at the conference of the New York State Studies Group, SUNY-Brockport, 1978), and her dissertation, "The Burned-over District Revisited" (Ph.D. dissertation, University of Virginia, 1974).

16. *Republican*, August 7, 1875. Based on reminiscences, this account fixes the beginning date as 1818, rather than 1817, and emphasizes the role of Presbyterians in organizing the effort, although most of the teachers were apparently not Presbyterians.

17. Charles P. Treadwell's diary, PAC.

18. See Whitney R. Cross, *The Burned-over District* (Ithaca, 1950), 128 ff., in addition to the works cited in note 15.

19. *Republican*, October 20, November 3, 1827; June 21, 1828; January 13, 1883.

20. *Republican*, July 10, 1841; July 9, 1842.

21. Marjorie Lansing Porter, *Plattsburgh* (1964), 23.

22. *Republican*, February 21, 1835; October 5, 1844.

23. *Republican*, November 25, 1837; February 24, 1838.

24. *Republican*, November 4, 1843; July 20, October 12, 1850.

25. *Republican*, June 4, 1814.

26. *Republican*, February 23, March 2, 1822; June 24, August 19, 1826; August 29, October 17, 1835; August 13, 1836; June 24, 1848.

27. *Republican*, February 13, 1892.

28. *Republican*, August 19, 1899; February 18, 1837; February 5, 1848; September 7, 1850.

29. *Republican*, April 13, 1822; NYSAS, *Transactions*, 1849, IX, 476.

30. *Republican*, February 3, 17, 1821; March 29, 1828; July 2, 1836; August 30, 1845; *Northern Intelligencer*, August 27, 1822.

31. *Republican*, September 27, November 29, 1834; June 5, 1886.

32. *Republican*, October 18, 1811; October 9, 1813; October 26, 1833; April 27, 1844; October 7, 1848.

33. *Republican*, December 31, 1814; July 14, 1832; November 19, 1836.

34. *Republican*, April 12, 1834; manuscript notes of Marjorie Lansing Porter, Elizabethtown, New York.

35. *Republican*, March 9, April 19, 26, September 27, 1834; September 26, 1835; January 16, February 20, 27, April 23, October 22, 29, 1836; March 4, 1837; November 6, 1841. Carl Bode, *The American Lyceum: Town Meeting of the Mind* (New York, 1956), is the standard work on the lyceum movement.

36. *Republican*, December 12, 1817; January 2, 1819; research paper by Paul C. Edwards, State University College, Plattsburgh, summarized in *North Country Notes*, no. 66 (June 1970).

37. *Republican*, January 16, 23, 1836; March 31, April 8, 1837; November 16, 1833; January 9, November 12, 1836.

38. *Republican*, May 19, 1836; September 7, 1844.

39. To Judge Platt, January 24, 1786, Platt Papers, Plattsburgh Public Library.
40. *Republican*, January 19, 1878.
41. Moore to Sailly and Charles Platt, March 26, 1800, Pliny Moore Papers in the possession of Charles W. McLellan of Champlain.
42. *Republican*, March 23, 1839; November 15, 1845.
43. *Republican*, April 16, 1813; July 19, 1817.
44. *Republican*, February 21, 1846; October 20, 1849; NYSAS, *Transactions*, 1851, XI, 489; 1852, XII, 374 ff.

8. Social Reform

1. John A. Krout, *Origins of Prohibition* (New York, 1925), passim. For more extreme affirmations of the same point, see Gerald Carson, "The Dark Age of American Drinking," *Virginia Quarterly Review*, 39 (1963), 94–103, and William J. Rorabaugh, "The Alcoholic Republic, America, 1790–1840" (Ph.D. dissertation, University of California at Berkeley, 1976). I am indebted to Edward Pessen for summarizing Rorabaugh's thesis for me. The dissertation is not available from University Microfilms.
2. John Lambert, *Travels through Canada and the United States . . . 1806, 1807, and 1808* (2 vols., 2d ed., London, 1813), I, 157.
3. *Republican*, August 19, 1815.
4. *Republican*, March 22, 1834.
5. *Republican*, December 16, 1815.
6. Krout, *Origins of Prohibition*, 85–88.
7. *Republican*, October 7, December 16, 1815. Joseph R. Gusfield, *Symbolic Crusade* (Urbana, 1963), 44, argues that the function of the temperance movement was "to restore a superior position to the declining Federalist elite."
8. *Republican*, February 21, 1818; Krout, *Origins of Prohibition*, 108–112.
9. *Republican*, September 8, 1827.
10. Original records in the possession of Addie Lawrence Shields of Beekmantown; New York State Society for the Promotion of Temperance, *Annual Report* (1830).
11. New York State Society for the Promotion of Temperance, *Fourth Annual Report*, 1833, p. 79.
12. Manuscript record at Hancock House, Ticonderoga, New York. Mrs. Thomas V. Lape kindly made this and other records at Hancock House available to me. On the county convention, see also *Republican*, January 11, 1834.
13. *Republican*, March 20, 1847.
14. New York State Society for the Promotion of Temperance, *Temperance Almanac*, no. 9, 1842, NYSL.
15. *Republican*, March 10, 1832.
16. *Republican*, February 22, 1834.

17. *Republican*, January 11, 1834.
18. *Republican*, March 11, 1837; March 17, 1838.
19. Krout, *Origins of Prohibition*, 280–283; NYAD, 1847, doc. 40, p. 16; Minutes of the town meeting of Beekmantown, April 27, 1847; *Republican*, May 1, 1847.
20. *Republican*, October 7, 1848.
21. *Republican*, November 11, 1837.
22. NYAD, 1847, doc. 180; 1848, doc. 193; 1849, doc. 242.
23. See chapter 5, note 42.
24. *Temperance Almanac*, no. 9, 1842; NYSAS, *Transactions*, 1851, XI, 486.
25. Sabbath violation is considered in chapter 6.
26. NYAJ, Special Session, 1828, pp. 7–9. Edgerton also worked in the same session for more effective suppression of dueling, but that cause seems to have stirred even less interest among his constituents.
27. *Republican*, October 4, 1828.
28. Flagg to Ingham, July 24, 1829, Flagg Papers, NYPL.
29. NYAJ, 1831, pp. 542–543.
30. A tendency to view the temperance movement primarily as a fore-runner of the national trauma of prohibition pervades both Krout's *Origins of Prohibition* and Alice Felt Tyler's engaging chapter on the subject in *Freedom's Ferment* (Minneapolis, 1944). Neither stressed the role of the movement in changing the mores of a large portion of the people. The same point applies to John J. Coffey, "A Political History of the Temperance Movement in New York State, 1808–1920" (Ph.D. dissertation, Pennsylvania State University, 1976), and to William J. Jackson, "Prohibition as an Issue in New York State Politics, 1836–1933" (Ed.D. dissertation, Columbia University, 1974).

9. The Constitutional Framework

1. Texts of the early constitutions of New York State appear in Robert C. Cumming et al., *The Constitution of the State of New York* (Albany, 1894). See also Charles Z. Lincoln, *The Constitutional History of New York* (5 vols., Rochester, 1906), and J. H. Dougherty, *Constitutional History of the State of New York* (New York, 1915). Four works of particular value to me were Nicholas Varga, "Local Government in Colonial New York: A Synoptic View," to be published in Bruce C. Daniels (ed.), "Town and Country," by Wesleyan University Press; Jean Peyer, "Jamaica, Long Island, 1656–1776; A Study of the Roots of Urbanism" (Ph.D. dissertation, City University of New York, 1974); John A. Casais, "The New York State Constitutional Convention of 1821 and Its Aftermath" (Ph.D. dissertation, Columbia University, 1967); and Langdon G. Wright, "Local Government

in Colonial New York" (Ph.D. dissertation, Cornell University, 1974).

2. Electoral data from the "several State Electoral censuses" are summarized in the New York State Census of 1855. My calculations are based on information in these successive censuses. Cf. Chilton Williamson, *American Suffrage from Property to Democracy* (Princeton, 1960), 197.

3. *New York Laws*, 1788, chap. 40, pp. 675 ff.; 1799, chap. 62, pp. 388 ff. For supplemental information on this subject, see Edgar J. McManus, *A History of Negro Slavery in New York* (Syracuse, 1966); also his *Black Bondage in the North* (Syracuse, 1973); and Leon F. Litwack, *North of Slavery: The Negro in the Free States, 1790–1860* (Chicago, 1961).

4. *New York Laws*, 1847, chap. 435; 1830, chap. 171; 1823, chap. 261. New York's restrictions on alien land ownership related primarily to the enormous land holdings of foreigners. Studies relating to this point are cited in chapter 1, note 43.

5. Ernest L. Bogart, *Peacham: The Story of a Vermont Hill Town* (Montpelier, 1946), 90.

6. *New York Laws*, 1823, chap. 244, pp. 329 ff.; the New York law quotes the major provisions of the federal law of 1792.

7. Hugh Hastings (ed.), *Military Minutes of the Council of Appointment of the State of New York, 1783–1821* (4 vols., Albany, 1901), I, 142, 638, 267; NYAJ, 1803, p. 67; 1804–1805, p. 346; 1812–1813, p. 80.

8. *New York Laws*, 1823, chap. 244, pp. 329 ff.

9. Ibid., 1834, chap. 70, p. 713.

10. Ibid., 1787, chap. 8, pp. 352 ff.

11. Ibid., 1801, chap. 70, pp. 134 ff.; 1788, chap. 31, pp. 643 ff.; 1824, chap. 331, pp. 382 ff.

12. Ibid., 1788, chap. 64 (town meetings); chap. 62 (poor relief); Minutes of the Clinton County Board of Supervisors, State University College Library, Plattsburgh.

13. *New York Laws*, 1785–1788, pp. 762, 769 (March 7, 1788); 1797–1800, p. 402 (April 1, 1799); p. 594 (April 8, 1800); 1845, chap. 180, p. 183.

14. The basic provisions of the law of 1788, chap. 65, pp. 769 ff., "for raising a revenue in the counties" remained unchanged.

15. *New York Laws*, 1788, chap. 62, pp. 731 ff.; records of the Overseers of Poor of Beekmantown, 1820–1835, in the possession of Addie Lawrence Shields of Beekmantown.

16. See, for example, the revised statutes of 1827, chap. 15, p. 303, relating to the accounting of school aid money.

17. Peter S. Palmer, *History of Plattsburgh* (Plattsburgh, 1877), 23.

18. NYAJ, 1798, p. 125; records of the Clinton County Board of Supervisors, State University College Library, Plattsburgh; Peter S. Palmer, *History of Lake Champlain* (Albany, 1866), 141.

19. *New York Laws*, 1810, chap. 61, p. 16; 1831, chap. 105, p. 146; NYAJ, 1819, appendix, p. 33; NYAJ, 1820, p. 464. Outstanding general

works on the role of state governments in economic development in this period are Oscar Handlin, *Commonwealth: A Study of the Role of Government in the American Economy, Massachusetts, 1774–1861* (New York, 1947); Louis Hartz, *Economic Policy and Democratic Thought: Pennsylvania, 1776–1860* (Cambridge, 1948); Nathan Miller, *The Enterprise of a Free People: Aspects of Economic Development in New York during the Canal Period, 1792–1838* (Ithaca, 1962).

20. *New York Laws*, 1785–1788, pp. 764 ff. (March 7, 1788).
21. Ibid., 766, 769.
22. NYAJ, 1808, p. 432.
23. *New York Laws*, 1815, chap. 129, pp. 129 ff.; NYAJ, 1824, pt. 1, pp. 146 ff.; see also NYSJ, 1824, pp. 31, 165–166, and *Republican*, April 6, 1822.
24. Ibid., November 30, 1822.

10. Roads

1. See George W. Roach, "Colonial Highways in the Upper Hudson Valley," *New York History*, 40 (1955), 93–116; *New York Laws*, 1797–1800, chap. 43 (March 21, 1797), 51 ff. Despite their obvious importance, roads have attracted little scholarly attention, but see also Roger N. Parks, "The Roads of New England, 1790–1840" (Ph.D. dissertation, Michigan State University, 1966); Michael S. Cross, "The Stormy History of the York Roads, 1833–1865," *Ontario History*, LII (1960), 213–233.
2. Records of Commissioners of Highways, Town of Peru, State University College Library, Plattsburgh.
3. Richard C. Ellsworth, "The Settlement of the North Country," in A. C. Flick (ed.), *History of the State of New York* (10 vols., New York, 1934), V, 191.
4. Beekmantown:

Year	Persons Liable	Days Assessed
1829	390	1,204
1830	421	1,304
1831	407	1,374
1833	413 .	1,387
1834	422	1,453

Persons liable in Beekmantown in 1830 were 18 percent of the census figure. Assuming the same percentage of Plattsburgh's population was liable, its 1820 assessments (3,920) were well over four times the 875 people liable (18 percent of 4,862).

5. Notation of these decisions is found in the Plattsburgh Town Meeting Minutes, 1811 and 1816 respectively, Clinton County Historian's Office.
6. NYAJ, 1808–1809, p. 186.
7. Ibid., 1811, pp. 59, 351, 355; NYSJ, 1822, pp. 60, 71–72, 115. Federal aid apparently stemmed from President Monroe's personal encounter with the road in 1817. See *North Country Notes*, no. 43 (March 1968).

8. NYSJ, 1822, pp. 60, 71–72, 115.
9. *New York Laws*, 1822, chap. 55, pp. 62–63; Peter S. Palmer, *History of Plattsburgh* (Plattsburgh, 1877), 41; *New York Laws*, 1843, chap. 38, p. 37.

11. Welfare

1. For a more detailed account, see chapter 4, "State Poor Laws, 1783–1825," in Raymond Mohl, *Poverty in New York, 1783–1825* (New York, 1971), and D. M. Schneider, *History of Public Welfare in New York State* (2 vols., Chicago, 1938–1941), passim.
2. Records of Peru's Overseers of the Poor are at the State University College Library, Plattsburgh.
3. NYSJ, 1824, appendix A, 11–12, 99. Most recent accounts of poor relief in this period tend to emphasize the concern of contemporary "liberal" reformers to instill self-reliance and better work habits among the poor by denying aid to the indigent unless they were willing to take up residence in the poorhouse and perform supervised labor therein. See, for example, Mohl, chap. 10; David J. Rothman, *The Discovery of the Asylum: Social Order and Disorder in the New Republic* (Boston, 1971), chap. 7; Blanche D. Coll, *Perspectives in Public Welfare: A History* (Washington, 1969), passim; Samuel Mencher, *Poor Law to Poverty Program: Economic Security Policy in Britain and the United States* (Pittsburgh, 1967), chap. 6; Benjamin J. Klebaner, "Poverty and Its Relief in American Thought, 1815–1861," *Social Service Review*, 38 (1964), 382–399; idem, "The Home Relief Controversy in Pennsylvania, 1728–1861," *Pennsylvania Magazine of History and Biography*, LXXVIII (1954), 413–423; M. J. Heale, "Humanitarianism in the Early Republic: The Moral Reformers of New York, 1776–1825," *Journal of American Studies*, 2 (1968), 161–175; idem, "Patterns of Benevolence: Charity and Morality in Rural and Urban New York, 1783–1830," *Societas*, 3 (1973), 337–359; idem, "Patterns of Benevolence: Associated Philanthropy in the Cities of New York, 1830–1860," *New York History*, LVII (1976), 53–79; and the pioneering work of Robert H. Bremner, *From the Depths: The Discovery of Poverty in the United States* (New York, 1956), chap. 2. For an account of the history of a county poor relief program quite similar to that which operated in Beekmantown, see Elizabeth Gaspar Brown, "Poor Relief in a Wisconsin County, 1846–1866: Administration and Recipients," *American Journal of Legal History*, XX (1976), 79–117.
4. Records of the Beekmantown Overseers of the Poor, 1820–1835, in the possession of Addie Lawrence Shields of Beekmantown.
5. NYSJ, 1824, appendix A, chart, 11, 17–18; Coll, *Perspectives*, 20. Beekmantown apparently conformed generally to the pattern in New England as characterized by Josiah Henry Benton, *Warning Out in New England* (Boston, 1911), and Edward M. Cook, Jr., "Social Be-

havior and Changing Values in Dedham, Massachusetts, 1700–1775,"
William and Mary Quarterly, XXVII (1970), 546–580.
6. NYSJ, 1824, appendix A, chart, p. 11.
7. Ibid., 95–96.
8. See Schneider, *Public Welfare*, I, pt. 4.
9. NYSJ, 1824, appendix A, 16.
10. *New York Laws*, 1828, chap. 155, p. 169. The law implementing the basic reforms was passed in 1824, chap. 331, pp. 382 ff.
11. *Republican*, December 16, 1826; April 21, 1827.
12. See notes 2 and 4.
13. Figures are from the annual reports of the secretary of state published among the documents of either the senate or assembly from 1830 through 1849.
14. NYAD, 1844, doc. 21, pp. 78–79.
15. Ibid., 79–81.
16. Peter S. Palmer, *History of Plattsburgh* (Plattsburgh, 1877), 45.
17. Schneider, *Public Welfare*, I, 369.
18. Quoted in Schneider, *Public Welfare*, I, 251. See also Coll, *Perspectives*, 29–32.

12. Schools

1. There is no modern scholarly work on the rural schools of New York State in the early nineteenth century. The best of the old accounts is S. S. Randall, *History of the Common School System* (New York, 1871). An excellent supplement to Randall is Edward Eggleston's novel, *The Hoosier School-Master*, also published in 1871. While it purports to concern Indiana, Eggleston did his research in the same New York State records upon which much of this account is based. Eggleston's portrayal of rural schools seems wholly persuasive except in one respect. The school district records examined for this study show little evidence of midterm replacement of teachers nor such preoccupation with physical threats to the teacher as provide much of the dramatic interest in his novel.
2. *Republican*, March 21, 28, 1885; E. Wilder Spaulding, *New York in the Critical Period, 1783–1789* (New York, 1932), 34–35.
3. *Republican*, January 19, 1878. Tredwell's first senate term was 1788–1789.
4. NYAJ, 1798, p. 282.
5. See W. C. Watson, *Military and Civil History of the County of Essex* (Albany, 1869), 210; Annual Report of the State Superintendent of Common Schools, NYAD, 1839, doc. 17, p. 18. These reports are cited hereafter as assembly documents for particular years.
6. Randall, *Common School*, 8.
7. Ibid., 9. See also Elsie G. Hobson, *Educational Legislation and Administration in the State of New York, 1777–1850* (Chicago, 1918).
8. *Republican*, November 27, 1886.

9. *Republican*, April 5, 1879.
10. Moore to School Commission, December 2, 1811, Pliny Moore Papers, in the possession of Charles W. McLellan of Champlain.
11. NYAD, 1845, doc. 100, p. 90.
12. *New York Laws*, 1812, chap. 242, pp. 600 ff.; Supplemented 1814, chap. 192, pp. 229 ff.
13. Annual Reports of the Superintendent of Common Schools have been collected in bound volumes by the education branch of the New York State Library.
14. Records of Beekmantown's School District Number Five, 1827–1839, are at the NYSL. Those of Chazy's second district are at the State University College Library, Plattsburgh. Beekmantown's fifth district was not one of the best. The minutes of the town meeting for 1821 stated that "they had not drew any money since they were organized as a district." In 1822 the district paid a teacher "not approved by the Inspectors."
15. NYAD, 1836, doc. 6, p. 25; 1844, doc. 34, table A; NYAJ, 1825, appendix B, p. 31.
16. See note 14. Cf. Richard M. Bernard and M. A. Vinovskis, "The Female School Teacher in Ante-Bellum Massachusetts," *Journal of Social History*, 10 (1977), 332–345.
17. NYAD, 1850, doc. 50, p. 21.
18. Beekmantown figures were calculated from reports in the minutes of the town meetings; the state average for 1830 is in NYAD, 1831, doc. 15.
19. NYSJ, 1827, p. 226.
20. NYAD, 1831, doc. 15; 1843, doc. 14, p. 33.
21. NYAJ, 1827, appendix A, p. 5; NYAD, 1843, doc. 14, p. 33.
22. NYAJ, 1827, appendix A, pp. 6–9.
23. NYAD, 1834, doc. 9, p. 16.
24. NYAD, 1836, doc. 6, pp. 41–43.
25. NYAJ, 1827, pt. 2, p. 970.
26. NYAD, 1838, doc. 13, pp. 20–24.
27. NYAD, 1845, doc. 30, pp. 126 ff.; Randall, *Common School*, 180 ff.
28. *Republican*, September 3, 1842.
29. NYAD, 1846, doc. 30.
30. NYAJ, 1827, pt. 2, appendix A, p. 9.
31. NYAD, 1836, doc. 6, p. 27.
32. NYAJ, 1814, pp. 34–35, 606–607.
33. NYAJ, 1818, p. 479.
34. NYAD, 1845, doc. 30, p. 127. This extreme example of the latitude allowed parents in choosing textbooks affords an interesting contrast to the "social control" emphasis in many recent studies, as also does the decentralization of control reflected in the great authority retained by the local school district (see below). Studies focusing at least to some extent on the social control thesis include Sidney L. Jackson, *America's Struggle for Free Schools: Social Tension and Education in New England and New York, 1827–1842* (New York, 1941); Michael B. Katz, *The Irony of Early School Reform* (Cambridge, 1968); idem,

Class Bureaucracy and Schools (2d ed., New York, 1975); idem, "The Origins of Public Education: A Reassessment," *History of Education Quarterly*, 16 (1976), 381–407; Frederick Rudolph (ed.), *Essays on Education in the Early Republic* (Cambridge, 1965); Carl F. Kaestle, *The Evolution of an Urban School System: New York City, 1750–1850* (Cambridge, 1973); idem, "Social Reform and the Urban School," *History of Education Quarterly*, 12 (1972), 211–228; idem, "Conflict and Consensus Revisited: Notes Toward a Reinterpretation of American Educational History," *Harvard Educational Review*, 46 (1976), 390–396; idem, with Maris A. Vinovskis, "Quantification, Urbanization and the History of Education: An Analysis of the Determinants of School Attendance in New York State in 1845," *Historical Methods Newsletter*, 8 (1974), 1–9; Stanley K. Schultz, *The Culture Factory: Boston Public Schools, 1789–1860* (New York, 1973); Ruth Miller Elson, *Guardians of Tradition: American Schoolbooks of the Nineteenth Century* (Lincoln, 1964); Timothy L. Smith, "Protestant Schooling and American Nationality, 1800–1850," *Journal of American History*, LIII (1967), 679–695; Raymond A. Mohl, "Education as Social Control in New York City, 1784–1825," *New York History*, 51 (1970), 219–237. Major criticisms of the social control thesis appear in R. Freeman Butts, "Public Education and Political Community," *History of Education Quarterly*, 14 (1974), 165–183; Sol Cohen, "The History of the History of American Education, 1900–1976," *Harvard Educational Review*, 46 (1976), 298–330; Marvin Lazerson, "Revisionism and American Educational History," *Harvard Educational Review*, 43 (1973), 269–283; and above all in Lois W. Banner, "Religious Benevolence as Social Control: A Critique of an Interpretation," *Journal of American History*, LX (1973), 23–41. Diane Ravitch, *The Revisionists Revised: A Critique of the Radical Attack on the Schools* (New York, 1978), appeared too late for me to use it.

35. See Randall, *Common School*, 180 ff. See preceding note concerning literature on education as social control. Katz has called the pattern of the rural communities "democratic localism" and contrasted it to the "paternalistic voluntarism" which prevailed in urban areas.

36. Charles Carpenter, *History of American Schoolbooks* (Philadelphia, 1963), passim; John A. Nietz, *Old Textbooks* (Pittsburgh, 1961), 16–17, passim. For a more general characterization of nineteenth-century textbooks, see Elson, *Guardians of Tradition*.

37. Nietz, *Old Textbooks*, 242. See also James Beckley Palmer, "Causal Factors in the Development of the New York State Elementary Course of Study from 1776 to 1904" (Ph.D. dissertation, Cornell University, 1930).

38. Nietz, *Old Textbooks*, 52–53.

39. Ibid., 218.

40. Ibid., 162–163; Carpenter, *Schoolbooks*, 131–139; NYAD, 1847, doc. 10.

41. NYAD, 1847, doc. 10; 1845, doc. 30, pp. 126 ff. See also Randall, *Common School*, 213.

42. NYAD, 1845, doc. 30, p. 127; 1847, doc. 10.
43. NYAD, 1843, doc. 14, p. 13; 1850, doc. 50, p. 7; 1849, doc. 20, pp. 30–32. Records of Beekmantown School District Number Five, NYSL.
44. *Republican*, November 17, 1849; Randall, *Common School*, 253 ff.
45. See note 14; NYAD, 1850, doc. 50; 1851, doc. 21.
46. Randall, *Common School*, 253 ff., has the best account. He was a participant in the struggle.
47. *Republican*, November 23, 1850.
48. NYAD, 1852, doc. 25.

13. Republicans and Federalists

1. For a more extended characterization of the Antifederalists as distinguished from their opponents, see Jackson Turner Main, *The Antifederalists: Critics of the Constitution, 1781–1788* (Chapel Hill, 1961); his more recent *Political Parties before the Constitution* (Chapel Hill, 1973); and "The Antifederalist Party," in Arthur M. Schlesinger, Jr. (ed.), *History of U.S. Political Parties*, I, *1789–1860: From Factions to Parties* (4 vols., New York, 1973), 135–169; Robert Allen Rutland, *The Ordeal of the Constitution: The Antifederalists and the Ratification Struggle of 1787–1788* (Norman, 1966); Cecilia Kenyon, "Men of Little Faith: The Anti-Federalists on the Nature of Representative Government," *William and Mary Quarterly*, XII (1955), 3–43, and her introduction to a selection of documents, *The Antifederalists* (Indianapolis, 1966). On New York Antifederalists in particular, see Linda Grant Depauw, *The Eleventh Pillar* (Ithaca, 1966); Alfred F. Young, *The Democratic-Republicans of New York* (Chapel Hill, 1967); Staughton Lynd, *Anti-Federalism in Dutchess County, New York* (Chicago, 1962); and Robin Brooks, "Melanchton Smith: New York Antifederalist, 1744–1798" (Ph.D. dissertation, University of Rochester, 1964).
2. See the works cited in note 1 concerning ratification of the Constitution in New York.
3. On Tredwell's political career, see *National Cyclopedia of American Biography*, III (1893), 158; Billy Bob Lightfoot, "State Delegations in the Congress of the United States, 1789–1801" (Ph.D. dissertation, University of Texas, 1958).
4. Jonathan Elliot (ed.), *Debates in the Several State Conventions on the Adoption of the Federal Constitution* (5 vols., Philadelphia, 1861), II, 404–405.
5. This and subsequent parenthetical page notations relating to Tredwell's views refer to the volume of Elliot cited above. See Edmund S. Morgan, "The Puritan Ethic and the American Revolution," *William*

and Mary Quarterly, XXIV (1967), 3–43, for an exploration of Calvinist thought patterns in this period.

6. Jabez D. Hammond, *The History of Political Parties in the State of New York* (2 vols., Cooperstown, 1846), I, 48.

7. Cf. Young, *Democratic-Republicans*, chap. 23.

8. Woolsey to "brother" [Gilbert Livingston], November 28, 1787, Woolsey Papers, NYSL.

9. Woolsey to John Williams, December 21, 1792, Williams Papers, NYSL.

10. T. Platt to Moore, April 18, 1796, Pliny Moore Papers, in possession of Charles W. McLellan of Champlain.

11. Woolsey to Moore, December 11, December 24, 1796, Pliny Moore Papers.

12. See Young, *Democratic-Republicans*, 461 ff.

13. Woolsey's autobiography, written to Thomas Macdonough, March 5, 1818, Woolsey Papers, NYSL; Woolsey to Moore, January 21, 1800, Pliny Moore Papers.

14. Minutes of Plattsburgh's town meeting are in the possession of the Clinton County Historian, Plattsburgh. On the intensity of political differences at this time, see Marshall Smelser, "The Federalist Era as an Age of Passion," *American Quarterly*, X (1958), 391–419.

15. NYAJ, passim.

16. Sailly and Charles Platt to Moore, March 24, 1800; Committee to Moore, March 22, 1800, Pliny Moore Papers.

17. Pliny Moore Papers, passim, especially T. Platt to Moore, March 9, 1801.

18. Woolsey to Moore, April 20, 1800, Pliny Moore Papers.

19. For example, see Moore to Assemblyman Hoyt, March 9, 1810, and reply, March 18, Pliny Moore Papers.

20. Moore to William Bailey, January 23, 1802, Pliny Moore Papers.

21. Bailey to Moore, March 3, 1802, Pliny Moore Papers.

22. Woolsey to Moore, May 2; Moore to Woolsey, May 4, 1805; Woolsey to Moore, February 19, 1807, Pliny Moore Papers.

23. Sailly to Moore, February 10, 1803; Woolsey to Moore, February 13, 1808; Hoyt to Moore, May 18, 1810, Pliny Moore Papers.

24. Woolsey to Moore, March 16, March 31, 1802; Sailly to Moore, February 18, 1811, Pliny Moore Papers.

25. Woolsey to Moore, March 31, 1802, Pliny Moore Papers.

26. Moore to Woolsey, April 3, 1802, Pliny Moore Papers.

27. Solomon Nadler, "Federal Patronage and New York Politics, 1801–1830" (Ph.D. dissertation, New York University, 1973), 32, 130.

28. Hicks, Mooers, et al. to "Friends of the Administration," November 25, 1803, Mooers Papers, Kent-DeLord Collection, State University College Library, Plattsburgh.

29. Moore to sister, Eunice, August 2, 1808; N. Z. Platt to Moore, April 15, 1809; Woolsey to Moore, undated account of celebrations marking the end of the embargo, Pliny Moore Papers; Sailly to DeLord, May 1, 1809, April 23, 1810, Kent-DeLord Papers, State University College Library, Plattsburgh.

30. On the sentiments in Dutchess County, see Lynd, *Anti-Federalism in Dutchess County*, passim.

31. *Republican*, April 12, 1811; May 11, 1878; May 4, 1889.

32. *Republican*, May 11, 1878; Peter S. Palmer, *History of Plattsburgh* (Plattsburgh, 1877), 40.

33. *Republican*, April 17, May 1, 1812.

34. Woolsey to Moore, November 21, 1806, Pliny Moore Papers; *Republican*, November 13, 1812. For perceptive characterizations of the Federalists, see David Hackett Fischer, *The Revolution of American Conservatism: The Federalist Party in the Era of Jeffersonian Democracy* (New York, 1965); Shaw Livermore, *The Twilight of Federalism: The Disintegration of the Federalist Party, 1815–1830* (Princeton, 1962); Linda K. Kerber, *Federalists in Dissent* (Ithaca, 1970); and James M. Banner, Jr., *To the Hartford Convention: The Federalists and the Origins of Party Politics in Massachusetts, 1789–1815* (New York, 1970).

35. *Republican*, April 22, 1815.

36. *Republican*, May 4, 1816.

37. *Republican*, February 22, April 5, May 10, 1817.

38. Hammond, *Political Parties*, I, 74. See also Dixon Ryan Fox, *The Decline of Aristocracy in the Politics of New York* (New York, 1919), 195 ff.; Michael Wallace, "Changing Concepts of Party in the United States: New York, 1815–1828," *American History Review*, 73 (1968), 453–491; R. W. Irwin, *Daniel D. Tompkins, Governor of New York and Vice President of the United States* (New York, 1968); Raymond J. Russo, "The Political Process in New York State, 1816–1824" (Ph.D. dissertation, Fordham University, 1973).

39. *Republican*, April 18, May 2, 1818.

40. *Republican*, February 20, 1819.

41. *Republican*, May 1, 1819.

42. *Republican*, March 25, 1820; Solomon Nadler, "The Green Bag: James Monroe and the Fall of De Witt Clinton," *New-York Historical Society Quarterly*, LIX (1975), 203–225.

43. *Republican*, November 23, 1820; Town Meeting Minutes, Plattsburgh and Beekmantown.

44. *Republican*, March 25, 1820.

45. *Republican*, March 10, 1821.

46. *Republican*, March 10, March 17, April 7, 1821.

47. Beekmantown Town Meeting Minutes; *Republican*, April 7, 21, 28, May 5, 1821. The *Republican* (April 28) gives the Beekmantown vote on the convention as 162 to 1, but the town meeting minutes record 192 to none.

48. Hammond, *Political Parties*, I, 569; *Republican*, February 24, 1821.

49. *Republican*, January 26, 1822. For a possible explanation of this seemingly anomalous behavior, see John Casais, "The New York State Constitutional Convention of 1821 and Its Aftermath" (Ph.D. dissertation, Columbia University, 1967), especially 208n.

50. *Republican*, September 21 to November 16, 1822.

51. E. Miller to Moore, April 22, 1806; Woolsey to Moore, February 13, 1808, Pliny Moore Papers.

52. Cf. Nadler dissertation (cited in note 27), 261, 289.
53. *Republican*, August 31 through November 2, 1822.
54. *Republican*, November 2, 16, 1822.

14. Democrats and Whigs

1. Most authorities now see this period of the 1820s and early 1830s as
   dividing the "first" from the "second" American party "systems."
   In this view the first system pitted the Jeffersonian Republicans against
   the Federalists; the second and significantly different system pitted the
   Jacksonian Democrats against the Whigs. The titles of the two political chapters in this study reflect that consensus view, but the Republican-Democratic political leaders of Beekmantown and Clinton
   County would, I suspect, have had some quarrel with it. In the 1830s
   and 1840s, they thought that their organization had been continuous
   since the early period of settlement. They were equally convinced
   that, despite the bewildering succession of party names under which
   their opponents had offered political battle, essential continuity in
   personnel, in organization, and above all in policies had existed there
   too. The leading proponent of the party systems' conception is
   Richard P. McCormick, *The Second American Party System: Party Formation in the Jacksonian Era* (Chapel Hill, 1966). Other outstanding
   works on the political history of the Jacksonian period include Arthur
   M. Schlesinger, Jr., *The Age of Jackson* (Boston, 1945); Lee Benson,
   The Concept of Jacksonian Democracy: New York as a Test Case (Princeton, 1961); Edward Pessen, *Jacksonian America: Society, Personality,
   and Politics* (revised ed., Homewood, Ill., 1977); Robert V. Remini,
   Martin Van Buren and the Making of the Democratic Party (New York,
   1959); idem, *The Election of Andrew Jackson* (Philadelphia, 1963); Frank
   Otto Gatell, "Money and Party in Jacksonian America," *Political
   Science Quarterly*, LXXXII (1967), 235–252.
2. See Clinton Rossiter, *The American Quest, 1790–1860: An Emerging Nation in Search of Identity, Unity, and Modernity* (New York, 1971),
   and Paul C. Nagel, *One Nation Indivisible: The Union in American
   Thought, 1776–1861* (New York, 1964).
3. The best study of Van Buren's role is Remini, *Van Buren*; but see
   also Jabez D. Hammond, *The History of Political Parties in the State
   of New York* (2 vols., Cooperstown, 1846). On Crawford, see Chase
   C. Mooney, *William H. Crawford, 1772–1834* (Lexington, 1974). For
   their cooperation on patronage, see Solomon Nadler, "Federal Patronage and New York Politics, 1801–1830" (Ph.D. dissertation,
   New York University, 1973), 224.
4. See the *Republican* editorials through September and October, 1823,
   especially September 20 and October 18. Flagg was a little less hostile

to Crawford in his letter to Van Buren, November 12, 1823, Van Buren Papers, LC.

5. Minutes of the town meetings of Plattsburgh and Beekmantown, 1823.
6. *Republican*, October 11, November 15, 1823.
7. *Republican*, November 13, 1824. On Flagg's role in Albany, see Hammond, *Political Parties*, II, 139 ff.
8. *Republican*, December 6, 1823. Cf. Remini, *Van Buren*, 38–39, 51–52, and Mooney, *Crawford*, 270–280.
9. *Republican*, September 15, 1827. Robert V. Remini, *The Election of Andrew Jackson* (Philadelphia, 1963), affords an astute analysis of the campaign of 1828.
10. *Republican*, November 15, 1825.
11. *Republican*, September 23, October 28, 1826.
12. *Republican*, November 18, 1826.
13. *Republican*, November 18, 1826. Ticket splitting as now practiced was not easy because each party provided its own ballots. Nevertheless, it was possible as some later election results (1838, 1839, for example) will show. Cutting one or more of the party candidates was of course very easy but did not occur at a significant level very often.
14. Remini, *Van Buren*, 157.
15. Mooers to A. C. Flagg, February 6, 1827, John Morgan to Flagg, December 4, 1827, Flagg Papers, NYPL.
16. Mooers to Flagg, February 6, 1827, Flagg Papers, NYPL; *Republican*, October 27, 1827.
17. William F. Haile to Flagg, September 3, 1827, Flagg Papers, NYPL.
18. John Morgan to Flagg, December 4, 1827, Flagg Papers, NYPL.
19. Ibid.; also Flagg to Ingham, July 24, 1829, Flagg Papers, NYPL.
20. *Republican*, November 3, 1827.
21. *Republican*, October 20, 1827.
22. *Republican*, November 10, 1827.
23. Tredwell to Van Buren, February 7, 1828, Van Buren Papers, LC.
24. Ibid., November 10, 1832; November 8, 1828. See also Winslow C. Watson's recollections of this campaign of 1828 which appear in the *Republican*, February 22, 1879. Watson's explanation of Peru's defection is referred to below.
25. John Morgan to Flagg, December 4, 1827, Flagg Papers, NYPL; *Republican*, February 22, 1879.
26. John Lynch to Flagg, April 14, 1828, Flagg·Papers, NYPL.
27. *Republican*, October 18, November 1, 8, 1828. The November 1 issue of the *Republican* charged B. H. Mooers with distributing Republican ballots in which his name appeared in place of the Republican incumbent Walworth.
28. *Republican*, February 22, 1879.
29. Flagg to Ingham, July 24, 1829, Flagg Papers, NYPL. Adams had appointed Sailly to succeed his father as customs collector in 1826. Although Sailly staffed his office largely with Jacksonians and enjoyed the support of local Jacksonian leaders, Jackson declined to reappoint him in 1830. See Nadler, "Federal Patronage," 278–279, 306.

30. *Republican*, February 22, 1879; October 7, 1837; September 8, 1838.
31. Charles McCarthy, *The Anti-Masonic Party*, Annual Report of the American Historical Association, 1902 (2 vols., Washington, 1903), I, 367–574, passim. See also Lorman Ratner (ed.), *Antimasonry: The Crusade and the Party* (Englewood Cliffs, N.J., 1969); Michael F. Holt, "Antimasonic and Know Nothing Parties," in Arthur M. Schlesinger, Jr. (ed.), *History of U.S. Political Parties* (4 vols., New York, 1973), I, 575–620; Ronald P. Formisano and Kathleen Smith Kutolowski, "Antimasonry and Masonry: The Genesis of Protest, 1826–1827," *American Quarterly*, XXIX (1977), 139–165; and Kutolowski's "Social Composition of Political Leadership: Genesee County, New York, 1821–1860" (Ph.D. dissertation, University of Rochester, 1973).
32. *Republican*, May 26, 1827.
33. *Republican*, May 26, 1827; March 15, 1828.
34. *Republican*, July 24, 1830; Beekmantown Town Meeting Minutes, 1830; Hammond, *Political Parties*, II, 336.
35. *Republican*, July 14, October 27, November 10, 1832; Beekmantown Town Meeting Minutes. On the political ramifications of the bank war, see Robert V. Remini, *Andrew Jackson and the Bank War: A Study in the Growth of Presidential Power* (New York, 1967); Frank Otto Gatell, "Sober Second Thoughts on Van Buren, the Albany Regency, and the Wall Street Conspiracy," *Journal of American History*, LIII (1966), 19–40; James Roger Sharp, *The Jacksonians versus the Banks: Politics in the States After the Panic of 1837* (New York, 1970); and John M. McFaul, *The Politics of Jacksonian Finance* (Ithaca, 1972). All four suggest that Bray Hammond, *Banks and Politics in America* (Princeton, 1957), exaggerated the importance of economic considerations and minimized unduly the political and ideological aspects of the struggle.
36. *Republican*, February 22, October 4, 1834.
37. *Republican*, August 23, September 6, 13, 27, 1834.
38. *Republican*, August 30, 1834.
39. *Republican*, November 9, 1833.
40. Beekmantown Town Meeting Minutes.
41. *Republican*, February 22, November 18, 1838.
42. *Republican*, April 7, 1838; November 11, 1837; Beekmantown Town Meeting Minutes.
43. *Republican*, March 10, 1838.
44. Hammond, *Political Parties*, II, 471. Peter Temin, *The Jacksonian Economy* (New York, 1969), affords significant insight on the onset of the depression.
45. *Republican*, November 12, 1836; November 18, 1837.
46. *Republican*, November 17, 1838.
47. *Republican*, November 3, 1838; August 31, November 9, 1839. For background on nativist tendencies, see Louis Dow Scisco, *Political Nativism in New York State* (New York, 1901), and Ray Allen Billington, *The Protestant Crusade, 1800–1860: A Study of the Origins of American Nativism* (New York, 1938).

48. *Republican*, September 28, 1839; August 29, 1840; October 16, 1841; July 12, 1844.
49. *Republican*, November 9, 1839.
50. *Republican*, October 31, 1840.
51. *Republican*, October 3, 17, 1840.
52. *Republican*, October 17, 1840.
53. Ibid.
54. *Republican*, October 3, 1840.
55. *Republican*, October 17, 1840.
56. *Republican*, November 7, 1840.
57. *Republican*, December 5, 1840. Robert Gray Gunderson, *The Log Cabin Campaign* (Lexington, 1957), is a colorful account of the 1840 election.
58. New York *Tribune Almanac* (1868).
59. *Republican*, November 6, 1841; November 5, 1842; November 11, 1843.
60. *Republican*, June 29, September 12, 28, November 23, 1844.
61. *Republican*, November 8, 15, 1845.
62. *Republican*, March 7, 14, 1846; New York *Tribune Almanac* (1868).
63. *Republican*, June 19, November 13, 1847.
64. D. S. Alexander, *A Political History of the State of New York, 1774–1882* (3 vols., New York, 1906–1909), II, 127n; *Republican*, May 6, 1848. The basic authority on the Barnburners is Herbert A. Donovan, *The Barnburners* (New York, 1925).
65. *Republican*, September 16, October 21, 1848. On the attitudes of the Free-Soilers, see Eric Foner, "Racial Attitudes of New York Free Soilers," *New York History*, 46 (1965), 311–329, and his *Free Soil, Free Labor, Free Men* (New York, 1970).
66. *Republican*, November 11, 25, 1848.
67. *Republican*, November 10, 17, 1849.
68. This is of course an essentially "Progressive" interpretation similar to that reached by Dixon Ryan Fox in *The Decline of the Aristocracy in the Politics of New York* (New York, 1919). The two themes most prominent in the work of the many scholars who have challenged Fox are that class differences did not figure significantly in the division of the electorate into opposing groups and that ethnic and religious factors were the most important influences on voting behavior. The leading advocate of the first point is McCormick, *Second American Party System*, while the "ethno-cultural" interpretation stems from Benson's *Concept of Jacksonian Democracy*. New York State studies which uphold McCormick in particular are Alvin Kass, *Politics in New York State, 1800–1830* (Syracuse, 1965), and Douglas T. Miller, *Jacksonian Aristocracy: Class and Democracy in New York, 1830–1860* (New York, 1967).

Works which have encouraged me to affirm the modified Progressive interpretation suggested by Beekmantown's political history include Richard Hofstadter, *The Idea of a Party System* (Berkeley, 1969); Shaw Livermore, *The Twilight of Federalism* (Princeton, 1962); Michael Wallace, "Changing Concepts of Party in the United States: New York, 1815–1828," *American Historical Review*, 73 (1968), 453–491; Richard H. Brown, "The Missouri Crisis, Slavery, and the Politics of Jacksonianism," *South Atlantic Quarterly*, 65 (1966), 52–72; Bruce Collins, "The Ideology of the Ante Bellum Northern Democrats," *Journal of American Studies*, 11 (1977), 103–121; Kalman Goldstein's rough but massively detailed "The Albany Regency: The Failure of Practical Politics" (Ph.D. dissertation, Columbia University, 1969); Judah B. Ginsburg, "The Tangled Web: The New York Democratic Party and the Slavery Controversy, 1844–1860" (Ph.D. dissertation, University of Wisconsin, 1974); Raymond J. Russo, "The Political Process in New York State, 1816–1824" (Ph.D. dissertation, Fordham University, 1973); and Richard P. McCormick's "Ethno-Cultural Interpretations of Nineteenth-Century American Voting Behavior," *Political Science Quarterly*, 89 (1974), 351–377, which points out that the ethno-cultural concerns alleged to be preeminent in the minds of voters were largely irrelevant to the major issues—very often economic issues—of public policy.

For thoughtful reflections on the massive Jacksonian scholarship, see Pessen's *Jacksonian America*.

Bibliographical Note

Throughout the text, notes have at times included comments on how the findings of this study relate to those of other inquiries. Too often, however, such comparisons seemed to require more space than was appropriate for a note. Consequently, I have chosen to use this Bibliographical Note to offer more extended comments on how the findings in some parts of this study relate to the conclusions suggested by other writers.

My finding that the first generation of settlers was of higher socioeconomic status than the second contrasts with the imagery made famous by Frederick Jackson Turner. In his original essay, most conveniently available in *The Frontier in American History* (New York: Henry Holt, 1920), Turner saw the "men of capital and enterprise" arriving only in the third wave of settlement, following the frontier squatter and then the landowning farmer. After considerable study of frontier land speculation, Turner revised his opinion in 1925. According to Ray A. Billington, *Frederick Jackson Turner* (New York: Oxford University, 1973), 458, Turner observed then that "often the economic stages represented by these waves of advancing population were blended or intermixed." Apparently, he never considered, however, that the first generation might rate higher on the socioeconomic scale than the second. In fact, neither Gene M. Gressley, "The Turner Thesis—a Problem in Historiography," *Agricultural History*, XXXII (1958), 227–249, nor Ray A. Billington, *America's Frontier Heritage* (New York: Holt, Rinehart and Winston, 1966), each a very thorough review of the voluminous literature, considered such a possibility. Frederick Merk's *History of the Westward Movement* (New York: Alfred A. Knopf, 1978) has speculators (p. 79) discovering attractive areas in the Allegheny Plateau but "semi-vagrant" pioneers (p. 125) developing them.

Three studies of New England towns have reported findings in accord with the thesis which I have suggested. Charles S. Grant in *Democracy in the Connecticut Frontier Town of Kent* (New York: Columbia University Press, 1961) found that the poor increased from 33 percent of the population at the founding of the town in 1740 to 42 percent in 1796 (p. 96) and that the percent of adult males qualified to vote decreased from 79 percent in 1751 to 63 percent in 1796 (p. 111). Similarly, Philip J. Greven's *Four Generations: Population, Land, and Family in Colonial Andover, Massachusetts* (Ithaca: Cornell University Press, 1970) presented a table (p. 225) showing that of the four generations which he studied it was the first, judging by the value of estates, which was the most prosperous. Both Grant and Greven attributed the decline in the level of affluence to the lowering of the amount of land available to each family as population grew. My more complicated explanation for the phenomenon appears in the Conclusion. Also, in *Salem Possessed: The Social Origins of Witchcraft* (Cambridge: Harvard University Press, 1974), Paul Boyer and Stephen Nissenbaum reported that the average landholding in Salem in 1690 was "just about half what it had been in 1660" (p. 90).

Several other studies included observations which seem to imply that the socioeconomic level may have been higher generally in the first than in the second generation in most frontier communities. Lewis D. Stilwell's superb study of *Migration from Vermont, 1776–1860* (Montpelier: Vermont Historical Society, 1948) noted in chapter 7 that emigrants in the second generation included disproportionate representation of the highly educated. Neil Adams McNall, in *An Agricultural History of the Genesee Valley, 1790–1880* (Philadelphia: University of Pennsylvania, 1952), observed (p. 76) that around 1825—that is, in the second generation—an "accumulation of poor debtors" began to be conspicuous in the Genesee country as wealthier migrants passed on farther west, and it was chiefly the poorer sort who stopped to settle. He noted also (p. 234) that among those leaving the Genesee country for the West were not only "malcontents" but also "many of the able and energetic." In *The Allegheny Frontier: West Virginia Beginnings, 1730–1830* (Lexington: University of Kentucky Press, 1970), Otis K.

Rice wrote (pp. 210–211) that "the first settlers of West Virginia . . . were apparently literate and interested in establishing schools." Later that interest seemed to have declined. Leslie E. Decker in "The Great Speculation: An Interpretation of Mid-Continent Pioneering," in David M. Ellis (ed.), *The Frontier in American Development: Essays in Honor of Paul Wallace Gates* (Ithaca: Cornell University Press, 1969), found that "on the mid-continent frontier . . . almost all the early comers to any area were speculators first and homeseekers second or not at all" (pp. 379–380). Michael S. Cross, in "The Age of Gentility: The Formation of an Aristocracy in the Ottawa Valley," *Canadian Historical Association, Historical Papers* (1967), 105–117, characterized the first generation of settlers as dominated by an elite which was highly conservative both socially and politically.

Resistance to this interpretive line, or at least to a corollary of it, came in particular from Paul W. Gates. In "Agricultural Change in New York State, 1850–1890," *New York History*, XLVI (1969), 115–141, he asked, "Must we assume, as Frederick Jackson Turner seemed to, that the element which went west . . . constituted the most dynamic, most energetic, the most discontented and left behind the easily satisfied, the less ambitious, the least self-driven?" In "Problems of Agriculture, 1790–1840," *Agricultural History*, XLVI (1972), 33–57, he cited as "unacceptable to me" the idea that the "best brains and the boldest spirits left" the older agricultural areas for the frontier.

My study also suggests two points concerning timber-based enterprises. The first is that the exploitation of timber resources was a more important factor in early American economic development than has been generally recognized. Douglass C. North, *The Economic Growth of the United States, 1790–1860* (Englewood Cliffs, N.J.: Prentice-Hall, 1961), for example, gave relatively little attention to forest products. They commanded still less attention in Stuart Bruchey, *The Roots of American Economic Growth, 1607–1861* (New York: Harper and Row, 1965).

The second is that because by its very nature the exploitation of timber resources was a business peculiarly associated with the frontier, it almost necessarily follows that opportunities afforded by timber resources were among the major attractions luring people to new and undeveloped regions. David C. Smith implied this as he castigated frontier historians for ignoring "The Logging Frontier," *Journal of Forest History*, 18 (1974), 96–106.

The "standard" work on lumbering in the United States is that of James E. Defebaugh, *History of the Lumber Industry in America* (2 vols., Chicago: *The American Lumberman*, 1906–1907). Defebaugh was editor of the *American Lumberman* and his work shows clearly the absence of professional training in history, but it has never been superseded. Similarly, a recent study on lumbering in West Virginia was the work of a biologist, Roy B. Clarkson, *Tumult on the Mountains: Lumbering in West Virginia, 1770–1920* (Parsons, W. Va.: McClain Printing Co., 1964).

Recent studies by professional historians which have focused on lumbering have been for the most part either state studies, biographies, or business histories. Among the state studies were several excellent mongraphs: Paul W. Gates, *The Wisconsin Pine Lands of Cornell University: A Study in Land Policy and Absentee Ownership* (Ithaca: Cornell University Press, 1943); Robert F. Fried, *Empire in Pine: The Story of Lumbering in Wisconsin, 1830–1900* (Madison: State Historical Society of Wisconsin, 1951); Agnes M. Larson, *History of the White Pine Industry in Minnesota* (Minneapolis: University of Minnesota Press, 1949); Nollie Hickman, *Mississippi Harvest: Lumbering in the Longleaf Pine Belt, 1840–1915* (Oxford: University of Mississippi, 1962); Richard G. Wood, *A History of Lumbering in Maine, 1820–1861* (Orono: University of Maine Press, 1935); and David C. Smith, *History of Lumbering in Maine, 1861–1960* (Orono: University of Maine Press, 1972). Recognition of the importance of timber products also appears in Richard L. Bushman's outstanding study, *From Puritan to Yankee: Character and the Social Order in Connecticut, 1690–1765* (Cambridge: Harvard University Press, 1967).

Of these the only ones to suggest conclusions similar to mine were Agnes Larson and Richard G. Wood. Professor Larson stated (p. 411): "Flour was always indebted to lumber in Minnesota, because it was lumber that first offered flour a market there. A number of outstanding lumbermen early began to invest their accumulated capital in flour milling." Wood observed (p. 95) that "pioneer farmers found a market for all their produce if they were established near a lumber camp."

The same point emerged from a recent Canadian study. Michael S. Cross observed in his "'Dark Druidical Groves'" (Ph.D. dissertation, University of Toronto, 1968), 280–282, that farmers on the Ottawa frontier "enjoyed a large and highly profitable market for their produce in the timber shanties." Because the hay and oats which they sold were too bulky to be brought from distant areas, farmers of the area enjoyed a local monopoly and charged monopoly prices.

Recent studies of the eastern frontier gave some attention to the importance of timber resources. Douglas Edward Leach, *The Northern Colonial Frontier, 1607–1763* (New York: Holt, Rinehart and Winston, 1966), affirmed flatly (p. 135): "There can be no doubt that the quest for timber was a major factor in the expansion of the New England frontier, especially in Maine and New Hampshire." Leach also found the making of potash and pearlash important as a supplemental source of income (pp. 85–86). Jack M. Sosin, *The Revolutionary Frontier, 1763–1783* (New York: Holt, Rinehart and Winston, 1967), attributed some importance to both potash and lumber but allocated only two sentences to the former and a paragraph to the latter. Charles E. Clark, *The Eastern Frontier: The Settlement of Northern New England, 1610–1763* (New York: Knopf, 1970), made occasional references to the importance of timber products but gave them no sustained consideration. Charles F. Carroll certainly affirmed the importance of timber products in his study, *The Timber Economy of Puritan New England* (Providence: Brown University, 1973), but his focus was broad and his treatment very general.

Ray Allen Billington's reassessment of *America's Frontier Heritage* (New York: Holt, Rinehart and Winston, 1966) had two interesting chapters on motives for moving to a frontier area. One was titled "Why and How the Pioneers Moved Westward"; the other, "The Frontier and the Migratory Compulsion." In the first he affirmed (p. 27) that "the most compelling attraction of the frontier was the hope of economic betterment." In the second he stated (p. 190) that "the basic urge in moving westward was for a better farm, more wealth, and a higher status in life." Nowhere did he mention timber resources as part of the frontier's economic opportunity. Furthermore, despite the observations quoted, one leaves the two chapters in question with the impression that Billington still accepted in large measure the Turnerian notion of men "'with the West in their eyes' who were impelled to move, they knew not why" (p. 26). The people who settled Beekmantown knew very well why they moved, and most migrated because they recognized in frontier circumstances an unparalleled opportunity to make money. Furthermore, it is clear that timber resources were a very important part of the money-making opportunity.

Agricultural historians have shown little disposition to look at the role of timber resources in affording a livelihood to frontier farmers. Percy W. Bidwell and John I. Falconer in their *History of Agriculture in the Northern United States, 1620–1860* (New York: Carnegie Institution, 1925) mentioned (p. 254) that farmers "carried on a wide variety of quasi-industrial pursuits . . . which in some cases were more lucrative than agriculture." In an earlier reference to such work (pp. 27–29), they suggested that while it might furnish the farmer an important source of income it "often interfered with farming operations and hindered the development of good agricultural practice." In *The Farmer's Age: Agriculture, 1815–1860* (New York: Holt, Rinehart and Winston, 1960), Paul W. Gates had an accurate paragraph on "wood ashes" (p. 34) but almost no other mention of timber-based enterprise. There was more recognition of the economic importance of timber products in his "Problems of Agriculture, 1790–1840," *Agricultural History*, XLVI (1972), 33–57. Clarence Danhof, *Change in Agriculture: The Northern United States, 1820–1870* (Cambridge: Harvard University, 1969), observed briefly (pp. 118–119) that farmers in some areas did derive money income from exploiting timber resources while clearing land.

In Canada, where lumbering has, of course, been of far greater relative importance in the development of the economy, historians have recognized fully how important it was. In the introduction to his "Lumbering in Eastern Canada" (Ph.D. dissertation, Harvard University, 1928) A. R. M. Lower, for example, observed not only that "the drama of Canadian history has been acted largely in a forest setting" but still more specifically that the Canadian forest was "a great mine of wealth, open to all who cared to come into it and hew out its riches." For nearly a century, he continued, lumber was "an easily available staple upon which . . . the major part of the economic framework of that colony was based." Comparing Canadian lumber to American cotton as a great national staple, Lower affirmed also that lumber production did "profoundly affect the manner of life of great numbers of people" and that indeed "nearly every farmer at one time or another made a venture in the trade." In a similar vein, Fernand Ouellet, *Histoire Economique et Sociale du Québec, 1760–1850* (Montreal and Paris: Fides, 1966), 192 ff., concluded that the timber trade, arising in a period of depression in the fur trade and in agriculture, increased employment, provided profits not otherwise attainable, and stimulated consumption incomparably. What I wish to suggest is that there were probably significant areas of the American frontier in the eighteenth and early nineteenth centuries in which forest resources may well have had similar importance.

Romantic attachment to the agrarian mystique may well account in part for the slighting of timber enterprises. The farming aspect of frontier life has so captured the imagination of American historians (see Henry Nash Smith, *Virgin Land: The American West as Symbol and Myth* [Cambridge: Harvard University Press, 1950]) that there has been some reluctance to conceive that the frontiersman may often have been a part-time lumberman as well. Reflecting the same agrarian bias was the general disapproval felt by nineteenth-century gentlemen for both lumbering and lumbermen. Lower's work and that of Richard G. Wood in particular reported, with complete sympathy in the first case, the resentment prevalent in most communities over the drunkenness, debauchery, and ostentation so common among lumbermen. Both made clear as well that lumbering's cash wages which financed such depravity were perceived as a devilish lure to which altogether too many farm folk succumbed.

Another factor contributing perhaps to explain the relative lack of emphasis on the importance of lumbering in frontier development is the concentration of recent study in the prairie areas of the Middle West, where of course there was no lumbering frontier. It may or may not be coincidental that by studying such areas, historians are free to concentrate their work on agricultural enterprise except of course for the diversion necessary to deal with the ubiquitous land speculators. It seems at least symbolically significant in this respect that when Merle Curti was selecting a Wisconsin county to study for his work on *The Making of an American Community: A Case Study of Democracy in a Frontier County* (Stanford: Stanford University Press, 1959) he went to great lengths to find one not dominated by the distinctive features of "the pineries," although the one selected was "on the fringe of this area" (p. 4). The proximity of his county to the pine lands, however, "enabled many agricultural pioneers to accumulate savings by winter labor with which to buy freeholds or equipment for improving lands on which they had squatted or homesteaded. . . . Proximity to the lumber frontier," Curti continued in his first chapter, "helped to equalize opportunity among agricultural pioneers with little or no capital" (p. 11). His conclusion, however, made no mention of the influence of lumber enterprise upon the community's development.

Relating this study to the growing literature on communities of the colonial and early national periods is too large a task to be undertaken here except in a very superficial way. Two excellent although now somewhat dated studies focusing on New England towns were John Murrin's review essay on "New England Town Studies," *History and Theory*, XI (1972), 226–275, and Jack P. Greene, "Autonomy and Stability," a similar review essay which appeared in the *Journal of Social History*, 7 (1974), 171–194. Clearly, Beekmantown was very much a part of the Atlantic world of commerce in contrast to what Greene calls the "backwater" aspect of the New England towns. Emigration rates seem to have varied in different New England towns, but in Beekmantown emigration was always high. Town autonomy, it would appear, tended to diminish in colonial New England; it scarcely existed in Beekmantown. Community cohesion was also declining in colonial New England; it, too, hardly existed in Beekmantown. In comparison with the New England towns, Beekmantown was more commercial, mobile, individualistic, and more fully integrated into the larger communities of state and nation.

For those with a particular interest in the history of Clinton County or of New York State, I commend Glyndon C. Cole's excellent bibliography entitled *Historical Materials Relating to Northern New York: A Union Catalog* (North Country Reference and Research Resources Council with the cooperation of the Adirondack Museum, 1968). Cole arranged his material topically and provided author and title indexes. To supplement Cole one should see Nell J. B. Sullivan and David K. Martin, *A History of the Town of Chazy* (Burlington: privately printed, 1970), and Allan S. Everest, *Moses Hazen* (Syracuse, Syracuse University Press, 1976). For New York State as a whole there is an all-encompassing annotated bibliography in David M. Ellis et al., *A History of New York State* (Ithaca: Cornell University Press, 1967).

Index